THE IMMIGRANT HERITAGE OF AMERICA
SERIES

Cecyle S. Neidle, Editor

California-born girl of Portuguese parentage, christening a U.S. Navy bomber in honor of the Portuguese discoverer of California. San Diego, 1942.

The Portuguese-Americans

by

Leo Pap

State University of New York, College at New Paltz

TWAYNE PUBLISHERS

A DIVISION OF G. K. HALL & CO., BOSTON

Published in 1981 by Twayne Publishers,
A Division of G. K. Hall & Co.
All Rights Reserved

Printed on permanent/durable acid-free paper and bound
in the United States of America

First Printing

Library of Congress Cataloging in Publication Data
Pap, Leo.
The Portuguese—Americans.
(The Immigrant heritage of America)
Bibliography: p. 283-92
Includes index
1.   Portuguese Americans—History.   I.   Title.
E184.P8P34   973:.04691   80-22256
ISBN 0-8057-8417-9

Contents

About the Author

Leo Pap, Ph.D., is a Professor of Linguistics at State University of New York, College at New Paltz. An immigrant from Switzerland, he first became interested in the Portuguese immigrants while doing his doctoral dissertation at Columbia University. That monograph, dealing with language adjustments among the Portuguese in the United States, was published in 1949 under the title *Portuguese-American Speech*. After some postdoctoral training in anthropology, he began delving more deeply into non-linguistic aspects of the Portuguese immigrant experience. His intermittent research on this subject, supported by several foundation grants, has extended over nearly three decades. Dr. Pap's scholarly affiliations include membership in the Immigration History Society, the American Anthropological Association, and several linguistic societies.

Preface

This is the first comprehensive account of an ethnic group which, although it represents only a small fraction of the total population of the United States, has woven itself into the fabric of American history since the earliest days of discovery and colonization: the Portuguese-Americans. Clustering together over the past hundred years in parts of New England and adjoining metropolitan New York, in California and in Hawaii, immigrants from Portugal have been the subject of a growing number of community studies and limited monographs in very recent years. But a major bibliography of American immigration history published as recently as 1956, and reissued in 1977, still contained only two entries relating to the Portuguese immigrants: one an old article dealing with an isolated episode, the other a sociological community study of the 1920s which elicited from the bibliographer this absurd annotation: "The study shows that the Portuguese are, by all accepted standards, a low-grade people. . . ."[1]

The present book, it is hoped, will show that the Portuguese element in the United States is not "low-grade," whatever that might mean. Neither high-grade nor low-grade, Portuguese-Americans in their overwhelming majority consist of "ordinary" laboring people with their distinctive traditions, as do all other ethnic components of American society. In writing this book, I have shied away from any glorification or vilification or any kind of justification. Anyone attempting to evaluate the "contribution" of this or that population segment risks conjuring up a biased distinction between givers and takers, hosts and guests, an accounting of who owes what to whom; whereas ultimately, in the amalgam of American society, which is largely the product of fairly recent immigration, all are contributors and recipients alike.

Aiming at the intelligent lay reader as well as the specialized scholar, I have tried to strike a balance between lively narrative and necessarily somewhat "dry" analysis. The more casual reader is free, of course, to skip over some of the statistics and other demographic details, as contained largely in Chapters 3—7. He may likewise disregard the more than 600 notes and the related bibliography, appended at the end of the volume for the purpose of scholarly documentation. (Many of these notes do, however, contain supplementary information in addition to bibliographical references.) Part I of the book is arranged chronologically, as a history of immigration and settlement. It is relatively sketchy on the new immigration of the last fifteen years, still awaiting detailed field study. Part II is organized more from the viewpoint of descriptive social science, outlining living conditions and the process of "acculturation" in the Portuguese-American communities.

The research on which this book is based began with the gathering of primarily linguistic material while I was a graduate student in the 1940s. This initial research resulted in my monograph *Portuguese-American Speech; an Outline of Speech Conditions among Portuguese Immigrants in New England and Elsewhere in the United States,* which was published by Columbia University Press (under the King's Crown imprint) in 1949. It has long since been out of print (but "on demand" individual reprint copies are again available from University Microfilms International). A necessary spin-off of that linguistic study was some general information on Portuguese settlement and immigrant life.

I started expanding upon that nonlinguistic material in the early 1950s, as I was becoming more interested in cultural anthropology and related social science. Off and on since that time, over the span of what is now a generation, I kept up this research, in the form of repeated field visits to many Portuguese immigrant communities in New England and around New York, in California, and as far away as Hawaii, interviewing many scores of informants, or acting as a "participant observer", at open-air festivities, in clubhouses, in the streets, and in private homes. At least equally important has been my regular perusal of many Portuguese immigrant newspapers, adding up to between 8,000 and 10,000 individual issues actually seen over the years. Persistent combing of libraries in many locations (but with my greatest debt of gratitude being due to the New York Public Library and the Library of Congress) led me very gradually to dig up hundreds of disparate primary and secondary sources, including governmental ones, that contained at least passing references to the Portuguese in the United States.

To make the results of this long-drawn-out library work available to other researchers while completion of my own book still seemed far off, I compiled a bibliography of 800 entries, three-fourths of them relating to the Portuguese in the United States and the rest containing background information on Portugal. It was published in 1976 under the title *The Portuguese in the United States: A Bibliography* (Staten Island, N.Y.: Center for Migration Studies). Another sixty items or so have been produced or have come to my attention since that bibliography went to press, and are available as a supplement on request.

Particularly in view of that separately published bibliography, topically broken down and in part annotated, I have not deemed it necessary to append to the present book a bibliography as complete as might otherwise have been desirable. Instead, the one at the end of this volume is no more than a partial list of sources used, limited to those which have been specifically referred to in the notes—in abbreviated form—more than once (up to twenty or even fifty times in some instances). Approximately 270 additional sources cited only once each are fully identified in the notes, without being listed again in the bibliography.[2]

The earlier stages of my work were supported in part by grants from the American Council of Learned Societies, the Instituto de Alta Cultura in Lisbon, Portugal, and the Research Foundation of the State University of New York. To all three institutions I herewith acknowledge my indebtedness.

Among individuals who have assisted me in the preparation of this book, I must thank in the first place the many informants, mostly of Portuguese birth or parentage, who graciously and patiently provided me with valuable data, in formal interviews or through correspondence, or sometimes unawares in casual conversation. Because of their very number, they must remain anonymous here; and I can only hope that they will feel somewhat repaid by seeing this book appear in print. A special word of thanks also to the publishers of several Portuguese immigrant newspapers who granted me complimentary subscriptions for varying periods; the daily *Diario de Noticias* of New Bedford, now defunct, came to me free of charge for well over twenty years!

Cecyle S. Neidle, editor of the Twayne Immigrant Heritage of America series, guided this manuscript through many minor revisions with unfailing tact and good judgment. My colleague Richard A. Varbero, a specialist in immigration history at State University of

New York College at New Paltz, read the entire manuscript and provided valuable critical comments. So did Antonio Simões, of Boston University, a specialist in the education of immigrant children and himself of Portuguese descent. Francis M. Rogers, of Harvard University, a lifelong student of things Portuguese, provided much encouragement for my research over the years, even though he did not see the final manuscript. Steven S. Ussach, of Bristol Community College, rendered assistance in an earlier revision of the first several chapters. Marie Cimino, of New Paltz, did a professional job of typing and retyping most of the manuscript. To all these persons I express my sincere appreciation.

Finally, an acknowledgment to my wife and son, who cheerfully agreed to postpone a long-planned trip to Europe so I could first finish this book, which had been too long in the making.

LEO PAP

New Paltz, New York
March 1980

PART I

History of Portuguese Settlement in the United States

Cape Cod fisherman of Portuguese birth. Late 1930's.

CHAPTER 1

From the Discovery of North America to the Early Days of the Republic

THE STORY OF THE PORTUGUESE IN AMERICA BEGINS WITH THE VERY first appearance of Europeans in the Western Hemisphere. Sturdy seafarers from the little kingdom of Portugal took a leading part in opening up the New World; Brazil, the third-largest country of the Americas (largest in Latin America), is the prime monument to their endeavor.

Christopher Columbus, though not of Portuguese birth, derived much of his nautical knowledge and interests from the Portuguese; in the words of Morison, "without the preliminary work of the Portuguese, the First Voyage of Columbus could not have attained its object."[1] He arrived in Lisbon in 1476 and remained there for several years, living in the midst of the greatest cosmographers and pilots of the age. It was there that he made up his mind to devote himself to maritime discovery, after having obtained the navigation charts and papers of his father-in-law, Bartholomew Perestrello, who was the Portuguese governor of Porto Santo, in the Madeira Islands.

There have been claims, open to doubt, to the effect that the Portuguese actually preceded Columbus in the discovery of America. A nautical map dating from 1424, now in the University of Minnesota library, was "found" in 1955 to show that some unknown Portuguese reached the Antilles in 1424. This matches the reputed discovery by the Soviet historian Tspernik, in 1959, of a letter from King Fernando and Queen Isabel of Spain which states that Columbus knew of the existence of land in the Antilles before starting out on his voyage, because he had heard about this from a sailor, Alonzo Sanchez, who had mapped the Antilles. A Portuguese by the name of Dualmo, if we are to believe the British historian A.

3

Davies, sailed from the Azores in 1487 and discovered America five
years ahead of Columbus.[2]

João Vaz Corte-Real, of Terceira (Azores), the father of Gaspar
and Miguel Corte-Real (see below), is reported by a contemporary,
the Azorean chronicler Gaspar Frutuoso, to have discovered Newfoundland and to have surveyed the New England coast in 1472 (or
1473); but little credit is given by most present-day historians to
Frutuoso's story.[3] Another Terceiran, João Fernandes, called *O
Lavrador* from his occupation as a farmer or small landowner, went
on a voyage of exploration to the North in 1492 (or 1499) together
with one Pedro de Barcellos. It has been surmised, chiefly from
maps showing a "Land of the Labrador," that Fernandes discovered
what is now known as Labrador; but closer investigation suggests
that the land he visited is the present-day Greenland—which had
been discovered and settled centuries before by Norsemen.[4]

Gaspar Corte-Real, rather than his father, João Vaz Corte-Real,
should probably be regarded as the real discoverer of Newfoundland.[5] In the spring of the year 1500, this young Terceiran nobleman
started out from Lisbon with two caravels, and he reached the east
coast of Greenland in June. Then, turned back by icebergs, he ran
up the west coast, and before the end of the year he was safely back
in Lisbon. In May of the following year, 1501, Gaspar set out again,
together with his brother Miguel, in three caravels. They steered for
Greenland, but ice packs prevented them from reaching their
destination. They then took a northwesterly course and finally
sighted Labrador. Turning south, they ran down the coast to Cape
Harrison, explored Hamilton Inlet, passed Sandwich Bay, and soon
found themselves off the coast of Newfoundland. Then, in September, Miguel Corte-Real sailed back to Lisbon with two of the vessels,
while Gaspar on his flagship continued the voyage, probably in a
southerly direction.

When the months passed and Gaspar did not return to Portugal,
Miguel resolved to go out and look for him. In May 1502 he left
Lisbon with three ships, and by June he was off Newfoundland
again. There the vessels parted, each going in a different direction
in search of Gaspar, and they agreed to meet again on August 20.
On that date two of the vessels met at the appointed place without
having found Gaspar; but the flagship with Miguel never returned.

Although no further trace of Gaspar was ever uncovered, the so-
called Dighton Rock is believed by some to provide a clue as to the
ultimate fate of Miguel Corte-Real and his crew. On the bank of the

Taunton River opposite Dighton, Massachusetts, at a point called Assonet Neck, there is a rock covered with washed-out pictographs, scratches, and apparent inscriptions. From this mass Edmund B. Delabarre, after long and careful study, claimed in 1928 to have isolated the following inscription: "MIGUEL CORTEREAL V DEI HIC DUX IND 1511" (Miguel Cortereal by the will of God here chief of Indians 1511), plus a design resembling a simplified royal arms of Portugal. Based on this reading, Delabarre hypothesized that Miguel Corte-Real was shipwrecked somewhere along the New England coast, became chief of the Wampanoag Indians, and was commemorated after his death (in 1511) by a surviving member of his crew, with this Latin inscription. If the hypothesis is correct, the first Europeans to set foot on New England soil were Portuguese.[6]

Some twenty years after the brothers Corte-Real had reached the North Atlantic coast of America, two other Portuguese seafarers followed suit and apparently extended their coastal explorations further southward. João Alvares Fagundes, a nobleman from Vianna do Castelo, conducted extensive explorations sometime around 1520 south and west of Cape Race, Newfoundland. There are indications that he even entered the St. Lawrence River and then sailed along the eastern and southern coast of Nova Scotia into the Bay of Fundy.

Estêvão Gomes, a native of Porto who had been a pilot under Fernão de Magalhães in 1519, was appointed by the Emperor of Spain, Charles V, to lead a small Spanish expedition in order to discover a western passage to the Moluccas. He started out from La Coruña at the end of 1524 or early in 1525 and steered for Newfoundland. Then, instead of continuing in a northwesterly direction, he sailed on to Nova Scotia and down the North American coast, perhaps as far as Cape May or even beyond Chesapeake Bay. On his course, he charted the coast line of the present-day states of Maine, Massachusetts, Connecticut, New York (Hudson River), New Jersey, and Delaware. In the autumn of 1525 he returned to Spain.[7]

Turning from maritime exploration along the North Atlantic coast of America to the southern part of the United States, we find that Portuguese men played a role in the exploration of this southern territory also, although in Spanish service.

Hernando de Soto, the Spanish adventurer, had been given permission by Charles V of Spain to conquer Florida at his own expense, and had been appointed governor of Cuba. In 1538 he sailed with a company of some 600 men, twenty officers, and twenty-four ecclesiastics, and he disembarked in what is now Tampa Bay. The ships were sent back to Cuba, and de Soto first pushed north as far as the Carolinas, then turned southward back to Florida, and finally headed west. Many of his men perished on the way. In the spring of 1541 he crossed the Mississippi, then turned south, tired and discouraged. He died on the banks of the Mississippi, and only a handful of his men succeeded in reaching the Spanish settlements on the Gulf of Mexico.

The expedition of Hernando de Soto is described by one of its participants, a Portuguese gentleman from Elvas, in a narrative published anonymously in 1557. From this narrative it appears that there were eight Portuguese from Elvas in the expedition (and perhaps many more from other places in Portugal). One André de Vasconcelos seems to have headed the Elvas group. He and at least two of his companions perished along the Mississippi in 1542, like de Soto himself. The author of the narrative, perhaps by the name of Alvaro Fernández, was one of the few survivors, and in his report we get the oldest description of the interior of the states of Florida, Georgia, North and South Carolina, Tennessee, Alabama, Mississippi, Arkansas, Texas, etc.; in it is also recorded the first discovery and navigation of the Mississippi River.[8]

About the same time another Spanish expedition crossed into the southern parts of what is now the United States, from Mexico. Francisco Vazquez de Coronado, a companion of the viceroy of New Spain (Mexico), Antonio de Mendoza, had been appointed governor of the province of New Galicia in April 1539. Later that same year he received from a returning exploring party glowing accounts about large Indian cities situated to the north, especially Cibola (near Zuni, New Mexico). On the basis of these accounts Coronado obtained from Mendoza a commission to lead an expedition into that territory. The expeditionary force, comprising some 300 soldiers plus a number of Franciscan friars, started out from Compostela, Mexico, early in 1540. They first captured Cibola, and then separate exploring parties went off to the west and to the east. One group pushing into Arizona discovered the Grand Canyon in September 1540. In April 1541, after having camped along the Rio Grande during the winter, Coronado led his army across northern Texas into Oklahoma and Arkansas; and then, with a smaller group, he pushed north into Kansas, reaching close to the Nebraska border in July.

From the muster roll of the expedition and other contemporary records it appears that there were five Portuguese among Coronado's men. One of them, André do Campo, was with the friar Juan de Padilla when the latter was killed by hostile Indians at Quivira; but de Campo himself escaped.[9]

The most celebrated Portuguese contribution to the discovery of North America was made by the navigator João Rodrigues Cabrillo. João Rodrigues, later known as Cabrillo,[10] was born in Portugal about the time Columbus made his first voyage to America. Attracted by legends of wealth, he came to Santiago, Cuba, in 1518, shortly after the conquest of that island by Diego Velásquez. At the end of that same year Hernando Cortés left Cuba with a sizable army, against the orders of Velásquez, to conquer Mexico. Early in 1520, when Velásquez dispatched a force under Narváez to capture the insubordinate Cortés and bring him back to Cuba, Cabrillo went along with that force as a captain. In Mexico, after Narváez had succumbed to Cortés, Cabrillo joined the latter and greatly distinguished himself in battling the Aztecs. Later we find him taking part in the conquest of Guatemala, under Pedro de Alvarado; and when Alvarado was killed in a revolt in 1541, Cabrillo entered the service of Mendoza, the viceroy of New Spain.

For some years the Spaniards had been hoping to discover a strait that would connect the Atlantic with the Pacific ocean. Mendoza chose the seasoned mariner Cabrillo to search for such a strait, somewhere north along the Pacific coast, and in June 1542 two vessels under Cabrillo's command set sail northward from Navidad, Mexico. The chief pilot of the expedition was Bartolomé Ferrelo, thought by some to have been Portuguese but actually described as a Levantine; one of Cabrillo's ship masters, Antonio Correa, was most probably a Portuguese.

At the beginning of August 1542 Cabrillo arrived at Cerros Island, the northernmost point visited by a European up to that time, and later in the month the expedition reached what is now Port San Quentin, in Lower California. On 28 September Cabrillo sailed into San Diego Bay and went ashore, thereby becoming the discoverer of present-day California and the first European to set foot on the soil of the future Golden State. After making friends with the Indians there, Cabrillo continued his voyage northward, discovering Santa Catalina and San Clemente Islands, Santa Monica Bay, and San Buenaventura; and by the middle of October he was passing through the Santa Barbara Channel. Encountering severe storms farther north, he had to turn back and take shelter on San Miguel

Island. While waiting for better weather on that island, Cabrillo fell accidentally and broke an arm, but the expedition moved on after a week.

Beyond Point Conception another storm separated the two vessels, and carried them past San Francisco Bay to a point near Fort Ross; there the ships met again and turned back south. By the end of November the expedition was back on San Miguel Island, where camp was set up for the winter. Cabrillo now suffered an infection in his broken arm; and, feeling the end approach, he charged his pilot Ferrelo to continue the expedition northward. On 3 January 1543, the Portuguese discoverer of California died, and was buried on that island.[11]

Ferrelo took up his task and sailed northward once more, reaching the present northern limits of California on 1 March 1543. During the return voyage the two vessels were again separated by storms, but on 14 April the entire expedition, except for its leader, was safely back in Navidad, Mexico. They had not found the hoped-for passage between the Pacific and Atlantic oceans; instead, by an extraordinary feat of navigation, they had discovered the entire length of the California coast.[12]

Some fifty years later, another Portuguese navigator, Sebastião Rodrigues Sermenho, was ordered by the Spanish viceroy in the Philippines to survey the California coast. Sermenho left Manila in July 1595 and arrived off northern California in November. Passing Cape Mendocino he occupied Drake Bay; then he proceeded south and recorded the coastline all the way down to San Diego Bay, which he reached on 15 December of that year.[13]

As we can see from the foregoing, the Portuguese not only led in discovering and opening up Brazil as well as parts of Africa and Asia, but they also made very essential contributions to bringing North America into the European orbit, chiefly by exploration along the coasts. The maritime skill and sense of seagoing adventure which they evidenced in those glorious times was again a notable element, centuries later, in setting into motion the stream of regular Portuguese immigration to the United States, particularly to New England.

Nothing is known of Portuguese settlers (as distinct from explorers) in the sixteenth century or the first third of the seventeenth century within the territory now constituting the United States, and we may assume that there were none. However, during that period the Portuguese kept in close contact with the northeastern corner of North America through fishing enterprises.

John Cabot, and then the brothers Corte-Real, had noted on their respective voyages an abundance of fish in the waters surrounding Newfoundland, and this news spread like wildfire along the coasts of western Europe. By 1506 codfish from Newfoundland waters was being brought into Portugal in sufficient quantities to be taxed, and for a quarter of a century Newfoundland was in fact almost a transatlantic province of the growing Portuguese empire. Later in the century, when the English became dominant there, up to 400 Portuguese, English, and other European fishing vessels swarmed around Newfoundland every year; even nowadays many Portuguese—and Portuguese-American—fishing boats visit the Grand Banks annually.

According to the *Tratado das Ilhas Novas,* written by Francisco de Souza in 1570, a company formed in 1521 in the Portuguese town of Vianna do Castelo (the home town of João Alvares Fagundes) was given a grant by the king and sent two vessels to Newfoundland waters in order actually to colonize the territory frequented by the fishermen. The colonists first settled at what is now Ingonish, a small village on the coast of Cape Breton Island. But after they had spent a winter there, they moved to another unknown location and built a town of some eighty houses. What happened to these settlers later is not known. According to one version, they made their way back to Portugal by 1526.[14]

The first documented instance of a Portuguese settler in the American colonies in the seventeenth century seems to be that of one Mathias de Sousa, who arrived in Maryland in 1634. He may possibly have been of Jewish descent, one of that group which had left Portugal under the pressure of anti-Jewish persecutions.[15]

When Father Isaac Jogues, the French Jesuit missionary, arrived in New Amsterdam (New York) in 1643, after escaping from Indian captivity, he found at least one Portuguese living among the 400 or 500 settlers there. One day, entering a house near the fort, he noticed a picture of the Blessed Virgin on the chimney piece, and it turned out that his hostess, the wife of a Dutch ensign, was a Portuguese Catholic; she could not speak any of the languages known to Father Jogues. That there were one or several Portuguese residents in New York at that time is also indicated, for instance, by the old marriage records of the Dutch Church.[16]

Holland, and later the Dutch possessions along the northeastern coast of South America, had become a haven to many of the Portuguese Jews who had been driven from Portugal, first by the forcible conversion order of 1496 and then by the continuous persecutions (even of those who had forcibly embraced Catholicism) throughout the sixteenth and seventeenth centuries. Other Jews of Portuguese descent, together with many originating from Spain, had found refuge in England and in eastern Mediterranean countries. During the second half of the seventeenth century, and through the eighteenth, many of these Spanish-Portuguese (Sephardic) Jews made their way to the American colonies. They deserve brief mention here because, although they were socially quite distinct from the non-Jewish immigrants from Portugal with whom this book is primarily concerned, and although many of them had grown up outside Portugal as descendants of the émigrés, they nevertheless did carry with them some of that Portuguese culture of which their ancestors had been an important part during the later Middle Ages. The most conspicuous mark of their Portuguese ancestry, even nowadays, is in their family names; as a matter of fact, the majority of Portuguese names that achieved prominence in colonial and modern American history belong to descendants of those Jewish refugees from Portugal.

The first group of Spanish-Portuguese Jews, consisting of twenty-three individuals, arrived in New Amsterdam (New York) in 1654, coming from Recife, Brazil. They had gone to Recife from Holland after the Dutch West India Company had conquered that part of Brazil from the Portuguese; but in 1654, following a lengthy siege, the Dutch returned the city to the Portuguese, and Recife's Jews, numbering in the hundreds if not thousands, had to take flight again.

The small group initially admitted to New Amsterdam was soon augmented by Jews arriving directly from the Netherlands. They lost no time in founding a congregation, Shearith Israel, and in petitioning the local authorities for the right to establish a Jewish cemetery in the city (1655); a small part of that cemetery, located near New York's Chatham Square, still exists. A second cemetery was established at West 11th Street, near Sixth Avenue. Some of the old gravestones showing Portuguese names are preserved; and among the wills filed between 1665 and 1796 in the Surrogate's Office of the County of New York we find mention of such genuinely Portuguese names (belonging to Jews) as Nunez, Rodrigues Marques, Pinheiro, Nunes Fernandes, Machado, De Tores, De Silva, Mendes Seixas, Pacheco da Silva, and de Mesquita. The earliest minutes and accounts of Congregation Shearith Israel (now the Spanish-Portuguese Synagogue at Central Park West, New York

City) were in the Portuguese language; but the use of Portuguese died out after a few decades, and Spanish likewise gave way to the use of English by the middle of the eighteenth century. In the earliest period, New York's Jews were known as the "Portuguese Nation."

A few of the Jewish group that had reached New Amsterdam in 1654 very soon moved on to Newport, Rhode Island, because the Dutch governor of New Amsterdam was reluctant at first to grant them the right to free and permanent settlement. (Some other Jewish residents left the city when it fell to the British in 1664.) Largely as a result of the activities of Spanish-Portuguese Jews, the small town of Newport became one of the important trading centers of the American colonies; these activities also contributed indirectly to the start of regular Portuguese immigration in the nineteenth century.

The first Jewish settlers at Newport were joined by some ninety Jews arriving from Curaçao in the last decade of the seventeenth century, and more came during the first half of the eighteenth century, some of them directly from Portugal (where they had managed to subsist by outwardly professing Catholicism, as so-called Marranos). The most important of these was one Aaron Lopez, born in Lisbon in 1731, who settled in Newport in 1752 (naturalized in Taunton, Massachusetts, in 1762 following Newport's refusal to grant naturalization to Jews). In 1759 Lopez and his coreligionists laid the cornerstone of what is now the oldest extant synagogue in America, the Touro Synagogue in Newport.

Aaron Lopez, and with him one Jacob Rodriguez Rivera, a Jew who had come to Newport about the same time from Spain, were instrumental in introducing the sperm-oil industry to America. Lopez went into the manufacture of spermaceti products, and he fitted out his own fleet of whalers and merchantmen to work the American shores, the West Indies, Portugal, Holland, England, and the whaling grounds. Whaling, largely controlled by the Dutch during the latter half of the seventeenth century, had become a predominantly British industry in the eighteenth century; but the development of Newport under Aaron Lopez and his associates helped pave the way for the leading role which New England was to take in whaling in the nineteenth century, with New Bedford as the center. It is likely that the whaling ships operated by Lopez, like those going out from Nantucket and New Bedford in later years, recruited part of their crews in the Azores, and thus provided the "jumping board" for some of the earliest Azorean settlers in the American colonies.

Newport's commerce was destroyed in the Revolution, and Aaron Lopez himself, who had sided with the Colonists, died during the war. Many of Newport's Jews then moved to New York or Philadelphia.

We have previously mentioned Mathias de Sousa, the Portuguese who had come to Maryland in 1634. Another native of Portugal, the physician Jacob Lumbrozo (definitely identified as a Jew), settled in the Maryland colony in 1656, where he purchased land, practiced medicine, and traded with the Indians until his death ten years later.

Yet another Jewish physician, Samuel Ribeiro Nunez, born in Lisbon, Portugal, arrived in the newly formed colony of Georgia in 1733, coming from England together with a group of some forty Portuguese and Spanish Jews who had escaped to England from the Inquisition. One member of this group in particular, Abraham de Lyon, is credited with having introduced the cultivation of grapes into Georgia in 1737; in his native Portugal he had become familiar with the art of viniculture.

The Portuguese Jewish congregation of Savannah, Georgia, established in 1734, suffered a severe crisis in 1740–41 when many of its members moved to Charleston, South Carolina, after a dispute which involved the question of slave labor. The trustees of the Georgia colony opposed Negro slavery, but numerous colonists, Christians and Jews alike, objected to doing all the hard work themselves while neighboring colonies had slaves to work for them. In Charleston the Jews founded a new congregation and built a synagogue in 1750; its initial members included such names as da Costa, Nunez Cardozo, and others of later fame. After some years, some of these people drifted back to Savannah, where the Jewish congregation was reorganized in 1774.

Elsewhere in the American colonies, Jews of Portuguese extraction settled in various Connecticut towns in the course of the eighteenth century. Most prominent was the Pinto family, first mentioned in the Connecticut records in 1724 (and in those of New York in 1736). Jacob Pinto, and his brother Solomon, who had become residents of New Haven in 1759, played a particularly active part in the Revolution, on the side of the Colonists. In the eighteenth century also some Portuguese and Spanish Jews settled in Boston, and there were important congregations in Philadelphia as well as in Richmond. In 1790 it was estimated that a total of about 3,000 Jews were then living in the United States, most or all of them of Spanish-Portuguese extraction.[17]

But what about non-Jewish Portuguese immigrants in colonial times? That there was a sporadic influx of small numbers may be inferred from various sources, although details are scarce. Father Jogues and other Portuguese Christians in seventeenth-century New Amsterdam have already been mentioned. It is reported, according to the records of the Pennsylvania colony, from 1727 to the Revolution, that there were some Portuguese, in addition to Germans, Dutch, French, and Swiss, among those to whom the oath to the British crown was administered (in that colony). Scattered lists of immigrants landing at Philadelphia from Lisbon or Amsterdam between 1769 and 1805 include a number of Portuguese names, some of these undoubtedly belonging to persons of Jewish descent. It is also claimed, according to the records of Robeson County in North Carolina, that a group of shipwrecked Portuguese sailors landed near Georgetown, South Carolina, shortly before the middle of the eighteenth century and gradually intermarried with Indians and Negroes; the prevalence of the names Cumba and Oxendine in that county among the colored population is usually traced to that group.[18]

This last report, about Portuguese sailors in the Carolinas, refers undoubtedly to the alleged origin of the so-called Melungeons or Croatans in the Smoky Mountains area of eastern Tennessee, western North Carolina, southwestern Virginia, and eastern Kentucky. These people of mixed race, numbering well over 20,000 persons at present, are still a mystery as far as their ancestry is concerned. Of dark complexion, they are classed neither as white, Negro, nor Indian; most of them seem to have a streak of all three races in them, and their social status is generally somewhere between that of whites and of nonwhites (they were always free, and are said to have owned slaves themselves as far back as colonial times). The term "Melungeons" (perhaps from the French *mélange*, mixture) is applied to them in many places, particularly in Hancock County, Tennessee. In the Carolinas, above all in Robeson County, North Carolina, they are generally called "Croatans" (presumably from the belief that their principal ancestors were Croatan Indians). But they are also known by many other popular names, particularly "Portuguese"; they themselves are said to have always insisted that they were of Portuguese ancestry, if only to escape the classification as colored people.

As to their alleged Portuguese origin (which because of their

racial appearance can only be considered as less than half Portuguese at best, unless we think of the possibility of a predominantly
Capeverdean strain), various traditions circulate locally. One of
them is the version reported by Holmes; a slightly different version
has it that the Portuguese ancestors of the group were mutineers
who had deliberately beached their vessel on the North Carolina
coast or that they had been left behind on the shore for some reason
by a Portuguese pirate ship; according to yet another variant, they
had been regular Portuguese traders who intermarried with Indians
and English settlers.[19]

Although the extent of their Portuguese ancestry and the exact
details of their past remain unknown, the persistent claim of these
mixed-bloods to Portuguese forebears can hardly be considered a
mere fabrication; the certain inference can be drawn that some
small group of Portuguese (other than Jews) actually settled near
the Carolina coast sometime before the Revolution.

Turning back to New England, we have records of the presence
of a few Portuguese settlers on the island of Martha's Vineyard,
Massachusetts, toward the close of the colonial period. At Edgartown on that island there lived, before 1790, one immigrant from
Portugal by the name of Emanuel Silvara (Manuel Silveira), and
another one known as Antony Chadwick (obviously an adopted
name); both had married local Yankee girls and had joined the
Protestant church of their wives. Yet another, Joseph Dias (José
Diaz), had come to Tisbury on Martha's Vineyard about 1770,
probably from the Azores. He, too, married a local girl, in January
1780, and immediately after that joined the cause of the Revolution-
aries. Captured by the British, he was sent to England as a prisoner
but secured his release after a few months and returned to Tisbury
in December 1780; in that same month he let himself be baptized
and joined the new Baptist church. Again he went forth to battle
against the British; falling into captivity a second time, he was
imprisoned on the hulk *Jersey*, where he died in 1781.[20]

What had brought these few Portuguese to New England shores
the records do not indicate; it may very well have been whaling, or
some other kind of fishing. The earliest United States customs
registers are said to indicate that some Portuguese crew members of
whaling ships may have settled at Nantucket around the turn of the
eighteenth century; but this leads us beyond the colonial period. In
1780, according to a report by the governor of the Azores, Antão de
Almada, large numbers of men in the western group of the Azores

islands embarked as crew members on some of the 200 whalers which were then cruising in the vicinity; many of these proceeded later to America.[21]

That there must have been at least several hundred Portuguese settlers—in addition to the Jews of Portuguese extraction—in the American colonies when they declared their independence from Britain is suggested by the results of the United States census of 1920, which recorded the national origins of the white population of the United States: in that year the colonial stock (descendants of the population enumerated in the first census, 1790) of Portuguese origin was estimated at 24,000 persons.[22]

Joseph Dias, the Azorean immigrant to Martha's Vineyard, was not the only Portuguese to stand in the front lines when the dispute between the American colonists and Great Britain flared into open revolution and war. When John Paul Jones set out in 1779 on the *Bonhomme Richard*, the first warship to fly the Stars and Stripes, to fight the British off the British Isles, he had with him among his crew twenty-eight Portuguese, recruited in the French port of L'Orient in August of that year. This Portuguese contingent, taken on partly to replace unreliable British elements (prisoners of war) among the original crew of the vessel, constituted some 15 percent of the enlisted personnel (with the officers, the total complement numbered 227 men, plus 137 French soldiers acting as marines). According to the muster roll taken after the famous battle against the British ship *Serapis*, eleven of the Portuguese sailors were killed in that battle and two more were wounded. At least some of the survivors are believed to have settled in the United States later on.[23]

In George Washington's armies, one of the most valiant and most colorful characters was a soldier of Portuguese birth. Peter (Pedro) Francisco, described by contemporaries as a towering giant of swarthy complexion, capable of lifting a cannon weighing 1,100 pounds, had joined the Continental Army at the age of fifteen, and during his four years as a private with various Virginia units he won legendary fame for his strength and fighting prowess. In one engagement, at Guilford Court House, he is said to have mowed down eleven men in succession with his five-foot blade sword. On another occasion, when he was surprised unarmed by nine cavalry-men of British General Tarleton, he managed by ruse and lightning action to disarm one of his captors and to put the others to flight.

According to his own recollections, Francisco had been born in Portugal about 1761, kidnapped when four or five years old, and taken on board a ship that sailed for America. When the ship arrived at Hopewell, Virginia, some sailors dumped the boy on shore and put to sea again. The waif was taken into the home of an uncle of Patrick Henry, in Buckingham County, and later was put to work on the estate of his foster parents until the Revolution broke out. After the end of the war, Peter Francisco became a shopkeeper, a blacksmith, a planter, and a wealthy country gentleman in succession, marrying three times in the course of his career. In later years, his reputation won him an appointment as sergeant-at-arms of the Virginia House of Delegates, and shortly before his death in 1831 he applied to Congress for a soldier's pension, which was granted. He was buried with military honors in Richmond, where a headstone marks his grave. The "strongest man in the Revolutionary armies" is also commemorated by a monument in Greensboro, North Carolina. Copies of an engraving depicting Francisco's encounter with Tarleton's troopers adorned many American homes for a generation (the original engraving is in Independence Hall, Philadelphia).[24]

Peter Francisco, it is true, was a Portuguese only in a limited sense, having been raised almost entirely among Yankees. But there were still other men of more genuinely Portuguese background who swelled the fighting ranks of the young American republic. Some of these show up in the records of the War of 1812, in which the United States reasserted its independence from Britain.

Early in that war, Commander Oliver Hazard Perry had been commissioned to organize an American fleet on the Great Lakes to oppose the British ships there. Among Perry's men who fought the successful Battle of Lake Erie, in September 1813, there seem to have been at least three Portuguese, to judge from the names appearing on the muster roll.[25] One sailor known simply as "Portuguese Joe," Captain of the Main Mast on one of Perry's ships, became a hero of the war: in one of the Great Lakes engagements, after the American flag on his vessel had been shot down by British guns, Portuguese Joe climbed the main mast under heavy fire and nailed the flag to the masthead. He survived that battle, to die in a fire in New Orleans toward the middle of the century.[26]

Some Portuguese had come to the environs of New Orleans right after the Louisiana Purchase in 1803, and perhaps even in the last years of the Spanish regime, according to the Louisiana Historical Society; they settled in the parishes of St. Bernard and Plaquemines. Some more appeared off the Louisiana coast as crew members of the famed French pirate leader Jean Lafitte, who was to prey upon British shipping in those parts. Lafitte made his headquarters on the shores of the Bay of Barataria, some sixty miles south of New Orleans. In 1814, when the British were preparing an invasion of Louisiana from their West Indies bases, they tried to bribe Lafitte into an alliance with them, but the Frenchman tipped off the Americans about the impending attack, and offered his services to Andrew Jackson. In the ensuing Battle of New Orleans, Lafitte's men, who are said to have included many Portuguese sailors and gunners, rendered most effective aid to the American side.[27] On the other hand, some fishermen on the shores of Lake Borgne helped the British as spies and guides. It has been said that these fishermen included not only Spaniards and Italians but also a few Portuguese, but the evidence for this is doubtful.[28]

CHAPTER 2

Beginnings of Postcolonial Immigration from Portugal

MARTHA'S VINEYARD AND NANTUCKET, THE TWO ISLANDS OFF THE NEW England coast, have already been mentioned as places where a few Portuguese from the Azores had come to settle from the close of the colonial period onward. The Azores, or nine Western Islands, stretching across 400 miles of the Mid-Atlantic from northwest to southeast and forming an integral part of the Portuguese homeland since the middle of the fifteenth century, had become an important way-station and rendezvous for whalers roaming the Atlantic. (The whaling ships fitted out by Aaron Lopez in Newport, we recall, may have been the first ones from New England to visit those islands.) The port of Horta, on the island of Fayal in the center of the group, was the place where they would stop, not only to take on fresh water and supplies but also to pick up local lads to complement their crews. Another archipelago constituting a Portuguese possession since 1456, the Cape Verde Islands, off the westernmost point of Africa, became such a calling station, and at the same time a source of manpower for New England whalemen toward the middle of the nineteenth century; there the Yankee vessels anchored off the island of Brava. It is in connection with the whaling business, then, that fishermen from Fayal became the first Portuguese to settle in southeastern New England over the first half of the nineteenth century; and they were soon joined by some Portuguese nationals (partly of African stock) from Brava. (In later years, when the Azorean settlers in New England included more and more natives from islands other than Fayal, many New Englanders continued to call the whole group "Fayalese"; the name "Bravas," on the other

Portuguese fisherman working out of Provincetown.

hand, has become the popular designation of all Capeverdeans in New England, whether hailing from Brava or from some other island in the Cape Verde archipelago.[1] What prompted the whaling captains from Martha's Vineyard and Nantucket, and particularly from New Bedford in later years, to pick up crews in the Azores and the Cape Verde Islands and to bring them to America? Life on the whaling ships was hard and often dangerous; cruises that took the men from their homes would last from half a year up to two and three years at a time, in pursuit of the sperm whale across the oceans. Yet wages were low. Thus the Yankee skippers found it increasingly difficult to recruit qualified labor among the New England population, and their crews became more and more international and exotic, including even Eskimos from the Arctic, Kanakas and Samoans from the Pacific islands, North American Indians, Negroes from the West African coast, and so forth, in addition to Americans and Europeans. Desertions en route depleted the original crews; more and more it became a practice to leave the home port with merely a skeleton crew, averaging about two dozen men, and to pick up cheap additional manpower at way stations later on.[2]

The sturdy islanders of the Azores, and also the Capeverdeans, were traditionally good fishermen and sailors, deriving much of their living from the sea. Plagued by chronic poverty, and of adventurous spirit, many of their young men were ready to grasp the chance that the visiting whaleboats seemed to offer them, to try their luck far from the narrow confines of their island—although they often had no clear idea of the kind of life that would await them on those vessels. In the Azores, there was still another motive, apart from the search for a livelihood, that induced many youngsters to join the whalers: the desire to escape military service, which was considered an oppressive hardship by the islanders, distant as they were from the mainstream of Portuguese life on the continent. Primarily to preserve the sources of military manpower, Portuguese laws restricted emigration from the islands; but while controls were stringent in the eastern Azores, about the middle part of the nineteenth century, it was not too difficult for young men on Fayal, and also for those from the small islands of São Jorge and Flores to the west, to sneak aboard a whaler at night and get away.

The Yankee captains admitted these youngsters eagerly, up to a dozen per vessel, to complement their crews, and they would assign them to tasks at the foremast or in the steerage, with little or nothing

being said on either side about remuneration. The further fate of
the new ship's hands depended largely on the skipper's generosity—
or brutality. After the Portuguese boys became experienced whalemen, the captains often signed them up in accordance with regular
procedure at some American consulate along the way, and as
seamen these foreigners could then enter the United States at the
end of the voyage. At that time they would receive a liberal
allowance from the proceeds of the voyage, if the captain was fair,
and eventually would either return to their native islands or, as
many did, would settle along the New England coast. There are
some known instances of Yankee captains who even adopted such
Azorean young men and took them into their homes later on. But
other whaling bosses pursued their trade with hard-boiled cruelty
toward the men under their command; brutal treatment during the
voyage, not merely the hardships inherent in hunting the whale,
was often responsible for desertions. Particularly Brava pick-ups,
later in the century when the whaling industry was fighting for its
life, were frequently the victims of unscrupulous practices, according to Chippendale. Lured aboard under false pretenses, many of
them were shanghaied from the Cape Verde Islands and, once the
vessel was on the high seas, were exploited with mounting brutality;
sometimes, we learn from Chippendale (a former whaleman himself), this brutality was calculated to drive the frightened men into
desertion shortly before the end of the voyage, so that their share of
the proceeds could be confiscated. Nevertheless, a good number of
these Capeverdeans reached America, and one by one they settled
down in the New Bedford area.[3]
   Of the Capeverdeans, many actually stuck to whaling until the
turn of the nineteenth century or beyond. The Azorean sailors,
however, were relatively quick in turning to other pursuits, once
they had worked their way across to the United States on whaling
vessels. Toward the middle of the century, some of them began to
send for their women and families back in the Azores and to
establish homes in New Bedford, Massachusetts. The women made
the voyage not on steamers, but on small sailboats that would take
one to two months to reach their destination, usually the port of
Boston. Yet by 1858 there were only a dozen Portuguese women
living in New Bedford, at a time when men from Fayal (and
occasionally from some other Azores island) were already "as plenty
as whales' teeth" in that whaling city,[4] numbering many hundreds.
   The first Portuguese name occuring in the customs register of

New Bedford actually dates from 1817; but quite a few Azorean sailors are thought to have visited the port even before that year. Commercial intercourse between New Bedford and the Azores came into full swing about 1830 or shortly thereafter; some ten years later the first Azorean family is said to have settled down in the town. In the peak year of whaling, 1857, when the New Bedford whaling fleet comprised some 360 vessels, a considerable number of these vessels were already in Portuguese hands, and most of the others had at least some Portuguese crew members aboard (not all of the latter, of course, could be considered residents of the city). By the end of the Civil War, the Portuguese population of New Bedford numbered "more than eight hundred" individuals.[5]

In nearby Fall River, Massachusetts, which was to become the second-largest Portuguese settlement in the eastern part of the country, immigration from the Azores had its bare beginnings about the time of the Civil War. The first Portuguese is reported to have arrived in 1855; local church records indicate a Portuguese wedding performed in 1857, and a few Portuguese names appear on the baptismal register from 1860 on.[6] Records in Providence, Rhode Island, show that Portuguese sailors started coming to that city in 1839,[7] but actual settlement in larger numbers did not begin until two or three decades later. In Provincetown, on Cape Cod, where the Portuguese element constitutes the absolute majority of the population today, the first Portuguese birth appears in the church records in 1853, but a few Portuguese may have settled in that fishing town well before the middle of the century; by 1869, forty-four of ninety-four children born in the local parish were of Portuguese parentage.

In Boston, where a Portuguese vice-consulate was in existence as far back as 1837, and through which most of the early Azorean immigrants (other than whalemen) entered the country, some forty Portuguese residents were officially counted in 1860, and another eighty in the neighboring counties of Middlesex and Norfolk. (One girl from Flores Island, in the Azores, is known to have arrived in suburban Cambridge in 1849 to marry a Portuguese there.) To the fishing community of Gloucester, on Cape Ann, a first small group of Azoreans came between 1845 and 1847, and larger numbers were attracted by the fisheries there in the next two decades. [8]

Census figures for Massachusetts as a whole show 855 natives of "Portugal" (which usually means the Azores in the first place!) as of 1855. Ten years later, according to the census of Massachusetts, there were a total of 1,883 "natives of Portugal" in that state (including 516 in New Bedford, 505 in Boston, and 237 in Provincetown). The total rose to 3,705 by 1875 (and by that time there were also quite a few American-born children of the immigrants).

In adjoining Rhode Island, according to the censuses of that state, the number of "natives of Portugal and Western Islands" rose from 58 in 1850 to 561 in 1875, at which time there were also over 300 American-born children of these foreigners. More than half of these lived in Providence.

In the state of Connecticut, 265 Portuguese-born residents were counted in 1860, according to the United States census for that year; ten years later they were down to 243. Presumably most or all members of this group were domiciled in or around the port of New London. In 1846 New London ranked second as a whaling center, after New Bedford; a few years later, however, its whaling business began to decline repidly.

Outside New England, a small Portuguese colony developed about the middle of the nineteenth century in New York City, which was experiencing a tremendous growth at that time. There had been some Jews of Portuguese extraction in that city since the seventeenth century, as we remember. Some who had gone to Newport returned to New York after the Revolution. But apart from them, there seem to have been at least a few Catholic Portuguese immigrants in the city about the time of the War of 1812.[9] By 1860, according to official figures, 106 males and 34 females of Portuguese birth (plus a dozen or two described as "Atlantic Islanders") were living in New York City. The year before, this small group had founded a Portuguese military company, in imitation of the Italian and other immigrant groups (the native American companies, i.e., National Guard units, were still reluctant to admit immigrants). During the Civil War, one New York regiment included a small company of Spaniards and Portuguese.[10]

In New Jersey, merely one or two dozen immigrants from Portugal were counted in the United States census of 1850 and that of 1860. However, sometime before 1830 a group of Portuguese hired to cut lumber for the Camden and Amboy Railroad are alleged to have settled in the Pemberton area and to have named their place Lisbon (now New Lisbon, a village about thirty miles east of Philadelphia).[11]

As for Pennsylvania, the presence of some Portuguese individuals toward the end of the colonial period has already been mentioned.

Shortly before 1820, a small Portuguese colony had formed in that state, probably consisting of political émigrés; a few more refugees from Portugal's civil war came from Madeira about 1830, according to one source.[12] But the census of 1850 reported no more than three or four dozen residents of Portuguese birth for that state; in 1860 their number had risen to about 100 (most of these probably living in Philadelphia and in its suburbs on the New Jersey side). During or shortly after the Civil War, some Portuguese families drifted into Erie, Pennsylvania (perhaps in connection with the completion of the second Erie canal), coming from the Western Azores via Boston.[13]

Far to the south, meanwhile, in Louisiana, a group of "a few hundred" laborers had arrived from Portugal about the year 1840, contracted by Louisiana plantation owners to work on their sugar plantations. They were mostly single men, and after a few years many of these intermarried with local Creole women. However, they did not give up their ethnic solidarity for some time, although they were completely isolated from their countrymen in New England. In April 1847 they founded the first Portuguese mutual-aid society in the United States, the Portuguese Benevolent Association, to pay sickness benefits and funeral expenses and also to organize their traditional Holy Ghost festival once a year. When some internal quarrel produced a split, a second such society was founded in August 1848, under the name of Lusitanian Benevolent Association. But both competing societies merged again three years later, into the Lusitanian-Portuguese Benevolent Association, which as of the 1950s was still in existence in New Orleans (although by then its membership of several thousand no longer included anyone of Portuguese descent).

Sources disagree as to whether these plantation workers hailed from the Portuguese mainland or from the Azores; we are inclined to accept the latter hypothesis (the Holy Ghost festival is primarily an Azorean tradition). As to why contract laborers from Portugal had been brought into slaveowning Louisiana, we can only speculate: In the last two decades before the Civil War the price of slaves was becoming very high; for this reason wage-earning Irish and other European immigrants received more and more preference as laborers in the New Orleans sugar refinery and elsewhere. Most of the Portuguese seem to have stayed on the sugar plantations until the Civil War. In the census of 1860, 109 natives of Portugal were counted in New Orleans. A few years later, we find half a dozen

Portuguese-born soldiers in one Louisiana company of the Confederate Army. In 1865, when the Civil War ended, and slavery with it, the majority of the Portuguese abandoned the work on the sugar plantations; some allegedly returned to Portugal, but the greater part moved into new occupations in New Orleans. Yet, before long the bulk of the latter moved to the new land of opportunity, California; and the only traces left of them today in the big Gulf city are the above-mentioned benevolent society and a few Portuguese family names among the local population such as Machado, Silva, De Fraites (Freitas), and Rocha.[14]

Entirely unique is the case of the Portuguese immigrant group from Madeira which arrived in Illinois in 1849. Tens of thousands of Portuguese were to settle in the United States over the years and to build new homes for themselves; practically all of these (with the exception of some Portuguese Jews and of a few politically conscious intellectuals in recent years) immigrated for economic reasons, and not primarily in search of religious or political freedom. The Madeirans who came to Illinois, however, professing the Protestant faith, were refugees from religious persecution.

In the year 1838 the Portuguese island of Madeira, off the northwestern coast of Africa, had received a visit from the Scottish physician and Protestant missionary Dr. Robert Reid Kalley, who had interrupted his voyage to China to recuperate from sudden illness on that island, famous for its heathful climate. Very soon Kalley decided to remain on Madeira and to expend his missionary efforts there rather than in China. His efforts were successful, for in the course of a few years, reading the Bible to the poor and oppressed islanders, he converted hundreds of them to Protestantism. The converts, deeply dedicated to their new faith, established a militant congregation; the local Catholic clergy, in turn, became increasingly worried and hostile. When the opposition of the Catholics flared into violent rioting in 1846, Dr. Kalley and his followers, by then numbering more than a thousand, took refuge on shipboard and sailed for Trinidad in the British West Indies, where there was an urgent need for plantation labor.

In Trinidad the Madeiran "exiles" tried hard to reestablish themselves, but over a period of two or three years the local climate and work conditions proved so disastrous to them that they began to look for a haven elsewhere.[15] In the United States, where their plight had been receiving wide publicity, the American Protestant Society finally took an interest, and arrangements were made with the American Hemp Company to bring the refugees into this country and to settle and employ them at Island Grove in Illinois, between the cities of Jacksonville and Springfield. However, when the first shipload of the Portuguese islanders arrived in New York in the spring of 1849, they found that their prospective employer had withdrawn from his commitment, and they were left stranded. Now the people of Jacksonville and Springfield themselves took over, offering asylum and a livelihood to the homeless. Gratefully the Madeirans accepted the offer. Charitable contributions from various parts of the country poured in to defray the cost of their westward journey; and, after some delay caused by a cholera epidemic in Illinois, an initial group of 130 persons moved to Springfield in November 1849. A similar group went to Jacksonville.

The prairies of Illinois became a permanent new home for these Protestants from Madeira. The first parties of settlers were soon followed by the rest, who had stayed behind in Trinidad; by 1855 close to 400 of their number were living around Springfield, and a slightly larger group near Jacksonville. There they founded their new church, which remained under the jurisdiction of the Free Church of Scotland until 1856; today this is an American congregation of the Methodist denomination. Portuguese traditions have faded into oblivion among the descendants of the "Madeiran exiles." But even in our day the hilly area between Jacksonville and Springfield where the colonists concentrated continues to be referred to as the "Portuguese Hill"; and among the present population of Jacksonville we find families with such Portuguese names as Sousa, Goncalves, Vasconcelos, Fernandes, Gouveia, etc.[16]

In Springfield, Illinois, at the time when the Madeiran refugees arrived, there was living a man destined to become America's greatest champion in the fight for human dignity and freedom: Abraham Lincoln. A small-town lawyer of rising fame, he took into his home about 1858 a "black-eyed" Portuguese woman by the name of Frances Affonsa to do the family washing; she stayed on to become the regular cook of the Lincolns. Her "man," Manuel de Fraita, we read in Sandburg's biography of Lincoln, "who said he would sometime take her for a bride," often came to see her, and the two had supper together in the kitchen. The Lincolns liked Frances's cooking, and she actually managed to get along well with the lady of the house—which was no mean accomplishment. Undoubtedly both Frances Affonsa and Manuel de Fraita (Freitas) were members of that refugee group from Madeira.[17]

Portuguese dairy farmers in Marin County, California, during milk cooling operation.

California, the land discovered by the Portuguese mariner João Rodrigues Cabrillo in Spanish service, had seen the beginnings of European settlement in 1769, when the Franciscans under the sponsorship of the Spanish crown had started the establishment of missions along the Pacific coast. By 1823, after the territory had come under the control of the new Republic of Mexico, there were twenty-one religious stations of this kind, from San Diego in the south to Sonoma in the north, with large plantations and cattle ranches. The Spanish government had also begun in 1777 to found a number of pueblos, or towns. Even before Mexico had established its sovereignty, some American pioneers from the east started arriving in northern California. In 1846, with the aid of the American settlers, the United States wrested this Pacific territory from Mexico. By that time, some natives of Portugal were already residing or doing business on the shores of California.

We have pointed out that men from the Azores had found their way onto whaling ships as early as the latter part of the eighteenth century; many of these whalers visited the California coast. There were Portuguese not only among the crews of these vessels, but also among the captains, as early records show. At various spots along the California coast the whaling companies established stations for the processing of whale oil, starting in 1789. The Portuguese seem to have played a prominent part in the operation of some of these whaling posts or factories, which were named after them. South of Los Angeles there are two points known as "Portuguese Cove" and "Portuguese Bend" since Franciscan times; melting pots and other equipment used in the past for separating the fatty substance from the flesh of the whale can still be seen in those locations. At Monterey there still stands a building dating from 1850 with a sign reading "Portuguese Whaling Station." Thus the whaling industry was instrumental in bringing the first Portuguese not only to New England, but also to California—as transients, at least, if not as permanent settlers. (In both areas, this industry became extinct toward the end of the nineteenth century).[18]

Apart from those engaged in whaling, very few individual Portuguese are known to have lived in California before the annexation of the territory by the United States. When San Diego, established as a Franciscan mission in 1769, was fortified by the Spaniards a few years later, the "presidio" was placed under the command of one José Manuel Machado, reputedly a Portuguese in Spanish service. The first foreigner to settle in the Spanish pueblo of Los Angeles was José Antonio Rocha, who arrived there from his native Portugal in 1815, or shortly thereafter, after landing at Monterey, and built a relatively large home on what is now Spring Street, at the corner of Franklin Street. In 1853, a few years after the town had been taken over by American forces, Rocha sold his house to the municipality, and it became the first city hall and county court house of the American city of Los Angeles. One Carlos Pedro Diogo Andrade, born in Portugal in 1825 to a Portuguese army officer, arrived in California in his childhood (presumably with his father) and became a pioneer in Amador County (east of Sacramento).[19]

It was from spots bordering on this county in California that the news flashed across the continent, and then around the world, in 1848: gold had been found! Gold, and unlimited riches, for whoever would get there first to grab the precious metal. Among the thousands of adventurers who rushed to northern California as the result of this news were small numbers of Portuguese. Some of these were sailors who had deserted their whaling ships at San Francisco and at other points. Others, a little later, came from New England, sailing around Cape Horn or cutting their voyage in two by crossing the Isthmus of Panama in mule-drawn carts. The discovery of gold was also the attraction for some who migrated to California directly from Portugal, shortly after the middle of the nineteenth century.[20]

After a few years, however, the gold fever subsided, and the settlers in California turned to other pursuits, disillusioned but nonetheless determined to remain on the new frontier. The Portuguese, whom the official census placed at 109 individuals in the year 1850 and at about 1,500 ten years later (mostly men from the western Azores), concentrated first in the proximity of San Francisco Bay, but they also fanned out as far north as Fort Bragg, and from the Sacramento area southward through the San Joaquin Valley as far as Hanford, going generally into wheat-growing, shepherding, etc.; a few, in the San Diego area far to the south, went into fishing after the close of the Civil War. The hope for gold was gone, but the blessings of agriculture attracted additional Portuguese immigrants from New England and directly from the Azores. It was after the close of the Civil War also, as we recall, that a group from Louisiana moved out to California.[21]

Here are a few individual sketches illustrating these developments: Carlos Pedro Diogo Andrade, whom we have already mentioned, moved to Sacramento in 1846, but a few years later he settled in Amador County, where he discovered a gold mine and

laid claim to it. Francisco José da Silva, born in 1826 on the island
of Pico, in the Azores, embarked on a whaling ship as a youngster;
when after years of roaming the oceans his vessel sailed around
Cape Horn and up to San Francisco, da Silva deserted it there in
1847. João Soito Freitas, born in the Azores in 1823, signed up on a
whaleboat at the age of eighteen, and at the end of his cruise settled
down in New Bedford; but in 1853 the adventurous young man
embarked again in New York, bound for California via Cape Horn.
In California he first went to work in a gold mine near Folsom,
accumulating some $2,000; then, in 1862, he purchased land in Yolo
County and in the following year married an Azorean girl, with
whom he gave fourteen children to his new country. A. de Costa,
born in 1830, left Fayal in the Azores as a cabin boy on a whaler
from New London. After a voyage of three years that carried him
around the world, his vessel called at San Francisco in 1849.
Promptly the crew deserted the ship—except for de Costa. Since the
captain could not find a new crew, he sold the ship as junk to a
Chinese company, and young de Costa secured employment on
riverboats running up to Stockton. In 1861 he married an English
girl in San Francisco, and the couple moved to Hawaii.[22]

A very few of the Portuguese frontiersmen in the California of
pre–Civil War days eventually drifted northward into Oregon, or
farther inland into the RockyMountain territories. One of these,
John "Portugee" Phillips, became a sort of Paul Revere of the West:
Born in 1832 as Manual (or João) Felipe, on the island of Pico in the
western Azores, he came to California shortly after the Gold Rush,
later moved inland prospecting, and in 1866 obtained a job as a
woodchopper with the quartermaster at Fort Kearny, along the
Bozeman Trail in Wyoming. The fort had just been built, in
connection with the federal government's resumption of a strong
stand against the Plains Indians, now that the Civil War was over.
Suddenly, a savage Sioux attack threatened Fort Kearny with
extinction, and a volunteer was needed to break through the siege
lines to seek help at the next fort, Laramie. This meant riding some
240 miles through hostile territory, in freezing snow. Phillips, known
there simply as "Portuguese John," accomplished the almost impossible task (which has been called a much greater feat than the
famous ride of Paul Revere during the Revolution). This action later
earned him special praise in Congress. After a government-sponsored return visit to his native Pico, he died in Wyoming in 1883.[23]

We cannot close this account of Portuguese immigration into the

United States through the Civil War period without referring to the Hawaiian Islands, then known as the Sandwich Islands, which became United States territory in 1898. During the last two decades of the nineteenth century, these were to develop into the third major area of Portuguese settlement on American soil, after New England and California.

Individual Portuguese nationals were living in the island kingdom of Hawaii as early as the year 1794.[24] But the earliest Portuguese visitor there of whom details are known was the adventurer John Elliot de Castro, who first came to those islands in 1814. Driven by a desire for quick wealth, de Castro had joined in speculative enterprises in various parts of the world, and in the year 1814 stopped off on Hawaii, where he so impressed King Kamehameha I that the latter retained him as his personal physician and favorite, presenting him with large tracts of land. After staying less than a year, the treasure-hunting de Castro sailed for Sitka, off the coast of Alaska, where the Russian-American Company, under the Russian Alexander Baranof, had established a trading post in 1799. At the time of de Castro's arrival there, Sitka's trade extended not only to the United States, but also to Hawaii, California, and China. Baranof hired the Portuguese adventurer to accompany one of his merchant ships to California; in California, however, de Castro, along with the entire crew of the vessel, fell into Spanish captivity. After his release or escape, he embarked again at San Francisco in October 1816, as guest of Otto von Kotzebue, the German explorer in Russian service who was setting sail for Hawaii; in the Hawaiian Islands de Castro was hoping to catch an American vessel that would take him back to Sitka. However, after his arrival there, de Castro settled down again and stayed on for at least another two years as secretary (foreign minister) to King Kamehameha.[25]

In 1827 two baptisms of Portuguese children were performed at Honolulu.[26] In the year 1828 there appeared in the Hawaiian kingdom a Portuguese by the name of Antonio Silva; local tradition has it that he was the first to grow sugar cane on the islands.[27] In the course of the next fifty years, prior to the onset of organized mass immigration in 1878, several hundred Portuguese settled on the islands, arriving singly or in small groups. Again, as in New England and in California, it was the whale fishery that brought most of these early pioneers to the distant archipelago in the Pacific. Sailors from Fayal, Graciosa, and São Jorge in the western Azores, and from the Cape Verde Islands off Africa, they jumped ship to try their luck among the cheerful natives of Hawaii rather than continue the rugged life aboard the whalers. In 1853, according to local statistics, there were 86 Portuguese on Oahu, including twenty Capeverdean blacks (yet these latter were commonly known as Portuguese— "Pokiki" in older Hawaiian pronunciation—not as Negroes!)[28] According to the same official statistics there were 436 Portuguese nationals on that principal island early in the year 1878. But the Portuguese consul in Honolulu reported in 1881 that the Portuguese colony in Hawaii, as of the earlier part of 1878, consisted of 420 Azoreans and 120 Capeverdeans; the Azorean group, he added, included sixty-six individuals who had come from California seeking employment. Most of the Capeverdeans and some of the Azoreans, it is said, married Hawaiian women, while other Azoreans secured wives from their native land.[29]

Thus, in our account of Portuguese settlement in the United States, we have come to the end of the early period of sporadic influx and to the threshold of a second chapter: mass immigration, large-scale settlement in southeastern New England, in California, and in Hawaii. By coincidence, perhaps, mass immigration started about the same time—a few years after the Civil War—on both the Atlantic seaboard and the West Coast (and hardly a decade later in Hawaii). The tempo of immigration, for the whole country, is illustrated by the following United States census figures covering the numbers of arrivals (not necessarily immigrants) from "Portugal" who were admitted to the United States (exclusive of Hawaii, of course) between 1820 and 1880:

| 1820–30 | 180 | 1841–50 | 550 | 1861–70 | 2,658 |
| 1831–40 | 829 | 1851–60 | 1,055 | 1871–80 | 14,082 |

On a year-by-year basis, these same census statistics, whatever validity we can attach to them, indicate some remarkable oscillations in the curve visualizing the movement of early Portuguese immigration: From 1820 to 1855, the number of immigrants admitted in any one year seldom exceeded two or three dozen and was always less than 100—but with the following exceptions: from 1832 to 1833, the figure jumped from 5 admissions to 633, and between the years 1849 and 1850, from 26 to 366![30] In 1855, 205 Portuguese were admitted; then annual figures sank again as low as 46, until the last days of the Civil War. In 1864, there were 240 admissions, and in the following two years 365 and 344, respectively. From 1869 through 1871, the number of annual admissions was between 500 and 1,000, but between 1872 and 1880 it climbed to between 1,000 and a little over 2,000 per year.

Actually these figures do not give an accurate picture of Portuguese immigration, for reasons that will be discussed in the next chapter. They are undoubtedly somewhat too low, chiefly because many Azoreans and Capeverdeans, when asked about their country of origin, must have indicated the Azores and the Cape Verde Islands, respectively, rather than "Portugal."

As against the numbers of persons who entered the country officially in a given year or a decade, the following United States census figures report the numbers of foreign-born persons that were counted as established residents in certain key years:

	1850 Born in "Portugal" (excludes Azores and Madeira?)	*1860* Born in "Portugal"	"Atlantic Islands"	*1870* Born in "Portugal"	"Atlantic Islands"
Mass.	290	988	433	735	1,947
R.I.	58	86	24	146	81
Conn.	74	265	—	49	194
N.Y.	194	353	96	237	112
N.J.	16	14	15	37	5
Penna.	34	90	27	89	45
La.	157	145	34	125	7
Ill.	42	395	453	76	782
Calif.	109	1,459	121	2,508	943
Other states	300(?)	321(?)	158(?)	540(?)	318(?)
Total U.S.	1,274	4,116	1,361	4,542	4,434

("Atlantic Islands" includes the Azores and Madeira, as well as the Spanish Canary Islands. Many Azoreans and some Madeirans were evidently placed under the heading of "Portugal." The figures for "Portugal" and "Atlantic Islands" are best combined to reflect natives of the Portuguese islands, plus a few from mainland Portugal and/or the Canary Islands.)

As for statistics compiled in Portugal and covering emigration to the United States, there are hardly any usable figures for this period.

From 1820 to 1871, figures for emigration from (the mainland of) Portugal were apparently confused and mingled with those for emigration from Spain (via Portugal), for some odd reason, while emigration from the Azores was tabulated separately. Probably one merely recorded the destination reported by emigrants at Portuguese ports of embarkation, without noting whether the emigrants were Portuguese citizens or Spaniards in transit. According to such Portuguese statistics, a total of 6,885 Azoreans went to the United States between 1820 and 1871 (which means, we assume, that this many were officially recorded as sailing from Azorean ports, bound for the United States—but clandestine emigrants and whalemen ignorant of their ultimate destination were naturally overlooked); in 1871, 785 Azoreans are reported to have left for this country.[31]

CHAPTER 3

The First Period of Portuguese Mass Immigration, c. 1870-1921:

The Process in General

AS NOTED IN THE PRECEDING CHAPTER, THE INFLUX OF RELATIVELY large numbers of Portuguese immigrants into the (continental) United States started about the year 1870. Portuguese mass immigration into the then sovereign Sandwich Islands, now the state of Hawaii, had its onset just a few years later. Official United States immigration statistics show five to six times more immigrants from "Portugal" during the 1870s than during the previous ten-year period. After 1870, Portuguese immigration increased steadily decade by decade, reaching a peak between the years 1911 and 1920. After 1921, quota restrictions legislated by the American Congress were to slow this influx to a carefully regulated trickle, until resurgence almost four decades later. Here is the actual official count:

1861–1870	2,658
1871–1880	14,082
1881–1890	16,978
1891–1900	27,508
1901–1910	69,149
1911–1920	89,732
1921–1930	29,994 (incl. 19,195 for 1921)

Out of the offical total of 241,916 "Portuguese" immigrants admitted into the United States from 1820 through 1921, barely 2 percent arrived up to 1870. About one-fourth of this number came between 1871 and 1900, and nearly three-fourths during 1901–1921.[1]

As for the regional origins of these immigrants classified as Portuguese, we can readily accept the estimate by Alvin R. Graves, based on Portuguese as well as American immigration statistics and other sources, to the effect that (at least) 65 to 70 percent of those who arrived between 1820 and 1921 were from the Azores, not from what most Americans popularly think of as "Portugal" (i.e., the mainland portion of that country). Inasmuch as Continentals did not arrive in the United States in appreciable numbers until after 1906 (chiefly in 1910–12 and again in 1919–21), the proportion of Azoreans coming in throughout the nineteenth century and into the first decade of the twentieth was probably above 80 percent, the balance being taken up largely by Madeirans (particularly if we include immigration to Hawaii) and by Capeverdeans.

In terms of preferred destinations of Portuguese immigrants to all parts of the world, Portuguese immigration statistics for 1892-1921 indicate that among the nearly 1 million Portuguese who (legally!) left their homeland during that thirty-year period, 86 percent of the Continentals chose Brazil, and so did 52 percent of the Madeirans—but only 16 percent of the Azoreans. Inversely, 82 percent of all Azoreans during that period chose "North America" (for all practical purposes the United States) as their destination, while only 34 percent of the Madeirans and barely 5 percent of the Continentals did so. (These figures exclude Hawaii, which took about 4.5 percent of all Madeirans but only 0.6 percent of emigrating Azoreans.) In terms of regional composition of the total contingent that did opt for North America between 1892 and 1921, 63 percent hailed from the Azores, 26 percent from the Portuguese mainland, and 11 percent from Madeira. (The Capeverdeans are evidently not covered in this statistic.)[2]

Why did so many Portuguese emigrate during the period under consideration? The following reasons can be adduced for Portuguese emigration in general, and for emigration to the United States in particular:

1. The principal reason at all times was poverty, a lack of economic opportunity at home.[3] For a fuller discussion of this leading motivation, see Chapter 9.

2. Another reason was the desire of young men to escape military service. This factor seems to have been of importance especially in the latter part of the nineteenth century, when the Portuguese

monarchy was beginning to totter under Republican opposition, and again immediately before and during the First World War. The escape from military service must, of course, be judged against the background of economic and political conditions existing at the time in Portugal, especially in the Azores and Madeira. The islanders, isolated and relatively neglected by the central government as they were, had little sense of involvement in the affairs of the mainland. Also in the north of continental Portugal, hotbed of Republicanism around the turn of the century, military service was felt to be an unjust burden.[4]

3. A general historical inclination toward (overseas) emigration, founded on the "spirit of adventure"[5] and maritime orientation, may have counted as an impulse, but only when combined with economic pressure.

4. At specific times, natural disasters such as volcanic eruptions or drought-induced famines, which have periodically plagued the lives of Azoreans and Capeverdeans, caused an upsurge in emigration. For example, a drought in the Cape Verde Islands in 1904 sharply increased migration to the United States. Volcanic eruptions in the Azores in 1958 sparked the recent renewal of mass emigration (see Chapter 7).

5. Throughout the period under consideration, as well as in more recent times, a desire to rejoin family members already settled in the United States (or for a woman to follow her suitor's call to marriage) was, of course, a major inducement to emigration.[6]

6. On the other hand, "spiritual" aspirations such as the search for religious freedom or for educational opportunities provided hardly any stimulus for Portuguese emigration. The exodus of the Madeiran Protestants mentioned in the preceding chapter is one documented exception.

As for the method of immigration, we have already seen that prior to 1870 many male immigrants came over as whalemen and sailors, their families frequently following later as passengers on sailing boats. Even after 1870, though the whaling industry was in decline, many Azorean and Capeverdean men continued to arrive in the United States as seamen.

A few biographical sketches will serve to illustrate the general process and to add typical details. One is the story of Francisco P. Soares, who was born on the Azorean island of Flores in 1872. His grandfather Antonio Soares had gone to California in 1849, sailing around Cape Horn. After working in the California mines for several years, he traveled to Boston to take ship and return to Flores. Meanwhile Antonio's son, João, had joined an American whaling ship in the Azores, at age sixteen, and after four years of voyaging he stopped at New Bedford, where he had heard his father was staying. Missing his father by a few days, João Soares hired aboard a sailing vessel and returned to Flores. There he married, but after some years left his wife and family to return to the United States, where he worked as a sailor on ships plying between Philadelphia and New Orleans. In 1870 he went to San Francisco, from where he sent for his wife and four children. But Senhora Soares refused to come to the land where "the Indians run wild. . . ." Eventually João himself returned to Flores, where he died in 1921. One of his sons, Francisco, in turn left Flores at age seventeen, and made his way to San Francisco in 1889—but now traveling from Boston by railroad.[7]

No less interesting is the story of Frank J. Gomes, also born on Flores in 1855. At age eighteen Gomes joined a whaling ship and voyaged four years under great hardship. He was given a mere $100 as his final share when he came ashore in San Francisco in 1877. Despairing of the sea, Gomes worked as a laborer in San Jose, then as a store clerk in Modesto, California. In 1884 he returned to the Azores, where he married Maria Rosa Gonsalves and took her back with him to California. By 1899 Gomes had become a prosperous dairyman and farmer and his eight children only knew about whaling ships from the stories of their father.[8]

For some, whaling continued to be a source of employment as well as a method of immigration. Antonio Fortes, born on São Nicolau, Cape Verde Islands, in 1890, shipped out on the New Bedford whaler *Pedro Varela* in 1908. After nine months on the seas, Fortes arrived in New Bedford. There he found a job in a rope factory and attended school at night. In 1910 he shipped out on that same whaler again. The cruise was aborted when the non-Portuguese part of the crew mutinied, and the vessel had to put into Baltimore. With a different crew, the *Pedro Varela* then cruised the Cape Verde Islands, returning to New Bedford in 1912. In 1913 Fortes signed aboard the whaling ship *Greyhound*, returning to New Bedford in 1916. He continued to ship out until 1921, when he finally settled down and married on Martha's Vineyard. There he worked as a gardener and estate custodian until his retirement in 1964 at the age of seventy-four.[9]

The island of São Nicolau was also the home of one Joseph Ribeiro, who signed aboard the famous whaler *Charles W. Morgan* in 1919 when that ship put into the Cape Verde Islands. Ribeiro, in an interview in 1975, recalled how fifty-six years earlier he had been first in line among many Cape Verdeans anxious to sign up on an American ship. After a cruise of nine months, the *Morgan* put in at New Bedford and Ribeiro went ashore. From New Bedford he went to Bridgeport, Connecticut, where some of his cousins had settled. There he went to night school and learned to read and write English, and eventually he settled down in Norwich. The *Charles W. Morgan* was taken out of service in the early 1920s for by then the whaling industry was practically finished—and with it a historic mode for Portuguese lads to reach the United States. Incidentally, when Ribeiro landed in New Bedford in 1920 no less than seven stowaways from the Cape Verde Islands were also found to be aboard.[10]

The increased movement and volume of people and goods between the United States and the Portuguese Atlantic Islands after 1870 resulted in the development of more regular maritime services. By the 1880s there were three or four sailing vessels plying five or six times a year from the Azores to Boston and New Bedford. In addition there was irregular service of English, German, and Portuguese steamers.[11]

C. Alice Baker, writing in 1882 about her summer vacation in the Azores,[12] tells how she first booked passage from New Bedford to Faial on a steamer "painfully rumored to be unseaworthy." She then switched to reserving a "stateroom" on a sailing boat whose itinerary included Flores, Faial, Terceira, and São Miguel. This was an American bark but, with the exception of the captain, manned by a Portuguese crew; in addition to the stateroom passengers, it carried Portuguese steerage passengers for the islands of Flores and Faial. According to Baker, there was then an "excellent" line of Portuguese steamers providing fortnightly service between the Azores and Lisbon;[13] and an American steamer, the *Mississippi*, from New Bedford, stopped at Ponta Delgada, from where it would go on to Madeira. For those who did not seek stateroom accommodations, the American bark *Iceberg* carried legal and clandestine emigrants from Horta to Boston (as of 1876, this took about twenty-five days) and returned to the Azores with smuggled United States tobacco and reemigrating Portuguese.[14]

In 1902, the American White Star Line set up regular twice-monthly steamer service to the Azores from Boston. These ships called at Ponta Delgada and sometimes at Madeira, but never at ports in continental Portugal. Probably as a result of this Boston-Azores connection, the Portuguese line(s) which had previously provided service from Lisbon to the Azores to Boston discontinued the Azores-Boston service in 1908.[15] In 1911 the Fabre Line started direct service from the Azores to Providence, Rhode Island; until 1920, Providence was the main port of entry for Portuguese immigrants.[16] The Fabre Line steamers went from New York to Providence, then to Lisbon, from there to Ponta Delgada, Angra do Heroismo, and Horta (the three principal Azorean ports), and then returned to Providence.[17]

Irregular service between the islands and the United States also increased during this period. In 1900, six Portuguese sailing boats and one Portuguese steamship entered the port of Boston.[18] In 1904, fifteen steamers entered Boston, and there were no less than nineteen ship arrivals at New Bedford, with Portuguese immigrants aboard.[19] In 1905, thirteen British steamers from the Azores made port in Boston; five Portuguese steamers arrived in New Bedford from Lisbon and the Azores, and fourteen sailing boats from the Cape Verdes. Similar numbers of arrivals are recorded for the years through 1909.[20]

Development of regular and irregular service can be seen as a response to the growing traffic of immigrants. In turn, it also stimulated immigration by making transportation more available. Particularly, it enabled women and children to emigrate more easily, and it opened up the eastern Azorean islands (in addition to the western and central ones) to emigration to America. Steamship passage from Ponta Delgada to the United States cost $23 in 1902 and about $30 a few years later;[21] many could barely afford this, and some tried to come over as stowaways. At any rate, the haphazard emigration of Portuguese males as whalers was quickly replaced by the large and frequent emigration of individuals as well as whole families as paying passengers in steerage. Some arrived penniless, having spent everything on the fare.

Regular shipping service also increased illegal emigration. The Portuguese government had issued strict antiemigration laws designed mainly to curb escape from military service. These laws required from every male emigrant over fourteen years of age a heavy deposit of money (the equivalent of about $300) as guarantee for his return in case of conscription. These fees, in addition to the passage costs, precluded legal emigration for many Azoreans, who were either too poor or unwilling to put up the guarantees. Hence, many tried to escape secretly. In the earlier part of the nineteenth century they boarded occasional whalers and traders, but, with the advent of regular shipping, often boys of fourteen years were smuggled into the vessels by their parents, who paid the passage money and a small fee to an agent.[22]

One of the best autobiographical descriptions of such clandestine emigration is provided by Lawrence Oliver, born on Pico in 1887, who in 1972 published his autobiography, *Never Backward*,[23] a long and charming account of his life from São Miguel to San Diego, California. Here is Oliver's description of his departure:

I don't see how any boy could ever have celebrated his sixteenth birthday in a more memorable fashion than I celebrated mine. I was lurking near a pier in the harbor of São Miguel in the Azores looking out on the one hand for the law and on the other for sight of a launch, which, God willing, would smuggle me and several other boys on to a White Star steamer whose destination was the United States.

I had in my pocket one five dollar piece—borrowed. Most of my clothes I wore on my back. I had never been to school, I could neither read nor write (Portuguese), nor could I speak or understand a word of English.

The launch arrived. We jumped in. The men rowed for dear life. Had we been caught, everyone would have been arrested. In a few minutes we met the steamer and boarded her as fast as humanly possible. The ship hoisted anchor. We were on our way to America, on my sixteenth birthday, March 27, 1903!

Oliver speaks of his father, Manuel Oliver, who first left on a whaling ship in the 1840s, jumped ship to work in the California gold mines in 1849, and returned to the Azores in 1858. Later Manuel made another trip to the States and returned. After Lawrence was born, the elder Oliver left again, but returned once more in 1891. All these years the family was living in poverty. When Lawrence's sister Mary left for New Bedford at age seventeen, Lawrence begged his father to let him go also; but it was not until 1903 that he agreed:

He would pay my fare, but there were complications. Because of my age, fifteen, the government would not give me a passport. The government wanted the boys to wait until they were eighteen, then go to serve in the army for two or three years. Maybe after that the officials would give you a passport. There was no guarantee. I didn't want to wait that long, so my father had to pay an agent to smuggle me out of the Azores.

I wasn't doing anything new. These agents were professional smugglers.

They operated regular services, for which young men paid a fee in order to get out of the islands. There was always the risk of being caught by the revenue cutter and being brought back to Portugal, in which case one paid a heavy fine. I decided that the risk was worth it. My father went to make the arrangements.

It was a complicated procedure. About a week later Lawrence was awakened at 6:00 A.M. by his father, who told him that it was time to leave. They walked four miles to the port of Ribeiras (Pico), where Lawrence boarded a steamer to go to the island of São Miguel. His father "loaned" him a five-dollar piece, which he promised to pay him back as soon as possible. Two days later Lawrence arrived at São Miguel, where he met the agent and twenty-one other boys, "all doing exactly what I was doing." At night the agent led the boys nine miles into the country to a house in the town of Ribeira Grande, where he instructed them to remain until it was time for the next move. The young men, ranging in age from twenty to thirty-five, remained at the house for six weeks, but Oliver, because he was so young, was taken to the house of the agent, in Ponta Delgada, where he served as the messenger between the agent and the waiting would-be emigrants. During that time the agent made a trip to Lisbon and upon his return he instructed the boys that they would be leaving in two weeks:

He told us that he had the plans set. We would walk the nine mines back to the city. When we arrived, we were not to stick together. We were to scatter, but at a certain time in the afternoon be waiting by the pier. When a launch came, we were to jump in. "Don't waste any time and don't say anything," he cautioned. When the right day came, we did as he told us.

Oliver's trip to Boston, in steerage, lasted seven days. In Boston he passed quickly through customs, "for all you needed was a little money in your pocket, so that the authorities could be sure that you wouldn't be on relief right away." So Lawrence Oliver, aged sixteen, with $5 to his name, arrived in the United States in 1903.

There were more impromptu means of smuggling people out of the Azores. Let us cite once more the summer tourist Miss Baker, cruising the Azores in 1882: As her ship was beating up behind Flores, far away from any sign of human habitation, she saw a thin column of smoke from a narrow ledge on one of the steepest cliffs of the island:

"Some poor fellow wants to come aboard," said the mate. To avoid the severity of the conscription laws, the young men of the Azores seek to escape from the islands on American vessels. They kindle bonfires as a signal for a boat. They are taken on board without passports, and stow themselves away among the cargo, out of sight of the custom-house officers. Last year [1881] a thousand were carried off in this way. We asked our Captain if he ever took them in. "Of course not," he said innocently; "but I noticed one singular thing on my last trip: I had passports for seventy steerage passengers and I landed one hundred and sixteen in America. It beat all, how they counted out so!"[24]

The Cape Verdeans also tried to emigrate surreptitiously, joining the crews of American whalers; some had saved enough money after a few whaling trips to buy a schooner of their own and to go into the business of smuggling Portuguese emigrants away.[25]

Exact estimates of the extent of this secret emigration are, of course, impossible. Lautensach[26] computes a tentative figure for the period from 1911 to 1920 by comparing the actual increase of the population of Portugal with the statistics for birth rate and mortality and arrives at an estimate for this period of between 70,000 and 100,000 secret Portuguese emigrants (to all parts of the world). Estimates as regards the United States are complicated by the fact that many Portuguese either legally or clandestinely first emigrated to other countries and from there illegally entered the United States. For example, in 1920 a number of young men from the small mountain village of Rio de Onor, near Bragança, on the Spanish-Portuguese border, entered the United States illegally after a brief stay in Argentina and Cuba.[27] The exact number of Portuguese who entered the States illegally or at least unrecorded between 1870 and 1920 (or before or after) can of course never be determined. It is safe to assume that that number was considerable.[28]

The figures on Portuguese immigration (by decades) given at the beginning of this chapter are problematic not only because a certain number of unrecorded immigrants have to be added, but also for the following reasons:

1. Up to and including the year 1924, the annual figures in question are defined as counting immigrants (during 1904–1906, immigrants plus nonimmigrant aliens) from "Portugal, including Cape Verde and Azores Islands." No mention is made of the "Madeira Islands" until 1925 and thereafter. This presumably means that immigrants from Madeira, during the 1870–1920 period, were counted under such rubrics as "Other Europe," "Other

Countries"—at least if the individuals in question reported their provenance as specifically Madeira, rather than Portugal.[29] Actually, a majority of immigrants from the Azores as well as from Madeira, and also from the Cape Verde Islands, probably identified themselves to immigration officials as quite simply "from Portugal," on the basis of their citizenship. (For this same reason, incidentally, a great deal of United States population statistics giving separate figures for residents hailing from "Portugal" [i.e., mainland Portugal] as against those hailing from the "Azores" etc. has made the ratio of Continentals to Islanders look much higher than it really was.) At any rate, even if some arrivals from Madeira were correctly included in the total figures for immigration from "Portugal," some presumably were not, and should be added.

2. From 1899 until well past World War I, immigrants were recorded not only by "country of birth or origin," but also by "race or people." Under this latter rubric, "Portuguese" was listed separate from "African (black)." Some official figures on immigration, and since 1908 on reemigration, have been using the term *Portuguese* in this restricted "racial" sense, thus excluding many Cape Verdeans; hence they are not entirely comparable to the overall figures listed above.[30]

3. Since this book includes the history of Portuguese immigration to the Hawaiian Islands, now a state of the Union, it is worth pointing out that official figures on Portuguese immigration to the United States, as those cited initially, do not include Hawaii. Figures for Hawaii make an important addition, at least for the years 1878–1910.

4. On the other hand, it is not entirely clear whether persons of Portuguese birth who entered the United States more than once— i.e., who after an initial stay in this country returned to their place of birth but then again came to America, perhaps repeating this process several times (as in the case histories mentioned earlier in this chapter)—were counted as immigrants several times or only once. Probably there have been some statistical duplications of this sort, which would realistically compel us to subtract something from official immigration totals covering entire decades.

As far as overall settlement pattern is concerned, most of the Portuguese immigrants throughout the half-century between the Civil War and the First World War kept clustering relatively close to the original ports of entry, the coastal and even insular locations, where the earliest footholds had been established prior to the onset of mass immigration: southeastern New England (with some minor southward extensions into New York-New Jersey), central California, and the Hawaiian Islands. Actually, much of the settlement on the West Coast was an outgrowth or extension of prior Portuguese contacts with New England, representing a sort of cross-country migration. Portuguese immigration into Hawaii, on the other hand, derived most of its impetus from events unrelated to settlement on the eastern and western seaboards of the continental United States. Portuguese maritime traditions have been coincidental rather than a major factor in these geographic developments.

Comparing the status of California as a Portuguese settlement area with that of the rest of the country (essentially southeastern New England), Graves points out that in 1870, California's 2,451 foreign-born Portuguese accounted for 27.3 percent of the United States total; but by 1880, California held slightly over 50 percent of the total Portuguese-born population of the country, because during the 1871–80 decade—and only during that decade—a marked majority of Portuguese immigrants newly arriving in the United States settled in California rather than in the East. In subsequent decades, California's relative importance dropped back, until by 1930 California's 35,395 foreign-born Portuguese accounted for barely 30 percent of the United States total.[31]

The 72,897 immigrants of "Portuguese" race (excluding "black" Capeverdeans) admitted during the twelve-year period 1899–1910 reported their final destinations by states (and "territories") as follows:[32]

Massachusetts	45,466
Rhode Island	7,040
Connecticut	964
New York	4,196
California	10,537
Nevada	255
Hawaii	3,470
Illinois	166
Ohio	109
All other states	694
(less than 100 each)	

During the eleven-year period 1911–1921, arriving immigrants of "Portuguese" race (thus again excluding small numbers of

Capeverdeans) reported their state of intended future residence
(i.e., destination) as follows:[33]

Massachusetts	59,827
Rhode Island	11,471
Connecticut	2,273
New York	8,669
New Jersey	2,186
Pennsylvania	1,716
California	14,426
Hawaii	1,923

The above figures give a reasonably accurate picture of the
relative distribution (or at least initial destination) of Portuguese
immigration during the half-century under consideration. In some
cases, the intended destination reported to the immigration official
was only a halfway station; for instance, some individuals declaring
for New York may have moved on to other nearby states soon, or
some Portuguese initially setting up in Massachusetts may soon
thereafter have gone on to California. But there can be no doubt
that (eastern) Massachusetts, together with adjoining little Rhode
Island, became and remained the principal compact Portuguese
settlement area. California took second place. Hawaii, an important
destination in the late nineteenth century, dropped behind the New
York metropolitan area.

Details about these major settlement areas are relegated to the
next chapter. At this point, let us merely note that a bare trickle of
Portuguese found their way into many other states of the Union—
not only into Nevada (an offshoot of the California settlement) and
Illinois (where the "Madeiran exiles" mentioned in the previous
chapter had established themselves), but also, for example, into
Ohio (perhaps drifting in from Erie), Florida (where there were 228
natives of Portugal by 1920, recent immigrants from New England),
and so forth. One episode relating to Louisiana deserves special
mention:

In Louisiana, where several hundred Portuguese had settled in
the 1840s to provide contract labor for sugar plantations (see pp. 24-
25), a second attempt to attract such labor was made in the early
1870s. Contracted for in Lisbon by agents of Louisiana sugar
planters, some 230 Portuguese (including some eighty children)
landed at New Orleans in early 1872, to work for three years on
plantations along the Latourche River. Because of bad work condi-

tions, many or all of these laborers fled the plantations within a few months, seeking jobs in New Orleans or sailing for Cuba.[34] (We recall how the "Madeiran exiles" had similarly fled from plantations in Trinidad, before settling in Illinois. . . .) But a few years later, starting in 1878, Madeiran labor arrived on the sugar plantations of Hawaii, for more permanent settlement in that archipelago.

Immigration does not necessarily lead to permanent resettlement. Many persons emigrating to the United States intended initially to remain only for a number of years, or long enough to accumulate some wealth, and then to return to their native land. Others immigrated planning to stay "for good," but sooner or later went back home because of lack of economic success or some other kind of disillusionment, or simply to live out their retirement years in relative prosperity where they had come from. The Portuguese are no exception to this phenomenon of reemigration, or voluntary repatriation. As a matter of fact, particularly in the case of the Azoreans and the Capeverdeans, there have been many cases of shuttling back and forth, perhaps partly because of the relative proximity of the Azores to New England shores, and/or because there was some tradition, for western Azoreans and for Capeverdeans as well, of naturally sailing back and forth in connection with whaling or other maritime pursuits.

Reemigration from the United States has been officially counted only since 1908. Here are some statistics for the Portuguese: During the three-year period 1908–1910, while 19,072 "Portuguese" (nonblack) immigrant aliens were admitted to the country, 2,620 departed, representing a ratio of fourteen reemigrants to 100 immigrants for this sample period. (Actually the total of emigrant aliens departing for residence in "Portugal," including Cape Verde [and Azores] Islands, i.e., including returning "African-black" Capeverdeans, was 3,163.) Of the 2,610 reemigrants of "Portuguese" race, about 72 percent had been in the United States for no more than five years, some 21 percent for five to ten years, and barely 7 percent longer than ten years.[35] From 1911 through 1921, arrivals of immigrant aliens from, and departures of emigrant aliens to, "Portugal, including Cape Verde and Azores Islands" (again apparently omitting Madeira!) added up officially to 108,927 arrivals versus 29,123 departures,[36] reflecting a marked relative rise in reemigration rate in the early part of and in the years immediately after World War I.

Since figures on the reemigration of aliens do not include that of naturalized American citizens, we undoubtedly have to add a substantial number of Portuguese immigrants who, after staying in the United States longer than five or even ten years and becoming naturalized citizens, chose to return to their place of birth in their later years. According to one source, there were in 1933 some 17,000 naturalized Americans living in the Azores, constituting the third-largest American colony in Europe after those of Paris and London.[37]. Even if this figure for 1933 is grossly inflated and certainly no measure of the (relatively low) naturalization rate of Portuguese immigrants during the 1870–1920 period, the "return traffic" had become heavy enough by 1908 to require a naturalization convention between the United States and Portugal to be concluded that year.[38] Naturalized or not, as of the end of World War I almost all the inhabitants of some of the Azores islands were said to have been in the United States at least once.[39]

Even more than the Azoreans, most Capeverdeans upon first arriving in the United States did not intend to settle permanently; they wanted to make some money in this country and then return home—or at least go back for visits. For many of them, especially single men from the islands of Brava and Fogo, it was simply a matter of seasonal employment in the States during the summer and fall (cranberry-picking around Cape Cod, for example), but spending the winter back home.[40] One Capeverdean author reminisces how in November the schooners (sailing ships typically capable of carrying about fifty passengers and crew) would come back to Brava from the United States, with emigrants returning to get married, for a vacation, or to stay for the rest of their lives. In March, after a round of weddings and baptisms, the ships would leave again to take emigrants back to New England.[41]

The permanent return, or return visits, of substantial numbers of emigrants from the United States (of *Americanos*, or of *Calafonas*, as those from California in particular came to be called) into the small, tradition-bound villages of the Portuguese islands were beginning to have some Americanizing or otherwise catalytic effect on local life-styles—a process which has naturally continued over the past fifty years. The Portuguese ethnographer Leite de Vasconcellos noted in the early 1920s that ". . . the continuous influx from America is gradually penetrating and transforming everything [in the Azores]: America even modifies clothing habits and the type of dwelling; in some houses one can see furniture and dishware imported from there; the local vocabulary has come to include

English words."[42] Similarly, an Azorean newspaper in the late 1930s acknowledges that repatriates used to American comfort have introduced modern houses and furnishings; they have bought land from the big landowners and thus transformed the Azorean economy; they have introduced English expressions and modernized farming methods and clothing fashions.[43] Another Azorean writer goes still further: repatriates have brought into the Azores American ideas of liberty, mutual respect, regional autonomy, and interest in schools and literacy.[44]

As much as successful repatriates were admired for their relative wealth, emigrants who returned to their native village about as poor as they had left were often scorned rather than pitied. Dinis da Luz tells the story of one Tio Moisés, a poor old peasant living in isolation in his Azorean village. He had been in the United States, worked in New Bedford cotton mills, become ill, and returned penniless. His fellow villagers now were heckling him about his lack of success, pointing to other *Calafonas* in the village who had returned with enough wealth to build a fine house, to own beds with real springs, two bicycles, and even a "machine" (car). In another story set in an Azorean village, Mariquinhas hardly dares to go out of her house to evade the heckling by her neighbors. During a year of famine, she had been lucky enough to get herself married to a local teacher, Mendes, who took her along on a sailboat voyage to the United States. There the couple worked in New England textile mills, then exchanged that "unhealthy" milieu for heavy farm work in California, did not like it there, either, and ended up in Honolulu. Mendes died there, and Mariquinhas returned to her native village, now a destitute widow.[45]

The feeling of isolation and neglect harbored by many inhabitants of the Azores with respect to mainland Portugal and the Portuguese government, together with the relatively heavy emigration to the United States and the presence of Americanized reemigrants and visitors from the States, gradually created a strongly pro-American sentiment in those islands. It was often strong enough to lead to more or less openly voiced interest in possible annexation by the United States as early as the turn of the century.[46] During the First World War, when the United States Navy established a coaling station at Ponta Delgada (1917–19), Azoreans were markedly more happy about this than was the Portuguese government; a Boston newspaper felt encouraged in the summer of 1917 to propose purchase of the Azores by this country.[47] (The idea has periodically

been debated again in more recent times.) But there is no documentation of similar sentiments having ever been voiced in the Cape
Verde or Madeira Islands.

We conclude this chapter with some figures on the total number
of "Portuguese" residents living in the United States at a particular
point in time between 1870 and 1921 (as against the number of new
immigrants arriving over a certain period).

If available sources differ sometimes to an exasperating extent in
their statistics, this is due more to the ambiguity of the term
Portuguese in this connection than to inaccuracies in counting. In
principle, the total number of "Portuguese" residents should equal
the total number of immigrant arrivals from "Portugal" (or arrivals
of "Portuguese race," or of Portuguese mother tongue?) since the
beginnings of immigration, minus the number of such individuals
who have either died or who have reemigrated. This number would
then exclude any American-born descendants of the immigrants,
and it would vary depending on whether "Portugal" is understood
to mean continental Portugal only, or also the Azores and Madeira,
or even the Cape Verde Islands (officially more a colony than part
of the Portuguese "mother country").

Actually, some of the figures cited here or there are intended to
cover only foreign-born residents; others include the so-called
second generation (children of immigrants born in the United
States), or even the third generation or ultimately the somewhat
nebulous "Portuguese colonial stock" (descendants of Portuguese
who immigrated in colonial times—identified as such by their
allegedly Portuguese-sounding family names, without regard to the
frequent process of Anglicization or other name changes . . .). At
the other extreme from the broad notion of "Portuguese stock," the
question has been raised[48] whether a count of the Portuguese in the
United States should include only nonnaturalized Portuguese citizens or the naturalized Portuguese-born as well. (How about cases
of dual citizenship? How about defining as Portuguese a person who
"feels" more Portuguese than American, using a criterion of socio-
political loyalty?) Swinging back again toward a broader notion that
includes certain American-born: it is easy to include children both
of whose parents immigrated from Portugal; but what about the
offspring of a father born in Portugal and a mother born in Ireland
(or the other way around)? Should such a person be included in the
Portuguese or the Irish "second generation"? If we want to divide
up the population of this country equitably by "ethnic" origins,

such an individual should obviously be counted as only half an individual in counts of the Portuguese element in the United States. Indeed we might be forced to quarter a person whose Portuguese ancestry is limited to one grandmother. . . .

Some official immigration was well as population statistics, as has already been hinted, have made a distinction between immigrants from Portugal of "Portuguese" or of "white" race, as against those of "African-black" or "colored" race. (The latter presumably covers all Capeverdeans—even though a certain proportion of them, especially on the island of Brava, are as "white" as most inhabitants of the Portuguese mother country.) Other special census counts have referred to persons of Portuguese mother-tongue (whether foreign-born or not). As far as geographic (as against generational, civic-attitudinal, lingual) definitions are concerned, federal and state or local population statistics tend to contribute to the same kind of confusion already noted for immigration figures: the category "Portugal" is often used to refer to the mainland portion of Portugal only; as regards the islands, some tabulations use a separate category, "Azores", but less often make separate reference to the "Cape Verde Islands" and to "Madeira." In some tabulations (e.g., the United States population census for 1920) there is a category "(Other) Atlantic Islands" in addition to "Azores" and "Portugal"; it presumably includes Madeira and the Cape Verdes— but also the Canary Islands belonging to Spain. Elsewhere (e.g., in the Massachusetts population census for 1910) "Atlantic Islands" is understood to include the Azores along with the other islands. The rubric "Western Islands" is sometimes found, alongside "Portugal" (e.g., in some Rhode Island population censuses), to refer to the Azores, or possibly to the Azores and Madeira jointly (but apparently excluding Cape Verde). To top it all, Madeira and the Cape Verde Islands may be found relegated to a broad category, "All other [countries]," together with Africa, etc. (as in the United States population census for foreign-born white, by country of birth, for 1930). At any rate, no reliance at all can be placed on separate figures purporting to distinguish continental from all or part of insular Portugal: many persons of insular Portuguese descent identified themselves to census-takers (or to immigration officials) as simply "Portuguese" or from "Portugal." Therefore, the safe thing to do is to pay attention only to totals for "Portugal" and "Azores," etc., together—at least where separate figures are available.

Last but not least, attention must be paid to whether statistics on

Portuguese-Americans do or do not include Hawaii. For example, United States census figures on the foreign-born population between 1870 and 1920 explicitly cover the continental United States only. However, figures from separate censuses conducted in the Hawaiian (formerly Sandwich) Islands are available.

It is with these several cautions in mind that the following census data for the (continental) United States have to be interpreted:

	Total Foreign-born				Foreign-born White	
	1870	1880	1890	1900	1910	1920
"Portugal"	4,542	8,138	15,996	30,608	57,623	67,453
"Azores"						33,778
"Other Atlantic Islands"	4,434	7,641	9,739	9,768	15,795	
						5,196
Total	8,976	15,779	25,735	40,376	73,418	106,437

By principal states of Portuguese settlement, the corresponding totals (adding up "Portugal", "Azores", and "Other Atlantic Islands") were:

	Total Foreign-born				Foreign-born White	
	1870	1880	1890	1900	1910	1920
California	3,451	8,064	12,446	15,583	25,287	33,409
Connecticut	243	244	413	655	747	1,410
Massachusetts	2,682	3,585	8,024	17,885	36,573	53,545
Rhode Island	227	395	1,380	2,865	6,571	11,615
New York	349	441	780	823	1,094	1,973
New Jersey	42	76	91	151	188	825

The figures for 1870–1900 include nonwhites—essentially, in our case, Capeverdeans. In 1910, 1,737 nonwhites of Portuguese birth were counted; in 1920, 2,528. These figures for Capeverdeans seem too low.

The census for 1910, in addition to counting the foreign-born, gave a figure of 111,122 for Portuguese white "stock," defined as

the sum of those born in "Portugal" and those born in the United
States of parents—or of at least one parent—born in "Portugal."
This breaks down into 57,623 foreign-born and 53,499 American-
born. For 1920, the corresponding figure is 134,794. (But this
excludes persons counted under "Azores" and "Other Atlantic
Islands"!)

The 1920 census, moreover, in connection with the establishment
of immigration quotas proportionate to the various segments by
"national origin" of the white population of the United States,
arrived at an estimate of 263,000 residents either born in Portugal or
descending—along a line reaching as far back as colonial times—
from (at least one? or more?) natives of Portugal:

"Colonial stock" (descended from persons enumerated in the 1790 census)	24,000
"Postcolonial stock" (descended from or consisting of immigrants coming to the U.S. after 1790):	
Immigrants	104,000
Children of Immigrants	105,000
Grandchildren of Immigrants	30,000
Total	263,000

From today's vantagepoint of viewing Hawaii as a state of the
Union, and since the Hawaiian archipelago had become an American territory about the middle of the 1870–1921 immigration
period, figures for the Portuguese stock residing in those islands
should properly be added to the above figures for the continental
United States:

	1890	1900	1910	1920
Born in Portugal	8,602	6,512	7,585	5,794
Born in Hawaii of Portuguese parents (or grandparents)	4,117	9,163	14,716	21,208
Total	12,719	15,675	22,301	27,002

CHAPTER 4

Portuguese Settlement in the
Northeast, c. 1870-1921

As indicated in the preceding chapter, most of the 200,000 or more Portuguese who immigrated into the United States during the last two decades of the nineteenth century and the first two of the twentieth settled down (and, with their descendants, have stayed put to this day, by and large) in locations relatively close to where the earliest Portuguese footholds had been established, prior to the onset of mass immigration: southeastern New England, central California, and Hawaii. Some more precise geographic and statistical details on these major settlement areas are provided in this and the next chapter.

As in the case of many immigrant groups other than the Portuguese, the build-up of these relatively compact clusters of Portuguese settlement resulted from the desire of recent immigrants to remain close to relatives or friends who had arrived earlier, and from economic opportunities located within, or at least supported by, such networks of ethnic contact. (Details on the economic and social structure of Portuguese ethnic communities are relegated to later chapters; but these cannot in effect be viewed separately from the more purely geographic picture, or vice-versa.) Mapped and measured against the vastness of the territory of the United States, the cities and rural places harboring substantial numbers of Portuguese-Americans in the Northeast (and similarly along the West Coast, or within the Hawaiian archipelago) do, of course, appear more narrowly clustered together into a few blotches than they would if transferred onto the map of such a small country as continental Portugal, let alone the insular world of the Azores. To an immigrant from Portugal, especially if he or she arrived before the age of superhighways and the airplane, going the short distance from Boston to New Bedford or from Providence to Cape Cod still felt like a real trip.

The arrival of substantial numbers of Portuguese coincided with and was part of what has been termed "the foreign invasion of New England," starting about 1880; the "invaders" were primarily non-English-speaking immigrants from French Canada, Italy, Czarist Russia, the Austro-Hungarian Empire, and Germany and Sweden, to mention the largest groups in order of importance. As a result, by 1920 a marked majority of New England's population of about 7,400,000 were immigrants of non-English mother tongue, or children of such immigrants. Moreover, by 1920 about two-thirds of the native stock of native parentage found themselves relegated to largely rural, weakly industrialized sections of Vermont, New Hampshire, and Maine; by contrast, about three-fourths of the foreign stock (plus a certain number of American blacks) were then settled in the urban industrial centers of Massachusetts, Connecticut, and Rhode Island. As far as the Portuguese are concerned, not only did they avoid the northern and western parts of New England; within the southeastern region, they formed their principal nucleus in what even early in this century could already be considered a single metropolitan district, stretching from New Bedford to Fall River to Providence.[1] To this, add the Boston area to the north and Cape Cod to the east, with offshoots elsewhere along or near the southern New England Coast.

In 1892, Henry H. Lang gave this summary picture:

In New England we have not less than seven Portuguese colonies, numbering at present more than twenty thousand. Of those seven colonies a large one is in Providence, Rhode Island, while the other six belong to the State of Massachusetts. Naming the latter in the order of their municipal strengths and importance, they are the following: New Bedford, Boston (including Cambridge), Taunton, Fall River, Provincetown, and Gloucester. For the most part these Portuguese colonists are natives of the Azores, chiefly from the islands of Fayal, Pico, St. George, and Flores; only a few are from Madeira, and still smaller is the number of colored Portuguese from the Cape Verde Islands.[2]

In 1912, the Portuguese consul in Boston reported to his government that in his consular district, covering the six New England states, there was now located the largest Portuguese colony in the world, after the one in Brazil. According to this report, it numbered about 70,000 native Portuguese and about 80,000 American-born descendants, some 90 percent of them living in Massachusetts, about 10,000 in Rhode Island, 1,000 in Connecticut, and hardly 300 in the three northern New England states. Of the total Portuguese colony in New England, Azoreans still constituted about 75 percent, although the number of mainlanders had by then risen to about 11,000. Two-thirds of the colony's labor force, the consul added, were factory workers—including 56 percent of the Portuguese women.[3] Checking the total population figures from these two sources against United States census data (for the foreign-born only) cited on p. 52, Lang's figure would seem to be in approximate agreement; but the later consular estimate is vastly in excess of census counts.

To focus more closely on particular New England communities, Massachusetts and Rhode Island state census reports provide some valuable details as to the number of residents born in "Portugal," including the "Western Islands" (but excluding American-born children):

County	Town	1885	1895	1905	1915
Massachusetts					
Barnstable		848	1,318	1,801	
	Provincetown	698	962	1,003	962
Bristol		2,506	7,263	17,938	
	New Bedford	1,445	3,861	7,352	15,145
	Fall River	313	1,707	7,020	13,360
	Taunton	276	536	1,425	2,772
Essex		621	1,020	1,379	
	Gloucester	466	711	758	943
Middlesex		538	1,523	2,814	
	Cambridge	351	825	1,237	2,216
	Lowell	43	310	924	1,930
Suffolk		1,150	1,266	1,289	
	Boston	1,122	1,215	1,233	1,507
Dukes Nantucket Norfolk Plymouth		420	852	2,641	
Total Massachusetts (incl. counties not specified above)		6,118	13,298	27,937	52,133

County	Town	1885	1895	1905	1915
Rhode Island					
	Providence	363	981	2,173	3,737
	East Providence	16	81	403	1,097
	Portsmouth	121	251	537	510
	Bristol	83	205	659	1,333
	Middletown	57	176	237	396
	Newport	22	99	256	657
	Tiverton	21	74	219	563
Total Rhode Island		814	2,241	5,293	10,449[4]

Within Massachusetts, as the above figures show, Bristol County contained the point of gravitation for Portuguese immigration from the start—and it still does today. New Bedford remained the leading community throughout the period, with Fall River coming to run a close second by 1905. The city of Boston, together with adjoining Cambridge, rivaling New Bedford in the 1880s, dropped to third place about the turn of the century; as a matter of fact, we note a shift from Boston proper toward "suburban" Cambridge. Portuguese settlements of minor scope developed in Taunton and Lowell. In all these places, textile works and other factories provided the main attraction. The Portuguese fishing communities in the towns of Provincetown and Gloucester, even though they have tended to get the most publicity, never attained numerical importance; the same is true of the Portuguese element on Martha's Vineyard and Nantucket islands, dating back to whaling days, and along the coastline from Norfolk to Barnstable counties.

New Bedford eventually acquired the nickname of "Portuguese capital of the United States." By 1905, the 7,208 natives of the Western Islands there, plus 144 Continentals and 4,610 American-born of Portuguese parentage, represented 16 percent of the city's total population; and their proportion kept on rising. One reminiscing member of "Batefete" 's Portuguese community, during a centenary celebration in 1932, put it this way: "It is here that a Portuguese usually starts out on his wanderings through Uncle Sam's territory. Whether he disembarks in Boston or lands in Providence or New York, he will not stop nor rest until he has made a jaunt to this city. It is from here, most of the time, that he moves on to other places where he has friends or relatives or where he hopes to find a better job."[5] From New Bedford, the Portuguese proceeded, for instance, to Provincetown or Gloucester, or to California. New Bedford served as the immigrant's collection point, the place in which he first experienced America, before moving on in many cases.

If we continue to follow Lawrence Oliver, after his arrival at the Boston Customs, we can gain an interesting perspective of "Bate-fete" in the year 1903:

> My destination was New Bedford, to the same people who had be-friended my sister, Mary. Since I could neither read nor write, nor speak a word of English, the interpreter gave me a slip of paper on which my destination was written. There, also, was a note to the policeman at the train station in New Bedford, asking him to guide me, or send me to our friends. The Portuguese interpreter put me on the train at the Boston depot. Soon I was on my way, with my five dollar gold piece in my pocket, and my clothes tied up in a bundle. For the first time, I was riding on a train. I hoped that it was the right train, for there was nothing which I could do to help myself.
>
> At New Bedford, I showed the paper to the policeman at the station. He read it, called a taxi and gave the driver instructions. All the way I worried. How much would the driver charge? How would I know how to pay him? . . . That five dollar gold piece was all I had, and I didn't want to change it. Also, I was chilled. The climate in New Bedford, although it was spring, was nothing like that of the Azores.[6]

Oliver found his way without incident and several days later he secured employment on a farm in Acushnet at five dollars a month, plus room and board. The farmer was a Portuguese from Flores who worked Oliver so hard he quit after two weeks and walked the eight miles back to New Bedford, keeping his eyes open for a peanut-roasting machine in front of a five-and-dime which he knew was close to where his older sister worked.

The next day Oliver went to visit a friend, one José Vitorino Machado, who worked in a cotton mill, and asked him to help him find a job. Oliver began working as a floor sweeper the next day, at $3.50 per week:

> I worked hard while there. Also, I watched the rest of the workers doing their jobs. Whenever I could, I helped them, with the idea in my mind of

learning the work, getting promotions, and more money. I was learning that in America gold wasn't being found in the streets, but that if I worked hard, I could achieve more than I ever could dream of acquiring in the Azores.
In a year I saved thirty dollars. . . . One thing I didn't like about my situation during that year was that I had no opportunity to learn any English. I worked with Portuguese people and lived with Portuguese people all during that time. Even my boss was Portuguese.
I remember, also, that I went through many cold days in New Bedford. The climate was not like Pico, and I was forced to buy warm clothes for the winter months. That was a big adjustment.[7]

Oliver did "adjust." About a year after he arrived in the States, his father sent for him and his sister from San Diego. Using all of his $30 savings of the previous year, Oliver crossed the United States by train to California in 1904. He never returned to New Bedford. Oliver's experience was not unique, however. New Bedford was the first stop for many.

Take Joaquim Borges de Menezes, for example, born in Altares, Terceira (Azores), in 1866. Menezes studied for the priesthood but left the seminary one year before graduation and entered the army. After three years in the military, Menezes emigrated to the United States, arriving in Boston. Shortly after, he moved to New Bedford, where he became the editor of a Portuguese newspaper. In 1896 Menezes moved to Hayward, California, where he took charge of the weekly *Amigo dos Catholicos*, which later changed its name to *Arauto*.[8]

Similarly, Alberto Moura, born in Chaves, Trás-os-Montes, in 1891, also studied for the priesthood, but then went through a military academy and became an officer. In 1914 Moura arrived in New Bedford and founded a newspaper there. After two years Moura moved on to Oakland (California), where he worked as editor of the *Portuguese Union*. By 1923 Moura had taught himself law and was admitted to the California bar.[9]

The earlier Portuguese settlers in New Bedford were mostly from the western Azores, particularly from Fayal. According to Henry R. Lang, writing about 1888, the Azoreans were occupying almost the entire southern section of the city, and a good part of the western section; this Portuguese quarter had become popularly known as "Fayal." There were also some Capeverdeans there by that time.[10] In the following decade, with the growth of New Bedford's cotton mills, many immigrants from the eastern Azores (São Miguel,

Terceira) drifted in. Madeirans and Continentals came mostly after 1910;[11] so did additional Capeverdeans.

To the east of New Bedford, Portuguese settlement along Cape Cod goes back to a relatively early date, as indicated previously. Church records in Provincetown show that in 1872, thirty-five out of 102 births in that fishing community were children of Portuguese; and according to a survey of the Provincetown schools done in the 1870s, 196 out of 812 schoolchildren were then Portuguese.[12] About 1880, the Provincetown newspaper *The Advocate* reported: "One third of the town's population of 6,000 are Portuguese, and these make remarkably good sailors."[13] In 1911, one of the old-time Cape Cod Yankees, Mary Heaton Vorse, noted that the Provincetown fishing business, "during the last twenty years," had passed almost entirely into the hands of the Portuguese. The Azores had started sending their "handsome, clean-blooded people over fifty years ago"; in recent years, "the Lisbons" (Continentals) had begun to come also. But, Vorse charmingly added, "If I say they came, that isn't quite true. The Portuguese immigration is unlike any other in one respect: It was we who needed the Portuguese and showed them the road to this country." And she concludes: ". . . The life of the Portuguese and the Americans is more closely woven together in Provincetown than in any other place I know of."[14]

Adjoining Cape Cod's Barnstable County to the south, across Buzzard's Bay from New Bedford, a small Portuguese colony survived from whaling days on the island of Nantucket (229 foreign-born in 1915). Another was established on Martha's Vineyard (near Cottage City) about 1880; it became popularly known as "Fayal," after the home island of these pioneer vegetable farmers who, in the words of one admiring writer, "succeeded in turning the barely disguised sand-hill into a blossoming bit of garden."[15]

Capeverdeans played a prominent part in supplying seasonal, or in some cases year-round, farm labor along various spots in Barnstable County, starting about the turn of the century. They would drift in from New Bedford, Fall River, or Providence for the cranberry- (and later also the strawberry-) picking season; many would spend winters back in the Cape Verde Islands. Some of these "Bravas" together with Azoreans actually pioneered the strawberry industry on the Cape (chiefly at Falmouth).[16]

The Portuguese community in Greater Boston (including Cambridge and Somerville) had its beginnings about as early as the one in New Bedford—apparently centering in Boston's North End.

From the barely forty native Portuguese counted in Boston in the 1860 census (cf. p. 22), the official count rose to 1,122 (exclusive of American-born descendants) in 1885. Between these dates, in early 1873, after a disastrous fire and smallpox epidemic in the North End section of town, the (Protestant) North End Mission discovered and provided relief for "hundreds of destitute Portuguese, chiefly women and children," hailing from Fayal; the men were mostly sailors, according to the Mission report, and many of the women did sewing in garment shops. The Mission people, relying on information supplied by the relief recipients, estimated Boston's total Portuguese community at 4,000 to 5,000—evidently too high a figure.[17] By 1895, only about 800 (foreign-born) Portuguese were left in the North End of Boston, scene of much interethnic strife at the time; together with the Irish and Jews, they were gradually moving into suburbs such as Cambridge and Somerville, yielding to the pressure of the more recent Italian immigration.[18]

Among the Fayalese in Boston about the turn of the century, one man stood out, nontypically, to rise from the status of poor factory worker to that of physician. Born into an upper-class family in Fayal, Garcia Monteiro decided as a young man to forego social privilege and to start from the bottom up by personal effort. After a sailing voyage of forty days, Garcia Monteiro landed in New Bedford in 1884. Dropping his initial plan to go on to San Francisco, he stayed in the whaling city to work on a Portuguese immigrant newspaper, which, however, for lack of subscribers barely yielded him a living. In a series of letters written to a friend back home between 1884 and 1890, and subsequently published,[19] he portrays among other things the dilemma of a relatively educated, intellectually ambitious immigrant moving within a circle of largely illiterate fellow ethnics of peasant mentality. His newspaper folded within a year, unappreciated by the "ignorant hippopotamuses" whom it was designed to uplift. So by 1885 we find Monteiro in Boston as a poorly paid printshop operative, complaining to his friend: "If you saw how a worker gets exploited in this country, you would be indignant and would very much change your opinion of the Americans." Almost near death for a while, from malnutrition and tuberculosis, he still refused to return to Fayal or to accept financial help from his family. He decided to prepare himself for medical school through self-study while holding on to his printing job, thus working from 5:00 A.M. to midnight. In 1887 he was actually admitted to a medical school in Boston (which was then tuition-

free). Living on $3 a week, he managed to graduate within three
years. He studied hard, he assured his friend proudly; American
schooling is efficient and severe! In a letter dated September 1890,
he announced his decision to remain in the United States: "What
would I now be doing back on my island? After having breathed
this wonderful air of work and independence for over six years, and
having steeled my character, I would die of boredom if I returned
home!" Shortly thereafter, Monteiro met and married an "American
miss" from upstate New York. . . .

Now back to a bit of geography and statistics, rounding out our
picture of Portuguese settlements in the Northeast. North of Boston,
the Portuguese attained a position of relative importance in the
fishing port of Gloucester, from beginnings dating back to the mid-
nineteenth century. As in the case of Provincetown, the first
Portuguese fishing folk there came from the Azores, but after the
turn of the century there was an influx of Continentals from such
Portuguese fishing ports as Figueira da Foz, Faro, and Olhão.[20]
Another Portuguese "colony" north of Boston, at Lowell, had its
start about the turn of the century; workers were attracted by the
cotton mills in that city. As of 1908, some 440 Portuguese families
(1,500 adults, 700 children) were living in Lowell's drab and
crowded tenements. By 1916 their number had risen to 3,000
persons.[21]

Not until about 1913 did any Portuguese settle in the western
part of Massachusetts—at Ludlow, near Springfield. They were
recruited at New Bedford, Providence, and Fall River by agents of
two Ludlow mills, and gradually, during the interwar years, a
sizable Portuguese community developed there, including many
Continentals along with Azoreans.[22]

The Portuguese community at Fall River has been the second
largest in the United States since the beginning of this century
(although rivaled at times in this position by Oakland, California, if
we include the immediate surroundings of that city). The Portuguese did not begin to settle in Fall River in any appreciable
numbers until about 1890, when they responded to the labor
demand of a rapidly expanding cotton industry. The Fall River mills
aimed direct recruiting efforts at the most populous Azorean island,
São Miguel, in the eastern part of the archipelago. As a result, Fall
River's Portuguese element assumed a predominantly São Miguelian or "Micaelense" character, as distinguishable from the western
Azorean type as from the Madeiran or Continental in dialect, local

traditions, and other traits. By 1920 the Portuguese constituted about one-fifth of the city's total population of 120,000, with Columbia Street (soon known as "Portuguese Street") serving as their main thoroughfare.[23] In the small state of Rhode Island, practically next door to the Fall River–New Bedford area, Portuguese settlement may be said to have started right after the Civil War (if we disregard some Portuguese Jews in colonial Newport). Like New Bedford and Boston, Providence, Rhode Island, was a gateway city for Portuguese immigrants. Many of them stopped there merely on their way to the textile cities of Massachusetts or the farming communities of California. It is important to remember that after 1911 the Fabre Steamship Lines regularly carried Azoreans to the United States via Providence; for instance, in 1914 vessels from Portugal docked about once a week.[24] The city also received transit immigrants arriving from New York City on coastal steamers such as those of the Fall River Line. While many immigrants moved on, a substantial number settled in Providence or its environs. The city's population of Portuguese birth rose from 2,173 (plus 403 if we add East Providence) in 1905 to 3,737 (plus 1,097) in 1915, numbering 2,588 (plus 1,505) in 1920, with a marked gradual shift from Providence proper toward East Providence. Like New Bedford and Cape Cod, but unlike most other places of Portuguese settlement, Providence attracted large numbers of Capeverdeans (who are probably at least partly included in the figures just cited). For a long time these "Bravas" congregated in a small area of cheap tenements along the waterfront, called the Lower East Side, working chiefly as longshoremen and sailors, often returning to the Cape Verde Islands in the fall and showing up again in the spring. The "white Portuguese" (Azoreans), according to an official survey about 1920, would live in a district immediately in back of the Capeverdeans, keeping carefully separate from their "black" compatriots.[25]

As for the rest of Rhode Island, small rural Portuguese communities with an emphasis on vegetable gardening grew up along the east side of Narragansett Bay: the 1920 census reported 2,295 Portuguese immigrants around Bristol, about 1,000 at Portsmouth, and 423 in Newport. In addition, toward the end of World War I new industrially oriented communities sprang up at Pawtucket and West Warwick, in the northern and southern outskirts of Providence. Those residing in Portsmouth had originally drifted in from Fall River after 1880, later augmented by immigrants from São

An average Portuguese-American family—"young" folks and visiting in-laws. Near Providence.

Miguel directly seeking an alternative to factory work more congenial to them, viz., farming.[26]

Apart from Massachusetts and Rhode Island, the only other state in New England to receive small numbers of Portuguese during the 1870-1920 period was Connecticut mainly along the coast of Long Island Sound, in such places as New London and Stonington. In 1870, according to the census, there were a mere 243 natives of ortugal in the entire state; in 1880, 244; by 1910, 747; and by 1920, 1,410 (see p. 52). Before 1870 some towns in Connecticut had effectively competed with New Bedford as whaling ports. Many Portuguese, such as João Rosa, rebaptized John Rogers by a well-meaning customs official, stepped ashore in New London or Stonington in the whaling era. John Rogers later married an Irish immigrant who arrived in Connecticut as a result of the potato famine and they moved to Massachusetts, where many years later their grandson, Professor Francis Rogers, was instrumental in establishing Portuguese studies at Harvard University.[27] But during the period of mass immigration, Connecticut held relatively little attraction for Portuguese immigrants, as these statistics indicate. In the state of New York, a very small Portuguese immigrant colony in New York City is attested to as of 1873,[28] numbering still no more than about 100 individuals (engaged in commerce) in 1898;[29] census figures for 1920 indicate 1,845 persons of Portuguese birth or parentage in that metropolis, and 2,559 for the entire state. One small Portuguese-American community in upstate New York during the period under consideration is worth mentioning. Sometime during the last decades of the nineteenth century, a group of Madeirans found employment at a foundry in Corning. When this foundry moved to Rochester about 1910, many of its Madeiran workers also moved along (some others found work at the Corning Glass Company). By 1919, the Rochester group numbered about 200.[30] Probably the original settlers had drifted into Corning from Erie, where a small Madeiran settlement had sprung up in the 1870s (and has retained its identity in splendid isolation to this day).[31] In New Jersey, finally, a few Portuguese settled down at Newark after 1904; but the Newark colony (and one at Elizabeth) did not have any real growth until the 1920s.

CHAPTER 5

Portuguese Settlement in California and Hawaii, c. 1870-1921

I *California*

ALTHOUGH THE GOLD RUSH OF 1849 AND SUBSEQUENT MINING EFFORTS brought a few hundred Portuguese to California, it seems more appropriate to set the initial date of Portuguese mass immigration into that state around the year 1870. Following the Civil War, the Homestead Act had set in motion a westward population movement, which also included an increasing number of Portuguese. From about 1,500 individuals in 1860, their number rose to 3,451 in 1870 and 8,064 in 1880 (foreign-born only), according to the United States census. But these official figures are probably too low: in 1876, the Portuguese consul in San Francisco estimated the number of his countrymen along the West Coast at 12,000 (presumably including the "second generation").[1] The truth may lie in the middle. In 1892 the consular estimate had risen to 15,000 to 20,000, and by 1908 to 30,000 to 40,000 (which is about in line with census figures, if we also count American-born children).[2]

The census for 1910 reported 51,731 persons of Portuguese birth or parentage for the state of California (plus 658 for Nevada, Washington, and Oregon). In 1920, the corresponding figure was 81,232. In relation to the total of California's population, what this meant was that in 1880, when fully one-third of that population was foreign-born (centering on the San Francisco–Sacramento area, with the Irish and Chinese in the lead there, later to be overtaken by Germans and Italians, and with Mexicans strong in the south), the Portuguese constituted a bare 2.7 percent of that foreign element. Their share reached its highest point in 1920, 4.4 percent; but by that year the foreign-born total itself had dropped to 22 percent, so that the Portuguese accounted for roughly 1 percent of

Queen of the Holy Ghost festival, in front of the altar in the Brotherhood of the Holy Ghost Hall, at Novato, California. She holds the crown which she will wear after the special mass is said.

the state's total population. While the vast majority of foreign-born whites have congregated in urban areas, especially in the twentieth century, the majority of the Portuguese in California first settled and have tended to remain in rural locations, farming.[3]

Mention has already been made of the early presence of Portuguese whalemen and fishermen in California—besides Portuguese participation in gold mining there. But by 1885, both mining and whaling were well-nigh extinct; various forms of farming, and to a very limited extent fishing, have been the major attractions for Portuguese immigration to California. The earliest settlers came by boat, as indicated in Chapter 2, partly from New England, where they had originally landed, and thence around Cape Horn or via Panama. From 1870, however, most immigrants used the railroad from the East, with Oakland as the western terminus.[4] Later, a third current of immigration (or migration), although small and intermittent, came from the Hawaiian Islands; for example, between 1911 and 1914 some 2,000 Portuguese arrived from Hawaii, having left their original settlement area because of poor working conditions.[5]

At the same time, reemigration (or "retromigration") to Portugal was proportionately less from California than it was from New England—partly because farming provided greater stability than factory work.[6]

As for regional origins, most of the Portuguese immigrants to California, like those who settled in New England, came from the Azores; these, up to about 1900, were almost exclusively from the western islands of Pico, Fayal, São Jorge, and thereafter also from Terceira. They were augmented by small numbers of Madeirans, and by groups of Capeverdeans as well.[7] By 1912 there were several thousand Capeverdeans in the San Francisco area, working on the San Francisco docks or on Sacramento riverboats; as of 1920 the largest Capeverdean colony in California was at Sacramento, where many of these people were employed by the Southern Pacific Railroad.[8] Immigration from continental Portugal was negligible, even slighter than in the Northeast, until after 1910.[9]

Most Portuguese who migrated to the West Coast had first landed in New England or New York, and in many cases had spent some time in the Northeast before moving on. This led to continuing personal ties and a certain amount of communication, even occasional migration back and forth, between these geographically widely separated settlement areas. We find a clear reflection of this fact in some of the Portuguese immigrant newspapers published at the time in California, and similarly in New England, with almost every issue reporting some local events or personal news from the other end of the country.

For some random examples, the weekly *Arauto* of Hayward, California, in its issue of June 20, 1896, carried a long story about a Portuguese priest in Fall River having left the church in order to get married, along with a dispatch from Santa Cruz in the Azores describing the latest Holy Ghost celebration there. The issue of April 16, 1904, gave much space to the Holy Ghost festival in North Oakland, California, followed by an item about a "basket party" (a dance featuring the auctioning off of donated food baskets) among the Portuguese farmers at Newport, Rhode Island; in turn followed by a dispatch from Yerington, Nevada, about the growth of a Portuguese colony there, and an admonition for all voters in Alameda County, California, to register for the November election. The issue of January 25, 1908, told with gusto of a New Bedford Portuguese newspaper having been sued by a Portuguese physician in Lowell because it had accused him (slanderously?) of breach of engagement with a girl from São Miguel, Azores. In the March 7 issue of the same year we read about a memorial service held in Honolulu's cathedral for King Carlos of Portugal, recently assassinated.

For some biographical sketches: Antonio Pereira came to New Bedford from the Azores in the 1840s, and in 1849 joined the gold rush, crossing the Continent with ox team and covered wagon. After some mining in Nevada and northern California he took up cattle raising at Panole, and finally went into fruit and vegetable gardening at Hayward till his death at age eighty-seven. In California he had married Maria Neves, who had arrived there by boat. Their son Frank first worked as a "cow puncher" and then as a clerk, finally opening a general store in Hayward. His wife was born in Hayward of an Azorean father who had reached California via Cape Horn and had then raised sheep in the San Joaquin Valley before retiring to Hayward.[10]

Joseph M. Avila, born on São Jorge in the Azores in 1852, came to the United States at age thirteen, worked on a farm near Boston for a while, and then went to New Bedford to ship on a whaler for nearly four years. Returning to New Bedford, he worked in a factory one year, then boarded a steamer to Panama, from where he reached California in 1870. Employed as a cheese maker for some time, he eventually prospered on his own dairy farm near San Jose.[11]

Joseph I. Barbeiro, born in the Azores in 1862, emigrated to California alone at age sixteen, worked six months on a farm, then fourteen years in mines in California and Oregon, and finally two years in railroad tunnel construction. In 1890, on the advice of a friend in San Francisco, he went to New York City to take a job as a hotel clerk, but after three months started west again. After working two years in Colorado mines, he was back in California in 1893 and became a storekeeper in San Leandro.[12] Manuel Daveiro, born on Madeira in 1864, went to Hawaii alone in 1883; there he worked on sugar plantations for eight years and married a girl from São Miguel. In 1891 the couple moved to California, went into the apple-growing business near Sebastopol—and also produced twelve children.[13]

Nicolau Miranda, born on the Island of São Nicolau in the Cape Verde Islands in 1888, came to the United States in 1908 to settle in Providence, Rhode Island, but after two years moved on to California. He worked six years on Sacramento riverboats, then as a longshoreman in San Francisco, and eventually stayed with the Berkeley Transportation Company for twenty-eight years, until his retirement in 1956. When interviewed by the present writer in 1962, he owned four houses in the Alameda area and was president of the Cape Verde mutual-aid society in San Francisco.

In 1870, according to a statistical analysis by Alvin R. Graves, California held 27.3 percent of the total Portuguese immigrant population in the United States, and New England about 70 percent. In 1880, California's share had risen to 51 percent because during the 1870s some 80 percent of all new Portuguese immigrants to the United States settled on the West Coast. Thereafter, California's comparative position waned again; by 1920 it was down to 30 percent of the United States total of Portuguese-born residents.[14]

By major regions, California's Portuguese foreign stock (foreign-born [F], and American-born of Portuguese parentage [A]), or else the foreign-born only, were distributed as follows:

Region		1860		1880		1900	1920
North Coast	(F+A)	53	(F) 153 (A)	66	(F) 410	(F)	927
North Central	(F+A)	156	(F) 393 (A)	201	(F) 396	(F)	226
Central Coast	(F+A)	606	(F) 5,542 (A)	3,867	(F) 11,010	(F)	18,353
Sacramento Valley	(F+A)	289	(F) 861 (A)	566	(F) 1,554	(F)	3,343
San Joaquin Valley	(F+A)	12	(F) 374 (A)	75	(F) 1,379	(F)	8,575
Sierra Mountains	(F+A)	577	(F) 539 (A)	292	(F) 465	(F)	387
Southern California	(F+A)	19	(F) 110 (A)	53	(F) 460	(F)	1,584
The State	(F+A)	1,717	(F) 7,990 (A)	5,169	(F) 15,704	(F)	33,409[15]

Whereas in 1860 the two foci of Portuguese settlement in California had been the Central Coast and the Sierra Mountains in about equal measure, by 1880 the Central Coast (San Francisco and Oakland Bay—especially Alameda, Contra Costa, San Mateo, and Marin counties) had become far and away the most important settlement area, holding 71 percent of all the Portuguese in the state, who were chiefly engaged in farming. The Sacramento Valley was next, but far behind (barely 10 percent). The Sierra Mountain area (originally important for mining) had attracted hardly any additional Portuguese during the 1860-1880 period. Throughout the period from 1880 to 1920, the Central Coast region maintained its vastly dominant position. However, after the turn of the century the San Joaquin Valley also attracted increasing numbers of Portuguese and became their second major area of settlement. In addition, Southern California (chiefly the San Diego area) with its fisheries began to attain some importance.[16]

Alameda County, stretching eastward from San Francisco Bay and comprising Oakland, San Leandro, Hayward, etc., may be considered the Californian counterpart of Bristol County, Massachusetts, in the East, as the hub of Portuguese settlement. San Leandro can boast the oldest Portuguese farming community in this country, going back to the 1850s—and the first mayor of Portuguese descent (a woman at that) in the 1940s.[17] An article in the *Saturday Evening Post* in 1911 said: "San Leandro, a little out of Oakland, is a city of orchards and gardens and is almost as Portuguese as old Lisbon itself."[18] Some of the Portuguese in Alameda County, and in Sonoma County to the north, are "immortalized" in Jack London's semiautobiographical novels, *Martin Eden* and *The Valley of the Moon*.[19] In the city of Oakland, the Portuguese first concentrated in the western section, near the waterfront, later spreading southeast; their number (first and second generation combined) was estimated at 4,000 in 1892, and in the 1920 census had risen to 12,260. Actually Oakland remained semirural for a long time; business activity centered in San Francisco. It was only during and after the First World War that Oakland turned into an industrial center (chiefly canning, also producing some cotton goods). San Francisco, like New York City, never invited substantial Portuguese settlement (even as of 1920, the Portuguese stock in "Frisco" proper totaled only 2,490). Yet consular reports about 1880 listed three Portuguese "hotels" (or boardinghouses) in San Francisco proper, plus four saloons, a restaurant, and not less than fifteen barbershops run by Portuguese.[20] After the big earthquake and fire of 1906, the

Portuguese consul reported that, since not many Portuguese lived in San Francisco proper, Portuguese property losses there were minor, although their favorite hangouts, with the several saloons and hostelries (along Jackson and Davis Streets), were completely destroyed.[21]

To the Sacramento Valley the Portuguese first flocked around 1870. As a matter of fact, according to one source, in this area they started out as contract laborers (probably the only instance of Portuguese contract labor in California): "In 1868 or 1869 Portuguese were brought from the Azores and set at work above the city of Sacramento. A few years later they were set at work farther down the river, working, it is said by the older Portuguese residents, for their board and lodging for about two years in return for their passage to this country." Near the villages of Freeport and Clarksburg, south of Sacramento, a large vegetable-growing area later became known as the "Lisbon district"; most of the early Azorean settlers in that particular location had come from Hawaii, after working in the sugar plantations there.[22] The Capeverdean colony in the city of Sacramento has already been mentioned. In 1914 the immigrant newspaper *O Arauto* claimed that the approximately 2,000 Portuguese in Sacramento then included a number of Portuguese nationals from the Portuguese colonies in East and West Africa, China, India, and Timor.[23]

Sacramento was the northernmost Portuguese settlement of consequence, and from that point the Portuguese (which, to stress this once again, essentially meant Azoreans) spread southward into the San Joaquin Valley, particularly the so-called "West Side" of the valley, through Stanislaus and Merced Counties (Modesto, Turlock, Atwater, Merced, etc.), Fresno and surroundings, and into Kings County, with heavy concentrations in the Visalia-Hanford-Tulare triangle, developing and eventually dominating the dairy industry there, as well as growing various crops. At Hanford, for instance, there is a record of Portuguese sheep-raisers as early as about 1870,[24] but most of the development in the San Joaquin Valley occurred after the turn of the century.

The fisheries, including whaling, which had brought a few Portuguese whalers to California's shores even before the Gold Rush (see p. 28), played a negligible role until almost the end of the period under consideration in this chapter. An official survey of United States fisheries undertaken in 1880 found two small companies of whalers with their respective shore stations at San Simeon and at

Whaler's Point, in San Luis Obispo County, dating since the late 1860s; the crews of both were almost exclusively Azorean. At Monterey, the survey encountered a group of Portuguese line fishermen operating about half a dozen boats. (One of Robert Louis Stevenson's friends at Monterey, in 1879, was referred to as "Joaquin the jolly Portuguese whaler."[25]) The fishermen of San Francisco, all of them then living near the end of Vallejo Street, also included a number of Portuguese.[26] It was at Point Loma near San Diego, close to where Cabrillo had first set foot on California soil in 1542, that a Portuguese fishing community of some importance was to develop, and by the 1930s to dominate the American tuna fisheries. Although practically all the Portuguese connected with offshore whaling had left the San Diego area before 1870, by 1893 there were again some Portuguese there, going after albacore in small boats. Starting about 1911, after the perfecting of canning methods, the colony grew, through accretions from the New England colony as well as directly from Portugal, and concentrated on the tuna catch.[27] To draw once more from the autobiography of Lawrence Oliver: upon his arrival from New England, Oliver had gone to Chico in northern California but was soon summoned by his father to join him in San Diego. Thus, in this final step of his American "pilgrimage," Oliver left Chico in the fall of 1906, traveling by train to San Francisco and from there to San Diego by sidewheel steamer. He found employment in the fresh-fish market of a distant relative, at $1 per day—to become eventually a tuna millionaire.[28]

II   *Hawaii*

The year 1878 marked the beginning of large-scale Portuguese immigration, on a contract-labor basis, into the present state of Hawaii, then the Kingdom of Hawaii (also known as the Sandwich Islands). For two or three decades prior to that date, there had been a sporadic influx of several hundred Portuguese, mostly Azorean and Capeverdean "jumpers" from American whaling ships (see pp. 31-32). After the American Civil War, the growing West Coast market and other conditions greatly stimulated the relatively young Hawaiian sugar industry. Developed and controlled by groups of Yankees who had been coming to the islands for the dual purpose of business and missionary work, this industry had initially relied on Chinese plantation labor. But as these Chinese tended to drift off into urban trades, the plantation men were looking for new sources of labor supply, particularly so after the conclusion of a reciprocity treaty in 1876 which opened the United States market to Hawaiian planters.

In the late 1860s a German botanist by the name of Hillebrand, surveying plant life in Hawaii and other parts of the world, had been retained by the sugar people to locate suitable labor while on a botanical trip to South Asia—without much success. Toward the end of 1876, one of the Portuguese old-timers, a shop-keeper named Jason Perry (Jacinto Pereira?), who also acted as a kind of consular agent for Portugal, urged the importation of laborers from the Portuguese island of Madeira, off the west coast of Africa. (On Madeira sugar cane had been successfully grown since the fifteenth century, transplanted from Sicily; the Portuguese also grew it in the Azores for a while in the sixteenth century.[29] In the Hawaiian kingdom itself, another early Portuguese settler by the name of Antone Sylva may have actually been the first to attempt sugar milling, on the island of Maui.[30]) In 1877 Dr. Hillebrand happened to be staying in Madeira to study subtropical flora, and he enthusiastically confirmed to his Hawaiian contacts that that overpopulated island, climatically so similar to Hawaii, might indeed be an ideal source of plantation labor. Somewhere along the line official Hawaiian interest also focused on the island of São Miguel, in the eastern Azores. Government-sponsored solicitation of contract laborers for the Hawaiian plantations was promptly undertaken, both in Madeira and in São Miguel. By 1878 the first boatload of 114 Madeirans (including entire families) arrived in Honolulu, followed by some 400 on a charter vessel the following year. In 1881 there were two ships bringing in over 800 men, women, and children from São Miguel. By 1888, when these importations were suspended for a while, a total of almost 12,000 Madeirans and São Miguelians (or Michaelese?) had thus made the long voyage halfway around the world to start new lives in a mid-Pacific island kingdom.[31]

The reasons why enough Madeirans and Azoreans could be found in those years willing to sign up for arduous penal labor contracts for five or more years in some distant land were the typical ones mentioned in the previous chapter: economic pressures, in the first place; also, in the case of young men, a desire to evade military service. The prospect of relocating on subtropical isles reminding them of home may have been an added attraction for venturing to Hawaii, despite the competition of Brazil and the United States as emigrant destinations. To quote from the life history of one Portuguese-Hawaiian women: "My father and mother were married in Madeira and came to Hawaii on a sailing vessel in 1884, arriving on the island of Kauai after a six months' trip around the Horn. My oldest brother had been refused permission to leave because he had to do military duty, but he stowed away and my parents hid him until the boat was far out to sea. In spite of his youth, he was put under contract with my father upon our arrival here."[32] In another autobiographical account, a Madeiran-born resident of Oakland named M. F. Olival recalls how in 1887, at age fifteen, he stowed away on a Hawaii-bound English bark calling at Funchal (Madeira's capital). Together with eleven other stowaways, he was soon put to work by the captain. After a grueling voyage of over five months (including thirty-three days just to get around Cape Horn in a heavy storm), during which time sixteen persons died and sixteen were born aboard the battered sailing vessel, they arrived in Honolulu, April 1888. Olival went to work on a sugar plantation (in this instance as a free laborer, not indentured). In 1894 he married a girl from São Miguel. A year later he quit plantation labor to join the new army of the Republic of Hawaii (the monarchy there having been overthrown); and upon annexation of the islands by the United States in 1898, he served as a volunteer in the American army there until 1902. Three years later he moved to California, permanently.[33]

The voyage around Cape Horn, typically with stopovers at Rio de Janeiro and Valparaiso, did not always last five or six months; the more common duration was three months. But even so, this was hard enough on the emigrants and costly enough for the importing Hawaiian planters[34] to put a damper on continued labor importation from the Portuguese islands after 1888. In 1911 the United States Immigration Commission reported efforts were being made to shorten the trip for future emigrants from Portugal to Hawaii by dispatching them via the Tehuantepec Peninsula or Panama, instead of via Cape Horn.[35] But actually the year 1909 proved to be the last one for group migration from Madeira and the Azores to the Hawaiian Islands. Following the one shipload from Madeira in 1888 (the one that included Mr. Olival), there were two more importations totaling 829 persons in 1895 and 1899. In 1899 and 1900, after American annexation of the islands had led to abolition of the penal contract labor system there, several hundred Portuguese from New England landed at Honolulu to work on the plantations; but, being used to factory labor, most of them quit their plantation jobs after a short while.[36] Direct importation from Madeira and São Miguel brought in an additional 3,403 persons in three large shiploads during 1906–1909.[37] After the fall of the Portuguese monarchy in 1910, labor recruitment for Hawaii shifted briefly to mainland Portugal: a total of 1,652 Continentals arrived in Honolulu in 1911, and another 228 (the last organized group from Portugal ever) came in 1913. These Continentals, hailing largely from cities (such as Oporto), did not adjust to plantation work as well as the Madeiran and Azorean peasants; many of them soon moved on to California.[38]

There had been migration from Hawaii to California, and less often the other way around, ever since 1888. For some individuals, there was even repeated moving back and forth; the Madeiran-Hawaiian lady cited above recalls: "I spent much of my childhood in California. After several trips between Hawaii and the coast, we finally settled on Kauai. . . ."[39] It was the rising wage rates in California after the exclusion of the Chinese that attracted a growing number of Portuguese from Hawaii to that state in the late 1880s and early 1890s (e.g., to the Sacramento area; cf. p. 72).[40] On the one hand, in the late 1890s many of these again moved back to the "Paradise of the Pacific" because the fall of the monarchy followed by annexation had created a boom there.[41]

Between 1901 and 1905, once more the pendulum swung in the opposite direction, drawing some of Hawaii's Portuguese to the West Coast.[42] In 1907–1908, special inducements by the Hawaiian Board of Immigration (such as free transportation) brought back some 500 of those who had moved on to California and also attracted small numbers from the New Bedford area[43]—which shows that official interest in the quality of Portuguese labor had not waned. In the balance, the Hawaiian sugar plantations had difficulty holding on to the Portuguese element; California farming on the one hand, and urban trades or independent farming within the Hawaiian Islands themselves, provided superior attractions. However, relatively few of the Portuguese emigrants to Hawaii returned to their native country, partly because of the high travel expense involved.[44]

As a result of the almost complete cessation of Portuguese immigration to Hawaii after 1913, by 1920 the proportion of Hawaiian-born of Portuguese parentage to Portuguese-born was nearly 4:1. Here are the "exact" population (as against migration) statistics:

Portuguese Stock in Hawaiian Islands, 1872—1920

	Born in Portugal	Hawaiian-born of (all-)[45] Portuguese parentage
1872	395	
1878	436	
1884	9,377	
1890	8,602	4,117
1896	8,232	6,959
1900	6,512	9,163
1910	7,585	14,716
1920	5,794	21,208[46]

Of course these figures are more meaningful if seen in relation to Hawaii's total population. In 1910 and again in 1920, the total "Portuguese stock" (exclusive of mixed-breeds) represented slightly over 8 percent of that population—proportionately much more weighty than in New England or California. This Portuguese element, moreover, found itself in a multi-ethnic setting in which East Asiatics (particularly Japanese, along with Chinese, Koreans, and eventually Filipinos) were increasingly predominant, as against Anglo American, "other" European, and aboriginal Hawaiian stock, and in which a growing proportion of people were of mixed ancestry.

As for the geographic distribution of the Portuguese stock within the Hawaiian Islands, the early arrivals (Western Azoreans and Capeverdeans employed in whaling) seem to have congregated at Honolulu, with some dispersal later on. The contract laborers from Madeira and São Miguel would naturally spread themselves around on sugar plantations located on several of the islands: Hawaii proper (the so-called "big island"—largest in size but not in population), Maui, Oahu (the most populous island and containing the capital city), and Kauai (where the Hawaiian sugar industry actually had its beginning). In addition to these four principal islands, a sprinkling of those Portuguese who eventually left the plantations made their way to the two or three smallest islands. For example, M. Madeiros had arrived with his parents from São Miguel about 1880, grew up on a plantation on the island of Hawaii, then lived in Honolulu (island of Oahu) for many years, keeping a tavern in the "Portuguese suburb" of Kakaako. But in 1912 we find him on the small island of Niihau (population about 300), managing a cattle ranch and on the side functioning as the island's "kaliau" (governor or supervisor).[47]

The principal development in terms of internal migration was the drift of the Portuguese from the various plantations into Honolulu, thus imitating the earlier pattern of the Chinese. In that city (and later on also in Hilo, second city of the archipelago) they would go into a variety of service and other trades. Another development, as an alternative to, or subsequent to, settlement in the Honolulu area, was a movement into small independent farming, in a variety of locations outside the plantation areas. The particular section of Honolulu that the Portuguese, and particularly the Madeirans, selected for residence as early as the 1880s exemplifies vividly the dream dreamt by so many immigrants anywhere from anywhere: that of being able to recreate in the new environment some cherished aspect of the old. For just as Funchal, the capital of Madeira, skirts and slopes up a volcanic mountain, so Honolulu spreads at the foot and up a hillside topped by a volcanic crater known as the Punchbowl. The Punchbowl district of Honolulu became the residential core of the Portuguese islanders, who soon converted this arid rock into productive gardens. By 1896, 4,000 of Honolulu's 28,000 inhabitants were Portuguese, clustering around the central hilly slopes, the majority living in their own homes. By 1902, there were over 5,000 Portuguese in Honolulu, as against a total of about 5,500 still living on the plantations and about 5,000 located elsewhere in the islands.[48]

CHAPTER 6

The Dormancy Period, 1922-1958

I The Throttling of Portuguese Immigration

PORTUGUESE SETTLEMENT IN THE UNITED STATES FROM THE EARLY
1920s to the late 1950s was marked by three overall developments:
(1) the gradual throttling of immigration, first by the legal requirement of literacy and then by nationality quota restrictions; (2) a
moderate and spotty extension of the eastern settlement area, from
southeastern New England down the Atlantic seaboard into Connecticut and the New York—New Jersey metropolitan area, with
tiny offshoots as far south as Florida; (3) the "freezing," by and
large, of the California and Hawaii settlements, with rapid deethnicization in the latter area.

The so-called Literacy Test, introduced in 1917, required all
immigrants to demonstrate a minimal ability to read and write.
According to the law, all aliens over sixteen years of age who could
not read any language (subjects were given a test of thirty to forty
words in their own language to read) were not admissible, with
some exceptions for close relatives of United States residents. One
immediate consequence of this innovation was that a very large
number of Portuguese subjects were henceforth barred from immigration due to the extremely high degree of illiteracy then found in
Portugal (see Chapter 8).[1] On the other hand, of course, Portuguese
emigrants arriving after 1917 have shown a higher average level of
formal education than earlier arrivals.

In addition to the literacy requirement, the Immigration Act of
1921 limited the number of aliens admitted annually of any
nationality subject to the quota law to 3 percent ("The Three
Percent Law") of the number of foreign-born persons of that
nationality already resident in the continental United States as
determined by the census of 1910. This was revised in 1924 to 2
percent based on the census of 1890. But the national-origins clause

of the Act of 1924, which became effective July 1, 1929, provided that the quota of any nationality should be computed by dividing 150,000 (the maximum annual immigrant number) by the ratio between the total inhabitants in the United States of all nationalities subject to the quota law and the estimated number of inhabitants in the continental United States in 1920 owing their origin to the nationality concerned. Under these provisions the minimum quota was 100.

Accordingly, the annual quota for Portugal (including the Azores, Madeira, and the Cape Verde Islands) as defined by the Act of 1921 had been set at 2,520 (revised to 2,465 in 1922). Under the Act of 1924 this quota was reduced to 503 immigrants a year, and in 1929 to 440 persons. Exempted from the quota restriction were children and spouses of United Stated citizens, immigrants from Western Hemisphere countries (such as Portuguese-speaking Brazil, which could easily and did serve as a halfway station for some Portuguese ultimately settling in the United States), and, of course, immigrants previously admitted but now returning from visits abroad. The number of Portuguese immigrants actually admitted under the quota between 1925 and 1929 was 2,449; from 1930 to 1934, 1,302; and from 1935 until 1939, 1,541. Some more immigrants were admitted outside the quota: from 1924 through 1946, 7,665 Portuguese came in legally under the quota, and 1,623 came in outside the quota. One interesting aspect of these figures is that, whereas the quota was rather fully utilized up to 1929, only 70 percent of the minute Portuguese quota was actually used from 1930 through 1946. Probably part of the reason for this latter fact lay in the changed conditions in Portugal (overthrow of the parliamentary republic and start of Salazar's fascist-oriented dictatorship in 1927, with tightened curbs on emigration and a promise of improved economic conditions), and part of it in the discouraging effects of the economic depression in the United States.[2]

By decades, the following numbers of Portuguese immigrants were admitted to the United States in 1921–1960 (apparently this includes nonquota admissions—but of course it excludes clandestine entrants!):

1921–1930	29,994
1931–1940	3,329
1941–1950	7,423
1951–1960	19,588

For appropriate comparison of these figures by decades it has to be kept in mind that 1921 was actually the peak year in the entire history of Portuguese immigration (19,195 admissions—thus leaving a balance of 10,799 for 1922–1930), and that 1959 marked the—albeit slow—beginning of the new Portuguese mass immigration, summarized in the next chapter (2,631 admissions in 1959 and 6,766 in 1960, as against an annual average of 1,000 to 1,500 during 1951–1958).[3]

Providence, Rhode Island, remained the principal point of entry, receiving up to 70 percent of the Portuguese immigrants until about 1935;[4] thereafter, New York became the main port of debarkation. As for areas of initial settlement, a breakdown of the total of Portuguese immigrants admitted during 1921–1930 by "states of intended future residence" (i.e., destinations as declared to immigration officials upon arrival) gives the overall picture:[5]

Massachusetts	13,340
Rhode Island	3,920
Connecticut	1,419
New York	3,736
New Jersey	3,021
California	4,243
Hawaii	18

The issue of clandestine, illegal immigration is, of course, tied to the existence of legal curbs on immigration. Although there had been some immigration restrictions in this country prior to 1917 (such as the exclusion of the Chinese), illegal immigration did not become a major issue until after World War I, and particularly after World War II. For instance, according to one unconfirmed estimate, about 6,000 Portuguese entered the United States illegally between 1920 and 1930, coming from Cuba.[6] In the years following World War II, Portuguese sailors repeatedly deserted their ships in American ports, or tried to; in June 1951, eight such sailors were found working as stevedores near Newark and were deported; this led to temporary prohibition of shore leaves for Portuguese seamen on their first visit to American ports.[7] In the fall of 1951, the Portuguese-American community was stirred by newspaper reports about two young men from São Miguel who, having tried to reach the United States in a 20-foot sailboat which they had secretly built, were picked up by immigration officials for deportation. Victor Caetano and Evaristo Gaspar, after crossing 2,400 miles of ocean in thirty days, had gotten into a heavy storm near Bermuda; they were rescued by an American freighter, only to be handed over to port authorities upon landing in Texas. Through the intervention of Portuguese-American organizations in New England, which collected funds for the two adventurers and enlisted the support of a senator from Rhode Island, deportation was stayed on appeal; a congressional bill to grant Gaspar and Caetano permanent residence was still pending two years later—by which time Gaspar had married a Portuguese girl in Fall River. (Caetano had left his wife back in São Miguel, and was now living in Cambridge).[8]

As regards the regional origins of Portuguese who immigrated during the "dormancy period," the Azorean element continued to predominate, even though Continentals (chiefly from northern Portugal) now also accounted for about one-fourth of the total. A large majority of the mainland Portuguese bent on emigration favored Brazil, as in earlier periods; but the majority of those from the "Adjacent Islands" (the official Portuguese term for the Azores and Madeira) continued to go to the United States (as well as to Bermuda, starting in the early 1920s).[9] American influence in the Azores kept growing, partly as a result of the many returned immigrants who had lived in the States. H. C. Adams, writing in 1935, reported: "American influence is apparent in the English spoken throughout the Azores. There seems to be a genuine liking for the United States. The Stars and Stripes are in evidence at every festival."[10] An American air-force base was established at Santa Maria in the Azores early in 1945. American military presence in the Azores was confirmed by treaty in 1948, and placed within the framework of the NATO alliance in the 1950s. The Cape Verde Islands, then enjoying only colonial status within Portugal's empire, continued to send immigrants, or in many cases just seasonal migrants, to America: as of 1930, there were some Capeverdeans in all but twelve states of the Union, totaling "over 8,789," according to a consular report. The United States census for 1930 reported 1,795 of them in the state of New York and 509 in New Jersey,[11] in addition to those in the more traditional habitats of New England (Providence, Boston, Cape Cod, the Boston area—and increasingly also Connecticut). Although sailing vessels had practically disappeared from transatlantic traffic by the turn of the century, some decrepit old schooners carrying migrants and cargo were still sailing between New Bedford and the Cape Verde Islands until about 1935.[12]

Since Portuguese immigration within the quota was now legally limited to a few hundred per year, those returning from the United States to Portugal (permanently or for lengthy visits) now tended to outnumber new arrivals considerably: for instance, in 1922 there were 1,950 arrivals, but 5,877 departures; in 1925, 619 arrivals versus 3,600 departures; for the eleven-year period 1922–32, 11,589 arrivals versus 25,466 departures. Actually there might have been even more departures were it not for the fact that some illiterate Portuguese settlers originally admitted before 1917 were now afraid that if they left the United States they could never gain readmittance.

According to the United States census for 1930, the population of Portuguese birth or parentage within the continental United States and Hawaii had by then risen to 121,955 foreign-born and 183,738 native-born, totaling 305,693. There were at least *some* Portuguese in every single state of the Union—down to one foreign-born each in North and South Dakota. . . . Broken down by states, but disregarding the states showing less than a total of 100, the picture in 1930 was as follows:

State	Portuguese-born	Amer.-born of Port. Parentage	Total
Massachusetts	48,942	63,843	112,785
Rhode Island	12,766	17,723	30,489
New York	7,758	3,398	11,156
New Jersey	4,411	1,798	6,209
Connecticut	3,271	2,708	5,979
Pennsylvania	1,563	893	2,456
Illinois	253	865	1,118
Ohio	286	347	633
Michigan	189	175	364
Indiana	98	55	153
Wisconsin	47	56	103
Maryland	168	110	278
District of Columbia	58	58	116
Virginia	107	118	225
Georgia	110	64	174
Florida	229	293	522

Continued State	Portuguese- born	Amer.-born of Port. Parentage	Total
Louisiana	80	161	241
Texas	98	198	296
California	36,343	64,617	100,960
Nevada	239	341	580
Washington	168	342	510
Oregon	145	338	483
Idaho	46	81	127
Territory of Hawaii	3,713	23,875	27,588

On the basis of the above census figures and those of previous decades, the then Poruguese consul in Providence estimated, not unreasonably, that as of 1930 there were at least an additional 45,000 "grandchildren of Portuguese immigrants" (i.e., persons having at least one Portuguese-born grandparent) and 26,200 persons of Portuguese "colonial stock," yielding an overall total of close to 400,000 persons, in the continental United States plus the Territory of Hawaii, who were either born in (insular or continental) Portugal or had at least one native Portuguese among their forebears.[13] (Whether there is any point in subdividing—dividing?—the American population into different "nationalities" beyond the second or third generation, and whether one out of four foreign-born grandparents is enough to assign a native American to some particular "ethnic" group is, of course, another question.)

By 1960 the total of Portuguese immigrants and their children in all fifty states (including Hawaii) had dropped by nearly 10 percent, as compared to 1940: 87,109 foreign-born and 190,293 native-born, making a total of 277,402.[14] Evidently the combined total of the slight amount of fresh immigration during these two decades and of the number of children born to immigrant residents was outweighed considerably by death and reemigration. Of the 1960 Portuguese population, about 35 percent were living in California, 48 percent in southeastern New England, 7 percent in New York and New Jersey, and a little over 3 percent in Hawaii. Over 87 percent of those in New England were in "urban" locations; so were 70 percent of those in California[15] (indicating a marked drop in "rural" living there).

II *Portuguese-American Communities in the Eastern United States*

As of 1960 New Bedford had retained its lead as the largest Portuguese-American community in New England, and as a matter of fact in the United States: 21,464 (first plus second-generation Portuguese stock), or about 30,000 if we include adjoining Dartmouth, Fairhaven, etc. The Azorean element continued its preponderance in the "Portuguese capital of the United States," but there were now also many thousands of "Lisboas" (Continentals) and Madeirans, and, of course, Capeverdeans. Actually, during the economic crises of the 1920s and later on New Bedford had seen close to a third of its Portuguese population drift away.[16]

The 1960 census figures for Fall River show a Portuguese stock of 19,787 there (at least 22,000 if we include Somerset and some other outlying sections). This cotton textile city, too, had at least temporarily lost part of its Portuguese population during the interwar crisis years, including many of the more recent immigrants from mainland Portugal. The Fall River Portuguese community not only retained its Azorean majority, but more specifically the prevalence of people from São Miguel. Taunton has remained the third major Portuguese community within Bristol County, Massachusetts, since before World War I, with a Portuguese stock of 5,695 in 1960. Actually it is outnumbered by the Portuguese "colony" in the Boston area, if we bracket together Boston proper with Cambridge and Somerville: 8,368 as of 1960, clustering in the northern suburbs and in South and East Boston.

In Provincetown, which during the "dormancy period" was becoming more and more of a summer resort town, the Portuguese element (in large part from São Miguel, Azores, and from Algarve fishing towns in southern Portugal) now constituted the marked majority.[17] The Portuguese in Falmouth and also in the Cape Cod area numbered 1,336 in 1960 (including many Capeverdeans); there were 1,172 up the coast at Plymouth, and 1,379 at Gloucester (down from 2,000 to 3,000 in previous decades, as some of the fishing people moved south to Georgia, Florida, etc.). Finally, within Massachusetts mention must be made of the (gradually declining) Portuguese settlements at Lowell, north of Boston, and the relatively recent communities at Peabody (attracted by the leather industry), Hudson, and especially at Ludlow, on the outskirts of Springfield. At Ludlow the majority of the Portuguese came from the Tras-os-

Montes province in northern Portugal, starting about 1912–1915, to work in a jute mill; by the 1940s they were forming a distinctive little "village" of some 1,500 people there.

In the small state of Rhode Island, the Portuguese remained concentrated along the eastern fringe, i.e., the Providence and Narragansett Bay areas immediately adjoining Bristol County, Massachusetts. The Portuguese "foreign stock" in that state numbered 29,155 in the 1960 census, representing about 3 percent of the state's entire population. Providence, together with adjoining East Providence, held the lion's share, 9,785 (slightly more than half located in East Providence). The drift into the northern and southern outskirts of Providence, begun toward the end of World War I, continued during the "dormancy" period: as of 1960, Pawtucket to the north had 2,746 Portuguese immigrants or children of immigrants, with an additional 2,000 or so in adjoining Central Falls, Valley Falls, and Cumberland; and there were 1,248 in West Warwick on the southern fringe. Many of the Capeverdeans in the Providence area, estimated at several thousand in the late 1920s (including many seasonal migrants), moved on to southern Connecticut, Westchester County (New York), South Boston, and as far as Ohio.

An interesting case of local parochialism or separatism developed on the northern fringes of Providence (the so-called Blackstone Valley) after the First World War: at Valley Falls, most of the Portuguese settlers were originally from Castendo, in the Beira Alta province of mainland Portugal; but in Central Falls, "beyond the bridge," they hailed from the island of Madeira and had their own exclusive Madeiran clubhouse. In the peninsular extension of Rhode Island southeast of Providence, the Portuguese element held its own as of 1960: 3,829 immigrants and their children in Bristol, 1,524 in Newport, and 1,083 in Middletown. In semirural Bristol and Portsmouth the regional accent remained on São Miguel; in Newport and Middletown, on Fayal.

Connecticut, which had counted only 1,410 natives of Portugal according to the 1920 census, had 3,271 of them (plus 2,708 of the second generation) by 1930 and 9,930 (first plus second generation) by 1960. The three main centers here are Bridgeport, Hartford, and Danbury, all of them heavily industrial. The majority of the Portuguese in the Hartford area had come from the Mira district above Lisbon; the majority of those in Danbury (some 300 families by 1954), from the Gouveia district, in north central Portugal. Other small Portuguese communities, with the emphasis on Continentals and Capeverdeans, developed at Waterbury, Naugatuck, and in the outskirts of New Haven. The old Azorean settlements at Stonington and New London, originally feeding on maritime activity, declined.[18]

For the state of New York, the census of 1940 showed 4,580 foreign-born whites from "Portugal" and the "Azores," to which we may add a certain number of Capeverdeans (classed as nonwhite) and Madeirans, and, together with the second generation, probably something over 8,000. Actually the Portuguese consul's estimate for 1935 was 7,504 "Portuguese citizens"; the large majority of these, the consul added, were males, from the northern mainland districts of Aveiro, Viseu, Guarda, and Vila Real; there were also 719 Madeirans and 916 Capeverdeans—but a mere 138 Azoreans.[19] New York City proper was the locus of most of this number: about 1,000 each in the boroughs of Manhattan and Brooklyn, nearly 500 in Queens, and 400 in the Bronx; in addition, there were about 1,000 in adjoining Westchester County to the north and 250 in Nassau County to the east. The Portuguese in Manhattan would cluster around Bleecker and Varick Streets, and those in Brooklyn around Court and Columbia Streets. The small number in the Bronx was to be found in the neighborhood of St. Anthony's (Portuguese) Mission, headed by one Father Cacella, the somewhat eccentric owner-editor of two little missionary newspapers. On a visit to the downtown Portuguese clubhouse on Varick Street, he was heard by the present writer to tell his banqueting compatriots, with sad humor: "Since you don't come up there [to my mission], I come down here." The Westchester group had its nucleus in Yonkers and Mount Vernon; it began arriving there from New England's textile mills and from Newark in the 1920s. Many moved away again during World War II.[20]

In Nassau County on Long Island, Mineola has become the site of a thriving Portuguese community of several thousand; this one started in the early 1920s, when some Portuguese men drifted in from New Bedford to apply for advertised summer construction jobs; returning to New Bedford for the winter, they eventually brought along other workers and their families. A similar pattern of job-induced migration had led groups of Madeirans from Erie, Pennsylvania, to Corning, New York, and from there to Rochester before World War I (see p. 65). Both in Rochester and in Corning— and in Erie, for that matter—comparatively small and isolated groups of Portuguese Americans, a few hundred each, have retained their ethnic consciousness, maintaining their own clubhouse and fraternal activities.[21]

In New Jersey, a relatively new compact Portuguese settlement area developed in the 1920s and 1930s with its hub in the Ironbound section of Newark (and with Ferry Street as the business center). Although a few Portuguese had settled in Newark before World War I, the real influx started in the early 1920s, from the direction of New Bedford and Pawtucket, where textile mills were in the throes of a heavy crisis. Once the new colony had grown its roots, there were thousands of additional arrivals, but now from continental Portugal—primarily from the fishing town of Murtosa but also from Chaves and some other spots in the Minho region (northern Portugal). The typical process was for the men to find jobs first, then to bring over their families. As of the 1940s, the Newark settlement had grown to an estimated 6,000 persons (including American-born children)—although the United States census for 1940 found only 3,821 foreign-born in all of New Jersey.

In Elizabeth, near Newark, and in a few other New Jersey towns within the ambit of metropolitan New York such as Perth Amboy and Lodi, additional small Portuguese settlements grew up during and after World War II. Apart from the Continentals, and a smattering of Azoreans and Madeirans in these locations, a group of Capeverdeans set themselves aside in Jersey City, and there is some puzzling indication of a few "Portuguese" (presumably Capeverdeans originally settled in New England) having drifted into cranberry and blueberry bogs, i.e., as berry-pickers, around Pemberton and New Lisbon at dates as far apart as the 1830s and the 1960s![22]

For Pennsylvania, the census figures show some 1,500 natives of Portugal in 1930, barely 1,000 in 1940. Mention has already been made of the small old settlement at Erie, founded by Madeirans in the 1870s but still ethnically distinctive (with its own clubhouse) in the 1950s. Of more recent origin is the Portuguese community at Bethlehem, consisting mostly of Continentals from the same areas as those in Newark; they were attracted by the steel industry there, first about 1914 and particularly in the 1920s. There is also a small group at Philadelphia.

No significant numbers of Portuguese have ever settled within the southeastern portion of the United States—nor, for that matter, in the Midwest or the Southwest (brief mention of which is conveniently included here, as a kind of appendix to coverage of the East). The few hundred natives of Portugal reported by the census of 1930 in Maryland, the District of Columbia, and Virginia presumably represent primarily persons in the employ of federal or international agencies or of the Portuguese embassy in Washington, D.C., or in the Virginia and Maryland suburbs of the nation's capital. A partial identification of the roughly 1,000 foreign-born Portuguese (as of 1930—or by now perhaps 2,000 to 3,000 of the first and second generation) living in Georgia, Florida, Louisiana, and Texas, is provided in a report by Georgia's inspector of coastal fisheries, about 1933: "The prawn fisheries of the South Atlantic coast constitute one of the country's leading seafood industries, and is practically entirely in the hands of Portuguese fishermen. The fishing is done between Southport, N.C., and Cape Canaveral, Florida. . . . The industry is also important on the Gulf of Mexico between Apalachicola, Florida, and Galveston, Texas, with Portuguese fishermen heavily represented in that territory as well."[23] Portuguese fishermen are known to have migrated from Provincetown to Brunswick and Savannah, Georgia, in the 1930s.

As for Florida, a California Portuguese newspaper reported as early as 1912 that fifty Portuguese from mainland Portugal and Madeira had left New Bedford for Florida in order to set up a colony there.[24] Others followed later, moving down from Gloucester and Provincetown, in search of a climate reminiscent of their native Algarve province in southern Portugal. They settled primarily at Fernandina and St. Augustine, to catch and can seafood. The search for a retirement haven motivated some other elderly Portuguese from New England to move after World War II to such places as St. Petersburg, New Smyrna Beach, Miami, Tampa, etc.[25] As of 1949, small Portuguese fishing fleets and canneries were reported not only along the Georgia and Florida coasts, but also at Morgan City and Patterson, Louisiana, and at Biloxi, Mississippi.[26]

In the midwestern states at least some of the approximately 1,000 persons (as of 1930) of Portuguese birth or parentage in Illinois are likely to have been attracted by descendants of the "Madeira exiles" referred to in Chapter 2. In the 1940s, a hillside on the outskirts of Jacksonville, Illinois, was still known as "Portuguese Hill," and the local telephone book still showed many subscribers with such typically Portuguese names as Sousa, Gonzalves, Vasconcelos, Fernandes, and Gouveia.[27] But undoubtedly it was the lure of various defense plants and other industries that drew several hundred persons of Portuguese birth (including Capeverdeans) to such places as Columbus, Ohio, and other midwestern locations.

III *California*

In California the total number of foreign-born whites from Portugal (including the Azores and "Other Atlantic Islands") rose slightly from 33,409 in 1920 to 36,050 in 1930, but dropped to 30,224 by 1940. At the same time, the 67,617 native-born of all- or part-Portuguese parentage enumerated in 1930 also dropped slightly, to about 63,080 by 1940. These figures suggest that Portuguese migration to that state, either directly from Portugal or after initial settlement in the East, continued on a small scale in the 1920s; but it practically stopped in the 1930s (with a population drop due to mortality and apparently some migration to other states). From 1940 to 1960, California's Portuguese stock (first and second generation together) rose from 93,304 to 97,489; this reflects a modest resumption of Portuguese movement toward the West Coast, during and after World War II, consonant with the general American population trend during that period.

Since the 1930s, California's urban versus rural population in general has sharply increased. At the same time, Californians have concentrated more and more around the two metropolitan centers of San Francisco and Los Angeles—but spreading outward from the central cities to suburban communities. Comparatively speaking, the Portuguese in the state have clung to a more rural life-style and have participated but little in the build-up of southern California. In 1940, the foreign-born white population as a whole clustered in urban centers even more than the state's general population (more than 80 percent); but nearly three-fourths of the foreign-born Portuguese, a larger proportion than among any other foreign-born group, were living in rural areas, mostly on farms. Portuguese living patterns, it is true, have also become more urbanized: In 1930, 59 percent of all the California Portuguese were "rural" (by census definition), but only about 30 percent were so classified by 1960. At the same time, while in 1930 the Portuguese accounted for 9.6 percent of the total foreign stock living on farms, by 1960 they constituted 14.7 percent.[28]

During the 1920–1960 period the densest Portuguese concentration in the state continued to be in Alameda County, off San Francisco Bay; other dense concentrations were in Santa Clara and

Contra Costa counties, adjoining Alameda County to the south and north. In 1940 these three counties (with Oakland and San Jose as their principal urban centers) accounted for 11,460, or over one-third, of all foreign-born (white) Portuguese. Between one-fourth and one-third, 8,631, were then spread out through the San Joaquin Valley (largely Merced, Stanislaus, San Joaquin, and Kings counties). The rest, approximately one-third, were distributed chiefly in the lower Sacramento Valley, around San Francisco and along some Central Coast portions (Santa Cruz, Monterey, San Louis Obispo). Within southern California, the Point Loma (San Diego County) fishing colony remained most important, but there were also several hundred Portuguese each in the Los Angeles and Santa Barbara areas. Along the northern coast, there remained small groups in Sonoma County just north of San Francisco, and much farther north in Humboldt County. (Equally small groups, offshoots of the West Coast settlement and totaling several hundred, were scattered in the states of Nevada, Oregon, and Washington; cf. p. 84.)

During the several decades under consideration in this chapter, with fresh immigration from Portugal practically at a standstill, the California Portuguese naturally experienced a certain amount of deethnicization, of "mainstreaming," as the American-born came to outnumber the foreign-born more and more, and as general socio-economic developments in American (and particularly in Californian) society encouraged horizontal and vertical mobility. Yet, with all this intermingling and leveling out among ethnic groups, a noteworthy amount of regionalism based on old-country origins continued to linger in the consciousness and in the actual residential patterns of Portuguese-Californians. For instance, as of the 1950s the small Portuguese colony in Scotia, Humboldt County, still was almost exclusively from the Algarve province in southern Portugal. The majority of the several hundred Portuguese at Santa Cruz were from the island of Graciosa, Azores—the capital town of which is also called Santa Cruz.

The Portuguese around Los Banos and Gustine, on the "West Side" of the San Joaquin Valley, traced their origins mostly to the islands of Terceira or São Jorge. Those from São Miguel in the eastern Azores were reported most heavily represented in Marin County (San Rafael, etc.). A marked majority of the Portuguese in the San Diego (Point Loma) area had come either from Paúl do Mar, on the island of Madeira, or from the Algarve (southern tip of mainland Portugal). The Capeverdeans in California continued to cluster at Sacramento (living largely within a few blocks bounded by 3rd and 5th, S and T Streets) and also in Alameda City, adjoining. Oakland. Set apart from the main body of Portuguese-Californians even more than were the Capeverdeans, a group of over 1,000 immigrants from the Portuguese colony of Macau were living mostly in the San Francisco area (as of the early 1960s). The large majority of these "Macaenses" had come from the Portuguese "concession" in Shanghai (rather than directly from Macau on the south China coast) after the Communist takeover in China; they were feeling more at home in San Francisco's Chinatown than among the Azoreans of San Leandro. . . .[29]

Some major shifts in occupational and residential pattern naturally did occur during the 1940s and 1950s, among California's Portuguese as among the rest of the population. The prime example is the Oakland area: earlier in the century, the Oakland Portuguese would cluster around Maria Auxiliadora church in the eastern part of town, and around St. Joseph's church in western Oakland. But as many blacks and Mexicans moved into these sections of the city, together with much industry, many of the Portuguese moved away, toward the southern part of Alameda County (San Leandro, Hayward, etc.). On the other hand, with the industrial and residential build-up of much of Alameda County, many of the "rural" Portuguese there gave up agriculture, selling their land at good profit and shifting into industrial occupations, so that by the early 1960s agricultural activities remained pretty much limited to the San Joaquin Valley and the Santa Clara area.

IV   Hawaii

Portuguese immigration had ceased earlier and more abruptly in the Hawaiian Islands than either in California or in the East, even before the start of the First World War. In 1920 there were 5,794 persons of Portuguese birth in that region, as against 21,208 Hawaiian-born of Portuguese parentage; i.e., three-fourths of the Portuguese stock were then already native-born. By 1960, there were altogether 764 foreign-born left. Moreover, through intermarriage that Portuguese component of the population had become more and more diluted.[30] A small amount of reemigration, or rather migration, from Hawaii to the continental United States continued in the 1920s and probably beyond.[31]

An urban trend, away from the plantations and into the city of Honolulu, had started among the Portuguese within a few years of immigration, as we have already noted. Nevertheless, as of 1920 56 percent of the Portuguese were still classified as rural; by 1930, 46 percent; by 1960, only 28 percent (25.3 percent rural nonfarm and 2.7 percent rural farm). Even so, urbanization was much slower among Hawaii's Portuguese stock than among the Chinese there: by 1930, 71 percent of the Chinese but only 45 percent of the Portuguese were living in Honolulu.[32] Even though "miniature ghettos" had formed in Honolulu as soon as the various ethnic groups arrived there, these would gradually disappear; by the 1930s the Portuguese and the Chinese in particular were already completely absorbed by Honolulu's cosmopolitan community.[33] Nevertheless, as of the early 1960s Honolulu's hilltop Punchbowl district was still a preferred location of many Portuguese-Hawaiians (and, perhaps significantly, on the islands of Kauai and Hawaii proper many Portuguese ranchers were also reported living in hilltop homes as of the 1950s).[34]

By the 1960s the Japanese had become Hawaii's dominant ethnic group, not only numerically but in terms of the economy and local governmental influence. The plantations had become largely mechanized, employing only a reduced labor force. Partly as a result of this, after World War II many persons of Portuguese descent were again moving to California in search of better jobs. The large majority of the Portuguese element, however, was well integrated and permanently settled in the "Paradise of the Pacific," now a state of the Union.

CHAPTER 7

The New Portuguese
Mass Immigration,
1958 to the Present

FROM THE TIME OF THEIR DISCOVERY AND INITIAL SETTLEMENT BY THE
Portuguese in the fifteenth century to the present day, the Azores
Islands have had a history of serious earth tremors and volcanic
eruptions on an average of at least once every decade or two,
centered at one or the other of these nine islands. This is what would
appear from a compilation of local historical events undertaken by
Porfirio Bessone, an Azorean immigrant at Cambridge, Massachusetts, who made his living there as a printer and piano tuner while
pursuing journalism and authoring dramatic skits as a hobby. Sifting
through a variety of sources including the archives in his hometown
of Ponta Delgada, Bessone found, for example, notice of an earthquake in October 1522 which swallowed up a hilltop convent and
209 nuns with it, records of no less than eight minor quakes in 1562—
63, and so on almost every few years. Bessone's list ends with eight
recorded tremors in 1930, which was shortly before he completed
his *Dicionário cronológico dos Açores.*[1]

And so it happened again—on a catastrophic scale, one day in
September 1957: a submarine volcanic eruption off the western end
of Fayal (a small but relatively populous island in the center of the
archipelago) struck widespread terror on that island. There had
been minor earthquakes on the island of Terceira in 1951 and at
Ponta Delgada, capital of São Miguel, in 1952. But this time a
submarine volcano temporarily coughed up an entire new island
near Fayal, and quakes continued for the remainder of the year,
with volcanic activity again reported in March and August of 1958.
The various eruptions in 1957—58 and another serious quake that

hit the island of São Jorge in February 1964 resulted in the displacement of some 25,000 Azoreans from their homes.

It was these seismic occurrences that set in motion a new wave of Portuguese mass immigration into the United States. But they could not have had this effect had they not coincided with two other broader developments within this country: on the one hand, the trend toward liberalization of immigration restrictions, or at least toward freeing the quota system from ethnic bias, in the wake of World War II and the "McCarthy era"; and on the other hand, the growing political strength of the Portuguese-American population, particularly within southeastern New England.

At the behest of Portuguese-American constituent groups, Senators John Pastore of Rhode Island and John Kennedy of Massachusetts cosponsored a congressional bill in the summer 1958 which became the so-called Azorean Refugee Act, permitting the issuance of 1,500 special immigrant visas outside the regular quota to family heads from Fayal (including their dependents), for use by June 30, 1960. A 1960 amendment to this act raised the number to 2,000 visas, to be utilized by June 1962. Under these special natural-disaster provisions, 4,811 Portuguese (family heads plus dependents) came to the United States—apart from regular quota immigrants. An additional 2,500 Portuguese arrived in the early 1960s under certain amendments to the general immigration legislation enacted in 1961 and 1962. When the island of São Jorge was victimized by a severe earthquake in 1964, Senator Edward Kennedy took up the cause of Azorean relief earlier advocated by his brother John, the late president. By 1965, special-quota legislation became unnecessary because of the new Immigration and Nationality Act.

The so-called Walter-McCarran Act of 1952, which replaced all previous immigration legislation, had already put big dents into the nationality-quota system adopted in the 1920s by greatly expanding the nonquota categories, or at least permitting such expansions. The Act of 1965 finally eliminated this quota system altogether (effective 1968); the new standard maximum for any one country was to be 20,000 immigrant visas per year. For the 1965–1968 transition period, all unused quota numbers from countries that were unable to fill their allotted maximums were put together in a pool and distributed among other countries.[2]

To understand the unusually stimulating effect that this new general legislation has had on Portuguese—largely Azorean—immigration in particular, the special position of the Azores in relation to the United States has to be stressed once again. There was, of course, the geographic proximity between these mid-Atlantic islands and New England—only about half the distance between the United States and the heart of western Europe—and the fact that more than half the population of the Azores had some personal ties, some relatives or friends, in the United States. Moreover, there was the growing strategic importance of this insular part of Portugal to the global defense system of the United States, and the equal importance to Portugal of friendly American support (especially now that the traditional alliance with Great Britain had lost much of its value)—leading to treaties authorizing an American air base at Santa Maria toward the end of World War II, and another one later at Terceira. And then there was, as previously mentioned, the basically pro-American sentiment of many Azoreans, the feeling that their own central government was neglecting them, as a far-off second-grade province, and that they should look to America for greener pastures.[3]

The main motive of Portuguese emigration, after World War II just as in earlier periods, has naturally remained the economic one— coupled with the desire, in many cases, of being reunited with family members who had emigrated earlier. In proportion to her small total population, Portugal in recent decades has continued to be one of the principal countries of emigration in the world. As a result of this emigration, plus the results of her colonial wars in Africa, Portugal's total population actually dropped 2 percent between 1960 and 1970 (with women eventually outnumbering men by 9 percent).[4] Between 1952 and 1962, according to official statistics, some 340,000 emigrants (not counting clandestine emigrants!) left Portugal—nearly 200,000 of these going to Brazil, about 40,000 to Venezuela, 30,000 to France, 25,000 to the United States, and 22,000 to Canada.[5] Statistics reported for the two-year period 1968–1969 show a considerable shift in the ranking of principal countries of destination: some 73,000 Portuguese now turned to France (or perhaps as many as 110,000 if clandestine departures are included), the United States was second, as the reported destination of about 24,000, followed by West Germany (18,000) and Canada (c. 13,300), with Venezuela and Brazil now ranking at the bottom (c. 6,800 and 6,000).[6]

In this chapter we are placing the beginning of the new Portu-guese mass immigration somewhat arbitrarily at the year 1958, simply because this was the date of the new Azorean Refugee Act. But actually, a truly major increase in annual immigration from Portugal (or, to be more precise, of persons of Portuguese birth, even though some of these might have come in via Canada or Brazil) did not take place until 1966, that is, immediately following the new Immigration and Nationality Act of 1965. This is shown by the following official figures:[7]

Year (i.e., fiscal year ending June 30)	Immigrants Born in Portugal
1958	1,635
1959	2,694
1960	6,968
1961	3,960
1962	3,730
1963	2,975
1964	2,077
1965	2,005
1966	8,713
1967	13,927
1968	12,212
1969	16,528
1970	13,195
1971	11,692
1972	10,343
1973	10,751
1974	c. 11,300
1975	c. 11,800
1976	c. 10,300

Counted by decades, the total for 1960–1969 of 73,095 immigrant arrivals compares with about 14,500 for 1950–1959—truly a considerable upswing, to about the same levels as during the first two decades of this century (69,149 for 1901–1910, 89,732 for 1911–1920; see p. 35). As a matter of fact, for the ten-year period 1965–1974, the total number of immigrants arriving from Portugal was approximately 120,000 (or c. 1,000 per month)—far more than during any previous ten-year period. By the late 1960s, Portugal had become one of the four leading sources of new immigration to the United States: in 1967, according to a *New York Times* survey, the United Kingdom led, with 23,071 arrivals, followed by Italy (c. 20,000), "China" (Taiwan, 16,505), and Portugal (12,137). In that same year, fiscal 1967, total immigration from all sources was 361,972, the highest since the imposition of quota restrictions in the early 1920s.[8]

While immigration from Portugal was thus in line with the general "zoom" in immigration, it actually outpaced that from many other countries, if we think in terms of proportion— proportion to size of country of origin, as well as proportion to size of total population within the actually receiving settlement area (southeastern New England, etc.). On the other hand, even though the new legislation was now offering fulfillment of the long pent-up demand for migration to Uncle Sam's territory to the tune of 20,000 immigrant visas per year per country, Portugal still was not taking full advantage of this maximum quota during any one year.

As regards regional origins of the new Portuguese immigrants, we have already alluded to the continuing prevalence of the Azorean element. Earthquake victims from Fayal in the western Azores had been the first group to mark the transition from "throttled" to revitalized immigration; but during most of the 1960s, because of the location of an international airport on the island of Santa Maria and a United States consulate at Ponta Delgada, São Miguel, people from the eastern Azores, i.e., those living on São Miguel and Santa Maria, provided a disproportionately heavy portion of Portuguese emigrants to the United States. Only since April 1971, when the military airfield at Lajes on Terceira was opened to Portuguese (but not foreign) passenger planes in transatlantic service, have residents of the central and western Azores been able to share more evenly in the renewed opportunities of emigration.

Madeirans, who did not (and do not at this writing) enjoy direct air connections to the United States, and who because of a new tourist boom in Madeira felt less economic pressure toward emigration than did the inhabitants of the Azores, did not press in quantity for United States visas, and, if emigrating at all, would tend to go (by ship) to Brazil or Venezuela. The new immigration has included some Capeverdeans (barely 1,000 during 1958–1968); and, above all, it comprises a substantial minority of people from the Portuguese mainland. For example, official Portuguese emigration statistics provide the following breakdown for emigrants to the United States during 1969–1972:

From	1969	1970	1971	1972
Continental Portugal	5,064	4,377	4,205	3,660
Eastern Azores (São Miguel, Santa Maria)	4,251	2,866	2,560	2,123
Central Azores (Terceira, Graciosa, São Jorge)	2,273	1,597	1,344	1,132
Western Azores (Pico, Fayal, Flores, Corvo)	1,503	844	717	612
Madeira	20	41	13	46[9]

The particular areas within the United States selected for settlement—at least initial settlement—by the "new" Portuguese immigrants constitute pretty much the same pattern of geographic distribution as during the earlier immigration, except that Hawaii no longer figures in the picture, and that the relatively recent settlement area of Connecticut—New York—New Jersey has begun to outweigh California markedly. For the sample years 1968, 1970, 1972, and 1974, Portuguese immigrants reported their "intended future permanent residence" to immigration officials as follows, by major recipient states:

	1968	1970	1972	1974
Massachusetts	4,695	4,335	3,313	3,655
Rhode Island	1,455	1,577	1,143	1,009
Connecticut	1,018	982	687	886
New York	855	1,183	1,015	999
New Jersey	1,149	1,871	2,001	2,319
California	2,591	2,361	1,603	1,671
All other states		886	581	765[10]

As these figures show, Massachusetts together with adjoining Rhode Island continues to hold the lead, attracting 45 to 55 percent of the new arrivals for initial or intended permanent residence. The contiguous areas of Connecticut and metropolitan New York—New Jersey have been receiving between about 25 percent and slightly above 35 percent of the total, most of the rest (15 to 25 percent) going to California. This is about the distribution one would expect: most of the newcomers, generally arriving at New York City airports

(Kennedy or Newark) and most recently at Boston's Logan airport, are met by relatives or friends already resident in nearby towns, and are thus driven to the centers of the previous mass immigration, especially Fall River, New Bedford, Greater Providence, Newark, Greater Boston, etc. As Francis Rogers observes, this means that because of family ties too many of these immigrants first settle down in areas relatively lacking in employment (and educational) opportunities, such as New Bedford and Fall River.[11] Most recently, many of them have moved on to the outskirts of Boston (10 to 15 percent of the population of Cambridge and Somerville are currently Portuguese), or to such places as Hudson, Massachusetts, and Waterbury and East Hartford, Connecticut.

Because of the continued importance of personal ties between new and older immigrants, narrowly localistic affiliation is still very much in evidence. For instance, Azoreans congregate in the northern outskirts of Boston; Capeverdeans, in the Roxbury and Dorchester sections; while those who recently went to Hudson are mostly from the island of Santa Maria. The initial clustering of new immigrants in or around the largest and most compact centers of the older immigration, such as Fall River, New Bedford, and Newark, is understandable not only because of family ties, but also because of what Raymond Breton, in a recent study of ethnic communities in Canada, has aptly called the "institutional completeness" of such centers:[12] the availability of shopping and consulting facilities, churches, newspapers, radio, etc., utilizing their own language and providing a gradual blending of old customs and new.

On the other hand it must be pointed out that the new Portuguese mass immigration, mostly a phenomenon of the later 1960s and continuing through the 1970s, has not simply swelled the total Portuguese ethnic communities in the United States but has added further diversity and even a modicum of tension and cleavage to them. For it is no longer just a matter of different regional origins, racial nuances, the generation gap, but of people from a new (although not very new) versus an old remembered Portugal; a crushingly large number of embarrassingly outlandish country cousins versus a heavily Americanized second and third generation— and in the end, in some cases, a matter of plain old economic competition and conflict where the job opportunities are limited.

This chapter, which brings the history of Portuguese settlement in the United States up to the present—a history which in its earliest stages (see Chapter 1) had to treat as a single area, North America, what now is divided into the United States and Canada (not to mention Mexico)—must not be allowed to end without at least a brief reference to the recent large-scale immigration from Portugal into Canada. In several respects this immigration was and is similar to the wave entering the United States. Moreover, its centers are geographically not very distant from the Portuguese settlement centers in the northeastern United States and along the West Coast, permitting some occasional visiting back and forth, by car or bus or otherwise, between Portuguese-born relatives and friends now residing, respectively, in the United States and in Canada.

Portuguese emigration to Canada had been negligible until 1953, when groups of Portuguese farm laborers were brought into labor-hungry farm areas in Quebec, and into railroad construction sites, through cooperation between the Portuguese and Canadian governments. This was because the industrial build-up after World War II had siphoned off much Canadian farm and road labor into better-paying city jobs. But before long most of the Portuguese farm laborers also moved into urban areas, such as Toronto. Some of them had originally planned to move on from Canada to California or to New England, but then decided to stay. By 1961, there were about 12,000 Portuguese in Toronto, over 4,000 in Vancouver, and some 3,000 in Montreal, all working in factories and various service trades.

Ten years later, the colony at Toronto had grown to about 40,000 to 50,000 (probably now the largest cluster of foreign-born Portuguese in any one city outside of Portugal and Brazil). As of 1971 the Portuguese settlement in Vancouver, on Canada's west coast, was estimated at about 7,000, and the one in Montreal at 12,000. A still more recent estimate, as of spring 1976, gave a total of about 220,000 Portuguese (including a small proportion of Canadian-born children of the immigrants, and a large number of clandestine entrants) living in various parts of Canada, with Toronto still far in the lead, followed by Montreal, Vancouver, and many other places. The majority, perhaps 60 percent, hailed from the Azores (the largest contingent being from São Miguel, as in emigration to the United States, followed by those from Terceira). Some 38 percent were estimated to be Continentals, with a bare sprinkling of Madeirans and Capeverdeans.[13]

Returning to the United States for a concluding bit of statistics: the United States census for 1970 reported a total of 318,458

Portuguese "foreign stock" (first and second generation) residing in the whole country. Of this total, 119,899 had been born in Portugal, and 198,559 in the United States with one or both parents born in Portugal.[14] (These overall figures include Continental Portugal and the Azores, but apparently not Madeira or the Cape Verde Islands!) The breakdown by principal states of Portuguese settlement was:

	Total Portuguese Stock	Born in Portugal	Born in U.S. of One or Two Portuguese-born Parents
Massachusetts	108,919	44,424	64,595
Rhode Island	35,730	14,582	21,148
Connecticut	15,218	7,214	8,004
New York	15,126	7,630	7,496
New Jersey	17,355	10,600	6,755
California	98,275	29,303	68,972
All other states	27,835	6,146	21,689
Total United States	318,458	119,899	198,559[15]

Evidently California, as compared to the other major states, is now moving in the direction of Hawaii as regards the high proportion of second to first generation Portuguese ethnics.

PART II

Socioeconomic and Cultural Aspects of Portuguese Immigrant Life

Typical Portuguese housewife in Provincetown. c. 1940.

CHAPTER 8

Individual and Family

I Demographic-Physical Traits

IN THE FOLLOWING PAGES WE BRING TOGETHER SOME DATA ON THE SEX
ratio and age structure of the Portuguese immigrant population, on
birth and death rates, health conditions, and on various bodily or
"racial" characteristics. Such essentially physical data, while interesting in themselves, are cited here chiefly because of their bearing
or dependence on social and cultural conditions.

In the earliest stages of Portuguese immigration in the United
States, most of the newcomers were males. This was certainly true
of the Azorean whalers and Gold Rush pioneers, the early ranch
hands out in California, and, to a lesser extent, the early Portuguese
mill workers in Massachusetts.[1] It was also true of the Capeverdean
longshoremen and berry-pickers in southeastern New England,[2] and
again, shortly before and especially after World War I, of those who
came from continental Portugal to settle in Newark and other spots
in the metropolitan New York area. But there were also early
instances of entire families migrating together, such as in the case of
the "Madeira exiles" who settled in Illinois and the contract laborers
who came with their families to work on Hawaiian sugar plantations.[3] Typically, within a relatively few years the single men who
had come alone or the married men who had temporarily left their
families behind would, respectively, have their fiancées or families
come over, or go back to the old village to get them—unless they
themselves decided to retromigrate. The immigration laws of the
1920s and especially of the 1960s gave priority to the admission of
close relatives of United States residents, which fact probably
contributed to the relatively even sex ratio of the more recent
immigrants. These came to join family members already established

in the United States, and with their help were absorbed into a work force in factories and service trades which, overall, was equally hospitable to both sexes.[4]

Nothing really significant can be read into the fact that the proportion of males to females among Portuguese immigrant arrivals fluctuated somewhat year by year. The males were always in the majority in the years for which separate immigration figures by sex are available, which is from 1869 onward. But the males never constituted more than about 70 percent of the total. (The one exception was the year 1917, when, probably because of war conditions, there was an excess of female over male arrivals.)[5] This agrees approximately with what was true for the total immigration into the United States from all countries combined: according to an authoritative compilation by the National Committee on Immigration Policy, "statistics of immigration show that males made up approximately 65 percent of the total immigration from 1820 to 1924. By 1930 the sex ratio had dropped to 100.6, and at the present time [1950] it is about equal."[6]

Nevertheless, there is a significant difference between the overall sex ratio of European immigrant arrivals, from all parts of Europe, 1899–1909, which was 69 percent male to 31 percent female, and the ratio of 59 percent male to 41 percent female for immigrants from Portugal for the same period.[7] The lesser preponderance of males among the Portuguese arrivals may possibly reflect, in part at least, the relatively more marked desire of Azoreans as a group, compared to certain other immigrant groups, to remain in the United States, and to establish their families there by single immigrant men marrying girls from the Islands who followed after them, rather than by intermarrying with women from other nationalities. Also, the Portuguese, whose mass immigration into the United States occurred during a relatively late period (as compared to the arrival of groups from northwestern Europe earlier in the nineteenth century), by 1940 were still far from having attained sex parity (except for those in Hawaii): the 1940 census of the American white population by mother tongue showed 46,360 foreign-born white males of Portuguese mother tongue (which actually included some Brazilians) as against 37,420 females. For United States-born whites of foreign or mixed parentage, the 1940 figures were 61,740 male versus 58,760 female Portuguese speakers.

Comparing the sex ratio of foreign-born whites from Portugal (continental Portugal plus Azores) by major states of Portuguese settlement, United States census figures for 1930 and 1940 further reveal that, whereas the male-female ratio had become almost even in the older immigration centers of Massachusetts and Rhode Island, males far outnumbered females in New York and New Jersey (the postwar destinations of many single men from Continental Portugal). Connecticut was in an intermediate position, and—most noteworthy—California also showed a far greater excess of males than was true for southeastern New England:

	1930		1940	
	Male	Female	Male	Female
Massachusetts	22,121	21,281	18,643	17,807
Rhode Island	6,068	5,611	5,025	4,751
Connecticut	1,585	867	1,383	869
New York	4,250	994	3,356	1,224
New Jersey	2,935	770	1,851	792
California	21,539	13,877	17,449	12,179

As for age structure, it is in the nature of voluntary emigration aiming at economic improvement that men and women in the most vigorous and productive age range (or in what used to be called the "prime of life" before the advent of euphemisms about age . . .), viz., between the later teens and the mid-forties, should heavily predominate. By and large this was also true of the Portuguese emigrating to the United States. However, whereas the age distribution of European immigrants to the United States from all countries, arriving during the sample period 1899–1909, was 12.3 percent under age fourteen, 82.6 percent at age fourteen to forty-four, and 5.0 percent forty-five years and older, the Portuguese included a significantly larger proportion of children: 23.7 percent under age fourteen, 68.5 percent at ages fourteen to forty-four, and 7.8 percent forty-five years and older.[8] (These figures do not even include Hawaii, with its importation of laborers accompanied by large families.)

The probable explanation of this fact is not only in the relatively strong inclination of emigrating Azorean men to take their families along or to have these follow after them a little later, but also in the widespread desire of these islanders to evade conscription into the Portuguese armed forces: In reports to his government in 1892 and again in 1893, the Portuguese consul in San Francisco emphasized, with some exaggeration, that, since the principal motive of Azorean emigration to California was the wish to avoid military service, the "majority" of the Portuguese in that state arrived before reaching draft age, after clandestine departure for the Azores.[9] By the year 1940, however, after some fifteen years of severely throttled immigration, the population pyramid for foreign-born white residents of Portuguese mother tongue (not the age distribution of new arrivals!), in the entire United States, was bulging around the middle:

Under age 25	2,260	45–54	24,140
25–34	8,720	55–64	14,680
35–44	24,360	65 and over	9,620[10]

In the Hawaiian Islands, when a need for new sources of plantation labor arose in the late nineteenth century, "white men of influence in governmental affairs . . . wanted more white people, fewer Chinese", even if this meant having to pay more passage money to bring in Portuguese women and children along with the men, and having to pay somewhat higher wages to Portuguese family men than to Chinese single men. "But the military laws of Portugal prevented the free emigration of able-bodied young men if they were subject to military service as reservists, and so it was necessary to accept a good many middle-aged men," in a reverse twist of the situation alluded to before.[11] At any rate, since the laborers from Madeira and São Miguel were imported together with their families, their age (as well as sex) ratio was nearly normal from the start. And as these people tended to have large offspring, the 12,780 Portuguese arriving during 1878–1899 included 4,930 children. Even as of 1930, out of a total of 29,117 persons of Portuguese birth or parentage some 12,000 were below the age of twenty.[12]

Instances of longevity (which need not have much bearing on average life expectancy) may have been and perhaps still are more common among Portuguese islanders than among the American population at large. Extensive mortality statistics are not at hand. As for longevity in Portugal herself, scattered census data indicate that in 1864, six in 10,000 inhabitants (0.06 percent) were ninety years of age or older; in 1878, seventy-five males and 134 females in a total population of about 4.5 million (one in c. 22,000) were above age 100; in 1911, 1 percent of the population was aged eighty or older.[13]

Instances of longevity among Portuguese immigrants in the United States were often highlighted in the Portuguese immigrant press (especially in California), as if to publicize sturdiness as one of the prized virtues of "the race:" for example, there was António José Gabriel. Born on the island of Flores in 1836, he came to the United States as a teenager, and after a brief stay with relatives at Cambridge moved to San Francisco in 1854. After some mining in Nevada, he worked as a restaurant cook in California, where he died at age 109 in 1945. José Mendonça dos Santos arrived in California in 1867; there he celebrated his one-hundred-eleventh birthday in 1938, after having gotten married for the third time at age ninety-seven. Frank Fisher (who had obviously Anglicized his Portuguese name), born on Santa Maria (Azores) in 1836, settled in Boston during the Civil War, and after marrying an Azorean girl there moved on to California, where a newspaper notice of 1938 reported him still well and alive at age 102.

Mrs. Genevieve de Brum Vargas, born on the island of Pico in 1830, similarly arrived at Boston in 1865, soon set sail for San Francisco, from there walked (yes, on foot) down the coast to Half Moon Bay—where she was still residing in 1944, at age 114. When interviewed that year, she confided she still had her original teeth, and had seen a doctor only once in her life. Joaquim S. Reis, born in the Azores in 1838, came to the United States on a whaler at age seventeen, and after spending some years in the Boston area took up farming near Clarksburg, California; there he died at age 114, under the name of King. (Port. *rei* = king!). In 1947, one Domingos Espinola was reported dead at age 105 in Peabody, Massachusetts; and the following year, Mrs. Maria Justina Simas, a native of São Miguel, mother of fourteen children, passed away in New Bedford at 102 years of age. In 1956 a New Bedford newspaper reported that a Mrs. Maria Santos, 104 years of age, had just returned to her native island of Fogo, Cape Verde, after forty-five years of residence in Massachusetts. In 1953 the oldest person in New Bedford, one Mrs. Ana Gomes, a native of Brava, Cape Verde Islands, who had come to the United States some eighty years earlier, was reported dead at age 119.[14]

At the other end of the scale, the issue of relatively high infant mortality among Portuguese immigrants was raised earlier in this century. Donald R. Taft, in his relatively influential study of the Portuguese communities in Fall River, Massachusetts, and Portsmouth, Rhode Island, termed the mortality of Portuguese infants in

New England "shockingly high" and implied a link to unsanitary living conditions at least partly due to ignorance.[15] Actually, a study in 1907 showed that infant mortality rates were generally higher among the foreign-born than among American-born parents.[16]

A detailed analysis of the annual Birth Reports of the United States Census Bureau for 1916–1921, by country of birth of mother (but not including the Portuguese), brought out that deaths per 1,000 live births, from specified causes, of children under one year of age, were seventy-nine among American-born white mothers, 136 among American blacks, 121 to 131 among immigrants from "Austria" and "Poland," sixty-seven among those from Scandinavia, ninety-four among those from Ireland and Italy, etc. This survey concluded that the influence of environment, and particularly the incidence of artificial as against breast feeding, rather than "race," was the main determinant of infant mortality.[17]

In Fall River specifically, a study of infant mortality during 1908 which did include the Portuguese in that city found a link between high infant mortality, a high incidence of artificial feeding (with use of solid foods rather than cow's milk, at that, particularly among the Portuguese), and mothers going to work after childbirth rather than staying home with the baby.[18] In New Bedford, in 1915, fully 25 percent of the 1,000 babies born to Portuguese parents there died under one year of age; the local Board of Health attributed this high rate of infant mortality to "the neglect of mothers, who . . . boarded their offspring with incompetent persons while they availed themselves of the opportunity to earn 'big' wages which were paid in the different mills of the city. . . ."[19]

A federally sponsored study of New Bedford's infant mortality problem, based on the year 1913, showed that the infant mortality rate among the city's foreign-born white Portuguese, 201 per 1,000, was then about twice as high as among the French-Canadians, the English, the Poles—and even among the "Portuguese Negroes" (Capeverdeans)! But it also revealed that the largest percentage of births attended by midwives rather than by physicians, about 57 percent, was among the Portuguese; that a much smaller percentage of the infants of white Portuguese mothers than of other foreign nationalities was breastfed; and that among this same ethnic group the infant mortality rate decreased strikingly as the length of parents' residence in the United States increased.[20] In Hawaii, finally, as of 1911–1913, infant mortality among the "Portuguese"—which in this case included the Hawaiian-born second generation—was about average, at 173 per 1,000 births (as against a staggering 746 for Filipinos, and about five for the British and Americans); by 1932 it was down to sixty-nine (compared to 206 for indigenous Hawaiians, 190 for Filipinos, and thirty-six for "other Caucasians," or northwestern European stock).[21]

All of these studies together provide ample evidence that the relatively high infant mortality rate noted among the earlier Portuguese immigrants in New England had nothing to do with hereditary physical traits or poor health of parents, but indeed resulted from inadequate infant care. Comprehensive data on health conditions among the Portuguese immigrants of recent years are not available; but a sample survey conducted in the Providence area about 1975 concluded that the "new" (post-1965) Portuguese arrivals were in better health, on the average, than the older immigrants and the native-born.[22]

Portugal has been and continues to be a country of relatively high birthrates, compared to the rest of Europe and to North America as a whole; the rate for 1920–1930 oscillated between about thirty and thirty-three (per 1,000 population), compared to seventeen to twenty-five in England and Germany, eighteen to twenty-one in France , and to twenty-five to thirty-one in Italy.[23] Among emigrant groups, where a high proportion of the high-fecundity age brackets may go hand in hand with a severe sex-ratio imbalance, birthrates need not necessarily be similar to those in the home country. Yet the Portuguese immigrants, along with various other immigrant groups, have indeed been noted for a markedly higher birthrate than that of the native American population, at least during the 1870–1920 period, but less so in more recent decades. For instance, in 1915, 1,147 out of a total of 3,724 births in New Bedford were of Portuguese parents, even though the Portuguese community in that city numbered only about one-fifth of the total population.[24]

Instances of prolific families have been noted with pride in the immigrant press; the record may well have been set by one José Silva from São Miguel, a bricklayer in East Providence, who upon his death at age eighty-eight in 1955 was reported to have fathered twenty-two children with his first wife and five more with his second, getting eighteen grandchildren from one son, seventeen from another, etc.[25] In Hawaii, as of the 1920s, the average Portuguese family included at least four children, and sometimes ten to fifteen; of the approximately 500 Portuguese-Hawaiian men whose biographical sketches were assembled by J. F. Freitas, at least

twenty-one had between twelve and seventeen children; eight of
these were born in São Miguel, seven in Madeira, two in other parts
of Portugal, and four in Hawaii of São Miguelian parents.[26] Only in
a very limited sense, of course, is family size a matter of fecundity as
a physical trait; sociocultural aspects of the family are relegated to
the end of this chapter.

The issue of "race" as a bundle of physical traits cannot be
ignored in describing the Portuguese-Americans, chiefly because
the concept of "Portuguese immigrant" has usually been understood, as it is in this book, to include immigrants from the Cape
Verde Islands, an archipelago off northwestern Africa which became
independent from Portugal only a few years ago. The term *race*
itself is not easily defined. The Portuguese, and Portuguese-Americans, are fond of referring to themselves as *a raça portuguesa*, e.g.
in extolling "the virtues of the Portuguese race," using the term in
about the same sense as did the United States immigration authorities, for several decades starting in 1898, when immigrants were
categorized in accordance with an official checklist of some fifty
"races"—actually a medley of nationalities, ethnic or minority
groups, i.e., groups defined by linguocultural or political as much as
by biological characteristics.[27] In more scientific and up-to-date
usage, which we follow here, a race is understood to be "a group of
people who possess the majority of their physical characteristics in
common." Such a bundle of characteristics is a result of population
blends and environmental adaptation and is never completely static;
some traits such as hair form or nasal contour are relatively more
stable over the generations than others such as stature and head
shape.[28]

Continental Portugal is regarded as one of the racially most
homogeneous countries in Europe, deriving largely from the pre-
Roman Lusitanians, blended with Celtic and Germanic groups
chiefly in the North and with Arab and Berber elements chiefly in
the South. The maritime discoveries of early modern times brought
a slight influx from India and Africa; and of course there has been
some intermingling with elements from Spain, France, etc. Strongly
dominant among the Portuguese is the "Mediterranean" racial
type: relatively short stature; longish head, with narrow face,
straight and fairly broad jaws; dark brown hair and eyes; skin color
ranging from light brown to brunet-white.[29] As far as the Adjacent
Islands are concerned, essentially the same racial type prevails
among Madeirans. However, in the Azores there is a somewhat

more pronounced admixture of "Nordic" elements from Flanders, also from France and England (especially in the western part of the islands). In addition, some Negroid admixture is present in the Azores, and perhaps in Madeira.[30]

Quite different is the racial composition of the Cape Verde Islands, off the coast of West Africa: there the mulatto element predominates, resulting from mixture of the original white Portuguese settlers with African slave labor brought in mostly from Guinea and the western Sudan and from subsequent miscegenation between white and colored. A small proportion of the population derives from west-central Europe (other than Portugal), Asia, and Brazil. In the 1937 census, to cite one statistic, 123,611 out of 165,540 inhabitants of the archipelago were classified as mixed-breeds, 35,444 as pure African blacks, and only 6,485 as whites. Racial composition varies considerably from one Capeverdean island to the next: e.g., the black African element predominates on Santiago and Maio, the white Portuguese admixture on Brava (from where most of the early Capeverdean immigrants to the United States came); Fogo, São Nicolau, and the rest of the archipelago occupy intermediate positions.[31]

Writers representing the viewpoint of the "average American," or perhaps more accurately of (white) mainstream America, have described Portuguese immigrants in the United States in terms like these: "Physically they [the Azoreans] are undersized, but are remarkably free from disease and physical defects."[32] The Portuguese in Provincetown: ". . . beautiful dark-eyed girls . . . handsome, strong-looking fellows. . . ."[33] "Now the whole Cape Cod is dark with the dusty skins of the Portuguese 'white man,' quite a shade blacker with the Portuguese nigger [i.e., Capeverdean]."[34] Azorean farmers in California: ". . . these small, brown-skinned immigrants. . . ."[35] "The modern young Portuguese in Hawaii constitute a dark and handsome group. . . ."[36] "Azoreans are fair of complexion, largely olive-skinned with straight black or brown hair. The Cape Verdeans range in color from brown to black, with hair varying from the long straight black to the short and 'different' variety."[37] The Capeverdeans along Cape Cod "are big, broad-shouldered fellows, not as coarse-featured as many southern negroes. . . . Except for dark skins, many of the men are not unattractive physically. . . . Many have a strain of white blood. . . ."[38]

Actually, as indicated in previous chapters, the nonwhite Capeverdeans constituted only a small fraction of the total "Portuguese" immigrant population. But since their presence in such places as New Bedford and along Cape Cod was very noticeable, and since the Capeverdeans tended (until fairly recently) to identify themselves as "Portuguese," the popular impression arose among many New Englanders earlier in this century that the Portuguese ethnic group in general, including the Azorean majority, was more or less "colored." What also may have contributed to this confusion is the fact that the Capeverdean immigrants, especially early ones from Brava, included quite a few light-skinned individuals along with Negroids, and that, on the other hand, the non-Capeverdean Portuguese were perceived as relatively swarthy anyway, compared to the pink-white Nordic type. (On intergroup relations between non-Capeverdean Portuguese and Capeverdeans, see Chapter 10.)

In the Hawaiian Islands, prior to annexation in 1898, the label *haole* (originally "stranger," non-Hawaiian) was at first applied by the natives to all visitors. But since most of the early visitors to the Islands were skilled and relatively affluent whites of North European and American ancestry, *haole* gradually came to denote only this (not only racially, but socioculturally defined) group, to the exclusion of unskilled laborers of whatever origin, such as the Portuguese. After 1898, Mainland racial definitions were officially applied to Hawaii's people, resulting in the combining of Haoles, Portuguese, etc., under the heading of "Caucasians."

However, in the census of 1910 and through the 1930s, to take account of the de facto distinction between Haoles and the plantation-imported Portuguese (and Hispanics), persons of European or American ancestry enjoying Haole status were classified as "Other Caucasians"; whereas the Portuguese were counted as a separate group—including a small number of black Capeverdeans among them. Since 1940 Hawaii's population of Portuguese ancestry has been categorized officially, and increasingly also in unofficial practice, as simply "Caucasian," or "Haole," or "white."[39] This development nicely illustrates how the popular perception of physical traits is often inseparably tied to the perception of cultural-behavioral traits.

But what this development probably also illustrates is the fact that, as already hinted above, some "racial" traits are less stable than others, and may actually undergo noticeable change within a generation or two: in an extensive physical-anthropological survey of various European immigrant groups, sponsored by the United States Immigration Commission about 1910, it was found that American-born children tend to grow taller, with smaller heads, than their eastern European parents, probably because of improved nutrition and hygiene.[40] Similar observations were made on Hawaii-born children of Japanese and among Texas-born children of Mexican immigrants (including even a lightening of pigmentation!) in the 1930s.[41] For the Portuguese in Hawaii, John Vandercook noted about the same time that ". . . the majority of the Madeira islanders bear the marks of an oppressive poverty. . . . They are characteristically of small stature, slender and dark-skinned. . . . The Portuguese in Hawaii, of identically the same stock and original background, are typically taller, paler and conspicuously stronger. . . . The application of American principles and the effect of American opportunities have produced in the case of the Portuguese in Hawaii what seems almost a mutation of species."[42]

And so, generally, second- or third-generation Portuguese-Americans are far less distinct in physical appearance from the "average white American" (whatever that means) than was true for their immigrant forebears.

II   *Education, Mentality, Beliefs*

The vast majority of Azoreans and other Portuguese who came to the United States up to the end of the First World War, and even many of the more recent arrivals, had emerged from a relatively closed and isolated peasant environment where the mental horizon was pretty much limited to the native village, or at best to a particular island or district. Awareness of a larger world was often more due to ties with relatives or friends who had previously migrated overseas than to a strong sense of Portuguese nationhood. "Ignorant," "simple-minded," and "superstitious" were common epithets applied to these people by authors of the late nineteenth and early twentieth centuries.[43]

Literacy, in the Portuguese countryside and even in the towns, was mostly the prerogative of a small upper class, the priests, and many tradespeople. The average farm laborer or fisherman did not see much value in a formal education: one did not have to read to know what was going on in the village. There might even be a disadvantage to literacy: those who could read and write were obliged to vote, and voting meant one must have a knowledge of politics, and surely politics was the realm of the witches.[44] Skills acquired in school were not generally perceived as improving one's chances for a livelihood. On the contrary, why should children waste years in school when they could help on the farm instead!

Portugal has been, and presumably still is at this writing, near or at the bottom of the scale among the countries of Europe as far as literacy is concerned. Since ability to read and write was generally not a selectional factor in emigration prior to the end of World War I, the same comparatively high degree of illiteracy that existed within Portugal also afflicted Portuguese immigrants to the United States prior to the introduction of the Literacy Test. In nineteenth-century Portugal, elementary education had been in the hands of the clergy, and it dwindled badly when the Church lost its properties. In 1894, compulsory free schooling for ages six to twelve was legislated on paper; but there was neither enough money nor enough parental interest actually to set up sufficient schools, particularly outside the major cities.[45] A new law of 1898 reducing the period of compulsory education to three years did not help much; not until the 1960s did Portugal raise that three-year period to a minimum of six years.[46] Taking account of the scarcity of public schools, the constitution of the Portuguese Republic of 1933 provided that, while elementary instruction was obligatory, it was the concern of the family, and of public or private institutions in cooperation with the same, so that it could be administered at home instead of in school.

According to the Portuguese census of 1878, 58 percent of the total population above ten years of age could neither read nor write. The illiteracy rate was even higher in Madeira and in part of the Azores. In the 1911 census, 48.5 percent of all males and 63.6 percent of all females above age seven were reported illiterate; in 1940, 41.2 percent of all males and 56.1 percent of all females (above age seven).[47] As of 1968, Portugal's illiteracy rate was still reported the highest in Europe[48]—which certainly suggests not just poverty, but a continuing and rather deep-seated popular indifference toward schools.

In accordance with the above picture, United States immigration statistics indicate that 68.2 percent of all Portuguese immigrants fourteen years of age or over admitted during the twelve-year period for 1899 through 1910 could neither read nor write. That was the nationality group with the highest rate of illiteracy (followed by the Turks, with a rate of 58.9 percent, and the southern Italians, with 54.2 percent). Between 1911 and 1917 the figure dropped to around 50 percent or a little less. Thereafter, the new Literacy Test precluded immigration of illiterate adults or adolescents, unless they came to join close relatives.[49] By regional grouping, immigrants from mainland Portugal exhibited a somewhat higher degree of literacy than those from the Islands. The Capeverdeans were reported doing even a little better than the Continentals (there were some good Protestant mission schools in the Cape Verdes). Western Azoreans had a higher percentage of literates than immigrants from São Miguel, with those from Madeira exhibiting the least proportion of literates.[50]

Not only did the requirement of minimal literacy for immigration (after 1917) hit Portugal harder than many other countries; illiterates, though admitted as immigrants, would be barred from naturalization unless they first acquired the rudiments of literacy. And while news in the village back home traveled mostly by word of mouth, in the United States there was greater need for letters and newspapers to expand one's net of communication. Typical is the recollection of Francisco Cunha, one of the early Portuguese settlers in Fall River: in the first years of Portuguese settlement in that city, nobody there could read or write Portuguese, so Cunha's father had to go to New Bedford whenever he wanted to have a letter read from, or written to, the folks back in São Miguel.[51] In the 1890s, another old-timer reminisces, many Portuguese in New Bedford used to gather in the shop of a cobbler to listen to the journalist Miguel Polycarpo read Portuguese newspapers to them.[52] Jack London, in his novel *Martin Eden,* has Martin ask his Portuguese landlady (somewhere around Oakland) to read his mail to him while he lies sick in bed. "No can," answers Maria Silva; "Teresa [her little daughter], she go to school, she can."[53] One Portuguese settler out in Elko, Nevada, in a newspaper interview reported in 1897, rejects criticism for allegedly having changed his true Portuguese name to Mellion: "It's not my fault if the Americans call me Mellion," because, explains Mr. Mellion, "I can neither read nor write. The fault is with the Portuguese government, for in my parish back home there wasn't any school. It's very sad that Americans call us by names different from those of our families."[54]

Portuguese immigrants arriving after 1917 were naturally better educated than earlier ones. As a matter of fact, in 1929 the Portuguese government prohibited the emigration of illiterates between ages of fourteen and forty-five (with a few exceptions) in the interest of Portugal's prestige abroad.[55] The new Portuguese mass immigration starting around 1960 has brought in a majority of people who have had at least a few years of elementary schooling. As of 1968, illiterates among them allegedly represented only about 15 percent of the total (presumably exclusive of children), while in

Portugal herself illiteracy continued at a level of close to 40 percent.[56]

In the earlier period of immigration, the prevailing attitude of Portuguese-born parents toward the formal education of their children was: let them leave school and go to work as soon as possible. That this attitude is rooted in a more complex set of factors than just a peasant or "working-class" background and a widespread tradition of near-illiteracy can be seen from the fact that, in the Hawaiian Islands, this low Portuguese valuation of the schools was in marked contrast to that of the Chinese, Japanese, and Korean immigrant groups, who at a very early stage sought for their children the benefits of an extended formal education.[57] For example, in 1926 only 15 percent of Portuguese boys and 15 percent of Portuguese girls fifteen to eighteen years of age were enrolled in Hawaii's high schools, as against 67 percent and 47 percent for the Koreans, 64 percent and 51 percent for the Chinese, and 33 percent and 20 percent for the Japanese. Proceeding to the college level, in 1930 15 percent of the Portuguese eighteen to twenty years old were attending school, as against 48 percent of the Chinese, 37 percent of the Koreans, and 26 percent of the Japanese.[58]

Switching to the industrial settings of New England, in 1914 only seventy-two out of 2,853 Portuguese public-school pupils in Fall River were above the fifth grade, and none was in senior high school. But in the 1930s the value of education began to be appreciated, and by 1940 103 out of 845 high-school graduates in Fall River were Portuguese ethnics; some were even attending college.[59] A similar upswing of interest in secondary and college education has been observed among the California Portuguese. Nevertheless, among the new wave of Portuguese immigrants, e.g., in the Providence area, there is again widespread parental resentment at having to keep children in school until age sixteen.[60]

In some ways related to the relatively low level of literacy, low valuation of formal education, conservatism, and reliance on physical labor that have characterized the large majority of Portuguese, at home as well as after emigration, are certain other personality traits attributed to them with near-unanimity by American and other observers. Of course such characterizations often reveal as much about the observers as about the observed. Also, personality traits are subject to change, in response to changing environment. Here are the epithets most commonly encountered in the literature (several scores of sources!), referring to Portuguese immigrant settlers in New England, California, and Hawaii:

(1) "Law-abiding," "obedient," "peaceful," "orderly." Sometimes a negative connotation is added: "docile," "subservient," "lacking in initiative." In this connection, also, crime statistics are cited showing the Portuguese ethnics to have a very low crime rate. (But a rise in juvenile deliquency among the second generation was noted on some occasions.) A low incidence of drunkenness is likewise pointed to in support of the notion of orderly restraint. (2) "Hardworking," "industrious"—particularly in relation to farm work. They rarely turn to public welfare or charity. (But some American-born descendants show less industry and do apply for relief.) [61] (3) "Thrifty," "frugal," "sober." (4) "Honest," "loyal." They don't like to go into debt and they pay promptly. (5) "Cleanly," "neat." They keep their homes clean despite poverty and slum conditions. (6) "Quick-tempered," "impulsive"; "melancholy," "gentle"; "generous," "hospitable."

On the issue of "intelligence" (in itself an ill-defined and controversial concept), IQ and similar tests have on different occasions yielded typically ambiguous evidence. In tests administered to over 1,000 children in Hawaii in the early 1920s, there was no significant difference in learning capacity between the Portuguese, Chinese, and Japanese—but all three groups scored considerably below the Anglos (perhaps due to language and environmental rather than intelligence differences). The Portuguese showed "the biggest percentage of [cases of] mental retardation" among the several races. In another set of IQ tests given to Honolulu schoolchildren about the same time, the Portuguese again scored far below the Anglo-Saxon and Oriental groups. A few years later, again in Honolulu schools, the Orientals surpassed the Hawaiian and Portuguese groups in arithmetical and verbal ability tests. In yet another analysis of test results in Hawaiian schools, the IQ scores of "Caucasians other than Portuguese" (Haole) topped the list (88), with the Portuguese and Puerto Ricans at the bottom (72 and 66) and the Orientals in between.[62]

In California, also in the early 1920s, IQ testing of kindergarten children placed the "American" and "North European" groups at 106 (the top), the "Spanish" at 78 (the bottom), the Portuguese and Italian ethnics at 84, and the Chinese at 97. Several other tests done on California schoolchildren were used to conclude that the "Latin"

(South Italian, Portuguese, Spanish-Mexican) pupils were inferior, on the average, to the "American" pupils in innate general intelligence (quite apart from language problems).[63] In Massachusetts, about 1925, three large nonverbal intelligence tests were administered to over 5,000 "second-generation" schoolchildren of sixteen different ethnic groups: the Portuguese scored lowest (83), just below the blacks, French-Canadians, and Italians; Polish Jews and Swedes topped the list (c. 102), with the "Americans" joining the Lithuanians (c. 98), etc.[64] In 1937, in a strange turning of the tables, some 400 (white) Portuguese schoolchildren aged seven to eleven in Lisbon, Portugal, were administered a Binet-Yerkes test battery; their average IQ was found to be superior to the average of American children (as determined by Yerkes in the United States)![65]

One must wonder about the validity or reliability of these various tests. What they probably do indicate is that, even where the language of the tests and of the respondents' homes is the same (English), differential intellectual stimulation in the children's "home and street" environment and other sociocultural differences between ethnic groups are bound to affect the ability to perform various intellectual tasks. Also, of course, while certain types of intellectual performance are heavily influenced by literacy (and by formal education in a fuller sense), illiteracy must not be confused with low intelligence!

Nor need superstitions be equated with stupidity. The culturally conditioned beliefs which Portuguese emigrants carried with them to the United States included many that readers of this book are likely to call superstitions, as well as others more respectfully called religion. As regards religion in the narrower sense, the overwhelming majority of the Portuguese settlers were and are, in a profound sense or at least nominally, Roman Catholics, incorporating in the offcial dogmas and rites of the Catholic Church a variety of regional Portuguese folk traditions. More about Portuguese-American religious and quasi-religious institutions will be said in Chapters 11 and 12. Some reference to small Protestant and Jewish Portuguese immigrant groups has been made in Chapters 1 and 2. As the Portuguese ethnics, particularly the American-born second and third generations, have moved toward the "mainstream" of American life, their Catholicism has naturally also undergone some degree of Americanization. Heavily under Anglo-American influence from the start have been the several small Portuguese Protestant groups, adding up to several thousand members. Apart from the nucleus in Illinois dating from the mid-nineteenth century, there are some along the East Coast (largely Baptist). These were originally inspired by Portuguese Protestant converts in Bermuda and in the Azores. Some conversions also occurred in California, starting about 1890. In Hawaii, a small Portuguese Protestant circle existed by the 1890s, with links to the Illinois group. A fair number of Capeverdeans in New England belong to some Protestant denomination.

It is difficult to form a comprehensive picture of folk beliefs or "superstitions" current at one time among earlier Portuguese immigrants, or possibly still alive among their children or among the more recent arrivals. Of course, one has to distinguish between beliefs actually held by informants and beliefs merely remembered and cited as curios. As one informant put it to the present author long ago: the fast-moving American life destroys the contemplative spirit underlying so many folk traditions; creeds and legends fostered by the romantic, slow atmosphere of the Portuguese countryside are here forgotten fast. (On the other hand, we might interject, modern American life breeds its own multitude of folk beliefs and legends. . . .) Moreover, low-prestige people harboring creeds which they know are decried and ridiculed by others as superstitions often get very defensive about revealing them to investigators. Elsie Parsons, who in the early 1920s roamed among Capeverdeans in New England in order to collect their native folklore, reported: "I have had requests for tales refused by Cape Verde Islanders on the ground that a narrator might find himself in jail. . . ."[66] Here are some of the most common beliefs attested to this writer by Portuguese immigrant informants:

Relatively deep-rooted and persistent are beliefs in the area of folk medicine. A wide range of ailments is popularly attributed to the "evil eye"; this involves the belief that certain individuals have the magical power to cast an evil spell through the glance of their eyes upon others whom they envy or have a grudge against, or whom they want to harm at the behest of some third party. The victim is then said to be suffering from a *mau olhado* or *olho ruim*, "evil eye," or from *quebranto* (literally, "a broken-down condition," from the verb *quebrantar*, "to break"; hence, a general feeling of illness, aching, etc.). The term *quebranto*, as in *deram-me um quebranto*, "someone has given me a __", may describe both the symptoms and the cause (viz., an evil eye). Less common, but of a similar nature, is the diagnostic term *ar ruim*, "evil air," "evil vapor," as in saying *um ar ruim passou por êle*, "an evil air, or vapor, passed through him", to explain someone's illness.

A belief in the powers of the evil eye is, of course, not specifically Portuguese, but is widespread also among other nationalities, such as the southern Italians. Similarly, many immigrants from Portugal share with others, including native Americans of various backgrounds, a fear of the number 13, and of Fridays, as potential harbingers of bad luck; and, above all, a belief in the devil and his evil powers. One way to protect oneself against the evil eye is to perform the gesture known as *figa*, "fig": protruding one's thumb between the middle and index fingers of the closed hand. To keep the devil away one may, of course, perform the sign of the cross, and in addition, avoid the very word *diabo*, "devil," perhaps by substituting for it the euphemism *nabo* (literally, "turnip"; cf. English *dickens* or *deuce*). More uniquely Portuguese, in the area of folk medicine, is the attribution of stomach troubles, chest pains from a cold, and the like to *espinhela caída*, "dropped sternum" (pressure caused by a dropping inward or downward of the lower end of the breastbone). A similar or identical diagnostic term is *arcas caídas*, "dropped ribcage." A stomach ache may also be diagnosed as *bucho virado*, "overturned stomach."

Extending into the area of folk medicine, but not confined to the diagnosing and treatment of disease, is the belief in what in English, for lack of a more precise term, can be called witchcraft. This is the field of activity of *bruxas* and *feiticeiras*, i.e., witches and sorceresses. These are usually old women, or pictured as such, although a *feiticeira* may also be a charming young girl. There are also, less commonly, male counterparts (*bruxos* and *feiticeiros*). These are not, as the English term *witch* tends to connote, supernatural evil beings. They are real people thought to be endowed with supernatural—or simply with unusual— powers, for evil as well as for good. As a matter of fact, they may not only do things like casting an evil eye, but, especially in the immigrant communities, may have healing powers, and in their healing capacity are also referred to as *curandeiras* or *curandeiros*, "healers." Therapeutic practices may range from incantations and various magic acts to the use of herbal medicines.[67] Apart from recourse to such folk healers, cures may of course be sought by some votive offering to one or the other saint, or to the Virgin herself—a practice where "superstition" and "religion" become rather inseparable. While these types of belief and practice are barely remembered by American-born descendants of the earlier immigrants, they have been restored to some limited currency in Portuguese-American communities by the new post-1960 wave of immigration.[68]

III *Marriage, Family Structure, Position of Women*

For most immigrants from rural Portugal, as for those from other countries, settlement in the United States meant, if not a temporary or permanent break-up of the immediate family, at least a loosening of bonds to the "extended" family, i.e., to the more distant relatives (including godparents, etc.), due to the very fact of spatial separation. But compounded with this was exposure to a (dominantly Anglo) milieu—particularly in urban New England, somewhat less so in rural California—which, in comparison to the old country, was marked by a trend toward individualism, shrinkage and democratization of the family, freer choice of marriage partner, separation of workplace and home, increasing job opportunities for women, and compulsory schooling for the young. Among poor immigrant families in the cities, the temptation or even the imperative need for women to hold outside employment along with the men was great. And there was the greatly increased possibility of a "generation gap" due to the language differential, the public school, and other factors.

All this added up to a considerable threat to the traditional structure of family life among Portuguese immigrants and their American-bred offspring. Of course American society as a whole has undergone some transformation, in its typical outlook on family and sex, during the full century spanned by the Portuguese influx into this country. Moreover, the environment faced by an Azorean family in, say, cotton-manufacturing Fall River was never quite the same as that on a Hawaiian sugar plantation or out in California's farm country. The amount or kind of change experienced by Portuguese ethnics has accordingly differed somewhat by period and region. It will be sufficient here to cite a mere sampling of testimony relating to marriage, the position of women, children's upbringing, and the like.

"Two thirds of the work in Portugal is done by the women," reported Aubrey Bell early in this century. Most women in Portuguese towns, added Lautensach a little later, still live in Islamic seclusion, and in the villages they do most of the field labor. In the Azores in particular, about 1880, upper-class women were said to

A Portuguese-born long-time resident of New Bedford proudly surveys the pictures of her seven sons serving in the American armed forces or in the war industry during World War II.

live in Oriental seclusion, strictly chaperoned. Still as of 1940, according to another observer, Azorean women, while exempted from the heavy labor done by men, were rarely seen outside the home, except in church.[69] Another author, about the same time, describes Portuguese peasant women as in a slavelike position, working alongside the men in the fields; in fishing communities, by contrast, the women "wear the pants" on land.[70] Portuguese courtship customs, during the period under consideration, involved rather strict chaperonage, although there was more freedom in the Minho region. The double standard tended to prevail in matters of marital fidelity. In the Cape Verde Islands, a kind of common-law marriage and instances of polygyny were and perhaps still are fairly common.[71]

The initial transfer of old-world courtship and family patterns to the new land of immigration is well illustrated in the reminiscences of some of Hawaii's Portuguese. One such informant had accompanied his family from São Miguel to Hawaii in 1883, and grew up in a laborers' camp on one of the sugar plantations there. At age twenty-two he got engaged to a sixteen-year-old Portuguese girl in another camp. Their courtship, he recalls, was always severely chaperoned; at first they were only allowed to look at each other without talking. Even after the engagement, the two young people could not sit close together; the girl's parents were always between them.

Another informant (let's call her D.J.), a Madeiran-born woman who had reached Honolulu with her parents in 1884 and who also spent part of her youth on a sugar plantation, reports: "My father was the boss in our home, but he handed my mother his paycheck every month and she took care of it. Every morning when we got up we had to kiss our parents' hands and ask for their blessing. This is still done [as of 1937] by many of the Portuguese families here, though parents are more insistent about their children paying this respect to grandparents and God-parents; however, some families require their children to do the same for uncles and aunts as well. . . . We were taught to respect each other in our family and especially our parents and guests. . . . When called by our parents, we always answered with the term for 'Sir' or 'Madam' in our language. Swearing was absolutely forbidden; there was no back talk allowed; we had to take punishment without a murmur and we feared the strap which my mother used for punishing us, for she was the disciplinarian in our home. . . . At night before going to bed, the whole family was led in prayer by my father. . . ."

D.J. was about fifteen when, accompanying her mother to a grocery store (on Kauai Island), she saw the young clerk who ten years later was to become her husband. During the years of initial courtship, he would send her occasional letters as he was not allowed to make social calls. When he finally wrote to ask her to marry him, "I told my mother about it, and she told my father about it as I couldn't talk about such things to him myself." The young man was then allowed to come to the girl's house to ask for her hand in person. "After he had told my parents that he wanted to marry me, my father called me in and asked if I wanted to marry the boy. . . . You see [D.J. explains to her interviewer], it was up to the girl to decide then and there as to whether or not she wanted to be married to the suitor. I accepted . . . [but] in spite of this we became engaged for two years before we were married. (The careful protection of the girls and the long engagements are gradually being dispensed with in Hawaii.)"

"As the time for my wedding approached," D.J. continues, "I was given much advice by friends and relatives but sex was not discussed. . . . For the wedding . . . we had three witnesses, a married couple for me and a best man for my husband. Today in Hawaii, Portuguese couples have abandoned this practice and have only two witnesses as in the American wedding. After the church ceremony, we had a dinner. We couldn't get away as couples here do nowadays, but had to stay until everything was over as our first duty was to our guests. . . ."[72]

Gerald A. Estep, writing in 1941, a few years after the above testimony in Hawaii was taken down, found that there was by then "a wide cultural differentiation between the Portuguese in the Island setting [Azores, Madeira] and those in California. . . . [Yet,] it is in Hawaii [where immigration had ended shortly after 1900!] . . . that the distinction from old-world patterns is most evident. On the other hand, the Portuguese in California have retained considerable of the old-world family pattern. The man is distinctly the head of the family. . . . Compulsory education is tending to break down family influence over children. In many Portuguese homes, however, the daughter is still merely an apprentice to the mother in the ways of being an obedient, faithful, diligent wife. . . . When her required school days are over, she is expected to remain in the home until she is courted and married."[73]

Yet at about the same time that Estep was painting this picture of relative conservatism in California, the city of San Leandro elected as its chief executive a woman of Portuguese extraction (during World War II); and a Portuguese government official, upon a visit to California about 1930, reported his impressions in these terms: "The Portuguese women [in California] participate in all activities of the colony, in sharp contrast to what happens in Portugal. . . . They are the ones that dominate and run things [with particular reference to fraternal society affairs, festivals, public receptions]. The Portuguese woman, in California, is not only American in her interest in fraternal societies; she has adjusted admirably to the sportive and pragmatic atmosphere of the U.S."[74]

An anthropologist studying Portuguese-American families (largely blue-collar middle class) at San Jose in the 1960s noted that, in contrast to the importance of "cousins" and various other relatives and of godparents in Portugal, these immigrant or second-generation families in California had become "almost exclusively nuclear." Nevertheless, as a rule, the Portuguese-American family is "functionally and emotionally embedded in a larger kinship network" than the typical Anglo family; it is remarkably free from "social or psychological stress," and is the "hub" of almost all community activities.[75] Another anthropologist, studying Portuguese-American kinship patterns in New England, also in the early 1960s, observed that Portuguese-Americans still attach relatively much importance to distinguishing between paternal and maternal relatives.[76] Still another researcher, a few years later, found a continuing reflection of the strong Azorean emphasis on the family unit in the fact that about half of the Portuguese dairymen in the San Joaquin Valley were in family partnerships.[77]

As against the traditionally subordinate position of women in the Portuguese household, the very fact of emigration and the need to adjust to the American environment frequently brought along some measure of emancipation. Even where an entire family emigrated together, the wife sometimes played a larger role than did the husband in actually making and implementing the decision to emigrate; and after resettlement, it was typically the wife's task to provide the family with a comfortable blend of the old ways and the new.[78] Some Portuguese women who emigrated alone did so not to join their husbands or fiancés in the United States, but primarily in search of emancipation. This latter motivation is vividly depicted in the autobiography of Laurinda C. Andrade, who had left her native Terceira alone at age seventeen to become a teacher in New Bedford.[79]

The kind of emancipation gained through outside employment was, of course, more readily available in urban than in rural settings. For example, in a sample survey of Portuguese immigrant households in the textile towns of New Bedford, Fall River, and Lowell, about 1905, some 43 percent of all the foreign-born women (sixteen years or over) were found to be employed in cotton mills and 56 percent were staying at home; 90 percent of the males were so employed.[80] At the same time, on Portuguese immigrant farms in Rhode Island, women were found to be helping the men in the fields, but without neglecting their housework.[81] In Hawaii, in early days on the plantations, the women generally took care of the household, but some also worked with their men in the fields or took in washing and sewing for the unmarried laborers.[82]

In rural California, according to Bannick, writing during World War I, most of the Portuguese women were doing very little work outside of their homes, in contrast to most of their "sisters" in the East; moreover, because of the relatively extensive and mechanized type of agriculture in California, women and children there were not as much employed in the fields as was the case on New England farms.[83] The traditional attachment of Portuguese women to their domestic roles has remained so strong, according to Steven Ussach, that those who took "men's jobs" during World War II rushed back to domestic activities as soon as they could afford to in the postwar years. On the other hand, still according to Ussach, in recent years the majority of the gainfully employed among the "new" Portuguese immigrants (the tens of thousands who have come to the United States since the mid-1960s), in the older settlement areas such as New Bedford and Fall River, have been women. This is because a large proportion of Portuguese males, centered in the construction industry, have been unemployed or only seasonally employed, whereas the women usually hold factory or service jobs near their homes.[84] One can only speculate about the emotionally and factually disruptive long-term effect this kind of situation may have on family structure, among the mass of recent Portuguese immigrants.

One index of the weakening or dissolution of traditional familial bonds and of ethnic ties is the incidence of intermarriage (outmarriage); another is the rate of divorces. Because of the regionalistic attitude prevailing among the Portuguese, there was a time when a union between an immigrant from, say, São Miguel and one from the Lisbon area was almost considered an intermarriage. Actual outmarriage to non-Portuguese was relatively rare among the first generation until after World War I; when it did occur it tended to involve Irish, French-Canadian, or Italian partners. except in the Hawaiian Islands, where the Portuguese might intermarry with various shades of native Hawaiian, Haole, or Oriental.

Here are a few bits of statistics: in 1895, in the state of Rhode Island, 1,005 American-born persons were of entirely Portuguese parentage, whereas 269 had a father born in Portugal but a mother born in the United States (possibly of Portuguese stock) or elsewhere; and presumably an additional number had a mother of Portuguese birth and a non-Portuguese father. The census of Rhode Island for 1905 showed 2,630 American-born persons of entirely Portuguese parentage; 521 had a Portuguese father and a mother born in the United States or elsewhere; and so on. In Fall River, a sample survey of French-Canadian families showed that intermarriages between French-Canadians within these families and Portuguese had risen from three in 1900 to fifty-six in 1943 (an increase proportionately far in excess of the increase of Portuguese and

French-Canadian ethnics in that city). Also in Fall River, the proportion of intermarriages among total marriages involving Portuguese rose from 6 percent in 1920 to 19 percent in 1930 to more than 60 percent in 1940.[85] In California, by 1940 only about 10 percent of Portuguese ethnics were reported marrying outside their own group (probably an underestimate), whereas in the Hawaiian Islands the outmarriage rate was then about 36 percent for "Portuguese" males and 51 percent for females.[86]

Divorce, generally prohibited by the Catholic Church, to which almost all Portuguese belong, was and still is quite rare in Portugal, although it became legal there after the fall of the monarchy in 1910.[87] An increasingly substantial divorce rate among Portuguese-Americans must therefore be interpreted, in part, as a mark of deethnicization, or Americanization. (This without overlooking the fact that in the United States, too, divorce was much rarer early in the century than it is today.) In Hawaii divorce was rare among the foreign-born; but among the second generation, by the 1930s, it became almost as common as among the general population. In California, as of 1940, the Portuguese divorce rate was still "very low."[88]

In sharp contrast to this, the frequency of divorce among the New Bedford Portuguese had become "a real epidemic" by 1944, when ten out of eighteen divorce cases pending in the local court on one occasion involved Portuguese-Americans; this shameful condition, exclaimed the *Diario de Noticias*, is due to the emancipation and masculinization of women![89] In neighboring Fall River, in 1957, fifty-eight out of a total of 218 divorces were between Portuguese (up from 1923, when only nine out of ninety-four divorces had involved that nationality).[90] By 1964, when the new waves of Portuguese mass immigration started rolling into Bristol County, Massachusetts, 60 percent of all divorce cases in that county were of Portuguese-Americans, even though only about 35 percent of the county's total population was then of Portuguese stock.[91] New concepts of marriage and family life were eroding ethnic tradition.

CHAPTER 9

Economic Conditions

ECONOMICALLY RELEVANT ASPECTS OF PORTUGUESE IMMIGRATION HAVE already been alluded to in previous chapters in the context of describing the settlement process as such. The present chapter focuses in a more systematic way, with illustrative detail, on the economic side of the Portuguese immigrant experience. The strictly economic side, of course, is always closely bound up with various sociocultural factors. Neither space nor the reader's patience would permit a full description of developments in all occupational fields that have attracted large or small numbers of Portuguese, at different times, in one or the other settlement area. We limit ourselves to giving some particulars about the most common economic pursuits during the earlier immigration periods: the fisheries, cotton-mill employment in New England, plantation labor in Hawaii, dairying and truck gardening in California. We conclude with some general remarks on the economic status of today's second and third generation—as well as on the situation of the new (post-1960) wave of immigrants.

The basic economic structure of insular and continental Portugal, during the earlier period of mass emigration to the United States (and continuing with relatively little change to the present), can be briefly described as follows: Portugal has been and remains one of the least industrialized and poorest countries in Europe, with at least 45 percent of the labor force engaged in agriculture and 2 to 3 percent in mining and fishing. With the exception of the east-central part of mainland Portugal (from where there has been hardly any emigration), the prevailing mode of existence has been that of small peasants intensively cultivating little plots with relatively primitive tools. In the Azores Islands, around the turn of the century, farming involved even as much as two-thirds of the labor force, while fishing occupied a bare 2 percent or so (the proportions vary from island to island). Crops, about that same time, included a variety of cereals and vegetables as well as (chiefly on São Miguel) citrus fruit and grapes, etc. The Azorean soil, by and large, was fertile enough to yield two or three crops a year. On Madeira Island, sugar cane and grapes (Madeira wine!) were leading crops; but poor soil typically required irrigation. Cattle raising and dairying gradually attained some importance in Madeira and in the western Azores. The tourist industry has been a major source of livelihood for Madeirans, but much less so for Azoreans. Light industry and commerce together have been engaging perhaps one-fifth of these insular populations. The Cape Verde Islands (a colony until recently), chronically plagued by droughts, with a rough and hilly topography, have kept their farming population at the margin of subsistence, yielding with difficulty a variety of garden crops.[1]

This, in a nutshell, was the milieu from which thousands upon thousands of Portuguese tried to escape to the United States in hope of economic betterment; they were practically penniless in most cases, with a low level of literacy and with few marketable skills. The issue of literacy has already been discussed. Immigration statistics for the sample period 1905–1909 indicate that of a total of 40,985 Portuguese legally admitted during those years, 13,508 showed no money at all on arrival; the average per capita amount of those who did was $23.60 (which works out to an average of $15.82 for the whole group).[2] As for occupational backgrounds, of all the Portuguese who arrived between the years 1899 and 1910, about 34 percent described themselves to immigration officials as "common laborers" (or were so categorized by the officials); only 5 percent were entered specifically as "farmers or farm laborers." Undoubtedly most of the "common laborers" can be bracketed together with the latter as having come from the farms. Some 20 percent described themselves as "servants," and about 5 percent as fishermen. Of the remaining 36 percent, about 34 percent declared "no occupation" (this undoubtedly included many women and children), leaving barely 2 percent for what from the official American point of view could be classified as "skilled" artisans (office clerks, seamstresses, etc.) and as "professional" (clergy, engineers, physicians, etc.).[3] A sample poll of 272 Portuguese males working in New England cotton mills about the year 1910 found that 62 percent of these textile operatives had been "farm laborers" or "farmers" in the old country; 84 percent of 259 Portuguese women workers similarly polled had had "no occupation" prior to emigration.[4]

I   Portuguese in the American Fisheries

Probably no aspect of the Portuguese presence in the United States has become so widely known, or even glamorized, as the role played by Portuguese in the early American whale fisheries and subsequently in the shore fisheries at such historically meaningful locations as Provincetown. Actually, in the total picture of Portuguese participation in American life, the fisheries and related maritime pursuits occupy only a minor and marginal position, on two grounds: although the American whaling industry provided the initial contacts or sparks that set into motion the stream of Portuguese immigration, the signing up of Azorean and Cape Verdean crews on visiting American vessels did not in itself constitute emigration or labor importation. Furthermore, the fisheries (onshore or offshore) have never occupied more than a small proportion of the Portuguese-American population. (For that matter, even in Portugal, known as a maritime country with a prominent interest in fishing, the fisheries employ only 1 or 2 percent of the total population, as indicated above.)

The American whaling industry, confined to New England during the colonial period, was at first carried on close to the shore in small boats, but in the eighteenth century began to follow the whales into deeper waters, in the Atlantic and ultimately as far as the Arctic and even the Antarctic. It supplied spermaceti oil for the manufacture of candles, and other products of the whale highly valued at the time. Truro and Provincetown on Cape Cod were important whaling ports until the Revolution, but then were far outstripped by Nantucket and, ultimately, by New Bedford. Major whaling grounds in the Atlantic, initially, were the waters around the Azores and the Cape Verde Islands. Not until the mid-nineteenth century did American whalers venture into Pacific waters, with Honolulu and San Francisco as way stations. (Portugal's fishing industry did not go into whaling on any scale, except for some small boats plying close to the Azores.) In the earlier period of Yankee whaling, the crews of the whaleships were largely recruited in the New England whaling ports. But as the industry expanded, and especially when the opening up of the West attracted more and more young New Englanders, it became increasingly necessary for the Yankee captains to look for labor in foreign ports—such as the Azores and Cape

Verde Islands. To natives of these islands, in turn, American whaling ships became opportunities not so much for reaping profits from fishing, but for eventually reaching America.

What were the wages of hunting the whale for the ordinary crewman? Days of strenuous work when a hunt was on, alternating with days or weeks of quiet boredom at sea; generally poor living conditions aboard; often cruel exploitation by officers—resulting in frequent desertions. There were no fixed wages; rather, two-thirds of the proceeds of a voyage would typically revert to the shipowners and investors, and the rest would be divided among the officers and crews. (The average whaleship would carry a total complement of some thirty to thirty-five men.) In the heyday of the industry, about 1850, according to Hohman,[5] an ordinary crewman's share, or "lay," at the end of a voyage of three to four years, after deduction of various charges, might typically amount to $200 to $300. In addition, of course, he had received free food (such as it was) and free equipment. The net lay about the year 1870, if we are to believe another source (probably a biased one: a shipowner defending his treatment of Portuguese sailors before a Portuguese consul), might amount to about $650 to $850, after voyages averaging three to four years.[6]

But by the year 1870, the American whaling industry had entered upon a severe and terminal decline, due to the discovery of petroleum in Pennsylvania in 1859 (to take the place of whale oil as a lighting fuel, etc.), the ravages of the Civil War, and exhaustion of many whaling grounds. The principal whaling had shifted to the Arctic Ocean; but in 1871, a whole whaling fleet out of New Bedford had to be abandoned in Arctic ice.[7]

Small numbers of Azorean and Capeverdean immigrants did hang on to whaling beyond the 1870s, even as late as the 1920s. Some of them continued to sign up as crewmen or lower-grade officers on deep-sea whaleships at San Francisco, until about the turn of the century.[8] In addition, at several spots along the California coast small shore-whaling companies composed of Azoreans were operating, much in the fashion of shore-whalers in the Azores, from the 1850s into the 1890s; the men would hunt in boats within a radius of perhaps ten miles from shore, where they themselves were living with their families, and where they extracted the whale oil in so-called "try-works."[9] In New England, the remnants of the once mighty New Bedford whaling fleet passed almost entirely into the hands of Azoreans and Capeverdeans; but eventually even the use of inexpensive old schooners could no longer yield worthwhile profit, and the last whaleship disappeared from "the Portuguese capital of the United States" in 1925.[10]

Apart from whaling, the American fisheries have attracted substantial numbers of Portuguese in Provincetown and Gloucester, Massachusetts, and, more recently, in San Diego, California. Western Azoreans started drifting into the Provincetown and Gloucester fisheries about the middle of the nineteenth century, and into Boston harbor shortly thereafter. Fishermen from mainland Portugal joined them after 1910. First in the employ of Anglo captains, and soon on their own account in many cases, they moved into the industry at a time of crisis. New England's offshore salt-fish business (going after cod and other species as far as Nova Scotia and Newfoundland) was hit hard by West Coast and Great Lakes competition using new fishing and fish-preservation techniques; and native New Englanders shifted into more profitable activities. (In Gloucester, the average annual earnings of a fisherman were $300 in 1880, and about $1,200 in 1930.[11])

Even a return to the earlier fresh-fish shore fishing, and a shift from hook and line to netting and trapping, plus motorization of vessels, have not been able to prevent the shrinking of the industry. Provincetown, with its largely Portuguese-American population, now lives more on tourism than on fishing. The same is true to a lesser extent of Gloucester.[12] Some Portuguese-American fishermen, in addition, are found in New Bedford, and in Stonington, Connecticut.[13] Some moved south, into shrimp fishing off Florida and Louisiana.[14] But real economic success in the fisheries has beckoned to Portuguese immigrants only in California.

On the West Coast, the introduction of canning in the 1860s, initially for Sacramento and Columbia River salmon and much later for sardines, tuna, etc., was to revolutionize the fishing industry. Several hundred Azorean Portuguese were involved in this type of fishery by the 1880s, the largest groups operating out of San Francisco and Monterey, alongside but separate from whaling. A few of them also settled near an old whaling station at San Diego, starting about 1885. It was at San Diego, in 1919, that one Manuel Medina, at the suggestion of a local fish canner, is said to have started specializing in tuna fishing down the Mexican coast. (Tuna has been a favorite catch along Portugal's Algarve coast and around Madeira for centuries.) Medina may also have been the first, about 1930, to use specially built, diesel-powered "tuna clippers" that could cruise as far as Peru and Hawaii, on month-long trips. Out of these beginnings evolved a tuna clipper fleet of some eighty vessels by 1940, the majority of them owned and/or operated by an increasingly prosperous Portuguese colony, compactly settled at Point Loma near San Diego.[15] Several of the San Diego Portuguese tuna entrepreneurs such as Manuel Medina (and the previously mentioned Lawrence Oliver, who was at least partly involved in the fisheries) are reported to have become "millionaires." The approximately 5,000 Portuguese-Americans in the Point Loma area currently own 100 tuna vessels valued at about $250 million. With the average crewman earning about $20,000 a year, this may now be termed the wealthiest Portuguese-American community in the country.[16]

II New England's Urban Portuguese: Mostly Factory Labor

Although the beginnings of Portuguese settlement in New England are associated with the fisheries, an increasing proportion of Azorean and other Portuguese men and women arriving after 1870 were drawn into factory labor, particularly into the cotton mills of New Bedford and Fall River. Others veered into maritime transportation, as merchant-marine sailors or longshoremen. Many of the women found outside jobs as garment workers or domestic servants. Relatively small numbers of Azoreans and Capeverdeans in New England, following their most natural inclination, were able to find a living in farming.

For a general picture of occupational distribution and income levels between 1870 and World War I, we can draw on some consular reports as well as on census statistics. Thus in 1872 the Portuguese vice-consul in New Bedford reported to his government that among the 1,100 Portuguese who had immigrated into his consular district over the previous ten years (three-fifths of them men, the majority single) farm laborers were earning $15 to $30 per month, plus food and board. Merchant marine sailors were getting $20 to $30 per month, plus food and board. Factory workers, generally unskilled, were receiving about $45 a month on a piece-work basis, without food or board. With these wages, the consul added, it is difficult to accumulate any savings: the only immigrants who do are those in whaling, because on the voyages there is little opportunity for spending. In a report from the Portuguese vice-consul in Boston, also of 1872, we read that most of the Portuguese men in his particular area were then employed in the merchant marine and fisheries, some in various crafts, earning $6 to $15 per week; the women were employed as seamstresses at $3 to $9 per week, or as domestic servants at $1.50 to $3 plus room and board.[17]

A little later, in the Massachusetts census for 1885, we find the following occupational breakdown of the state's Portuguese immigrant population, then numbering about 6,100: the largest category, about 26 percent of this total, were "housewives." Of those holding outside employment, almost one-third were in "manufacturing," including about 8 percent in cotton mills and 8 percent (all female) as garment workers; one-sixth in the fisheries (but hardly any in whaling!); almost 10 percent farm laborers and farmers; about 11 percent domestic servants; 5 to 6 percent transportation workers (mostly on sailing vessels); 3 to 4 percent barbers and male hairdressers.[18]

In 1900, when there was a labor force of close to 10,000 persons of Portuguese birth or parentage in Massachusetts, we find about 20 percent of the total employed in "cotton goods manufacture" (60 percent men, 40 percent women), a full 20 percent in various other manufactures, close to 25 percent classified as farm or factory "laborers" (which may include some unskilled cotton mill labor), a little over 15 percent still in the fisheries and in (mostly maritime) "transportation," 10 percent in domestic and other personal service, and the rest in commerce, etc.[19] In the neighboring state of Rhode Island, as of 1905, 20 percent of the labor force of Portuguese birth or parentage consisted of farm laborers or farmers, and 10 percent of longshoremen (mostly Capeverdeans on the docks of Providence); nearly 20 percent were classified as nonfarm laborers, and another 20 percent were doing miscellaneous factory work, the rest falling into various other categories.[20] Although these statistics are approximate, with shifting definitions of occupational labels, they suggest that the occupational distribution of Portuguese ethnics in southeastern New England, up to at least the turn of the century, was somewhat more varied and their entry into the cotton mill industry more gradual than has previously been assumed.

In 1913, the Portuguese consul in Boston summed up the situation in his district (all of New England) like this: 67 percent of the "colony" (persons of Portuguese birth or parentage) were then factory workers and other "manual" workers; 3 percent, farm workers; 2 percent, in maritime work; 3 percent, in commerce and the professions; the remaining 25 percent (largely women and children), without occupation. Thus, in effect, close to 90 percent of the gainfully employed were in factory-type work, according to this source. The consul further pointed out that (1) 56 percent of the "Portuguese" women (43 percent of those born in Portugal, 70 percent of their United States–born children) were working in factories—which was the highest percentage of employed women among the various foreign groups in the district; (2) the majority of the Portuguese workers (as of 1913) were found in the cotton mills of New Bedford, Fall River, and Lawrence, with the men earning an average of $8.71 per week, and the women $7.38; (3) these factory workers were not only earning less than those in farming and in the fisheries; they also suffered from a high incidence of tuberculosis and other illness.[21] Finally, according to the Massachusetts state census for 1915, about 75 percent of all gainfully employed Portuguese immigrants were by that year involved in "manufacturing and mechanical industries"—fully 55 percent in the textile mills. Only 6 to 7 percent were engaged in some kind of farming, 3 percent in fishing, 5 to 6 percent in domestic and personal service, etc.[22]

To focus more closely on the Portuguese immigrant's place in the cotton-mill industry: the first successful cotton mill in the United States had been established as early as 1790, in Pawtucket, Rhode Island. In subsequent decades, New England became the center of the country's cotton industry, with over 500 mills (usually quite small) operating by 1860 in such places as Lowell, Lawrence, Manchester, etc. These mills drew on native labor, largely farmers' daughters, until about the 1850s; then Irish and other immigrants began to step in, particularly so after the Civil War, when many native workers refused to return to these low-paying jobs.[23] At New Bedford, then the leader of the whaling industry, the first cotton mill (Wamsutta) was set up in 1848, and a few more were added after the Civil War, as whaling declined and the big shipowners were looking for new investment opportunities in that city. Some of the very labor coming out of whaling readily drifted into the new mills—including the earliest Portuguese mill operatives.

A major expansion of New Bedford's cotton industry occurred shortly after 1880, and an additional one shortly before and after the turn of the century.[24] It was this growth of cotton-goods manufacture, in the very home port of whalers whose search for booty had led them into Azorean waters, that almost accidentally turned New Bedford into the leading Portuguese immigrant community that it still is today. (Typically, few emigrants are really pioneers. Little more than accident often determines the place of settlement even for the early arrivals; friends and relatives tend to follow after them, in a continuing "network of contacts."[25]) First migrating from New Bedford, and later also through direct labor recruitment in the eastern Azores and parts of Portugal, additional Portuguese were drawn into the expanding cotton industry at nearby Fall River, starting in the 1870s and particularly in the 1890s and beyond. Mostly as offshoots of these developments in New Bedford and Fall River, thousands of Portuguese found their way into textile mills at Lowell, Taunton, and the Pawtucket area. By about 1900, Fall River had become the largest cotton manufacturing center in the United States (about eighty mills), overtaking New Bedford, Lowell, and the rest.[26]

When the United States Immigration Commission made an extensive sample survey of the labor force of the cotton manufacturing industry in the North Atlantic States (chiefly New England), shortly before 1910, immigrants from Portugal (mostly from the Azores) were the third-largest foreign-born group, after the French-Canadians and the Poles. But a larger proportion of the Portuguese immigrant population as a whole was committed to this type of work than was true of any other nationality. In the Fall River mills, the Portuguese immigrants equaled the French-Canadians (c. 19 percent each); in New Bedford, they were holding first place (c. 25 percent.)[27] By and large, the Portuguese (i.e., Azoreans and Cape-verdeans), together with Poles and Italians, were then holding the lowest-paid positions—below the average level of the French-Canadians and Irish, who had gotten there first.[28] Indeed the Immigration Commission, in its broad survey of the role of immigrants in various branches of manufacturing and mining, found that the average weekly earnings of all foreign-born "races" in all industries as of 1908–1909 were $11.92 for males and $7.90 for females; in the cotton-goods industry the average was lower, $9.28 and $7.93—but for the foreign-born Portuguese in that industry it was still lower, $8.05 and $7.28.[29]

One Portuguese old-timer in Fall River, by the name of João Tavares, in a recent newspaper interview, recalled that when he first went to work in a cotton mill in that city about 1908 he was paid $5.63 per week for working from 7:00 A.M. to 6:00 P.M. six days a week.[30] Another, José Gonçalves Correia, who had started out as a whaleman and ended up as a bird stuffer for the Museum of Natural

History in New York (!), is quoted as saying that as a "packer" in a New Bedford cotton mill in 1901–1905 he earned $6 to $8 per week; even a foreman then got only $14.[31] A third informant, Laurinda Andrade, who had emigrated alone from Terceira Island as a young girl to become a high-school teacher and community leader in New Bedford, recalls in her autobiography that on her first job in that city, as a helper in the "speeder-room" of a cotton mill, she earned all of $4 a week—yet bed and board alone cost her $6; as a machine operator in another mill a little later, she advanced to $8 to $9 per week.[32]

No wonder that many Portuguese immigrant parents in Fall River, according to the recollections of one Portuguese consul, tried to get their children into factory jobs before the legal minimum age of fourteen by securing falsified birth certificates from the Azores. (The same consul, to put these various earnings figures into focus, reminds us that about the year 1906, $6 bought a man's suit, or bed and board for a week; 10 cents bought a beer and sandwich, or a movie ticket.)[33] In a survey in Lowell, some years before World War I, a typical Portuguese immigrant family was found to live on the man's earnings of $10, having to spend $7.60 per week on food and $6 per month on rent (in some dilapidated, overcrowded tenement); the work week was fifty-eight hours.[34]

These harsh working conditions in the cotton mills soon led to unrest and to the formation of labor unions—although the Azoreans, typically averse to any impersonal collective action, were slow to develop union spirit. In Fall River, where there had been intermittent brief strikes since 1879, a half-year strike in 1904 to resist wage cuts led many workers to the brink of starvation. But, in the words of one of them: "The Portuguese was lucky—them as had the little vegetable gardens."[35] (Oh for the Azorean's love of tilling the soil!) During that strike in 1904, some 13,000 workers left Fall River, only to be replaced by more recent immigrants. By the end of World War I, the work week in the cotton mills had been reduced to about fifty hours, the average hourly wage had been pushed up from 10 cents to 48 cents—only to fall back to 24 cents by 1932. A nine-month strike wave in New England's textile industry in 1922 was followed by one in New Bedford, in 1928, lasting half a year. In this one, immigrants from continental Portugal, in contrast to the Azoreans, were very active.[36]

Many New England cotton mills finally moved south for a surer supply of cheap labor; of 153 mills in 1923, there remained only about thirty in 1937. The total labor force in this New England industry, so vital for Portuguese immigrants, shrank from 34,000 to 12,000 during that same period. The majority of the Portuguese textile workers in Massachusetts and Rhode Island had to find their way into other jobs, after much unemployment and hardship. Many managed to move into a variety of retail trades, or into municipal employment, etc., without relocation. But thousands eventually migrated to the Newark, New Jersey area, to industrially expanding Connecticut, or even to California—and some back to Portugal.[37] All in all, for those Portuguese who over a period of half a century had drifted into New England towns (and into metropolitan New York) to make a living in factories, or in various urban trades, economic advancement was painfully slow. There are no rags-to-riches stories; and even a modest rise from proletariat to lower middle class frequently did not come until the "second generation" had gone through American schools, where they were prepared for better jobs than had been available to poorly trained non-English-speaking immigrants.

III *Portuguese in Agriculture: Mostly in California*

Describing the island of Martha's Vineyard off the New England coast in 1874, one writer exclaimed:

> The land is of an excellent quality, quick to answer any legitimate demands upon it. . . yet agriculture here, as everywhere else in Massachusetts, is in decay. . . . Here, where Irish and Canadian-French have not found their way, the old folk die and leave empty houses. The few of sturdy age here look to the sea for their gain. . . . So between the inefficiency of the old, and the lack of interest in the few youths who remain, an admirable soil continues to be entirely neglected. . . .[38]

Thirty years later, referring to the same portion of New England, another writer commented:

> With the ominous drift of American population . . . from countryside and village to crowded city, and with the appalling flood of European immigration sweeping into the eastern long-shore towns, it is heartening to find a colony of newcomers possessed of a genuine instinct for land culture and an unsentimental love of cottage life. Such is the small but richly characteristic community on the island of Martha's Vineyard known familiarly . . . as "Fayal."

It was about 1880, we learn from the same source, that the first Fayalese-Azorean settler came to Martha's Vineyard and, purchasing a tiny plot of land, "succeeded in turning the barely disguised sand-hill into a blossoming bit of garden." Soon there was a whole little Azorean farming community: cottages closely surrounded by well-kept vegetable gardens, clustering loosely about a small Catholic church.[39]

There were not going to be many such Portuguese-American farming communities in the Northeast, the vast majority of Portuguese arrivals in New England indeed having been sucked into crowded cities with their factories and shops. But in several spots along the New England coast, Azoreans as well as Capeverdeans did manifest and did manage to stick to their preference for farming rather than industrial labor. For many of them, taking a job in a cordage or cotton mill upon landing at New Bedford was only a first step enabling them to save some money, so they could then buy or at least rent a small farm.[40] The persistence of these people in returning neglected soil to productivity gave rise to the saying, in parts of southeastern New England, that "a potato will not grow unless you speak to it in Portuguese." On the other hand, the willingness of these transplanted peasants to rely more on hard manual labor than on modern implements also gave rise to a somewhat invidious pun, among some Anglos along Cape Cod: to belittle a person's intelligence, one might say of him: "He is so ignorant that he thinks Manual Labor is a Portuguese." (A play on *Manuel*, the stereotyped first name of Portuguese males!)[41]

At Truro and other spots near Cape Cod, some Portuguese islanders started growing fruits and vegetables shortly before World War I on what had been considered barren wasteland. Strawberries around Falmouth and cranberries around Plymouth and Barnstable became particularly successful crops, heavily dependent on Azorean and Capeverdean labor. Capeverdeans at first drifted in from Providence and New Bedford for the berry-picking season only, doing factory or maritime labor the rest of the year. Eventually many of the migrants settled permanently on the Cape. They and their descendants remained a controlling element of the berry industry well past World War II.[42] Farther west along the New England coast, a few hundred Azoreans found their way into farming around Portsmouth, Rhode Island, beginning about 1890, coming from Fall River mills or directly from the Azores. Here the main crop was potatoes (and this is where the above-quoted saying probably originated). Typically, these settlers started out as farm laborers, then rented some land, and eventually bought a few acres themselves. Aided by their wives and children in the fields, working longer hours and living more frugally than native Americans, they succeeded where, in the words of the United States Immigration Commission investigators (c. 1910), the non-Portuguese potato grower felt doomed.[43] Nevertheless, by the time World War II rolled around, few Portuguese-Americans in the area resisted the temptation to quit agriculture for more lucrative industrial jobs. In postwar years, some Portuguese were still engaged in truck gardening on Long Island and in the Connecticut Valley.

But California is where the Portuguese element attained real importance, and a measure of real wealth, in agricultural pursuits. As indicated in Chapter 2, small groups of Azoreans had first found their way to the West Coast during Gold Rush days, and in connection with whaling. As of 1860, over 800 of them were engaged in gold mining, most in the Sierra Mountains east of Sacramento, and some farther north. But to a laborer without adequate capital equipment, the "Mother Lode" yielded little; within a decade or two most of these Portuguese had switched to agriculture. The only largely Portuguese mining settlement that held out until the end of the century was at Hawkinsville in Siskiyou County.[44] As a matter of fact, intensive vegetable and fruit farming had begun to attract people from the Azores as early as the 1850s, chiefly in Alameda and Contra Costa counties, east of San Francisco Bay. So eager were these people to rent or even buy land that, as the San Leandro Gazette complained in 1858 and again in 1865, they were falling easy prey to unscrupulous price gougers.

But, despite such exploitation, "the Portuguese [went] on renting, and from renting to buying, until many of them [were, as of c. 1875] well off and all of them making something."[45] Starting about 1868, some Azoreans moved from San Francisco Bay to the area around Sacramento, took up bottomland along the river, and stayed to become excellent vegetable growers there. In the 1880s, others took up farming in Fresno County or went to work in the vineyards of Santa Clara County. Still others moved farther into the San Joaquin Valley, also in the 1880s, and took up relatively large leaseholds of from 120 to 600 acres to grow field, feed, and grain crops; these were operating in companies of six to fifteen men, usually unmarried. One of the Azorean vegetable farmers near Merced, John B. Avila, introduced the sweet potato, a staple food in the Azores, into

California about that time.[46] Sheep husbandry, for the production of meat and wool, also attracted a fair number of Portuguese, especially south of Fresno, in the closing decades of the nineteenth century.[47]

In 1892 the consul of Portugal at San Francisco summed up the economic situation of his "flock" this way: It cannot be called excellent, but it is not bad either. In financial wealth the Portuguese settlers in California are way below the Irish and Germans, who are leading, and even below the French and Italians. In contrast to immigrants from other countries, who tend to cluster in industrial and commercial centers, the Portuguese in the state show a marked preference for farming. One of them, although illiterate, is said to have accumulated property worth $1,500,000. There are quite a few owning about $20–30,000 each.[48]

In 1891 an agricultural scientist touring California observed: "The Portuguese are already the peasantry of the rich valleys."[49] Symptomatic of the growing economic strength of the Portuguese-Californian population was the establishment in 1905 of the Portuguese-American Bank, in San Francisco.[50] Equally symptomatic, perhaps, is the fact that the Portuguese weekly newspaper *O Arauto*, then being published in the Oakland area, carried advertisements from as many as eighteen different savings banks in a single issue, with occasional advice on securities and other investments.[51]

As of 1915, when there were roughly 25,000 to 30,000 persons of Portuguese birth (i.e., not counting the second generation) living in California, the consul at San Francisco reported (on hearsay) that this number included about fifty individuals worth $50,000 each, twenty with assets of $200,000 each, four with $500,000 each, and one estimated to have $3 million—all of this mostly in the form of (rural) real estate.[52] (And those were days, of course, when a dime bought more than today's dollar.) Even if we do not consider this proportion of very wealthy people (one-fourth percent of the total) overly impressive, we must remember that almost all of them had started out in this country as penniless peasants—and that among their more numerous countrymen in New England, at that same time, there apparently was not a single individual who had risen from factory worker or small storekeeper to the status of "capitalist."

Focusing on the role of various immigrant groups in California's fruit and vegetable production (i.e., intensive rather than extensive farming) about 1910, the United States Immigration Commission noted the following characteristics of the surveyed Portuguese population samples: Few who have been farming more than ten years do not own the land they till, as they are quick to accumulate savings. But in contrast to Italian and Oriental immigrants, they are extremely individualistic and seldom form partnerships or cooperatives. They engage more extensively in the growing of crops requiring hand labor (rather than machinery) than do the native (American-born) and north European farmers. Frequently while improving their lands, as about San Leandro, they obtain two or more crops from the same field in the course of the year, e.g. by planting vegetables between rows of bearing trees. They invariably raise some crops for the market, while from the cows, chickens, and pigs, and the orchard and garden almost invariably found on the Portuguese farm they obtain the larger part of their food supply. They are much more eager to put women and children to work, in outside employment (e.g. in canneries) as much as on the farm, than are native or north European farmers.[53]

Almost thirty years after this official testimony, an Englishman visiting northern California in the late 1930s observed: "The Portuguese farmers near here [around Eureka] are sometimes laughed at by their neighbors, but on little postage stamps of land they manage by intensive cultivation to gain a better living than many Americans with twenty times the area. . . . The land-hungry European peasant has a solid respect and love for the land. He tends it with an evident affection, putting back into the land as much as he takes out."[54]

It was this tender intensive care of the land, bred by necessity into Azorean and Madeiran islanders, that paid handsome dividends for many Portuguese settlers in central California (dividends that labor at the factory loom could not). But actually it was the dairy industry more than gardening that produced the relative wealth of California's Portuguese ethnics. Immigrants from São Jorge, Terceira, and Flores in the central and western Azores, where dairying (at least as a home industry) had a long tradition, in contrast to other parts of Portugal, led in developing this line in California. The start was made in the 1870s in Marin County, which then had abundant natural pasturage, close enough to the burgeoning San Francisco–Oakland area for convenient marketing. Other Portuguese soon followed suit, in nearby Contra Costa and Alameda counties, as well as around Sacramento.[55]

From there, about the turn of the century, the industry spread into the San Joaquin Valley, as land values in the Central Coast area were rising and as irrigation opened up the dry interior valley to a longer grazing season—and ultimately to alfalfa culture. Dairying in California was based on the tenantry system pretty much from the start: large landowners would lease land and cattle to dairy operators who had little capital. Poor immigrants thus had a chance to work themselves up from lowly milking and other ranch jobs to tenantry, and from there gradually to independent dairy farming. With the invention of milking machines, cream separators, refrigeration, etc., dairy production became more and more of a specialized, factorylike operation.[56]

The Azorean settlers followed through on this; by 1915 they owned about half of all the dairy land in the San Joaquin Valley, and together with compatriots in coastal areas were then producing well over half of all the milk, cream, and butter (but not cheese) in California. In 1923, many of them formed a relatively powerful cooperative, Associated Milk Producers, with plants in six towns— one of the rare instances of cooperative business venture (as distinct from mutual insurance or fraternal associations) among Portuguese-Americans. In the early 1930s the Portuguese in California were estimated to control 60 to 70 percent of the state's dairy industry.[57] "There are more dairy cows on the ranches of California's Portuguese," a visitor from Portugal exclaimed in 1929, "than there are in all of Portugal: about 200,000, as against 20,000 from the Minho to the Algarve!"[58] As of 1938, total Portuguese holdings in the state were estimated at 450,000 heads of dairy cattle, representing a capital in excess of $30 million.[59] Here, for further illustration, are a few biographical sketches:

(1) Frank J. Gomes (already mentioned on p. 38) left his native island of Flores at age eighteen, spent four years in whaling (to earn a total of $100), then went ashore at San Francisco in 1877. After working as a store and hotel clerk, he entered the sheep business in Modesto, failed, then spent six years raising cattle in Nevada with a partner. Returning to Modesto, he bought thirty acres of land (at $30 each), raised alfalfa, and eventually became a successful dairy farmer.[60] (2) Born on São Jorge, J. S. Cardoza sailed for New York alone in 1873, at age fourteen. After a few years as a farm laborer in Rhode Island, he moved to California by sea, landing at San Francisco with 25 cents in his pocket. He found a farm job in the San Joaquin Valley and by 1881 had saved enough to lease 1,000 acres to raise grain. Eventually his leasehold of grainland grew to 2,500 acres. In 1885 he bought 160 acres to grow alfalfa and sold the

land two years later to build another homestead of similar size. There he manufactured cheese for shipment to San Francisco, until 1902. Then he installed a separator and switched to making cream. As of 1905 he had 130 cows and cut about 400 tons of alfalfa a year to feed them.[61] (3) Antonio A. Rodrigues, born on Terceira in 1905, left for Lemoore, California, at age fifteen. There Manuel Soares, himself an earlier emigrant from the same Terceiran village, found a job for him on a dairy owned by Tom Bettencourt. For four years Rodrigues milked cows there, until he had set aside enough money to start a dairy of his own. In the 1950s he diversified his agricultural operation to include deciduous fruits, grapes, and cotton, along with a milking herd. The farm is now run by himself and his son as partners; all labor is exclusively of Azorean descent.[62]

IV   *The Portuguese in Hawaii: From Plantation to City and Small Farm*

The process whereby most Portuguese originally reached Hawaii, viz., sporadically at first as whalers, and then in organized groups as indented laborers for the sugar plantations, has already been described (see Chapters 2 and 5). The several hundred who came from the Azores and Cape Verde Islands in connection with whaling, up to the 1870s, found miscellaneous jobs in Honolulu or on ranches; eventually many of these old-timers became independent stock or dairy farmers (owning up to 400 heads of cattle each) or small tradesmen. They introduced the manufacture of butter and the growing of corn (maize) to Hawaii.[63]

The record is not clear as to how many, if any, of those who went to work on Hawaii's sugar plantations had had previous experience with this type of labor. Certainly on the island of Madeira, from where about half of the imported laborers came, cane sugar was grown and exported to European markets as early as the fifteenth or sixteenth century; but exports became insignificant by the end of the seventeenth because of competition from sugar growers in Brazil. As of the 1870s there were eighteen sugar mills on Madeira— but apparently none on the Azorean island of São Miguel, the other source of Portuguese labor for Hawaii.[64] We recall that groups of Madeirans, and perhaps other Portuguese, had previously gone to work on sugar plantations in Louisiana and Trinidad.[65] The fact is that many of the Madeiran and Azorean contract laborers imported in 1878–79 turned out to be coopers, smiths, clerks, etc., rather than laborers. Yet these and the rest of them adapted well to plantation life—so well that the planters, in an effort to retain them after expiration of the initial three-year contract, raised wages from the original $10 a month plus board to $16 a month (with cottage and garden plot, but without food).[66]

Nevertheless, many would not renew their contracts or even stay on as free-lance day laborers, but preferred to become free farmers and tradesmen.[67] Additional imports then took their place on the plantations. In 1890 the Portuguese labor force in the Hawaiian Islands (among a total Portuguese population of 8,602, including women and children) was occupationally distributed as follows:

	Male	Female
Laborers (all or nearly all on sugar plantations)	2,653	3
Farmers	136	—
Fishermen	3	—
Mariners	10	—
Drivers and teamsters } (skilled plantation labor)	63	—
Mechanics	165	2
Planters and ranchers	17	—
Merchants and traders	56	—
Clerks and salesmen	35	—
Professional persons and teachers	10	1
Other occupations	118	5
Total	3,266	11[68]

It is noteworthy that, in sharp contrast to what was then true for the Portuguese in New England, hardly any females were counted among the gainfully employed in Hawaii (at least if we can rely on the above statistic).[69] The women were taking care of home and children, on the plantations and elsewhere. Probably this was not just a matter of free choice among the Hawaii Portuguese: plantation jobs involving hard physical labor presumably simply were not offered to women—whereas there was a tradition of female labor in cotton mills and garment shops.

From a report of the Portuguese consul at Honolulu for 1888 we learn that the Portuguese in the islands continued to be considered the best plantation workers, more robust and diligent than the Asiatics. On the other hand, under a Homestead Act just then adopted many of these Portuguese laborers had begun to purchase cheap public lands in the environs of Honolulu (island of Oahu), paying off faster than required, and had built up a whole little village. Also in the Hamakua section of the "Big Island" (Hawaii proper) many Portuguese families had bought land, near the plantations, to grow coffee. Others were going into small farming on land rented or bought from private parties, particularly around Kona (island of Hawaii), to produce cattle, coffee, and lumber. Around Hilo, some plantation laborers were growing sugar cane for themselves, in their free time, on plots of land ceded by their employer; but the lack of cooperative spirit among "our" people, the consul predicted, were dooming these miniature enterprises to failure. Plantation wages had dropped slightly because of the large number of Japanese coming in: foremen were then getting $30–50 a month, ordinary field laborers $20–24, plus free use of a cottage with bed and a piece of land for growing things on their own account.

In 1888, the consul's report continued, the total value of property (real estate and chattel) owned by Portuguese was estimated at about $1 million (exclusive of public homesteads), almost all of the real estate being on Oahu.[70] In a growing number of Portuguese families, another consular report added in 1890, the man kept working on the plantation while his wife and children tilled the soil on their nearby homestead. At Hilo, some of the independent little cane growers formed a milling cooperative—a symptom of modernization. In Honolulu, Portuguese construction workers were then earning $2 to $3 per day, tailors $12 to $15 per week; the growing affluence of the city siphoned off plantation labor.[71]

Again in 1897 the Portuguese consul at Honolulu supplied valuable details that round out the picture for us: There were at the time some 2,700 Portuguese still laboring on the sugar plantations— side by side with 12,000 Japanese, 4,000 Chinese, and 1,600 Hawaiians. The Portuguese on the plantations now fell into two distinct categories: the year-round employees (formerly on contract), and the floating day laborers who only worked on the plantations when they could not find work in Honolulu. Neither group liked the newly arrived Japanese with their "foreign" customs. Outside the plantations, some wealthy farmers and merchants could now be found among the old-timers (those who came in whaling days), who were forming a distinct group. In a surprisingly short time, the young people educated or born in Hawaii had developed into a separate class under American influence; these now shunned personal service jobs as demeaning, and showed modern entrepreneurial attitudes.[72]

About 1910, shortly after the last organized labor importation from Madeira and the Azores, and when the large majority of Hawaii's Portuguese ethnics could look back on twenty years' residence in the islands, or were born there of immigrant parents, there were still at least 3,700 Portuguese ethnics employed on the sugar plantations (probably at least a third of this number brought in during 1906–1909). But, we read in a report by a Portuguese turned Russian consul (!), intended to show the Czarist government what serious workers could accomplish in the Territory of Hawaii:

A goodly proportion [of the Portuguese] have already gradually branched out in different ways, many as independent storekeepers, quite a number as typographers, while an important percentage are found in Honolulu, in responsible positions, in banks and large trading or business houses. Thus, at the great firm, Honolulu Iron Works, we find 117 Portuguese employed . . . with wages from $6.50 down to $3 a day . . .; the Honolulu Planning Mill employs an average of 75 Portuguese, with daily wages ranging from $5 down to $1.50. . . . The Oahu Railroad Co. and the Rapid Transit Co. give employment to a large number of Portuguese laborers. Forty-four Portuguese, men and women, are employed in public and private schools, and quite a number of young Portuguese women are steadily employed as stenographers, cashiers and saleswomen. Other members of this colony occupy high positions of trust and responsibility on the bench, in the legislative, and in the County Boards, or as lawyers and notaries public, etc.[73]

In fact, for the Portuguese as for other ethnic groups in the Hawaiian Islands, economic advancement meant primarily an exodus from the sugar plantations into other occupational areas, urban or rural; on the plantations, too, many Portuguese did rise from the lowest to better-paid intermediate positions. (In a classic case of what has been called "economic succession," Japanese immigrants moved into the lowest-paid plantation jobs as Portuguese and other older settlers moved up the scale; later, the Japanese on their way up and away from plantations were supplanted by more recently arrived Filipino laborers, etc.) As of 1926, only 1,341 Portuguese were still employed on sugar plantations (as against 3,807 in 1908). Very few Portuguese moved into the more recently developing pineapple industry. In 1930, 45 percent of all Portuguese ethnics (first and second generation) were concentrated in the city of Honolulu; another 10 percent were located in Hilo, the second city of the archipelago. Their overall occupational distribution, according to the 1930 census, was as follows:

	Male	Female
Agriculture	1,749	60
Domestic and personal service	205	530
Forest and fish	22	—
Extraction of minerals	14	—
Manufacturing and mechanical	1,921	187
Transportation and communication	1,280	31
Trade	633	105
Clerical occupations	413	117
Public service	425	—
Professional service	180	244

Thus about 20 percent of the Portuguese labor force were now females—mostly domestic servants, teachers, nurses, and factory workers.

As a further index of economic advancement, the per-capita assessed value (for tax purposes, a mere fraction of true value) of real estate owned by Portuguese had risen from $105.80 in 1911 to $522.62 in 1930 (which, even allowing for inflationary change, still meant a doubling or trebling of true value).[74] Yet, to see all this in proper balance, we must recall that over the years, especially prior to World War I, thousands of Portuguese who had settled in Hawaii were so dissatisfied that they moved to California in search of better opportunities.

To conclude, here are a few biographical sketches: José Alves (a pseudonym) tells an interviewer in 1935 how he grew up on a Hawaiian sugar plantation, having left São Miguel with his parents and siblings in 1883. His father, as a contract laborer, was paid $9 the first month, $18 per month later on. The family was lodged in a house in a laborers' camp, where six families including a Portuguese one were already living. The kitchen was outside and the floor was dirt. The family slept on "stick-beds" (like benches); parents and sister in one room, he and two brothers in another. Other than the beds and one table, there was no furniture. Mother did washing and sewing for unmarried laborers, thus earned about $10 per month; and they were able gradually to buy some furniture and clothes. There was, however, plenty to eat, "and everybody was good to us."

When José reached age ten, he went to work in the fields, too, 6:00 A.M. to 4:00 P.M., earning $8 a month at first and $10 by the time he was seventeen. After his marriage to a Portuguese girl in another camp, he found a better job on a different plantation. (He also took English lessons nightly, paying $1 per month to a Portuguese man who knew English.) In 1909, the plantation manager gave him a twelve-acre plot of land to grow sugar cane on his own, with five helpers. Gradually the helpers left; he and a brother together with their wives then worked the land for themselves, making "good money." On the side, they always kept a fat cow, sold part of the milk, netting up to $25 a month from it. His children went through school in Hawaii; a daughter of his got married near San Francisco, and "now" (as of 1935) owns a big house. José is glad he came to Hawaii, for, he says, in São Miguel they all would have remained poor peasants, whereas here "I know that my children are not going to be plantation workers."[75]

Manuel Caetano Pacheco arrived at Honolulu from São Miguel as a child the same year as the above-mentioned "José Alves." He became a bookbinder in the city and took an early interest in government; by 1930 he had behind him three terms as supervisor of the city of Honolulu, and one term as senator of the Territory.

Louis R. Medeiros, also a native of São Miguel, became a schoolteacher in Honolulu as early as 1894, but eight years later entered commerce. During World War I he organized the National Guard of Hawaii, held the rank of captain, and as of 1930 was a credit manager and insurance executive.

M. A. Silva, a native of Madeira who arrived in Hawaii in 1884 at age sixteen, became owner-editor of a Portuguese immigrant newspaper at Hilo, and for several years worked for the Territorial Board of Immigration, recruiting plantation laborers in Portugal and Spain. In 1921 he was one of those who preferred to move to California.[76]

John Freitas Rapozo, born in the Azores in 1882, went through school in Hawaii, worked some years on a sugar plantation and as a cowboy, managed a hardware department, and finally set up his own general-merchandise store on the island of Kauai, doubling at the same time as local postmaster.[77]

V   Summing Up: The Last Fifty Years, East and West

Now for a brief outline of developments since the 1920s or 1930s. In Hawaii and California, and less so in the East, the past several decades have seen the foreign-born Portuguese element dwindle in proportion to the American-born descendants; the life-style of the latter, and even of many of the older immigrants, has generally come to approximate what may be loosely described as that of the mainstream lower middle class, with even a good sprinkling of middle middle and rare instances of upper middle. On the other hand, chiefly in New England, the tail end of this fifty-year period has witnessed the arrival of a new mass of working-class Portuguese immigrants, occupationally in a state of flux and initial adjustment; no comprehensive, up-to-date statistics about their economic condition are as yet available.

In California, during the interwar period and again after World War II, agriculture underwent increasing mechanization, factory-type large-farm specialization with migrant labor, and "urbanization" in the sense that a growing proportion of those working on farms would actually live in urban communities. A decrease in the land area given to agriculture was counterbalanced by an increase in productivity. Measured against this overall trend, a large proportion of the Azorean Portuguese, particularly dairy farmers, stuck to a relatively rural life-style and a more personal kind of small-to-medium farming operation longer than most other groups, selecting hired help among fellow ethnics. Some dairying was extended to the Los Angeles metropolitan area, and to the north around Eureka, but the center of Portuguese dairy operations remained in the San Joaquin Valley (especially on its "West Side"). Tenant farming, still widely used among the Portuguese in the 1920s, generally became outright ownership of land.[78]

About the year 1970, half of the 2,000 dairy farms in the San Joaquin Valley, at least a third of the state's total, continued to be owned or operated by persons of Portuguese descent.[79] On the other hand, the spreading urbanization around San Francisco Bay (particularly after World War II), with a resulting rise in land prices, caused many Portuguese-Americans in that area to quit farming or to shift operations up the Sacramento and San Joaquin valleys. An increasing number around Oakland, also at Sacramento, moved into a variety of factory and commercial jobs, or into city government; many hundreds own small businesses. This is particularly true of the second generation, and of Continentals (who generally have avoided agriculture). But quite a few here remained in truck gardening in selected locations. As a matter of fact, in parts of the San Joaquin Valley where irrigation made the land more fertile and costly, a switch took place from dairying to vegetable and fruit growing, even to cotton. The Portuguese community at San Diego has retained its strong position in the fishing industry.[80] Only a small proportion of the new immigrants who arrived in New England have found their way to California in recent years, usually to join relatives or friends there.

In the Hawaiian Islands, as of the 1960s, the large majority of the population of Portuguese (or part-Portuguese) extraction had well-nigh lost its ethnic distinctiveness, and was found primarily in a variety of urban occupations, around Honolulu and Hilo. Some Portuguese-Hawaiians on the islands of Maui and Hawaii were still working on the sugar plantations (where the need for manual labor had been reduced by the invention of the mechanical cane-cutter). Others were employed in the growing and canning of pineapple. In addition, on the islands of Hawaii (around Honokaa), Maui (at Makawao and Kula), and Kauai (at Kalaheo and Lihue) there continued to be clusters of small independent farms where one could hear Portuguese spoken.[81]

At the other end of these far-flung United States, thousands of Portuguese (the majority from continental rather than insular Portugal) have continued to shift around in a variety of industries and small businesses in the New York metropolitan region, including industrial New Jersey (Newark, Kearney, Elizabeth, etc.), New York City, Long Island (Mineola), and as far as the eastern fringe of Pennsylvania (e.g., Bethlehem, with its steel plants, and Greater Philadelphia). This includes people who had moved in from southeastern Massachusetts during the recession in the cotton mills there, as well as some of the fresh immigration of recent years. Particularly among the more recent settlers one again observes the natural tendency to cluster together at work as well as residentially; for instance, at Elizabeth, no less than a thousand Portuguese are employed in the United States Refining Company. In the industrial belt of southwestern New England, thousands of factory and service workers of Portuguese birth or parentage are concentrated around Danbury, Hartford, and Springfield.

In what is still and again the heartland of Portuguese immigration, stretching from New Bedford to Fall River and Providence, a major economic dislocation closed down the rest of the once-dominant cotton-goods industry just before the onset of the new mass immigration from the Azores (1958). Industry in this area is now greatly diversified, ranging from apparel manufacturing to electronics parts, rubber products, construction materials, etc. In

New Bedford, the leading places of employment for recent Portuguese immigrants—chiefly for women—are now the clothing factories, into which many of the old cotton mills have been converted. There and in the rest of southeastern New England, it has generally been easier in recent years for the Portuguese women rather than for their men to find stable employment. The women's skill as seamstresses is much in demand; but many men, often with an agricultural background, have had to hunt after (seasonal or out-of-town) jobs in the construction industry and the like.[82] Efforts to unionize the relatively new immigrants have been noticeably more successful among the Continentals than among the Azoreans, as had been true earlier in the century.

To conclude this chapter, we may ask why the Portuguese immigrant experience (we are thinking of the earlier mass immigration, not the recent one) has been generally more favorable in California, in an economic and social-status sense, than it has been in the East. For one thing, as Eduardo de Carvalho pointed out long ago, the Portuguese in California became more prosperous because there they had more of a chance to do the kind of work for which their "aptitude" or background had fitted them, viz., agriculture; whereas most of those in the East had to adapt painfully to factory work, in an alien industrial setting.[83] It is also true, we might add, that California in the late nineteenth and early twentieth century still offered much more of the opportunities of a "frontier" society, a rapidly expanding economy, than did the New England–New York region. However, getting in on the "ground floor" does not automatically assure one's growing with the company; there must be the freedom to develop and use the skills, and the camaraderie, for stepping upward. To quote Oscar Handlin:

> There was, in the factories, no hierarchy of skills through which the untrained could progress to ever-higher levels by developing proficiencies. On the contrary, the labor force was decisively divided into self-contained segments of managers, the skilled, and the unskilled. The unskilled had no opportunity for acquiring skill. Completely segregated from those who were more fortunate inside and outside the plant, often barred from the trade unions, they could hardly hope to advance their positions.[84]

The distinction between "trap jobs" and "step jobs" used recently by Grace M. Anderson in analyzing the job-seeking methods and job advancement of Portuguese immigrants in Toronto also seems highly suggestive in this connection: Some jobs, such as those of janitor, cleaner, kitchen help, are "traps", i.e., do not permit advancement to higher skill levels. Other jobs, especially in the demolition and construction industries, are "steps" toward advancement. Most of the recent Portuguese immigrants in Toronto, particularly Azoreans, have been using "networks of contact" consisting of relatives and friends to find jobs; this, Anderson believes, tends to isolate them from the wider community and usually leads to "trap" jobs (i.e., at the same level as these relatives and friends); the Continentals, Anderson found, are much more successful in job advancement, as they often get into construction jobs through trade unions.[85]

Perhaps we can say that in New England the Portuguese were drawn (very often through referral by relatives or friends) into "trap jobs," viz., in the cotton mills and the like; there was little or no possibility of promotion on the basis of skills—let alone the possibility of renting or buying such capital equipment as cotton-mill machinery for independent operation. In California, being drawn into farm labor—or the tuna fisheries, for that matter—provided "step jobs," at least in the sense that through thrift and application of skills one could gradually rise to economic independence. That, at least, seems part of the story.

CHAPTER 10

The Portuguese Immigrant Community and Its Institutions

I   Factions, and the Reshaping of Communal Conscience

WE ARE ALL GUIDED IN OUR THINKING BY LABELS—INCLUDING IDENTITY labels. One of the earliest labels we grow up with, at least in modern Western societies, is that of a last name; it helps us to identify ourselves as members of a family, including past and projected future generations. Soon, many of us also acquire a nationality label: I am an American, I am a Swiss, I am a—Portuguese? There are also intermediate stages and labels in a person's hierarchic inclusion in a group, from ego to family to nation, or beyond that. For most, if not all, "Portuguese" immigrants, i.e., immigrants identified (by outsiders if not by themselves) as Portuguese, one aspect of the specific "immigrant experience" was a sharpening, questioning, and frequently reordering of identity labels. This process is, of course, common in some measure to all immigrant or "ethnic" groups. The group that this book is concerned with, although relatively small compared to such immigrant nationalities as the Italians or Germans, provides an instructive example of the original complexities, and of their subsequent realignments within the American setting, that may be hidden under a simple nationality label.

It has already been emphasized that the large majority of Portuguese immigrants, particularly prior to World War II, came from rural peasant backgrounds, i.e., from villages, or at best from semirural small towns, narrowly confined on some small island or within a mainland district, where relationships would center on what sociologists call "primary groups," or face-to-face dealings with kin and neighbors—to the near-exclusion of more abstract affiliations with shifting interest groups, the members of which one would seldom or never see face to face. There was little change and little moving about (even though there was some awareness of far-flung maritime tradition). This does not mean that time had been standing entirely still in the Portugal from which most of the immigrants came; an Azorean in 1920, and certainly in 1950, was not quite the same as one in 1870—but not much different, either. Because of this confined horizon and relative conservatism (complicated by illiteracy, as a further barrier against relating to a wider community), the average Azorean, Madeiran, etc., tended to think of him/herself as primarily a native of this or that island rather than as a Portuguese citizen.

Extreme regionalism, or *bairrismo* (from *bairro*, "quarter of a town, neighborhood"), exclaimed a Portuguese writer in 1942, exists in the Azores as well as on the Portuguese mainland, with rivalries even between individual villages. First, there is opposition between islander and mainlander, then between Azorean and Madeiran, and finally there is rivalry between islands, and between localities on an island.[1] About the year 1900, according to the Portuguese census, over 94 percent of all inhabitants of the Azores were living in the "municipality" of their birth. Such residential immobility, Graves comments, promoted strong allegiance to a particular village and island.[2] Even today, Handler claims, most Azoreans do not think of themselves as Portuguese, or even as Azoreans, but identify with their particular village or island.[3] The unfamiliarity with the concept of nationhood among many of those islanders is well reflected in the strange expression current in the speech of São Miguel, and attributed to the influence of repatriates from the United States, *gente da nação*, literally "folks of (or from) the nation," in the meaning of "people from America, Americans": apparently the emigrants who introduced the term in this sense were unaccustomed to the Portuguese word *nação*, "nation," in its generic sense, let alone as a synonym of "the Portuguese nation, Portugal"![4]

In the United States, as has been indicated in earlier chapters, this *bairrismo* often pervaded residential patterns, with immigrants from the same island or continental district tending to cluster together. Quite naturally, many emigrants (except for early pioneers) picked their destination in the United States so as to rejoin relatives and/or friends who had preceded them. Not only in choice of residence, but in a variety of organizational activities this immigrant regionalism would persist.[5] Some examples have been given in previous chapters; here are a few more:

In the early period of Portuguese settlement at Ludlow, Massachusetts, there was so much friction between immigrants from Trás-os-Montes and Entre-Minho-e-Douro (two provinces in northern Portugal), with fistfights over women, etc., that eventually the "Minhotos" moved away, into Connecticut. The vast majority of the members of Espirito Santo (Holy Ghost) church in Fall River, as of the 1940s, came from Bretanha parish, São Miguel. In late summer throughout the 1940s and 1950s, immigrants from Moimenta da Serra, a parish in Beira province, would hold their annual picnic in the Providence area; those from Esmolfe would have theirs at Valley Falls; still others from the town of Ferreiroz would gather for an outing at Danbury.

In California in the 1960s, the UPEC (a statewide fraternal society) had two separate local lodges at Hanford, one for settlers from Terceira Island, another for those from Pico Island, as these two groups could not get along. The IDES fraternal society, at the same time, had a lodge chiefly for Pico people at Hanford, another for Terceirans at nearby Tulare. When Portugal's foreign minister visited California in 1955, the banquet in his honor was held in Hanford; but to square accounts, when the Portuguese ambassador to the United States visited the area a few years later, the organizing hosts were careful to select Tulare as the banquet site.

In New Bedford, as late as 1977, Portuguese-Americans from the Continent, Madeira, and São Miguel who had originally been attracted by the cotton mills located mostly in the northern part of the city, were still congregated in the northern sector; whereas those originating from Faial and Pico, who had first come in connection with the whaling industry headquartered in the south of New Bedford, continued to live primarily in the southern sector.[6]

One major division within Portuguese immigrant communities has always been that between Islanders—primarily Azoreans—on the one hand and Continentals on the other. Inhabitants of Portugal "proper" and of the Azores, Madeira, and Cape Verde Islands are not only separated by vast stretches of Atlantic ocean; they also know little about each other. The Azoreans in particular, as has already been indicated, have tended to resent the central government in Lisbon, and by extension mainlanders in general, for taking a neglectful and supercilious attitude toward them. Probably more important than political aspects of the problem, to the average immigrant, are the plainly observable differences in dialect, festive traditions, and various customs between people from his own home district and those from other parts of Portugal.

When the "Lisboas" (which is the Islander's popular name for the mainland Portuguese in general) began settling in numbers in various parts of New England, the older Azorean settlers described them as ill-mannered, irreligious, etc. Some feuds seem to have arisen when single men from mainland Portugal paid "too much attention" to the girls from Azorean or Madeiran families. When fishing people from the Algarve, Portugal's southernmost province, settled among Azoreans in Provincetown, some of the latter would call them "Guineas" (in this case not a reference to Italians, but to the somewhat "rough and rustic" blacks of Guinea, then a Portuguese colony). Many Continentals, speaking a Portuguese relatively close to the educated standard of Lisbon, would make a point of sneering at the nonstandard dialect spoken by many Islanders. In some locations, at some periods, the line-up was not Continentals versus Islanders, but rather Continentals plus Madeirans versus Azoreans (especially versus those from São Miguel). Among Azorean immigrants, some cleavage developed between the older "refined" group from Fayal and the more recent arrivals from São Miguel; the "Migueis" are strongly marked by their nonstandard speech and have a reputation for "coarseness."[7]

If there are typical differences between the inhabitants of different Azorean islands, there are also those between different islands of the Cape Verde group, to which we have already alluded in Chapter 8. In 1920 Capeverdeans in New England told Elsie Parsons that "inter-island marriage is disapproved. . . . In this country [the United States] there is a marked tendency for immigrants from the same island to keep together. A group of Fogo men will board in a Fogo family, S. Antão men in a S. Antão family, etc."[8] Archibald Lyall, after a journey to the Cape Verde Islands in the late 1930s, reported that "the lighter-skinned 'sampalhudos' of the Barlavento look down on the more negroid Sotavento people. A Santiago man, for example, would be very carefully vetted indeed before he was allowed to marry into a family from São Nicolau. . . . The people of Santiago and its neighboring appendage of Maio are the negroes of the Islands, and as such are looked down upon by their 'mestiço' neighbors, who call them . . . good-for-nothings."[9]

One Capeverdean woman in New England recalls that her light-skinned foster parents in the Islands hid her when visitors came because she was dark. David Baxter, in a study of New Bedford's Capeverdean community a few years ago, found this picture essentially confirmed. Also, he reports, the relatively light-skinned immigrants from Brava Island are referred to by other Capeverdeans as *batateiros*, "potato growers"; both groups use the disparaging epithet *nhambobo*, "yam grower," for immigrants from the Azores (where the sweet potato, alias yam, is a staple!), and by extension even for Madeirans and Continentals there. In California, a native of Brava Island in that state tells us, light-skinned Capeverdeans anxiously avoid contact with dark-skinned ones—not only because of the race problem in the United States but, to some extent, at least, also as a reflection of attitudes existing back in the islands.[10]

While a certain amount of race prejudice, or more specifically a status differential placing the light-skinned above the dark-skinned, is thus attested for the Cape Verde Islands (and, from the same root cause, for Portugal proper as well as Brazil), there can be no question but that in the United States the issue of skin color became considerably sharpened for immigrants from the Cape Verde Islands (until recently a Portuguese colony, relatively close to the status of an overseas province). And since Capeverdeans in the United States tended to categorize themselves to outsiders as Portuguese (rather than as Capeverdeans or as "Creoles"), this issue of skin color also acquired a very personal significance for the non-Capeverdean Portuguese immigrants who wanted to avoid being considered nonwhite. Official American census statistics have used the distinction between white and nonwhite Portuguese; but this distinction, somewhat questionable in itself, naturally tended to get blurred for the population at large, for the reasons stated above (see pp. 113-14). Thus there was the possibility of incidents like the one reported in the press in the early 1920s: During a melée following a soccer game between the (Portuguese-American) Lusitania team of Cambridge and an Irish team, a blond woman yelled at a Portuguese woman (who was just as fair-complexioned as the former): "You g . . . Negroes!" The Portuguese woman promptly reacted by slapping her in the face.[11]

During most of the period of Portuguese immigration, therefore, in southeastern New England as well as in central California, and perhaps occasionally in Hawaii, relations between the mass of "white" settlers and their Capeverdean compatriots have been more distant and cool than could be explained on the basis of "bairrismo" alone. For instance the Portuguese Continental Union, the largest Portuguese-American fraternal society in the East, refused to admit Capeverdeans to membership until 1959. (It is true that until 1931 the same society also excluded Azoreans and Madeirans, admitting only Continentals. . . .) "The Capeverdean colony [in New England] lives completely isolated," noted Eduardo de Carvalho, Portuguese consul at Boston in the 1920s.[12] Describing the population of Providence, Rhode Island, shortly after World War I, Shippee noted "the well-defined division between white and colored Portuguese. . . . These two groups . . . refuse to mingle in their colonies, although in Providence these colonies are adjoining."[13] In September 1932 the press reported a protest meeting against the exclusion of the Capeverdean colony in Providence from participating in a local celebration of the five-hundredth anniversary of the discovery of the Azores.[14]

In 1948, during a public meeting at the Sport Club Português in Newark, New Jersey, the present author witnessed the reluctance with which the representative of a Capeverdean club was seated on stage among delegates of various Portuguese-American organizations. Similarly, in 1962, during field interviews at Sacramento, California, this writer was told by white Portuguese that the Capeverdeans in that area "are just very different," "not really Portuguese," "no good to do business with." On the other hand, according to Francis Rogers, the new (post-1958) Continental and Azorean immigrants reject racial bigotry and want to draw the Capeverdeans here into the overall "Portuguese" community.[15] (But in the meantime, the Cape Verde Islands have severed their political tie to Portugal. . . .)

Speaking of the longtime cleavage between "Bravas" (as Capeverdeans are popularly known in New England) and the "white" Portuguese immigrant population, we also recall the concern of Portuguese settlers in Hawaii about their relation to the local "Haole" (Anglo white) population. In the continental United States, it was the presence of Capeverdeans that posed the principal (although not sole) threat to the "white" status of Portuguese ethnics; but in Hawaii, it was the fact of one's being a non-Anglo plantation laborer in close association with Asiatic laborers, and eventually the growing incidence of mixed marriages between Portuguese and non-Haole that seems to have been perceived as such a threat by some.

As of 1910, the bylaws of the Sociedade Portuguesa de Santo

António in Honolulu stipulated that membership was open to men of Portuguese descent, "except those whose father or mother is of Asiatic race." In 1902 an amendment to the bylaws of this same mutual-aid society had been proposed to the effect that membership should also be open to sons of a Portuguese mother and an Asiatic father, but this had been voted down. In 1922 membership was extended to include women (not only men) of Portuguese descent; and according to the 1951 edition of the bylaws of Saint Anthony's, "all persons of Portuguese descent or Americans of the white race" are admitted. However, in the Sociedade Lusitana Beneficente de Hawaii, the other Portuguese-Hawaiian fraternal organization of the period, membership was open to "all Portuguese regardless of color or nativity" as early as 1916.[16]

To return once more to the Capeverdeans: for a long time their position within American society was complicated by the fact that, like most colored immigrants from the West Indies, they felt even less at home with American blacks than with whites; all the more they (even the second generation) preferred to call themselves Portuguese, rather than Americans (as this might equate them with United States blacks). At one time, American blacks in the San Francisco Bay area would disparagingly call the Capeverdeans there "whites." A study of New Haven, Connecticut, in the 1930s found that the "Portuguese Negroes" kept aloof from American blacks although mingling with immigrants.[17] But in the wake of World War II, and with the civil-rights movement of the 1960s, the attitude of Capeverdeans in the United States (now mostly second generation) changed to closer identification with American blacks—and with Africans.[18]

Of very little importance in a numerical sense is the division of some Portuguese immigrant communities into Catholics and Protestants, since Protestant denominations never won over more than a minute percentage of the total group (with the exception of those Madeirans in Illinois). But it is worth pointing out that these Protestants, particularly prior to the growing up of a broadly Americanized second generation and the incidence of intermarriages (usually interethnic rather than interreligious), stood out as a rather determined faction. Calling themselves simply *cristãos*, "Christians," implying that Catholics are non-Christians, they moved away from the immigrants' cultural traditions and toward a new communal identity more rapidly than the Catholic majority. Another small "faction" generally keeping aloof from the mass of

Portuguese immigrants consists of well-educated upper-class Portuguese engaging in business or a profession, in New York or other cities.

Along a different dimension, already implied in some of the foregoing, there have been the inevitable cleavages, found in all ethnic groups, between relatively well-established, more or less assimilated "old-timers" on the one hand and "greenhorn" recent immigrants on the other—ultimately, between immigrants and American-born descendants. For instance, in Hawaii, by the turn of the century, the old-timers from the western Azores and Cape Verdes who had been residents since whaling days were quite a distinct element from the Madeirans and Michaelese brought in as plantation labor more recently.[19] At San Leandro, California, about the same time, the relatively assimilated longtime Portuguese residents resented the influx of "poor and foreign" Portuguese migrants from Hawaii, and derided them as "Kanakas" (an old term for indigenous Hawaiians).[20] In New England at the present time, many Portuguese-Americans from the older immigration period tend to scorn the new immigrants as embarrassing greenhorns, who should be interested in quick Americanization rather than in bilingual education programs.[21]

In general, then, "Portuguese" immigrants and their American-born children have been going through a change of identity labels, a change in their sense of belonging to a particular community, a redefinition of what constitutes "we" as against "they." For many of those arriving from the Azores or from other areas controlled by Lisbon, the fact of being officially classified as Portuguese, regardless of what particular island or province or parish they grew up in, and the fact of coming into close contact with fellow immigrants from different Portuguese regions, was a kind of jolting experience. Slowly—very slowly, in many cases—there developed a growing conscience of Portuguese nationality, in competition with or superimposed upon a person's allegiance to his more specific "home town."

In the area of language, in particular, this also involved becoming more conscious of a national language standard, of standard Portuguese (roughly corresponding to Lisbonese) as against non-standard regional varieties or dialects such as the popular speech of São Miguel or of the Algarve or of Madeira—let alone the Creole dialect (practically a separate language) of Capeverdeans. Now, in their new country of residence, these immigrants were simply called

"Portuguese" (perhaps even white versus colored Portuguese, or at best hyphenated Azorean-Portuguese, etc.), in their interaction with "Americans." For the Capeverdeans this was particularly difficult, on the grounds already explained. (Some of the latter were even confronted with the necessity of learning two new languages, not only one: not merely English, but also standard Portuguese, on top of their native Creole.)

To many Portuguese immigrants, American-born children of Portuguese parents were and are "Portuguese," whereas those of non-Portuguese foreign parentage are simply "Americans." The same kind of observation would undoubtedly apply to other ethnic groups in this country. On the other hand, of course, American-born children of Portuguese immigrants tend to stress their American identity. Ultimately, then, there arises the problem of the hyphenated "Portuguese-American." (More generally, indeed, what is the meaning of the hyphen to any hyphenated American? In a sense, we are all hyphenated this or that, members of subgroups down to the family level, an array of overlapping, superimposed, hierarchically ordered identity labels.)

The point has recently been made by David Handler that what new Portuguese immigrants gradually adapt to is not really American culture, but Portuguese-American culture (including, at a very early stage of adaptation, Portuguese-American speech, which includes many Anglicisms). There is no uniform American culture; rather, Handler observes, a certain amount of "ethnicity," of variations corresponding to different cultural ancestries, is built right into American culture.[22] Eduardo de Carvalho made a similar point in the 1920s, namely, that Portuguese immigrants, during a transitional stage, develop a new kind of allegiance that may be termed "colonialism," i.e., not a love of the old country, but of the "colony," the Portuguese-American community—a community which at times represents a piece of the old fatherland but at other times is like a former colony now emancipated and separate.[23]

At any rate, we can agree that before a Portuguese immigrant (or any kind of immigrant) comes to identify himself as an American, he usually develops a sense of belonging to his immigrant community, or rather, since this soon includes his American-born children and perhaps even grandchildren, a sense of belonging to his "hyphenated" or "ethnic" community. But this presupposes a close clustering of immigrants from the same country or even from the same native region in a delimited space (such as New Bedford, or

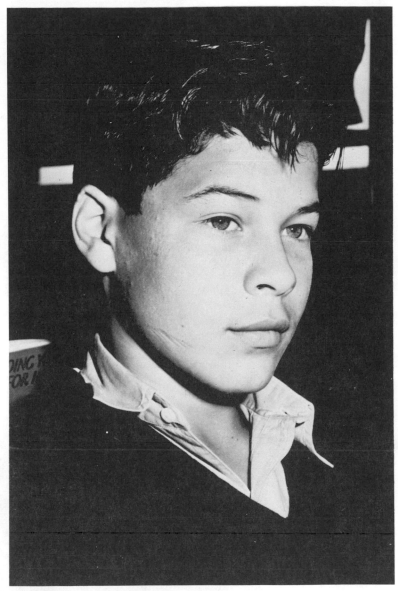

School boy of Portuguese parentage, San Leandro, 1950.

the San Francisco Bay area), permitting face-to-face contacts and, usually, a sharing of such institutions as the immigrant church, the clubhouse, and the neighborhood grocery which sells old-country foods.

II Mutual-Aid, Social, and Civic Organizations

Like other immigrant groups, and partly in specific imitation of what other such groups were doing, the Portuguese who settled in the United States lost very little time in organizing themselves for minimal economic assistance in case of emergencies, as well as for religious and/or secular socializing. Most obvious was the need for some mutual aid—particularly financial, but also emotional—in cases of sickness and death. Equally essential were organized opportunities for exchanging information, joint deliberation, and companionship. Because of the high degree of illiteracy, immigrants depended heavily on the oral face-to-face distribution of news, as had been the case in the home village; nevertheless, enterprising literate individuals also soon provided immigrant newspapers for the minority able to read. Religious services in Portuguese, eventually within churches built by the Portuguese immigrants themselves, had to await the approval of the Catholic hierarchy and the availability of Portuguese-speaking clergy.

As the various immigrant institutions characterized by use of the Portuguese language grew and developed, they amalgamated in varying degree cultural traditions of the homeland, facilities fulfilling specific needs of immigrants (such as instruction in language, American citizenship, ethnic self-assertion), and features borrowed from the new mainstream culture. These institutions were thus important vehicles and reflections of the transformation of Portuguese immigrants into Portuguese-Americans—Americans.

Modern mutual-aid societies started in Portugal around 1850, but their predecessors can be traced back at least as far as the fifteenth century. There was an upswing in the number of modern mutual-aid societies around the year 1900, chiefly on the mainland, with several hundred to several thousand members each, distributed over one town or a cluster of small towns, paying regular premiums for sick and death benefits. In the Azores, there were as of 1909 sixteen mutual-aid societies and fifty charitable institutions; there was a similar number in Madeira. By 1933, when Portugal was a fascist-type corporate state under the dictatorship of Salazar, mutual-aid societies in that country had a total membership of about 570,000 persons.[24] Nevertheless, it may be true, as has been claimed, that Portuguese emigrants generally had no interest or experience in "joining," in cooperative association, for mutual insurance or other purposes, until after they had settled in the new country and observed the example of other immigrant nationalities.

In the United States the first Portuguese mutual-aid society was founded as early as 1847, by a group of (former) sugar plantation workers near New Orleans (see pp. 24-25). The second such society was the Sociedade Portugueza de Beneficencia de Massachusetts, organized in 1866 at Boston; by 1872 it had over 400 members, and not untypically already had a local competitor in the Sociedade de Beneficencia, Instrução e Recreio União Lusitana, founded in 1871 (complete with music band).[25] In California, the Portuguese fraternal movement had its start in 1868, when the Associação Portuguesa de Beneficiencia de California was formed by Azoreans in San Francisco, in direct imitation of the organization set up in Boston two years earlier. Within a few days, a quarrel over the admission of a crippled fellow-settler produced a splinter group, under the leadership of a barber turned dentist, taking the name Associação Protectiva. But in 1871 the two rival factions reunited, under the new name Associação Portuguesa Protectiva e Beneficente; soon this society had several branches or subordinate "councils" in different communities around the state, establishing a "federate" pattern.[26]

In chronological order there followed the Associação Portugueza da Santissima Trindade de Beneficencia at Erie, Pennsylvania, organized by two dozen Madeiran families in 1874; unique in its isolated location and longevity, this small society was still functioning with its own clubhouse in the 1960s. In Hawaii, the Sociedade Portugueza de Santo António was established in 1877 by some early settlers who had been whalers; but it only really got off the ground after the arrival of the first groups of plantation laborers.[27]

For an example of the financial protection and other provisions of such societies in earlier days, we can cite the União Portuguesa do Estado de California, chartered in 1880 at San Leandro. Members (all male) were assessed $1 for each member's death, and 50 cents for the death of a member's wife. In 1892 this was amended to a fixed death benefit of $1,400 per member, $400 when the wife predeceased a member. (Wives were not admitted to membership, with voting rights, until 1952.) From time to time there were special collections for charity, to aid needy members and particularly for disaster relief in the Azores or in the United States. Sick benefits could be added to death benefits by individual local lodges ("councils"). An annual convention for delegates of the lodges was instituted in 1887, when there were four such subordinate units; their number rose to about 150 by 1918. An increasingly important feature of the annual conventions was a certain amount of pageantry including the UPEC band, drill teams, and officers parading on foot or on horseback in colorful Portuguese-style uniforms.[28]

For another example, take the Sociedade Portugueza de Santo António, of Honolulu. The original bylaws of 1877 state as its purpose the subsidizing of sick or disabled members; arranging burials and dispensing death benefits; promoting high moral and intellectual standards among the Portuguese of Hawaii. Members were assessed a regular quota of $1 per month, plus $1.50 a month for death benefits. They had to attend funerals of members, and heed the doctor's orders when sick. Sick members unable to work received $1.25 a day and free medical treatment—unless disability was related to drunkenness or venereal disease. The death benefit amounted to as many dollars as there were members. (By 1951 the sick benefit had dropped to $1 a day, and the death benefit ranged from $150 to $750.)

The association at Erie, according to its constitution of 1891 (drawn up in both Portuguese and English), provided not only sick benefits ($5 per week) and funeral expenses ($40 for members, $20 for wives) but also accident insurance for members who as sailors might suffer shipwreck (on Lake Erie?). Apart from funeral expenses for a deceased member, each surviving member was to contribute $1 to his widow if she had a good moral reputation, otherwise to his children or parents, or to have Mass said for his soul. Members were fined 25 cents for failing to attend meetings (which were to be conducted in Portuguese) or for leaving the meeting place without permission, and $1 for failing to attend a funeral or procession. As of 1962, meetings at Erie were being conducted in English; the clubhouse was open to "non-Portuguese," but only "Portuguese" men were eligible for sick and death benefits.

The Sociedade Cabo Verde was organized at San Francisco in 1914 to pay sick benefits ($7 per week) to Capeverdean men in that area, all members also being obligated to visit the sick, to attend a fellow member's funeral, and to contribute $1 for the death benefit. Meetings, according to the constitution, were to follow a "ritual" which prohibited discussion of religious matters. Members divulging "secrets" of the society would be fined $10, or even expelled.

This last point reminds one of Masonic practices; and indeed, in California all kinds of fraternal societies have leaned toward Masonic-style ceremonials, perhaps because there were many Masons among the Gold Rush companies. Portuguese mutual-aid societies in California generally followed this trend, too, to a greater extent than those in the East, in order to attract members and to compete with other population groups.[29] Such ritualistic features included the use of secret passwords by which members would gain admission to meetings, and the way members would address each other as brothers or as sisters. Officers of the "supreme council" (central committee) and of subordinate lodges were given such Masonic titles (and corresponding ceremonial functions) as "Marshal," "Inside Guard," "Outside Guard." This was true not only of the UPEC, but also of the equally statewide Irmandade do Divino Espirito Santo (IDES, founded in 1889 at Mission San Jose) and the Sociedade Portuguesa Rainha Santa Isabel (SPRSI, founded in 1898 at Oakland, for women).

Because the Holy See had forbidden Catholics to join Masonic and similar secret orders, adherence to such quasi-Masonic rituals aroused some initial opposition in Portuguese ranks. Early in 1887 a Portuguese priest in California warned in the immigrant newspaper at San Francisco against losing one's soul to Satan by joining a Masonic society, as its meetings were devoted to secret orgies, etc. This alarmed the wives of some UPEC members so much that another Azorean-born priest of more liberal persuasion, Fr. G. S. Gloria (who later left the priesthood to get married, and who became the prime poet of the California Portuguese), thought up the idea of composing a hymn extolling patriotism and religion, and having that hymn added to the UPEC ritual. This reassured the ladies of the community about the orthodoxy of their husbands' fraternal activities.

The same kind of suspicion also beset the early days of the IDES, although its avowed principal purpose, besides mutual aid, was the annual celebration of the Holy Ghost festival; to combat the suspicion, in 1898 it became compulsory for members of the IDES Supreme Council to attend mass prior to their meetings. In 1908, similarly, two lodges of the Ancient Order of Foresters which were composed entirely of Portuguese in Hawaii and in California had to defend themselves against accusations of anti-Catholicism. However, in the wake of World War II if not before, most of the Portuguese fraternal lodges in California and elsewhere dropped the earlier rituals for initiating new members and the like.[30]

Other aspects of the earlier Portuguese immigrant societies—state or nationwide fraternals as well as some local clubs—which have undergone limited change in the course of the twentieth century are regionalism and male predominance. For example, the União Portuguesa Continental dos Estados Unidos (UPC for short), now the only major nonlocal mutual-aid society in the East, headquartered in Massachusetts (over fifty lodges there and elsewhere), and originally an offshoot of the União Portuguesa Continental da California, admitted only men from Continental Portugal in its early years. In 1931 the membership base was broadened to include all white Portuguese (including Azoreans, Madeirans, women—but not nonwhite Capeverdeans).

The Real Associação Autonómica Micaelense de Massachusetts (1895–1936), which in its heyday had some fifty branches spread from the East to California and Hawaii, and which in 1904 had received from King Carlos of Portugal the privilege of calling itself *real*, "royal," was open only to men born on the Island of São Miguel and to their descendants. As a matter of fact, the stated major purpose of the association, beyond supplying modest sickness and death benefits, was to promote the cult of Santo Cristo, an image revered in São Miguel. But the successor of this association (which was wiped out in the East by the Depression), the Irmandade do Senhor Santo Cristo de Socorros Mortuários, founded in 1937 in Alameda County, offered membership to any Portuguese regardless of place of origin.[31]

At the same time, the Madeirans have clung to some exclusive organizations of their own: the Associação Protectora União Madeirense da California, founded in Oakland in 1913, but with branches spreading into New England and Hawaii; by 1964 it was nontraditionally headed by a woman, the American-born daughter of one of the founders. . . . Also, organized in New Bedford in 1920, there is the Associação Protectora União Madeirense de Massachusetts. Some old and some new organizations are inevitably limited to Capeverdean membership (covering one or several states, as in the case of the now-extinct Liga Fraternal Caboverdeana, with branches throughout New England, or just local, e.g., the Associação Caboverdeana Santo António in Providence). Capeverdeans were generally not admitted to (other) Portuguese immigrant societies, so had no choice but to stick to *bairrismo.* Regionalism is still very evident with a number of local clubs, devoted more to socializing than to mutual insurance; for instance, the Centro Madeirense in Newark, the Clube Santo Cristo in Cambridge, and the old Clube Dramático Continental in Lowell.

The "home-town spirit," an extension of one's concern for kin and neighbors, has naturally permeated many special charity drives organized by Portuguese-American organizations, newspapers, or ad hoc committees. A newspaper appeal to natives of Corvo in California yielded $1,000 for victims of a shipwreck off Corvo Island. The Coimbra Club in Providence collected twenty-five tons of clothing for the poor in the city of Coimbra. A benefit dance among immigrants from São Jorge around Gustine, California, netted funds to repair the roof of a church on that island. California settlers from Santo Amaro parish, Pico Island, contributed $1,300 to restore the high altar in Santo Amaro's church. Terceirans in New England and California joined hands to send $8,000 to charity institutions on Terceira. Capeverdeans in the United States dispatched $10,000 worth of foodstuffs to the famine-stricken Cape Verde Islands. Natives of Murtosa in Newark provided X-ray equipment for the Misericórdia (hospital for the poor) in Murtosa.

On a larger and periodic scale, the Madeiran Day (instituted in 1934 and still observed annually, with picnics and entertainment) collected contributions in the East, and later also in California, for charity institutions on Madeira. This soon also whipped the sons and daughters of other islands into action. A Dia Faialense was started in 1947, yielding charity money for Faial, as well as for neighboring Pico, Flores, and Corvo. Not to be left behind, the annual Dia Terceirense sent proceeds of its festivities to Terceira, São Jorge, and Graciosa. A Dia Micaelense to benefit São Miguel also entered the calendar of events for a while.[32]

That immigrant fraternal societies and clubs have been primarily men's business, with the women playing a subordinate or no role, is a perfectly natural reflection of the traditional function of the man as the "bread-winner" and, in a formal sense, as the family's principal decision-maker, etc. However, in the American environment and particularly in the East, a large proportion of Portuguese immigrant women have also actually acquired, and are just now performing, the role of bread-winners through outside employment. Moreover, the restructuring of the family and the logical implications of individualistic democracy have gradually led American society toward some equalization (uniformization?) of sex roles; this development was bound to rub off also on the foreign-born, and certainly on children of immigrants. Women's clubs had their beginnings in Boston and New York about 1868; thirty years later, there were 800 of them, with 100,000 members in twenty-one states, stressing self-education and local civic activities.[33]

Among the New England Portuguese about the year 1898, there were eighteen mutual-aid societies (counting individual lodges of multiple-lodge fraternals); two of these were for women members. In 1912 the number of these associations or lodges in New England had risen to about thirty-five, eleven of which were exclusively for women.[34] In that year, the Associação de Socorros Mutuos das Damas Portuguezas in New Bedford suffered a secession over the issue of whether or not to have a chaplain. . . .[35] In Honolulu as early as 1892, there was a Portuguese Ladies Society.[36] But California provided the principal forum for the rise of women's voices— despite the relatively conservative rural setting:

In 1901 the Sociedade Portuguesa Rainha Santa Isabel (SPRSI) was born in Oakland to promote Portugese culture, charity, the Catholic faith, and to pay benefits in case of death or illness; as of 1960, it had nearly 14,000 members in 158 "councils." Also in 1901, a competing women's society was set up under the name União Portuguesa Protectora do Estado da California (UPPEC), for charity and mutual life insurance; in the 1960s it had grown to 9,000 members in 102 councils; and, in a reverse twist of the widespread existence of women's auxiliaries within male-dominated organizations, this society now also admits men as "social members."[37] In 1938 the *Jornal Português* in Oakland could write; "The Portuguese woman has replaced man in community life." And the *Diário de Notícias* in New Bedford echoed a few years later: "The Portuguese organizations in the U.S., weakened by the Depression, have been saved by their women's auxiliaries, who create new income by arranging for festivals and entertainments.[38]

A dilution of Portuguese tradition or ethnicity, equivalent to some degree of "Americanization," can be seen not only in the rise of women's societies and auxiliaries, but also in the fact that a number of Portuguese immigrants (and their children to a greater extent) have joined essentially Anglo or at least non-Portuguese fraternal associations. Mention has already been made of the two lodges of the Ancient Order of Foresters, in California and Hawaii, composed of Portuguese ethnics.[39] For another more recent example, at Ludlow, Massachusetts, Portuguese set up a branch of the Knights of Columbus; and the local Unity Club has a mixed Portuguese and non-Portugese membership. The second generation, of course, freely joins all kinds of ethnically neutral social clubs and fraternals. On the other hand, the rise of intermarriages has introduced the presence of non-Portuguese elements into Portuguese-American organizations. More important and more surprising, many non-Portuguese in California (including former Governor and Chief Justice Earl Warren) joined Portuguese fraternal societies on purely business grounds, particularly early in this century: these fraternals had a reputation of low premiums and safe management. For instance, as of 1918, 1,295 out of 10,844 members (c. 12 percent) of the IDES were not of Portuguese descent.[40]

Emphasizing the function of socializing and entertainment, rather than mutual aid in emergencies, there have been and continue to be a large variety of local clubs, meeting on their own or rented premises. Most of these Portuguese clubs are found in the urban centers of the East; in California, this function is largely performed by the lodges of the statewide mutual-aid societies, and by ad hoc committees organizing annual festivals and picnics. About 200 such clubs were counted in the early 1950s, between thirty and forty in New Bedford alone (with a factionalistic splintering effect in this large community). They have been greatly revitalized by the arrival of thousands of new immigrants in more recent years.

Not counting the local association at Erie, the earliest—but shortlived—instances of this type of organization may have been two "literary" clubs founded in 1880, in Boston and Philadelphia, respectively, on the occasion of the three-hundredth anniversary of the death of Camões, Portugal's top literary figure.[41] Two years later, the Monte Pio Luso-Americano in New Bedford, still extant, had its beginning. In 1899, for some unrecorded reason, it received from President McKinley the unique privilege of flying the Portuguese flag from its building without at the same time displaying the American flag.[42] An example of a particularly well-endowed club is the Sport Club Português in Newark, founded by Continentals in 1921, now with over 1,000 members including women. It has a large, modern building, also utilized by other organizations in that city, including a spacious auditorium for stage performances and dances, a band, a drama group, a soccer team, a Boy Scouts unit, etc.; in 1936 a Portuguese-language school was added. Some of the clubs, trying to stress educational objectives, have minute libraries besides the inevitable bar and game room.

Drama, folklore, and musical groups, keeping alive some of the old cultural heritage, connected with one or the other club or fraternal society or else independent, were of some importance earlier in the century; but they went into a decline after the 1920s with the rise of the second generation and the availability of such new forms of entertainment as phonograph records, the movies (including the occasional showing of Portuguese films), radio, and finally television.[43] On the other hand, the presentation of Portuguese popular songs and instrumental music by amateurs or semi-professional performers received a new lease on life from the Portuguese-language radio programs starting in the 1920s. These programs of modest quality, broadcast over local stations in southeastern New England and in central California, continue to the present day, supplying a mix of local community news, some news from Portugal, commercials, and folkloric entertainment.

The first such program was heard in 1922 over a station in New Bedford, with California following a few years later. Actually this type of Portuguese immigrant institution experienced a much fuller development in California than in the East or in Hawaii, including the formation of auxiliary radio clubs (which in turn provided for socializing). Several of the California programs became daily ones; most of those in New England were limited to weekends, until very recently. As of 1959, there were still some ten daily programs on the West Coast, but only one daily program along with a dozen weekly ones in New England. (Inversely, at the time there was a daily Portuguese-language newspaper along with one or two weeklies in the latter area, but only one weekly newspaper in California.) As August Vaz puts it, in California, radio together with the automobile has ended the rural isolation of previous decades.[44] The latest development along these lines, incorporating the possibilities of the former drama and folkloric groups, is the appearance of Portuguese-language programs on television once or twice a week in Connecticut.

Finally, besides setting up associative mechanisms for emergency financial assistance and general fraternizing, Portuguese immigrant communities have made limited cooperative efforts of a civic-political and educational nature. The prevailing motivation in this is to improve one's socioeconomic position through greater political leverage, which in turn depends to some extent on a more advanced educational level. At the same time, among the foreign-born not yet deeply rooted in this country some political activity has been, and again currently is, oriented toward conditions in Portugal. For example, the Club Republicano Português in New Bedford, founded in 1911 in the wake of the fall of the Portuguese monarchy, derives its name from an interest in setting up a republic in Portugal, not in espousing the Republican versus the Democratic side in American politics. There used to be, to counterbalance that club, a Centro Monárchico Portuguez in several New England towns well into the 1920s; and much of the debate and schism in the Portuguese immigrant intelligentsia of those days, spilling over into the newspapers, had to do with monarchy versus (leftist) republic in Portugal, which generally also meant for or against the Church. The change in political interest, related to the rise of the second generation and its profound involvement in World War II, was reflected in part by the appearance of new clubs in the 1940s calling themselves Portuguese-American Servicemen's Club, Portuguese-American Citizen's Club, and the like.

In the first period of mass immigration, several clubs and societies were formed in New England to advise newcomers and to help them become American citizens. For example, a Naturalization Club was formed by voters in the small farming community on Martha's Vineyard as early as the turn of the century.[45] During World War I, there existed a Portuguese Immigrants' Protective Society in Providence.[46] A Portuguese-American Civic League was founded in Massachusetts in 1913 and was reorganized in 1928, to grow to thirty-two local branches by 1944. A Portuguese Civic League was organized in neighboring Rhode Island soon thereafter.[47] To promote the study of the Portuguese language and culture in the United States (i.e., for ethnic self-assertion), a Portuguese Educational Society was set up in New Bedford in 1944, followed by a Luso-American Education Foundation in 1963. In 1966, a new Luso-American Federation came into being in New England, for the dual purpose of helping new Portuguese immigrants to adjust to American life and to encourage Portuguese-American youths through scholarships to go on to higher education.

In California, a Portuguese-American League was founded at Oakland in 1911 to promote naturalization and entry into local politics. (In that same year also, the first Portuguese-American was elected to the California state assembly). But that organization was shortlived, and nothing further happened along those lines until the creation of the League of Portuguese Fraternal Societies of California in 1937. This League proceeded to finance Portuguese-American representation in the 1939 Golden Gate Exposition, including purchase of a monument to Cabrillo (see Chapter 1), and in 1942 raised some $10,000 to donate two antiaircraft guns to the United States Armed Forces, "as a sign of Portuguese-American solidarity with this country then fighting World War II."[48] This is a perfect example of ethnic self-assertion.

Separate from the League, and about the same time, a chain of Cabrillo Civic Clubs started forming itself to promote the commemoration of the Portuguese discoverer of California and to foster naturalization among the Portuguese immigrants in the state. In recent years a further activity of these Cabrillo clubs, joined together under a grand council in the fashion of the mutual-aid fraternals, has been to grant college scholarships to deserving Portuguese-American youngsters.[49] Apart from these specific organizations, a certain amount of civic education, i.e., of initiation into democratic political processes, has been performed indirectly by the above-mentioned mutual-aid societies; for it is at their local council meetings and statewide conventions that many Portuguese immigrants, unaccustomed to participation in governmental processes in their country of birth, have learned parliamentary procedures and the holding of public office, etc.[50] The same is true on a much smaller scale of some mutual-aid and social organizations in the East.

In Hawaii, where several Portuguese had attained positions in Territorial government early in the century, Portuguese fraternal societies went out of business shortly after World War II. However, several Portuguese civic clubs came into existence in the 1930s and were weakly joined together in 1940 as the Associated Portuguese Welfare Association, to promote "good citizenship," employment leverage, the college education of youngsters—and official inclusion of the Portuguese ethnics in the Caucasian (Haole) "racial" group.[51] This last goal was indeed accomplished by 1940.

CHAPTER 11

Portuguese Immigrant Institutions
(Continued)

I Churches

FOR THE AVERAGE PORTUGUESE VILLAGER, AND PARTICULARLY FOR THE
people of the Azores, the local (Catholic) church has been a very
vital institution—not entirely or necessarily on religious grounds in
the narrower sense, but as a focal point of social relationship and as
a prop for a whole cluster of cultural traditions. At least until the
abolition of the monarchy early in this century, the parish priest,
practically tenured for life and only weakly supervised by the
bishop, wielded considerable local power, not merely as a spiritual
adviser but as head of the local administrative council. In the
Azores, ecclesiastic authority was (and is) centered at Angra, seat of
the bishop and of the only seminary of the archipelago, subject in
turn to the Patriarch (archbishop) of Lisbon.[1]

The early Azorean immigrants in the United States, once they
were constituted as families and had clustered together in some
number, soon felt the need for a sacerdotal figure to conduct
services in the Portuguese language and to assist in the observance
of such regional traditions as the annual Holy Ghost festival. In the
absence of a Portuguese-speaking Catholic priest, to attend Catholic
services in an Irish or Spanish or "nonethnic" neighborhood might
only increase one's sense of alienation. (Or one might even prefer to
identify with a Portuguese-speaking Protestant minister, as happened in many cases of conversion in Bermuda, Hawaii, Newark,
and Fall River.[2]) The ultimate ambition was to have one's own
church building; but whereas in prerepublican and again in Salaza-
rian Portugal one could depend on a state-supported church for

funding, in the United States the immigrants had to build and support their churches at their own expense.[3]

Moreover, in accordance with Canonic law, the churches erected or purchased with the immigrants' own money would become the property of American bishoprics, and might be deethnicized or even turned over to other ethnic groups at an American bishop's discretion. This occasionally caused serious friction. In 1884 a group of Azorean settlers in Gloucester, Massachusetts, bought land to build what was going to be their Church of Our Lady of Good Voyage (a fitting invocation for a fishing colony). But they did so for their own account instead of in the name of the Archbishop of Boston, and the resulting dispute had to be settled in court. After the turn of the century, the Portuguese in Bristol, Rhode Island, although twice as numerous there as the Irish, had to attend the local Irish church for a long time because the bishop at Providence refused their requests for a Portuguese church; they only got their way after a new bishop took over, in 1913.

Shortly after World War I the Portuguese community at West Warwick, Rhode Island, having failed for years to get the bishop's permission to set up their own parish, went ahead anyway and built a church against his will. The bishop, of Irish extraction, countered by refusing to bless the new church and to appoint a pastor. A public interethnic row ensued, until an emissary of the Pope "persuaded" the bishop to drop his resistance.[4]

Over the years, Portuguese immigrant communities in New England and California did manage to finance and build a fair number of new Catholic churches (or, in some cases, to purchase old buildings for this purpose). The annual cost of maintenance would now be partly defrayed, in the American fashion, by membership contributions, by benefit affairs such as bazaars, clambakes, dances, and by proceeds from Holy Ghost or other similar celebrations (proceeds which in the Azores and Madeira were used more to assist the poor). Competition between pastor and parishioners over the control of such festivities and their proceeds did sometimes develop.[5] More or less independent from the churches, Holy Ghost brotherhoods and similar fraternal groups have been performing quasi-religious functions as part of the annual festivities in their charge. In California, the statewide IDES and SPRSI fraternal societies, both of them specifically devoted to the organizing of Holy Ghost festivals (apart from mutual insurance), are assisted by a "spiritual moderator" appointed by the Archbishop of San Francisco.

A shortage of Portuguese priests, allegedly due to a reluctance of ecclesiastic authorities in Portugal to appoint personnel to American posts, has been held responsible for delays in the creation of some Portuguese immigrant parishes and for the premature "denationalization" of some churches built with immigrant money. Yet among this relatively small number of Portuguese-born clergy in the United States, one, Humberto S. Medeiros, managed to rise to the rank of Archbishop of Boston, and from there to Cardinal; the other, Stephen Alencastre, to Bishop of Hawaii.

The first Catholic priest who left Portugal to officiate among immigrants in the United States arrived in New Bedford in 1867, followed by a second one in 1869; and by 1875 the newly founded parish of São João Baptista (St. John the Baptist) had its own little church. At about the same time a Portuguese parish was formed in North Boston, and, in 1885, one in Providence.[6] In California, a Portuguese shepherd in the literal sense became the first shepherd in the figurative sense, or to be exact, the first pastor of the first "national" Portuguese church there: one Manuel Francisco Fernandes from Pico Island, employed in sheep-raising and in mining in that state, returned to the Azores in 1877 to study for the priesthood at the Angra seminary, and then was ordained at Santa Barbara. After a few years of missionary work which took him to Hawaii and as far as the Portuguese colony of Macau off the China coast, Fernandes served as assistant pastor at a church in Centerville. Services in Portuguese were occasionally conducted by different priests at San Leandro and at other locations starting about 1880. In 1892, St. Joseph's Portuguese Church in Oakland was completed under the stewardship of Father Fernandes; but this restless man, who also founded a Catholic propaganda weekly, died in the prime of life, and "his" church was turned over to the care of the Salesian Fathers (an Italian order) in 1902.

In Hawaii, the first Portuguese Catholic cleric to appear on the scene was the self-same Father Fernandes. His unannounced arrival in 1889 stirred up a hornets' nest. The well-entrenched Congregation of the Sacred Heart, a Belgian order in charge of things Catholic on the Islands, refused to admit him to the local clergy; a petition by over a hundred local Portuguese to let them erect their own church under Fernandes was rejected by the (ethnically German) bishop. The following year, after Fernandes had sailed on to Macau, three Protestant Portuguese ministers from Illinois showed up at Honolulu and were able to turn the discontent of some of the rebuffed petitioners into conversion. Alarmed, the local

Catholic hierarchy now invited over a few Portuguese priests from California for mission work, ordained Madeiran-born Stephen Alencastre, and had some of the Belgian brethren learn Portuguese to meet the Protestant challenge. No Portuguese-Catholic ethnic church was ever built in Hawaii, although one on Maui Island and one at Honolulu assumed a strongly Portuguese character.[7]

Returning to California: about half a dozen more churches were built there with Portuguese immigrant money, in addition to St. Joseph's in Oakland. Some of them were later handed over to "Irish" or "American" pastors, at least partly due to a shortage of Portuguese-speaking priests (there were only eight of these in the whole state as of 1945, compared to at least forty in New England). St. Joseph's, after having become multi-ethnic (with services conducted in Italian and Spanish as well as in Portuguese and English), was razed in 1965 in connection with urban redevelopment, and this left only two such churches, in San Jose and Scaramento, respectively.[8] In New England, by contrast, there were nineteen Portuguese-built churches as of 1912; and twenty-seven in 1941 (actually thirty, but three became "denationalized" because of a lack of Portuguese priests). Since World War II no less than eight new Portuguese parishes have been established in the East, with their own churches, including three in Connecticut and two in New Jersey.[9] In Fall River, the Portuguese Catholic community still maintains seven different churches, as against three in New Bedford. The separateness of the Capeverdeans is dramatized by the fact that, in New Bedford at least, they have been attending a non-Portuguese church since 1905, most of the time under a Belgian pastor.

All but one of the eight Portuguese churches inaugurated between 1948 and 1973 are called Our Lady of Fatima, alluding to the alleged apparition of the Virgin at Fatima in Portugal, during the First World War.[10] The Portuguese church at San Jose, California, chose *Cinco Chagas* (Five Wounds) for its name; the Five Wounds of Christ are the heraldic symbol of the Portuguese nation. One of the Fall River churches, Santo Cristo, is consecrated to an image worshiped in São Miguel. Architecturally, at least a few of these immigrant churches have Portuguese characteristics. The one in San Jose is partly a replica of a church in Braga, Portugal, and includes Azorean details of style. St. Elizabeth's at Sacramento resembles a church at Angra, Terceira. Our Lady of Fatima in Ludlow has a chapel imitating the Chapel of the Apparitions in Fatima, Portugal.

The present Church of Our Lady of Good Voyage in Gloucester, partly a replica of a structure in Portugal, is famous for its Portuguese-inspired carillon. The Holy Ghost Church near Kula, on Maui Island (Hawaii), built mostly for Portuguese parishioners although apparently never under Portuguese control, is of octagonal shape, suggesting a crown as used in the Azorean Holy Ghost festival. The first Portuguese church in New Bedford (1875), although not the larger one that replaced it later, was built in Azorean style. All Portuguese-American churches contain images of St. Anthony of Lisbon (i.e., born in Lisbon, although better known for the place where he died, Padua) and of Our Lady of the Immaculate Conception (Portugal's patron saint).

While on the subject of churches as Portuguese immigrant institutions, we cannot neglect brief mention of church-related schools. No parochial schools were ever created by the Portuguese in California and Hawaii; but there are several in New England. The oldest one was founded by the Holy Ghost parish in Fall River in 1912. St. Michael's parish in the same city followed suit much later. In New Bedford, both the parish of St. John the Baptist and the one of our Lady of Mt. Carmel opened elementary schools in 1941. These schools were conducted almost entirely in English for many years, rather than as genuine bilingual undertakings. (Bilingual education programs for the new wave of Portuguese immigrant children have recently been set up by public-school systems in southeastern New England and Long Island, as well as in California.) In the wake of World War II, no less than three Portuguese parishes in Rhode Island (at West Warwick, Bristol, and Newport) also inaugurated schools of their own.

As regards the religious organization of the relatively few Portuguese Protestants in the United States, a few words must suffice (in addition to what has been said on pp. 120-21). Strictly speaking, the story begins in the Presbyterian church founded in 1850 for "Madeiran exiles" at Jacksonville, Illinois, and its subsequent offshoots.[11] Apart from that, the first Portuguese Methodist church was organized in New Bedford in 1891, followed by a Baptist one in 1893, and by a second Methodist one in Fall River. By 1935 there were fourteen small missions (chapels) or churches spread over a dozen towns in southeastern New England and in Newark, curiously divided among half a dozen denominations, and totaling perhaps a thousand parishioners. The movement had its growth period from about 1890 into the 1920s, but has pretty much stagnated since then. In California, there have been two small churches in the Oakland area. In the Hawaiian Islands, two Portuguese Protestant Congregations were formed in the early 1890s, at Honolulu and Hilo, growing to about 700 members in the 1920s. Because Catholicism is so deeply embedded in Portuguese cultural tradition, for immigrants to join one or the other Protestant denomination meant in itself a major step of "denationalization," requiring only a small further step for joining an English-speaking American congregation. One may assume, therefore, that between 1920 and the present an undetermined number of Portuguese-Americans have found their religious berth in "Anglo" Protestant churches—just as a good proportion of the Catholic majority has merged into the mainstream of American Catholicism, or into multi-ethnic parishes—or into the fold of the unchurched.

II   Newspapers

Although a marked majority of Portuguese immigrants prior to the 1920s were illiterate or nearly so, the group has included a sufficient number of enterprising individuals with journalistic inclination or ambition (although not necessarily with any special training) to set up and operate several scores of newspaper enterprises. Some of these Portuguese-language newspapers—usually weeklies—have been very shortlived; a few stayed in business for up to half a century. With all their limitations, these periodicals, including a few magazine-type publications, have filled (and continue to fill) a vital need for those immigrants able to read, and through them for those dependent on oral spread of news and commentary. Since the late 1920s, Portuguese-language radio programs (chiefly in California) have joined the newspapers for a small part of the function the latter are trying to perform, i.e., to supply local community news and commercials. Also since the 1920s, the proportion of literates in the Portuguese immigrant population has increased; but this was outweighed, until the onset of the new Portuguese mass immigration in the 1960s, by the dropping number of foreign-born and the preference for English-language media on the part of the second generation.

The first Portuguese-language newspaper founded by immigrants in the United States was the weekly *Jornal de Notícias*, published at Erie, Pennsylvania, from 1877 to 1884 by Flores-born João M. Vicente, who had first settled in Boston after a whaling cruise, and by his brother (or older son?) Antonio. Antonio Vicente moved on to San Francisco in 1884, to found the weekly *Progresso Californiense*, which did not last long. Three years later, with a partner, he established the weekly *União Portuguesa*—which was to remain in publication at Oakland until 1942.[12] In New England, the Portuguese immigrant press may have had its beginning, according to one source, with a paper called *Luso-Americano*, published in Boston and New Bedford from 1881 to 1889.[13] Or else first claim belongs to a paper by the name of *A Civilização*, which appeared in Boston in 1883 or shortly before.[14] At least three other very shortlived publications followed in the early 1890s, as well as three longer-lasting ones; one of these, the *Independente*, survived until the 1940s.

In California, Portuguese journalism was initiated by the *Voz Portuguesa*, a weekly established in 1880 by a Brazilian in San Francisco; it expired after six years.[15] But the anti-Catholic feeling of the 1880s prompted the appearance in 1888 of *O Amigo dos Católicos*; this paper, in which Father Fernandes and at least two other clerics had a hand, became *O Arauto* in 1896 and *O Jornal de Notícias* in 1917.[16] In the Hawaiian Islands, one source only mentions a newspaper called *A Liberdade* founded sometime after 1882; in 1896 it merged with the new *O Luso*, which continued until the 1920s.[17] According to other sources, the first paper in that area was the weekly *Luso Hawaiiano*, which opened shop in 1885 and served the Portuguese community until 1891. It was joined or followed by the *Aurora Hawaiiana* (1889–1891 or later), the *União Lusitana Hawaiiana* (1892–1896 or later), and three more shortlived papers in the 1890s—apart from the more successful *O Luso*.[18]

Thus, in all three major areas of Portuguese settlement in what is now the United States, Portuguese-language weeklies started entering into the communications network of the immigrants in the early 1880s, barely a few years after the onset of mass immigration. After the initial period, many new mastheads appeared after the turn of the century until the 1930s, to add to the variety of papers, to replace defunct ones, or to signify some reorganization. A full listing would make for dry reading.[19] As of 1910–1912, there were seven weeklies of small circulation in New England (two each in Boston, Fall River, New Bedford, and one in Lowell), three in California, and four or five in the Territory of Hawaii.[20] As of 1940 there were four or five in California, eight (including one daily) in New England and in adjoining metropolitan New York—New Jersey, and none in Hawaii. By 1960, what was left over was the daily *Diario de Noticias* in New Bedford (it ceased publication in 1974, after half a century) and one weekly each in New Jersey and California (plus a bimonthly Catholic propaganda paper in New York). On the other hand, the new mass immigration starting in the early 1960s has brought about a temporary revival of the Portuguese immigrant press, in the form of the *Portuguese Times* (written in Portuguese despite its title) in New Bedford, the *Jornal de Fall River*, and two new weeklies in Rhode Island and California.

Here is a characterization of this immigrant press written some thirty years ago:[21]

The Portuguese newspapers [like those of various other immigrant groups] have suffered from . . . poverty, from the relatively low educational and intellectual level of most of their actual and potential readers, from extreme factionalism, and from a scarcity of journalistic talent. There have been few professional journalists; quite a number of newspapers have been published or edited by poorly educated men possessing little journalistic skill and hardly any literary ability.[22] Quite often the functions of publisher, editor, printer, business manager have been united in one person, the whole enterprise being located in a shack-like workshop.[23] In addition to editorials and to other articles and feuilletons (often reprinted from other sources), there are, in varying proportion, news items of different categories: local news, especially about what is going on in the Portuguese-American community; Americana and international developments; news from Portugal. The local news from the various settlements is usually reported by volunteer correspondents domiciled in the different localities; many of them are simple workers without any journalistic background. National and international news is reprinted from the English-language press or is infrequently supplied by news services and direct correspondence. Newspapers received from Portugal furnish the source for local news from that country.

The Portuguese immigrant periodicals vary widely in character, trend and quality, and they have done so in the past. Some have pursued a rather neutral and liberal policy and have been open to discussion of opposing viewpoints. Others—the majority—have been more militantly ideological and representative of certain groups. Some papers have maintained a more literary and impersonal tone, while others have been given to sharp personal polemics.[24]

To further convey the flavor of this kind of journalism, and also to evoke with a few brush strokes the times and places and preoccupations of the people this book deals with, we conclude with a very sketchy content analysis of a few random newspaper issues (a less than representative sample!) that happen to be at hand:

(1) *A Voz Portuguesa*, San Francisco, August 5, 1880 (first issue!): Lead article by the editor-owner, exhorting the California Portuguese to organize for greater political strength, to vote against the Republicans and for the exclusion of Chinese immigrants. Article on Camões (Portugal's poet laureate), reprinted from a Brazilian newspaper. First installment of a serial on the history of Portugal. Miscellaneous local and international news. Advertisements from Portuguese immigrant hostelries in San Francisco and Boston, from quack physicians, etc.

(2) *O Arauto*, Hayward, June 27, 1896: Front-page obituary for Father Fernandes. Six columns of brief news items, mostly about Portuguese individuals and fraternal lodges in California, also New England (real-estate transactions, lodge meetings, farewell to the Irish pastor of Mission San Jose's Portuguese, accidents, theft in Chinatown, court actions, visitors, etc.). Nine columns of foreign news, including five from the Azores, one from Lisbon. Appeal for unity of the Portuguese settlers; bits on their history. Forecast of McKinley election. Serial installments: one page from a book on Portugal's past and present; one page, translation (by the *Arauto's* editor) of a French novel; one page, translation of an English book on Madeira. A visitor's praise of Hayward. Business section (three pp.): produce prices on San Francisco market, ads, list of Portuguese books for sale, etc.

(3) *O Luso*, Honolulu, December 31, 1910 (first three pages only): Front page: photo of Christmas tree outside Honolulu's Executive Mansion. Dynamite attack on a foundry in Los Angeles. Wedding of a Japanese with a white girl (shocking!). Portuguese club in Hilo starts literacy classes for naturalization. Glorious episodes in Portugal's history. Hunger epidemic in China. Lynching attempt in West Virginia. Revolts in Mexico and the Caroline Islands. Train robbery in Peru. Page 2: suicide of Portugal's mint director; a religious parable and poem; elections in Portugal; commercial ads. Page 3: ads; reprint article from a Lisbon paper on proposed change of Portuguese flag.

(4) *O Popular*, New Bedford, January 9, 1919: Long article (reprinted from Lisbon paper) on assassination of Portuguese prime minister. Editorial on question of independence of Azores. Summary of a speech by President Wilson. Departure of commander of United States naval base in Azores. Commercial ads and notices. Local

community news: reports of club meetings and of a talk on naturalization requirements, personals, ads of forthcoming entertainments, etc. Serial installments (a Portuguese novel, translation of a French novel). Brief notice of death of ex-Pres. Roosevelt. List of Portuguese books for sale. News items from Azores, island by island.

(5) *Diario de Noticias*, New Bedford, December 1, 1944: Front page: war news of the day (Europe, Pacific, home front). "Cover girl" pictures of three Portuguese-American girls from Ludlow in WAC uniforms. Installation of Portuguese priest in Fall River. Daily "Points of View" editorial column: salute to Ludlow's Portuguese-American G.I.s. Inside pages: several items on Portugal's Independence Day today (Dec. 1). Minor news, items from Portugal. Three Portuguese-American soldiers wounded. Ads. Separate Fall River page: ads, news of local G.I.s, obituaries. Serial installment (love-and-crime story). More ads, War Bond appeals. Daily column, "The Portuguese in America": personal and fraternal-activities news, sent in by local correspondents (Bethlehem, Wallingford, Valley Falls). Special-issue supplement, 3 pp.: pictures of eighty-three Portuguese-American G.I.s from Ludlow; filler war news.

(6) *Jornal Português*, Oakland, June 28, 1962: Brazil becomes world soccer champion. Portuguese church in Oakland gets new pastor. Benefit whist party, for Portuguese radio program. Many news items from Portugal and colonies (stale, supplied by ANI Portuguese news agency). Schedule of Portuguese film showings in California. Madeiran Day picnic. Expansion of local Port.-Am. factory. Port.-Am. G.I.s feted on Lisbon visit. Picture report on anniversary of (Port.-Am.) pentecost association. Ads, and more ads, focused on California dairy industry. Jackie Kennedy visits India. Serial installments (novels, translated from French, Spanish). Obituaries. Sports news (from Portugal).

(7) *Jornal de Fall River*, Fall River, June 27, 1979: Front-page spread, continued inside: statement by State Senator (a Port.-Am. woman). Port-Am. fashion shop opens in local shopping center. Short story, in English, translated from Portuguese [front-page bait for second-generation readers!]. Editorial salute to high-school graduates. Truckers strike. United States journalist murdered in Nicaragua. Ads. Gasoline shortage. Many local news items (about half of them without specific reference to Portuguese ethnics). Photo essay (2 pp.) on recent local Santo Cristo festival. Sports news special insert (12 pp., including ads), stressing sports events in Port.-

Am. community and in Portugal. Obituaries, births, other Port.-Am. personal news. Women's page (fashion, recipes). Ads.

And so, a century of Portuguese immigrant journalism, feeding its readers a mélange of information and entertainment, and some sense of community.

CHAPTER 12

The Holy Ghost Festival and Other Celebrations

THE "FESTAS" ARE AT LEAST AS CLOSE TO THE HEART OF THE PORTUGUESE as the "fiestas" are to the heart of many Hispanics. R. Gallop writes, with reference to continental Portugal: "All the long year through, an unending succession of religious festivals are held, some of general, some of purely local observance. These 'festas' and 'romarias' are most numerous during the summer months, from May to September. The 'festas' do not differ greatly from the festivities held in other Catholic countries in honor of the patron saint of town, village or parish. More characteristic of Portugal are the 'romarias,' pilgrimages to particular shrines, often remote from human habitation, which attract the faithful from miles around."[1]

In M.F. Smithes's description: "The 'romarias' are annual pilgrimages to some shrine either in a church or chapel on a hilltop, or where a saint is reputed to have performed a miracle." Usually individual prayer in the chapel is followed by a procession around it and by the priest's blessing. In the afternoon there is dancing and courting, for the "romarias" serve at the same time as pleasure outings and religious performances. "Every Sunday," Smithes writes, "there is a 'festa' in some church of the neighborhood. All the afternoon, rockets go up at intervals from the village, and crowds of people come from the neighboring hamlets, and even from the towns. . . . It is a huge picnic party, and when the pilgrimage is over, they [the people] enjoy themselves thoroughly."[2]

In the Azores and on Madeira the "festas" are just as popular as on the continent, if not more so. L. H. Weeks testifies, with some exaggeration: "The Azorean's holidays are all holy days. He has over a hundred Fourth-of-Julys every year, and each one celebrated by a church festival. It becomes impossible for him to conceive of a holiday without its patron saint and procession. All these processions are very much alike, —differing only, according to the day, in the statue that is hauled out from its resting place."[3] And Drexel Biddle reports: "A fête day or a religious celebration—at either of which times there is always a legal holiday—takes place on the general average of once a week throughout the entire year, in Madeira. On these occasions kite flying is indulged in as the principal amusement."[4]

These few quotations from travelers' accounts paint the general background against which we have to view the several festivals still celebrated by the Portuguese immigrants and their descendants in the United States. These festivals have indeed remained one of the salient features of Portuguese-American community life and culture. Their popularity, however, is more marked in southeastern New England and in central California than in the relatively recent settlements of Connecticut, New York, New Jersey, and Pennsylvania.[5] This is not surprising, for in these latter areas the Azorean element, particularly faithful to traditions of this kind, is in the minority.

Actually, the term *festa* as used in the United States has a very broad meaning. It may designate a real festival in the sense of a public religious or secular celebration, usually with an established ritual, recurring at a specific time of the year. But a "festa" may also consist of a modest outing or picnic, or of a little banquet or informal party held in a clubhouse, without any historic background or any special spot in the calendar. Such informal "festas" (less elaborate than what the English term *festival* would indicate) may, of course, be part of a more elaborate celebration; but even by themselves such parties are very popular. Many clubs and societies arrange picnics and outings during the summer months as well as dances, little banquets, or dramatic and musical performances, mostly during the colder season.

As in Portugal, the "religious" festivals celebrated in this country are by no means purely or even predominantly religious, but have an important social and entertainment function. While the old generation assembles for chatting, eating and drinking, and for chamarritas and other folk dances, the younger people love to exhibit themselves in processions and parades and to flock to the "arraial" for some youthful fun or, as several informants put it, "*para namorar-se*" (in order to fall in love, court each other). As to the religious element, some festivals seem to have become even more secularized here than they were in Portuguese territory; for instance, the devotion and religious enthusiasm manifested by most onlookers and participants of processions in the Azores or in continental Portugal are seldom in evidence at a procession in this country. Actually, processions are much less frequent here than in the old country. Instead of parades through the streets, there are often only processions inside the church or around the church grounds. The purely liturgic part of religious celebrations, which does not interest us here, may be considered to be the same in the United States as in Portugal.

I   *The Holy Ghost Festival*

The Holy Ghost festival (*festa do Espirito Santo*) is the most popular and most colorful social-religious event in the Portuguese-American settlements. It is a specific national tradition and has little or nothing to do with the universal Catholic holiday devoted to the Holy Ghost. A relatively detailed treatment of its history and of its present forms is therefore justified.

The Portuguese Holy Ghost festival as celebrated in the United States, which has been considerably transformed in the course of the centuries, is generally traced back to Isabel (Elizabeth) of Aragon, wife of Portugal's poet king Dom Diniz. Isabel has been canonized by the Church and is usually referred to as the Holy Queen. She lives in Portuguese tradition as the prototype of the pious and charitable woman, and various legends have been woven around her since her death in 1326. In the beginning of the fourteenth century, at Alemquer in Portugal, Queen Isabel built a church dedicated to the Holy Ghost, and when this divinely inspired work was completed she instituted a cult called the "Coronation of the Emperor." Out of this cult the ceremonial of the present Holy Ghost festival is said to have grown, at least in its main characteristics. Here is an outline of the original ceremony celebrated at Alemquer, as related by the seventeenth-century historian Correia de Lacerda:[6]

On Resurrection Day (Easter), the man who is to represent the emperor goes to the Church of São Francisco, vested with all the honors and accompanied by the nobility and the people. He has with him two men acting as kings and three pages carrying as many crowns; one of which the Holy Queen had left for this ceremony. On reaching the altar they offer the crowns to God, and a priest in full canonicals deposits one crown each on the head of the emperor and of the kings. Then all set out in majestic array to join the procession held on that festive morning in honor of Our Lord Christ the Resurrected. In the afternoon the emperor leaves the Holy Ghost Church preceded by trumpeters and other players as well as by two pages carrying the crown of majesty and the rapier of justice respectively, and he goes to the same convent (of São Francisco) to be crowned again. Then bouquets of flowers are distributed among the nobles of his retinue, and the latter dance with some maidens who are in the company of the emperor as his ladies-in-waiting. These maidens are presented with marriage portions and thereafter the emperor with the same array of splendor returns to the Holy Ghost Church. There he offers his crown on the altar, but receives it again from the hands of a priest. Then he sits down on a throne under a canopy, and the noblemen treat him with as much reverence as if his rank were real and not fictitious.

In this form the "império" [empire, i.e., empire festival] is repeated on each of the following Sundays, until the Day of the Holy Ghost (Whitsunday), on the eve of which the emperor leaves the same convent in full pomp, accompanied by a man who carries in his hand two skeins of blessed wax, one extremity of which is left burning on the altar of this church. The procession comes out of the church through the oak door and passes through the streets and with it the skeins of wax extend all the way to the altar of the Church of Our Lady of Triana. There the wax is again rolled up and then placed on the altar, where it burns throughout the following year. The procession now turns to the Holy House of the Holy Ghost, in which the bread and meat to be distributed among the poor on the following day is given the blessing.

Isabel founded this cult, in Lacerda's interpretation, to symbolize the unification of the world under the Portuguese crown, so that there would be only one shepherd and one flock. However, this cult, which spread from Alemquer to Cintra and then all over Portugal,[7] has also been interpreted differently. Thus Walker thinks that it was evidently intended to symbolize the Trinity.[8] Gallop ties the election of an "emperor" to the time when the functions of king and priest were united in one person and he sees a probable connection with the ancient tradition of the "King for a Day."[9] Also Braga delves into the pre-Christian era when he writes: "The festival is a transformation of old polytheistic cults; its introduction or development was connected with the religious ceremonies against the pest."[10]

There are several oral traditions circulating among Americans concerning the origin of the Holy Ghost festival. One usually well informed Azorean-born priest, when questioned by the present author, could not go beyond saying that the festival derives its character from the fact that Isabel was particularly devoted to the Holy Ghost and that she wanted to state an example of charity in the annual distribution of food to the poor. Another informant, a worker born in the Azores, declared that Isabel once vowed to give a meal to the poor and to crown them; but he knew no reason for that vow. A priest from continental Portugal explained that Isabel, while catering to the poor on Whitsunday, used to honor them by putting her crown on a poor man's head. A fourth informant reported that the "emperor" in the festival represented the Holy Ghost and as such distributed meat and bread to the poor, as the holy queen herself had done. A fifth one, also a priest from continental Portugal, stated that the Holy Ghost festival is referred to as the *império* (empire) because it commemorates the rule (empire) of Queen Isabel. One further tradition has it that the coronation ceremony is held in remembrance of the miraculous cures which Isabel performed by placing her crown on the heads of the sick.

Two relatively elaborate additional accounts of the circumstances surrounding the creation of the Holy Ghost festival have been collected among immigrants. The first, heard at Gloucester, is connected with the so-called "miracle of the roses." There was a famine in Portugal, and often the gentle Isabel would smuggle bread out of the palace and distribute it amongst the needy. One day as she was leaving the grounds on her errand of charity, she was stopped by her cruel husband, King Diniz, who demanded to know what she had in the basket. "Roses," she replied, and when her husband opened the basket the bread (the *rosquilhas*, i.e., small loaves of bread in the form of rings) had been transformed into roses. At that moment a dove alighted on the queen's hand, signifying the approval of the Holy Ghost for her deed. The crown used in the ceremonies today is symbolic of this event.[11]

The other story has two variants, heard respectively in Provincetown and Lowell, Massachusetts. According to the first, a famine occurred in Portugal during Isabel's rule. The queen then made a vow: if aid were forthcoming she would place her crown on the poorest family in the land and set a sumptuous dinner before them. Soon thereafter a storm broke out and three ships laden with wheat were hurled up against the shore. The wheat relieved the famine and Isabel fulfilled her promise. According to the second variant, Isabel was just praying for relief from the famine ravaging the land, when suddenly a ship with a cargo of food was thrown ashore. While this was happening, a dove (symbol of the Holy Ghost!) appeared over the crown of the Holy Queen, and therefore the miracle was later on commemorated in the sign of the Holy Ghost. Two Azorean-born priests whom the writer questioned about this food-ship tradition denied ever having heard of it, and one of them added that he did not know of any event, in Isabel's time, in which a dove should have played a role.

The Holy Ghost festival, with the "coronation of the emperor" as its main characteristic, gradually fell into disuse in the greater part of continental Portugal, but became very popular all over the Azores,[12] as attested by the Azorean proverb *A cada canto seu Espírito Santo* (To every corner its Holy Ghost). Indeed every locality in the islands has one or more Holy Ghost brotherhoods entrusted with organizing the festivities in a given district. Historically the *Império dos Nobres* (Empire of the Nobles) celebrated at Ponta Delgada on the island of São Miguel is significant as one predecessor of the present Azorean Holy Ghost festival; it commemorates the miraculous appearance of a little dove which stopped the plague then ravaging the island.

In the western Azores, too, tradition connects the Holy Ghost festivities with the fight against the plague and other natural catastrophies: In the year 1522, when the plague was on Terceira, the city council of Faial vowed to celebrate the Holy Ghost festival in order to arrest the evil; actually the Fayalese escaped the plague, but soon forgot their vow. A volcanic eruption in 1672 was taken as a reminder, and since then the celebration has been faithfully observed.[13] The frequent volcanic eruptions in the Azores together with the extreme poverty prevailing in those islands are considered the main reason why the festival with its charity features has grown such strong roots there. Generally speaking, the modern Azorean form of the festival includes more symbols pointing directly to the Holy Ghost (dove, flag, hymn, etc.) and puts greater emphasis on feeding the poor than did the Alemquer cult.[14]

In the United States the Holy Ghost festival seems to have had its first reenactment at Half Moon Bay in California, where it was celebrated in 1874. An immigrant woman by the name of Rosa Pedro had made a trip to her native island of Corvo, and on her return to California she brought with her a little silver crown. During the first year she kept it in a little chapel in her home, inviting the Portuguese settlers to join her in worship and to spend the rest of the night in singing and dancing. During the weeks immediately preceding Trinity Sunday the crown was transferred to other homes, in each of which the same prayers and frolics were repeated. On Trinity Sunday various offerings were auctioned and the proceeds distributed among the poorest families. Four or five years later a plot of land was acquired for the construction of a "hall," and since that time the Holy Ghost festival has been celebrated every year.[15]

In 1887 a handful of Portuguese farmers around Mission San Jose, encouraged by their pastor, decided to celebrate the Holy Ghost feast; in 1889 they organized the first "council" (lodge) of the Irmandade do Divino Espírito Santo (Brotherhood of the Divine Holy Ghost), a society which, as its name indicates (and as was mentioned in Chapter 10), was founded not only for mutual-aid purposes, but also specifically for the propagation of the Holy Ghost festival.[16] With the expansion of this and similar organizations (Sociedade do Espírito Santo, founded 1895; Sociedade Portuguesa Rainha Santa Isabel, founded 1898) the festival became increasingly popular, thoughout the Portuguese communities in California.

As for New England, there is no record of a Holy Ghost celebration before the turn of the century. There was one at Gloucester, Massachusetts, in 1902 for the first time. In that year a fishing schooner found herself in great peril in a wintry gale. The skipper, Captain Joseph P. Mesquita, started praying and vowed that if he and his crew were spared he would reenact the coronation ceremony instituted by the Holy Queen. The craft did return to port safely, and thereupon Captain Mesquita sent to Portugal for a crown. On Whitsunday the Portuguese settlers in the fishing town filed in procession from the skipper's home to the church, where after Mass the priest set the crown on Captain Mesquita and then in turn on all the members of his crew. After this multiple coronation blessed loaves were distributed among the worshipers, and the captain and his crew returned to their homes and entertained the members of the community. The crown was entrusted to the captain's keeping until the following year, and this same ceremony, with Captain Mesquita as the central figure, was repeated annually until 1931. Since then the Gloucester festival has more closely followed the lines of the traditional ceremonial, with a banquet in the afternoon at the "hall," etc.

By the 1920s, Holy Ghost feasts were regular annual occurrences in all the principal Portuguese settlements in eastern Massachusetts and Rhode Island. They have remained so to this day, receiving renewed impetus from the new mass immigration. In California, there is less of this renewed impetus, and some waning of interest in the event. In Hawaii, where the first celebration of this kind took place in 1891, there were at one time no less than four different Holy Ghost brotherhoods competing with each other in Honolulu alone, with additional celebrations in full splendor on Maui and Hawaii Islands throughout the summer; but by the 1960s the custom had all but disappeared.[17]

As celebrated in New England and California, the festival generally followed Azorean practice. Variants observed from place to place are often due to the fact that the organizers in one locality came from a different Azorean parish or island than those in another. The festivities may be scheduled for any weekend from the week following Easter until the end of July, rarely August or later. In the larger settlements there may be several celebrations following each other, organized by different parishes or clubs. Until the respective weekend of the festival, the crown together with other emblems of the Holy Ghost is kept in the local church, or at the "hall of the Holy Ghost" (a little building usually doubling as clubhouse and tabernacle), or at the home of the *mordomo* (the person in charge of a given celebration for one year).

During the week preceding the festival, the crown is often exhibited on a little altar, for the faithful to gather around it and say the beads in the evenings. (As a variant, seven families chosen by lot may take turns in keeping the crown for one week between Easter and Pentecost, the first of them guarding it for the rest of the year.) A day or two before the festive Sunday, a priest blesses the food donated by parishioners or brotherhood members or by the mordomo himself, for distribution to needy persons or, more often nowadays, for a community banquet on Sunday afternoon. The *arraial* (open-air entertainment, a kind of fair or carnival) may also start one or two evenings prior to the Sunday in question.

An essential part of most Holy Ghost celebrations is the procession on Sunday morning, before the crowning ceremony and / or after it. This procession has as its core emblems of the Holy Ghost (crown, dove, scepter, banner) and the "empress" or "queen" with her retinue wearing the crown or about to receive it in church. There may be all kinds of uniformed groups, including a band, bearers of the American and Portuguese flags, etc. After the service in church, the priest places the crown on the head of the day's celebrity (as a variant, there may be several crowns with several crownees); the worshipers then sing a hymn to the Holy Ghost (usually the Azorean *Alva Pomba*). The subsequent "arraial" may extend from Sunday afternoon until Monday morning, starting with a feast which has as its most traditional ingredients the so-called Holy Ghost soup, meat, and a sweet kind of bread. After the banquet, various donations are auctioned off, with at least part of the proceeds going to the church and / or to the festival organizers. Dancing into the night typically emphasizes, or used to emphasize, the Azorean folk dance called *chamarrita* (so much so that in some locations, the whole festivity came to be known among non-Portuguese as the annual Portuguese chamarrita).

Over the decades, the Holy Ghost festival as celebrated by Azorean-Americans (with the participation of Madeirans and Continentals, and even of some non-Portuguese) naturally underwent some modifications that may be loosely characterized as "Americanization," or perhaps simply as a weakening of tradition. For instance, in 1958 a fourth-generation Hawaiian-Portuguese in her thirties pointed to the following changes that had occurred since her youth: the chapel (in the hall of the Holy Ghost Brotherhood) is no longer respected like a church; grown-ups and children play games in it, instead of retiring to the basement or the yard for such profane purposes; the distributing of blessed food to the poor has been discontinued, and the bread is no longer made by the brotherhood women but is bought from bakeries; the young no longer look forward to marching in the procession but are almost ashamed to be seen in it by their school friends; the original (religious-charitable) purpose of the ceremony is all but forgotten.[18]

In newspaper reports of Holy Ghost celebrations in California, we read as early as 1915 of one Holy Ghost celebration at the end of May that in its procession featured a drill team dressed in United States Marine uniforms, and which was combined with a Memorial Day parade to the cemetery.[19] For another example, in 1924, the festival procession at Gustine included drill teams of the American Legion and the Knights of Columbus; and in various locations the "arraial" was described as featuring "dancing in English" as well as a "chamarrita in Portuguese."[20] In the 1930s, as one Californian pointed out to the author, many poor people still lined up for free soup, etc., during the Holy Ghost feast; but as of 1962, with public relief and unemployment insurance, there was no longer a need for food distributions. Years ago, another informant commented, food for the "arraial" was donated in kind, but now donations are in money and the banquet food is purchased. In some celebrations of recent times, the central coronation ceremony (sometimes opposed by the clergy as nonliturgical and pagan) may be missing; or else the procession may be skipped.

II *Devotions to Jesus and Mary*

Similar to the Holy Ghost festival in its regional and folkloric character is the one devoted to *Senhor Santo Cristo dos Milagres* (Lord Holy Christ of Miracles), or in brief, the Santo Cristo festival. This one is characteristic not of the Azores as a whole, but of the island of São Miguel, and thus of such centers of Michaelese immigration as Fall River (where one of the Portuguese churches is consecrated to Santo Cristo). It revolves around veneration of an image preserved in the Convento de Esperança at Ponta Delgada, the present capital of São Miguel. This image represents Jesus during the scene of "Ecce Homo" (when, at the palace of Pilate, he was exposed to the jeering crowd as a usurper of royalty). It is alleged to have been brought back from Rome by two local nuns in 1514, and became an object of devotion, reputed to perform miracles, about a century later; the fifth *dominga* (weekend) after Easter was fixed for its celebration. At Ponta Delgada the festival attracts thousands from all over the Azores, as the image is taken from the convent to the nearby church for Saturday-night worship, and is carried in procession on Sunday.[21]

In the United States this cult was popularized primarily by the Real Associação Autonómica Micaelense, a mutual-aid society formed in Massachusetts in 1903. Small replicas of the image were placed in various churches of New England. As this society also set up branches in California (and Hawaii), the cult spread to churches in Oakland and South San Francisco. The story is told of an immigrant woman from Flores who during a stay in São Miguel in 1903 had acquired a Santo Cristo statuette. When her little jewelry store in San Francisco was robbed one day, she vowed to decorate the replica image with jewels if the thieves were caught. They were, and she did; and the image was placed in a specially built chapel in Oakland's St. Joseph Church in 1910.[22] But Fall River has remained the principal locale of this festival; in June 1977 attendance was officially estimated at more than 40,000, with excursion groups coming from California and Canada as well as from Connecticut and New Jersey.[23]

For most participants, festivals like that of Santo Cristo serve more as social gathering points for friends and relatives, or as symbols of regionalism, than as genuine Catholic devotions. It is not surprising, therefore, that an image called *Bom Jesus* (Good Jesus), representing Christ at the same "Ecce Homo" stage of his Passion as the one in Ponta Delgada, imported from Brazil into the parish of São Mateus on the Azores island of Pico, became the focus of an annual gathering for Pico people, on the island itself as in some places in the United States (East Taunton, New Bedford, Hayward, Hanford, Bakersfield, etc.).[24] Another similar image, called *Senhor da Pedra* (Lord of the Stone), venerated at Vila Franca do Campo, the former capital of São Miguel, prompted the introduction of an annual festival by that name in New Bedford in 1919 (or 1924) by four immigrants from that part of São Miguel. This minor celebration has come to be viewed as a reflection of the localistic rivalry between Ponta Delgada, site of the Santo Cristo image, and Vila Franca do Campo![25]

The principal festivity consecrated to Jesus Christ is, of course, Christmas. Special mention of this universal holiday would not be justified here were it not for some special customs characterizing the Portuguese-American celebration, popularly called the *Festa do Menino Jesus*, feast of the Child Jesus. Basically these customs are rooted in Continental Portugal as much as they are in the islands; but there are regional variations. For Madeirans, Christmas is *the* "festa" of the year, with the ubiquitous display of *lapinhas* (little grots, mangers) containing gifts, etc.; in the United States, the leading Madeiran mutual-aid society, the APUMEC in California, was at first called Irmandade da Lapinha.[26] On Christmas Eve, there is or used to be serenading in the streets, and after (or before) Midnight Mass (*missa do galo*, "mass of the rooster") a festive meal. The traditional mangers containing tiny porringers with wheat have been replaced by "foreign" Christmas trees in much of modern Portugal;[27] but they are still seen in Portuguese homes in the United States.

In Provincetown, reminisces one Yankee writer in 1942,

the loveliest of all local customs was Menin Jesu, the little Jesus, brought by the Portuguese from the Western Islands. The older Portuguese people in Provincetown once kept open house from Christmas to New Year's. Every window in their houses had a candle behind it. In the front room was a pyramid of graduated shelves. One candle on top, on the next shelf two saucers of sprouted wheat; on the next, two candles; on the next, four saucers of sprouted wheat, and so on. These represented the Resurrection and the Light. At the bottom was a creche of little figures brought from the Western Islands. To everyone who came was given a tiny cordial glass of homemade wine—peach, plum, elderberry, or dandelion—and a tiny cake. . . . In some houses they would have both the Menin Jesu and a Christmas tree—the Christmas tree, with its presents, looking materialistic and Teutonic beside the sprouted wheat and the lights. Little by little the custom of Menin Jesu has vanished. . . .[28]

In Hawaii, similarly, one third-generation Portuguese recalled in 1960, a custom followed in her youth was the planting of wheat for the Menino Jesus about three weeks before Christmas; "at Christmas the wheat would have grown and was placed on the altar of the home, along with lighted candles, oranges, apples, and nuts. The family would attend Midnight Mass."[29] On Maui Island, the present author was told in 1962, many Portuguese families still put up mangers of the Christ Child in their homes. At Point Loma in California, where a major portion of the Portuguese community hails from the parish Paúl do Mar on Madeira, a Christmas custom typical of that parish is still observed (or was as of 1962): on Christmas Eve, groups of serenaders in regional costumes enter the local church, deposit their offerings (fruit, etc.), and sing a carol one by one as they move around the manger set up in the church. The day after Christmas, the carolers return to the church to pick up their offerings and have them auctioned off at the Portuguese clubhouse for the benefit of the church. From Christmas up until New Year's, there is serenading in the streets every evening.

Invocations of the Virgin are many, particularly in the Portuguese tradition. One that deserves special mention in this context, already referred to in the previous chapter (p. 180), is that of Our Lady of Fatima. Fatima is a little village in central Portugal where the Virgin is claimed to have appeared on May 13, 1917, to three shepherd children, to whom she recommended prayer and penitence, promising to appear again on the thirteenth of each month until October, when a miracle would happen. (On May 13 she is also supposed to have forecast the conversion of Communist Russia. . . .) On October 13, witnesses assert, they observed the sun making extraordinary motions, and a spring of healing water burst forth from the cave where the children had had their "apparition." Nowadays that spring and sanctuary attract thousands of tourists, as well as ailing pilgrims (especially on October 13) in search of a miraculous cure.

The devotion to Our Lady of Fatima has become a generally

Catholic one (since about 1950), promoted by a growing number of non-Portuguese churches in the United States along with the few Portuguese ones, and there is nothing in its liturgical observance that would have any relation to Portuguese immigration (except that some of its propagandists here have been Portuguese). However, it is noteworthy that in Portuguese immigrant circles the observance soon began to incorporate features from the Holy Ghost and other more or less ethnic celebrations. For example, when a *Festa de Nossa Senhora de Fatima* was first celebrated at Los Banos, California, right after World War II, it included Azorean-style bullfighting and dancing (subsequently suppressed by the clergy). At Artesia and at Fresno, California, in 1953, the celebration highlighted a "queen" with two "ladies-in-waiting" (as in the Holy Ghost ceremony), a procession to the Holy Ghost hall, followed by a roast beef dinner, an auction sale of offerings, and dancing.

Nossa Senhora dos Milagres (Our Lady of Miracles) is the patroness of the island of Corvo in the Azores, her image being worshipped in the church of Vila Nova; the annual festival is also attended by people from the neighboring island of Flores. Immigrants from Corvo started sponsoring an annual celebration at New Bedford about 1940 or earlier; but the major feast of Our Lady of Miracles in the United States is held at Gustine, California, where it is also known as the *Festa da Serreta*. (Serreta is a village on Terceira Island. Apparently the Gustine festival promoters decided somewhere along the line on a combined devotion to two different local invocations or images of the Virgin.)[30]

The Gustine event stretches through a whole week in early September, starting with a novena in church and leading up to a *Bodo de Leite* (Milk Feast) on Saturday at noon. This involves the distribution of milk, freshly drawn from festively assembled dairy cows, and of sweet rolls. (Gustine is a center of the dairy industry, and so is Terceira Island!) The procession on Sunday morning, opened with the American and Portuguese flags, may include up to seventeen different images from the local church and up to two dozen different "queens" (young girls representing different Portuguese communities and organizations throughout California). Entertainment includes several *cantorias ao desafio* (extemporaneous song contests, where participants take turns in improvising verses on a selected topic) and a Terceiran-style *tourada à corda* (roping bullfight, consisting of attempts to rope wildly running bulls), along with a Holy Ghost—style Sunday-afternoon banquet, chamarrita, and modern dancing, etc. This event, then, represents an amalgam and rearrangement of a variety of "traditions" and new regional features—somewhat comparable to the dialect mixture and Anglicization in Portuguese immigrant speech, to be described in the next chapter.

Other invocations of the Virgin lend themselves to such locally delimited annual celebrations as that of Our Lady of Good Voyage at Gloucester, Massachusetts, which each June attracts many tourists as it features the colorful blessing of the fishing fleet by the Archbishop of Boston (a blessing ceremony also dear to Italian and Greek and other fishermen, of course).[31] Or there are the annual get-togethers, principally of Madeiran immigrants, under the sacred sponsorship of Our Lady of Loreto (at Norton, Massachusetts, and also around Castro Valley, California), and of Our Lady of the Mount (or better, of Monte, as this is the name of a specific parish in Madeira). The latter invocation or image used to be feted occasionally in the Oakland area, but was—and probably still is—particularly popular in Hawaii: the hillside in the Punchbowl district of Honolulu easily reminded the Madeirans there of the hillside, or mount, overlooking Madeira's capital city of Funchal.[32]

III   *Other Periodic Celebrations*

The Madeiran festival par excellence in the United States has come to be the *Festa do Santissimo Sacramento* (Feast of the Most Holy Sacrament, i.e., of the Eucharist), now concentrated in New Bedford, so much so that it is locally often simply referred to as the *Festa dos Madeiras*. This annual affair, which must not be confused with the universal liturgic holiday of the same name, takes place on the first Sunday in August. (Worship of the Blessed Sacrament on the first Sunday of August is a tradition in the parish of Estreito da Calheta, Madeira.) Initiated about the year 1915 by four members of New Bedford's largely Madeiran parish of the Immaculate Conception, it is now considered the largest single social gathering for Portuguese-Americans (between 40,000 and 80,000 people) and the main tourist attraction of New Bedford—on neither religious nor folkloric grounds, but primarily as a huge shindig. There is a church service with procession, all right, but the emphasis is—even more than in the case of other celebrations already mentioned—on the amusement park, where *carne de espeto* (meat roasted on the spit, a Madeiran-style shishkebab) is much in evidence.

One interesting aspect of the history of this event is that it seems to have been a regionalistic response of Madeiran immigrants (who only started coming to the United States in any numbers about the turn of the century) t the dominance of Azoreans (with their Holy Ghost festival) which they encountered here.[33]

The three popular saints of the Portuguese people, particularly of those living on the mainland, are Santo Antonio (St. Anthony the Franciscan, born 1195 in Lisbon, died 1231 in Padua), São João (St. John the Baptist), and São Pedro (St. Peter). More popular beliefs are connected with them than with any other saints. St. Anthony is believed to restore lost objects to their owners—including lost affections. St. John is the favorite matchmaker. St. Peter, too, is given credit for romantic powers. Connected with such folk beliefs is the festive use of fireworks, bonfires, and water displays such as little cascades. The annual festivals of all three follow each other in close succession in the month of June, and they are an occasion for great revelry. Among Portuguese-Americans, these traditions have never enjoyed much popularity, primarily because of the prevalence of Azoreans, who have devoted most of their attention to the specifically Azorean festivals of the Holy Ghost and Holy Christ, etc. Yet in immigrant communities with a large contingent of Continentals one may encounter little parties in honor of St. John or St. Anthony in clubs or private homes, on the approximate dates in June, featuring regional folk dancing in a setting of lampions for illumination; or an artificial waterfall; small fireworks; special flower arrangements; use of foliage for "he loves me—he loves me not" games, and the like. St Anthony and St. John are also celebrated in special ways by Capeverdeans, back in the islands as well as in New England.

Purely secular celebrations or commemorations occasionally observed by Portuguese-American organizations, involving speechmaking and rarely some folkloristic enrichment, are the First of December (the date in 1640 when Portugal regained her independence from Spain), the Fifth of October (the date in 1910 when Portugal became a republic), and Camões Day (June 10), recently renamed Day of Portuguese Communities or Portugal Day (officially intended to reaffirm ties between the Portuguese at home and abroad). Generally speaking, Portuguese immigrants have shown little interest in these old-country patriotic dates but have been remarkably quick in participating in the major American observances: Memorial Day, Fourth of July, Thanksgiving. In California, mediating between old- and new-country ties there is the annual Cabrillo Day, promoted by a whole chain of Cabrillo clubs.

CHAPTER 13

Portuguese Cultural Traditions in Daily Life

I   *Language*

UNDOUBTEDLY THE MOST PERVASIVE AND SYSTEMATIC PART OF A PERSON'S cultural heritage is his or her mother tongue, impressing itself upon the growing person and coming to express that person's innermost thinking day by day. A language serves not only the practical function of communication but to an important extent shapes and guides one's way of looking at the world. Within an individual's mind a particular language becomes associated with specific life experiences, with memories and feelings about them. Learned in interaction with kin and neighbors, one's native tongue becomes an important symbol of ethnic and family loyalties, of group cohesion.

A large majority of immigrants who have settled in the United States over the past 100 years or longer have been of non-English mother tongue. For these millions of immigrants, whether Portuguese or Italian or Norwegian or whatever, a major part of the "immigrant experience," of the problems of adjusting to a new environment dominated by English speakers, has been one of language differences. For most non-English-speaking immigrants there was a practical need, in varying degree, sooner or later, to communicate with English speakers, either through interpreters or, if one was willing and able to learn English as a second language, directly. True, no actual laws were encountered in the United States that would compel a Portuguese immigrant to learn English (except for a bare minimum in connection with naturalization, an optional process). But especially in an industrial urban environment, there were severe economic and social disadvantages connected with inability to understand or speak English.

Certainly there were no official restrictions on the continued public or private use of Portuguese (or any other immigrant language), side by side with English. But there were strong subtle pressures toward "Americanization," toward espousal of "majority" patterns in language, as well as in many other ways, particularly once there was a second generation—children going through American public schools. Should one resist those pressures, at least to the extent of maintaining "loyalty" to the Portuguese mother tongue for limited uses within the family and among fellow Portuguese? Or should one actually be eager to switch to English, even in the home? This was partly (but only partly) a question of how much value an immigrant, or child of an immigrant, attached to the old ways as against the new. It was also a question of family relationships, of language learning aptitude in individual cases, and of other factors.

By and large the Portuguese, like immigrants from many other countries but somewhat in contrast to the Chinese, the Greeks, the French and French-Canadians, have been quick not only to learn some English for outside communication, but to sanction and even encourage the use of English within their own homes, and among themselves when in the public eye. As early as 1895, when immigration from the Azores into New England was in full swing, a Portuguese consul reported to his government that the American-born children of these immigrants were speaking only a mutilated Portuguese mixed with English.[1] In another consular report, of 1912, we read that the majority of this second generation, in such New England towns as Fall River, hardly knew any Portuguese, partly because school and outdoor sports activities left little time for these children to spend within their families.[2]

With respect to California, similarly, a Portuguese consul complained in the early 1900s that many of his countrymen there felt it was useless to continue speaking the Portuguese language, and were avoiding use of that language with their own children.[3] In 1913, the California newspaper *O Arauto* commented that the Portuguese in that state were not as respected as other immigrant groups because they themselves were ashamed of their background, and too embarrassed to speak Portuguese to one another in the presence of, say, some Irishman.[4] In Honolulu, it was felt necessary as early as 1890, barely ten years after the arrival of the first labor groups from Madeira and São Miguel, to start a private school to teach Portuguese to children of these immigrants.[5]

In 1932, an observer of the scene in Gloucester, Massachusetts, wrote: "Until recently, one Portuguese would not permit another to speak to him in his mother tongue in public. To his mind, this would have meant a profanation of American soil, an affront to his patriotism with regard to the adopted fatherland."[6] Ten years later, the *Diario de Noticias* lamented editorially: "The Portuguese-American boys and girls have had to learn the Portuguese they know by listening to their mothers and grandmothers, who could not speak English. Their fathers, as a rule, as soon as they know how to utter the 150 words constituting their English vocabulary, talk English with their children even at home. . . . In their turn, the Portuguese-American youngsters, not knowing our language well, avoid speaking it in public. They are ashamed to use the Portuguese they know. . . ."[7] The good-neighbor policy toward Latin America professed during World War II and especially the mounting prestige of Brazil since that time reduced this sense of "shame" somewhat, but without any long-term effect on the preservation of Portuguese speech in the United States. Even for the massive new wave of Portuguese immigrants of the 1960s, more literate and proud than those who had come two or three generations earlier, and despite the coincident enactment of bilingual education in public schools, it was still true that the children among them tended to consider Portuguese "inferior" to English.[8]

In Hawaii, where there are hardly any foreign-born Portuguese left, regular use of the Portuguese language is now a rarity. In California and particularly in southeastern New England and metropolitan New York, the recent enormous increase in the number of native Portuguese speakers has kindled among the American-born a limited interest in learning or relearning the language of their forebears. But this is a transitional interest; few traces of Portuguese speech survive past the second generation, except for family names and the designations of some traditional foods or folkloristic objects.[9]

Also transitional is the very form of the Portuguese spoken by immigrants, primarily in the sense that their native regional speech undergoes changes under the influence of English, and also in the sense that contact between settlers from different parts of Portugal may produce some dialect mixture. In the end there is the kind of speech, among longtime residents of this country, that involves a good deal of "code-switching," back and forth between Portuguese and English—one step short of shifting to English altogether.

Typical of this doubly transitional language situation are two newspaper items that appeared almost simultaneously some years ago. In the one, the announcer of a Portuguese immigrant radio program (in New England) defended himself against criticisms of his "incorrect" Portuguese speech by pleading that an announcer has to use the kind of language that the largest number of listeners understand, including all kinds of Anglicisms; for "many Portuguese-Americans just don't understand good Portuguese anymore." The other newspaper item told of the replacement of a long-established Portuguese-language radio program (in California) by one conducted in English, with Portuguese and Brazilian music, aimed at the thousands of Portuguese-Americans who do not speak Portuguese.[10]

English influence in Portuguese immigrant speech is mostly a matter of vocabulary, rather than of pronunciation or grammar. The borrowing of words, or entire little phrases, or particular meanings of words, from English is most often induced by the fact that whatever is designated by the English expression seems to the immigrant novel in some degree, characteristic in some way of American life, outside his preemigration range of experiences. Some of the most obvious examples relate to modern technical devices, typically American social institutions, as well as to the more homely area of foods, items of clothing, home, and street:

Taias (from English "tires"); *frisa*, "freezer"; *raivar*, "to drive" (a car); *papelano*, "pipeline" (for carrying milk from milking shed to storage tank); *boifreno*, "boyfriend"; *ceriol*, "cityhall"; *dide*, "deed"; *papel*, "(news)paper;" *ramborga*, "hamburger"; *bi(rr)a*, "beer"; *sopa*, "supper"; *clamchauda*, "clam chowder"; *alverozes*, "overalls"; *daipas*, "diapers"; *robas*, "rubber shoes"; *mecha*, "match"; *tanamento*, "tenement"; *alpesteres*, "upstairs"; *estoa*, "store"; *saiboque*, "sidewalk"; and so on. Although most Anglicisms are nouns, there are also verbs like *jampar*, "to jump"; *bordar*, "to board"; adjectives like *naice*, "nice." Loan translations (where English ways of combining meanings rather than English words are borrowed) include *escola alta*, "high school"; *apanhar frio*, "to catch cold"; and the like. Some Anglicisms cannot be explained by an immigrant's need to label something previously unfamiliar to him, but rather they reflect frequently heard exclamations that somehow convey the flavor of American-style conversation: okay! all right! shut up! never mind![11]

A different sort of Anglicization involves the surnames of Portuguese immigrants. In many cases but not all, this is due to the desire of an immigrant, or of his descendants, to appear Americanized, i.e., to conceal his non-Anglo origin. But sometimes the Anglicization results simply from inability on the part of some authority person (such as an immigration official, teacher, judge) to pronounce a Portuguese name, or to guess the correct spelling from hearing it pronounced. Either way, Anglicization usually consists in substituting the spelling of an Anglo name that sounds reasonably similar to the Portuguese one. In some instances, where the Portuguese surname also has a generic meaning, the name-bearer has resorted to "translating" it into English, i.e., selecting an English name with a similar generic meaning. Thus various families originally called Mello have become either Miller or Mellow; Rodrigues has become Rogers (Rodgers); Correa, Curry; Pereira, Perry. But through the process of translation, White may hide an original Alves; Wood, a Madeira; Peacock, a former Pavão.[12]

Traditionally the Portuguese common people, spending their lives in a relatively small circle of kin and neighbors, have paid much more attention to first names and nicknames than to family names. On the island of Fayal, from where many of the earliest Azorean immigrants came, the local post office and local businessmen used to file letters alphabetically by baptismal, not family, name.[13] At Porto Santo (Madeira), everybody is known by some nickname.[14] A descendant of Portuguese immigrants in Hawaii recalls: "In grandma's homeland a nickname was an affliction that plagued not only the victim but all the members of his family from generation to generation. . . . When the early Portuguese immigrants arrived in the Hawaiian Islands in 1878, many of them had secret hopes of casting off their family nicknames . . . but these names were not to be easily shed for at least two generations. . . . Those few who had escaped this affliction at home received nicknames in the Islands. There was Torto da Manoa ('The Cockeyed from Manoa Farm'), . . . and A Roza Braba ('The Wild Rose'). . . . A few illiterate families were registered by their family nicknames and their grandchildren now bear these names."[15]

Among Continentals around Providence, Rhode Island, members of the Andrade family were for two generations known as Fumegas ("Smokers"). In another family in the area, the mother (whose surname is Rodrigues) has always been known as Raposa ("Fox").[16] In the Portuguese community at Point Loma, a Mr. Mata chose his nickname, Frizado ("Curly"), to go into his naturalization papers—this despite the fact that two other individuals in that community officially surnamed Silva are also known as Frizado. There is also traditional instability in the official surnames, inasmuch as an individual may pick either his father's surname(s) or his mother's maiden name(s) or (part of) both in any order. Of two brothers, Pereira Mendonça, in Erie, Pennsylvania, one chose his father's name, Pereira (later changed to Perry), and the other his mother's name, Mendonça.[17]

Thus the Americanization process has included for many Portuguese ethnics a change in names or naming customs. However, what about any influence, not of English in Portuguese, but of Portuguese in (American) English? As is to be expected, it has been negligible. The names of a few Portuguese culinary specialties, such as *lingüica* (or lingreese) and *malassada*, have attained some currency. In Hawaiian English, the term *piccaninny* (small child) derives from Portuguese, and so probably does *bagasse* (pulp of the sugar cane).[18] A few intonational and syntactic features in Hawaiian regional speech are possibly due to Portuguese influence. There are, of course, non-Anglicized Portuguese surnames that have become part of American English (if we consider proper names part of a language); de Sousa, dos Passos, Cardozo, and Silva are among the better known. As for place names in the United States, there are or have been some thirty different places called Lisbon (after Portugal's capital), and a few called Brazil; but as far as can be determined, adoption of these geographic names had nothing to do with Portuguese immigration.[19]

II   Verbal Art, Music, and Dance

Since this chapter is concerned with the survival of Portuguese traditions, it is only traditional verbal art, custom rather than recent individual creation, that warrants brief mention here. Of course there is a relatively large body of Portuguese literature (poetry, novels, plays, etc.), produced over centuries by writers of great distinction (Camões, already referred to, is one of them). Some of this has been read and is remembered by the rather small minority of immigrants literate and intellectual enough to be interested in belles lettres. Some of the older literature can be said to have become part of the socially shared heritage of the Portuguese people; Portuguese immigrant newspapers and magazines have occasionally reprinted well-known poems or works of fiction. As for literature of a creative nature written by Portuguese immigrants (while residing in the United States), or even by children of immigrants as far as it incorporates some aspect of Portuguese

Folklore scene reminiscent of northwestern Portugal, as enacted at Portuguese club in Newark, N.J., 1945.

culture, there is some, but very little.[20] Most of the published output is buried in newspaper files, described in the previous chapter.

What comes closest to verbal art in the folkloristic sense is the performance of little plays by dramatic groups, usually amateur members of one or the other Portuguese immigrant organizations (see Chapter 11). There is hardly any live dramatic production of this sort going on now, with motion pictures (including an occasional Portuguese one) and television supplying most of the entertainment needs, even for non-English-speaking immigrants. There was a fair amount of it during the first half of this century, in New England (but hardly any in California or Hawaii, except for some Portuguese radio programs on the West Coast).

According to Camilo Camara, an erstwhile Portuguese consul who chose to make the United States his permanent home, there were in the early 1900s little groups of Azoreans in New Bedford and Fall River who performed *desafios*—historic episodes interspersed with songs and the like—in a very amateurish way. A little later (especially in the 1920s), Continentals formed regular dramatic groups, of real artistic talent, performing episodes of Portuguese life for patriotic or charitable causes; members of the second generation often learned Portuguese to take part in such plays.[21] In the 1930s, performances of full-length plays and short *autos* by established authors were still a fairly important part of Portuguese immigrant community life; for example, between late February and early April in 1937, five different dramatic groups presented nine different plays in New Bedford. In those years theatrical activity was also extended to New York City and Newark.[22] In the 1940s, taste veered from serious dramas to musical reviews.

The form of entertainment called *cantoria ao desafio*, already mentioned (p.200), popular in the Azores, was a common feature of festivities in California until the 1950s, and may have been revived by recent immigrants: two contestants alternate in singing improvised verses on a given topic, accompanying themselves on a viola or guitar (Portuguese-style); the one who can respond without faltering and in good rhythm while sticking to the subject is declared the winner by the audience.[23] Another form of Portuguese verbal art has attaracted the attention of some researchers in this country recently: traditional ballads or "romances." These are short narrative songs that tell a story, usually anonymous, passed down orally from generation to generation, and eventually circulating in a number of different versions. They represent a type of folk poetry that probably spread into Portugal from Spain, a spin-off from longer medieval epic poems. Many of these ballads, it was found, are still well remembered by older Portuguese immigrants in California. In the late 1960s, Joanne Purcell collected about seventy-five variants of some thirty ballad-types among such immigrants, who would sing the texts for her, usually with *viola* and *guitar* accompaniment. There also used to be dances and certain games to go with the ballads; but these, as well as the texts themselves, are being forgotten by the younger generation. Some of the material as gathered in California is in prose form rather than in verse; Manuel C. Fontes, following up on Purcell's work, has collected about fifty of these folktales, in addition to some 200 ballads in verse form.[24] In a similar project during World War I, Elsie Parsons had collected a great many folktales and riddles among Capeverdean immigrants in New England.[25]

Disregarding modern Portuguese songs, as written mostly for the movies or for records and usually shortlived, the traditional type of Portuguese song is often associated with a particular dance form and instrumental accompaniment, or a religious occasion such as Christmas, representing a particular region. Immigrants usually remember folksongs of their region, and in the United States they become familiar with those of other regions. A number of Portuguese clubs, chiefly in the East, have promoted folklore groups donning regional costumes and presenting such songs on special occasions. The one type of tune that non-Portuguese are most likely to think of as typically Portuguese, viz., the passionately plaintive *fado* (combinable with any improvised quatrain or other verse), is not rooted in the Portuguese countryside at all, but was introduced in Bohemian-style cafés in Lisbon and Coimbra in the early nineteenth century, perhaps derived from the Afro-Brazilian *lundum*; it is rarely heard in immigrant circles.[26] Classical Portuguese music, instrumental or choral, used to be presented now and then in New Bedford and Newark.

Popular Portuguese musical instruments deserve special mention here in connection with the ukulele, usually believed to be a native Hawaiian instrument but actually the product of Portuguese immigration to the Hawaiian Islands. Some of the Madeiran men who had immigrated to Hawaii in 1879 had brought along their favorite instruments for their private amusement: the six-stringed *viola*, the five-stringed *rajão*, and especially the four-stringed little guitar known as a *braguinha* or *machete* in Madeira (better known as *cavaquinho* in the Azores and Continental Portugal). The Hawaiian natives soon took a liking to the *rajão*, more manageable than the big *viola* which had already been brought to Hawaii by whalers. As the Hawaiians started playing the *rajão* during work breaks in their taro patches, this instrument acquired the nickname *taro patch fiddle*.

More successful even was the Madeiran *braguinha*: King Kalakaua became fond of its gentle sound, and this started a trend. Three of the Madeirans, Augusto Dias, José de Espirito Santo (or Santos), and Manuel Nunes, set up a business manufacturing braguinhas in Honolulu, as soon as they could get out of their plantation labor contracts (two of them had been instrument makers in Funchal). Their product sold well, soon under the nickname *ukulele* (meaning "jumping flea" in Hawaiian). There are several versions about how the instrument acquired this new name; at any rate, from Hawaii the braguinha, alias ukulele, spread across the continental United States (largely as a result of its being shown at the Panama-Pacific Exhibition in San Francisco in 1915), becoming the craze of nightclub and radio audiences. Manuel Nunes himself, or else his son, later moved to California to set up a ukulele factory there. Yet another "Hawaiian" instrument evolved out of Portuguese immigration: the steel guitar, which came about when a native Hawaiian boy hit on the idea of strumming a *viola* or Portuguese guitar with his pocketknife, for special sound effect.[27]

A few words about dances: best known in this country, because of the prevalence of Azoreans, is the *chamarrita*, or *chama-rita*, already mentioned. It combines with a particular tune by the same name, and is the old standby at all kinds of socials catering to the older folks. Actually this dance is more characteristic of Fayal, Pico, and Flores than of São Miguel, which features the *pèzinho* and the *furado*. The chamarrita starts out with couples dancing separately in a kind of valse or mazurka; then men and women line up, joining hands and walking in the round; again couples waltz off separately; then each woman circles halfway around her man; finally man and woman join one hand and hop around on the spot; and so on, with variations, accentuated by intermittent chanting. This is accompanied by one or several *viola* players and one *rabeca* player.[28]

The *pèzinho*, far less popular in this country, is a round dance in 4/4 time; the *furado*, in which a line of women slip through a parallel line of men, is danced in 8/8 time. Madeiran immigrants may indulge in their own regional specialty, especially the *cha-*

ramba with its syncopated, sexually suggestive rhythms, the *ca-macheiras* (derived from the English counterdance), and the *mourisca* (originally mimicking combat with the Moors). Continentals, in their New Jersey clubhouses for example, may favor one or the other variant of the *vira*, a dance in which women move in an inner circle, men in an outer circle, or vice-versa. Among Capeverdean immigrants, finally, the tangolike *morna* is by far the most popular dance, accompanied by a nostalgic melody.

III *Food Habits and Culinary Art*

Culinary art constitutes an important part of the national traditions of any foreign-born group in the United States. While non-English immigrant tongues tend to die with the foreign-born, many a recipe from the land of the ancestors will remain a favorite in the homes of later American-born generations and may even become part of the general American cuisine. The relative persistence of national cooking habits is easily explained by the fact that cookery is essentially a part of individual home life, of low public "visibility"; also, American culture does not discourage a passing interest in the

Mint leaves together with bread and spiced gravy go into the traditional soup served at Portuguese-American Holy Ghost celebrations, after the coronation ceremony.

exotic, such as a "foreign" dish—as long as one also does like apple pie.

The Portuguese immigrants and their descendants have preserved a fair number of culinary items from the old country, or rather, from their particular corner of it. Some of these items more or less characterize the daily fare in many homes; others are reserved for festive occasions. Any recipe, of course, has its variations and depends on the availability of ingredients. The American milieu, while permitting the maintenance of old food habits, also required some major adjustments where customary ingredients could not be obtained, or where an immigrant had to board, or eat in a canteen. For many foreign-born, living and working in this country soon meant a general improvement in living standards, reflected in a more varied and attractive diet than one had been able to afford in the old country. Thus American-style foods were readily adopted, along with the preservation of some old-country specialities.

We will forgo the temptation here to describe a large number of specific Portuguese dishes. Hundred of recipes are available in several Portuguese-American cookbooks published in recent years.[29] Instead, we present only a few details about the Portuguese immigrant's initial adjustments in food habits, and a brief character-ization of the most popular traditional food items commonly a part of festive occasions.

In the 1880s, Weeks described the standard diet of the Azorean peasantry as follows: "The staple article of food is Indian corn ground and mixed in cakes with water, and baked on flat hearth-stones. . . . Fish of all kinds is abundant in the neighboring areas and very cheap. A small sardine is most common. . . . Add to these two articles of diet a few vegetables, cabbages, and yams, garlic soup . . . and meat once or twice a year, and you have the average bill of fare of the Azorean peasant. . . ."[30] And Walker added: "The Azorean peasant is a prodigious bread-eater. . . . On rising at day-break, he at once sets about preparing the *açorda d'azedo*, by mixing onion, garlic, vinegar, lard, and a pinch of saffron, all boiled in sufficient water to moisten the half of a maize loaf. About eight o'clock he partakes of a second breakfast at the spot where he may be at work, consisting of a bit of saltfish, washed down by spring water; at noon he again eats his saltfish and bread, and on returning home in the evening, he takes 'en famille' the last meal, consisting of bread and chopped greens, the whole boiled with lard, salt and red peppers."[31]

As to the mainland of Portugal, the basic diet of the peasant has been described like this: bread, olive oil, haricot beans, cabbage, a little *bacalhau* (codfish), and wine. Sardines, bacon, and beef can only be tasted on the rarest occasions, such as some big feastday or wedding.[32] Above the level of the poor laborer, a meal consisting of soup, beef, and rice has been called the classical Portuguese dinner.[33] The various mealtimes in the Portuguese countryside are as follows: an early-morning bite, consisting of olives, bread, and some brandy, starts the day for the laborer in the Beira Alta region. Then follows the actual breakfast. Between it and the noon dinner a little snack is eaten in some areas. At nightfall one sits down to supper. During the summer months the laborers get also a little luncheon in the afternoon, and in the Minho region, when threshing is done late in the evening, the work day is ended with a helping of bread and sardines.[34]

On the basis of interviews in Portuguese immigrant households in Massachusetts in the 1920s and 1930s, nutritionists concluded that, in the process of moving from an old-country environment of fishing and gardening to one of grimy factory labor, these immigrants have had to change their diet, too, "not because a new one has been thoughtfully planned to fit the need, but because foods are too expensive. Fruit and vegetables are not grown near at hand, and therefore, cost more. Fish, too, is three times the price paid in the Azores islands. There are few goats in the city neighborhoods into which [the immigrants] come." One of the problems with children was that, if they were brought up on goats' milk in the homeland, they had to be taught to like the flavor of cow's milk.[35] The immigrants' food habits included much use of greens and fish, all right, but too little milk and butter; the cornbread of the old country was replaced by white bread; they drank too much coffee here and generally had a poorly balanced diet.[36]

In a more or less rural setting, immigrants were freer to recreate their old-country food habits. One Capeverdean woman recalls how, in the Cape Cod area, her mother used to raise all kinds of vegetables in the family garden. In the fall, she would kill a pig or two and make *linguiça* and *chouriço* sausages in the accustomed way. These sausages were eaten as breakfast with *cuscus*. A large wooden mortar imported from Brava Island was used to pound the corn here and make the customary *manchupa* (or *kachupa*). Frequently the family also ate *jagacida* (which was made with lima beans, onion, and rice).[37]

In Hawaii, Portuguese sausages (*linguiça* and *chouriço*) have become breakfast favorites of the general population. Portuguese sweetbreads (*pão doce*) and doughnuts (*malassadas*), too, are quite popular.[38] The diet of the Hawaii Portuguese, we are told, stresses corn meal, pork, fish, sweet potatoes, and green vegetables—items they were used to in the old country; but now they have added rice. They still observe the old habit of placing all the food on the table at once in serving dishes, and members of the family help themselves.[39]

The *linguiça* and *chouriço* sausages have also become popular in southeastern New England and in California. The former is made with the small long gut of the hog, and is stuffed with loin of pork. *Chouriço* is made with the large short intestine of the animal, and is strongly spiced. Another brand of pork sausage found in Portuguese-American homes is the *salpicão*, containing pork loin seasoned in garlic and wine. More popular is the *morcela*, a blood sausage that includes some pluck, fat, and bread.

A typically Azorean dish served in New England is the *caçoila*, a stew of the liver and heart of the pig, served with beans or potatoes. A tidbit favored by Continentals is *isca de fígado*, beef liver seasoned with vinegar, pepper, garlic, etc., then fried in olive oil or lard. The culinary specialty of immigrants from Madeira is *carne assada no espêto* (meat roasted on the spit). Festive occasions among Continentals may call for fried chicken with rice, or a *cozido* (boiled chicken or beef, with rice and cabbage, etc.). A mainstay of a good everyday meal, for any Portuguese, is cod or some similar fish.

The *açorda d'azedo* or vinegar soup of the poor man's diet in Portugal is all but forgotten. But the Holy Ghost soup, containing all kinds of meat, bread and potatoes, and various spices is as popular in the United States as the Holy Ghost festival itself. A less festive everyday soup is the *caldo verde* or green broth, made with boiled strips of cabbage and potatoes.

Seasonings play a great role in Portuguese as well as Portuguese-American cookery. The Azoreans like strong spices such as pepper-fruits, saffron, garlic, and vinegar; Continentals are more used to olive oil. *Vinha d'alhos* is a sauce made of garlic, vinegar, and other spices.

Favorite legumes include the broad beans which New Englanders sometimes call Portuguese beans. Stewed beans and toasted beans are well liked, as are *tremoços* (lupine seeds, soaked in salt water for several days), chick peas, toasted corn, etc. From corn is made the *papa de milho* of Madeirans, and the *cuscus* of Capeverdeans in this country. Azoreans are partial to yams or sweet potatoes.

Several Portuguese-American bakeries sell the kind of Portuguese bread made entirely from flour, much salt, water, and yeast (without eggs, milk, or fats). *Massa sovada*, a kind of sweet bread, is served at Holy Ghost celebrations—sometimes in the shape of human limbs or heads as votive offerings. A Christmas pastry is called *filhós*.

A major adjustment for many Portuguese immigrants has been the substitution of beer for wine, used almost daily in much of Portugal. Homemade wine, however, is not uncommon among the Portuguese in California.

CHAPTER 14

From Portuguese to American:
A Synthesis and Appraisal

THE TERM AMERICANIZATION IMPLIES CHANGES IN LIFE-STYLE, IN attitudes and habits, in the direction of what is considered characteristic of the American way of life. But attitudes and patterns of every-day living in the United States are not and never have been uniform; there are variations by time and by place. Individualism—and thus potential diversity in many areas—is itself part of the American creed. The United States today is not the same, neither materially nor attitudinally, as it was at the beginning of Portuguese mass immigration a hundred years ago. There are more than just geographical differences between life along the northeastern seaboard, in California, and in Hawaii. How, then, can we precisely measure the degree of Americanization of any immigrant?

There is a further logical difficulty. If Americanization means learning to do as Americans do, what segment of the population of the United States at any given time actually constitutes "the Americans"? All the inhabitants—including immigrant aliens? Presumably not; the alien resident in the process of adjustment cannot as yet be counted. Those inhabitants who are American citizens? If so, an immigrant can become a co-determiner of the American norm by simply naturalizing. More probably, that portion of the United States population actually born in this country? Including, perhaps in first place, the American Indians, and, at least in third place, the the American-born children of immigrants? Perhaps. Yet some native-born inhabitants are judged more "typically American" than others, in some respect or other. Who, ultimately, sets the norms for what is to be understood by Americanism?

In short, this concept is necessarily vague and shifting. Which is not to deny that there is a certain amount of agreement on a certain

New Bedford high school girl, of mixed Portuguese-Yankee parentage, displaying her girl scout honors.

number of behavioral traits that are, or should be, characteristic of the American way of life. More or less. In any case we may conclude that immigrants, to the extent to which they pass on some of their heritage to their American-born children and grandchildren, and bring an accumulation of small changes into the living habits of the natives at large, ultimately contribute to shaping what at any given period may be called "American society." In other words, immigrant groups not only adjust, but in small measure or large are also adjusted to. They not only take, they also give.

Various kinds of sociocultural adjustment, or Americanization, undergone by Portuguese immigrants and their children have been described or at least alluded to in previous chapters. They need not be mentioned again. To trace all areas of change would be an impossible task, anyway. In this chapter, we touch upon the development of social relations between Portuguese immigrant groups and their immediate neighbors, and upon the gradual entry of the Portuguese ethnic population into political processes and participation in American society at large. Viewing the process of social integration as one of give and take, we will conclude with an appraisal of the general contribution, and some specific individual contributions, of the Portuguese element to American society.

Because of the many facets involved in the process of assimilation, from superficial change in clothing habits to deep-seated beliefs, any statement about the comparative speed of assimilation of this or that immigrant group must be taken with a grain of salt. It has been said that immigrants from the Azores have been quicker to identify with America than those from mainland Portugal, and those from the western Azores quicker than those from São Miguel. Actually those from the western Azores started coming first, followed by those from São Miguel and then by Continentals. The Azoreans as a group have had less of a sense of Portuguese nationality than the Continentals to begin with.

There have been contradictory opinions about the comparative rate of Americanization of the Portuguese in urban New England as against rural California. Those in Hawaii are said to have assimilated more rapidly than the ones in California; but Portuguese immigration into California continued long after influx into Hawaii had ended. It is too early to appraise the rate of Americanization of the tens of thousands who have come from the Azores and the rest of Portugal in recent years; this large new wave of immigrants is therefore left out of account in this concluding chapter.

Generally speaking, it is the "second generation," the American-born (or American-raised) children of any immigrant group, that have the most decisive influence on the Americanization of the foreign-born adults. As these children go through American public schools, usually perceiving themselves as a "minority" and mingling with "other" children, they tend to become more subject to peer pressure than to parental control and present their elders with the choice of a widening generation gap or else parental willingness to adjust at least partially to majority patterns. This is also true for the Portuguese ethnics.

The American way of life where father and mother work away from home all day tends to break up traditional family life, one Portuguese informant told this author. According to another Portuguese critic, the children of immigrants think the "ignorance" they see at home reflects the status of Portuguese culture. They then hasten to get away from this old culture in order to raise their social status, and they even put pressure on their parents to get naturalized.[1] William C. Smith tells the case of a nine-year-old son of Portuguese immigrant parents who came to his father about a class in weekday religious instruction and said: "Dad, I don't want to go that class—they're all Portuguese!"[2]

Edward Ross, writing about the Portuguese as of 1914, reported: "Owing to their extreme clannishness, assimilation is slow. . . . The chief agents of assimilation are the children. Having mingled with other children in the public schools, the young people are taken into fraternal orders and share the social life of the community. Moreover, the parents unconsciously raise their standard of living through their efforts to gratify the wants inspired in their children by contact with schoolmates coming from better homes."[3]

Christian Bannick, in a study of Portuguese immigrants during the First World War, stated: "In the east they [the Portuguese] are much more clannish than those in California, possibly because the natives of the east are more conservative than those in the west. . . . There is no race prejudice [against the Portuguese in California]. . . . The assimilation which has slowly taken place has come chiefly through the contact incidental to business, and through the association of the children while attending the public schools."[4] Eduardo de Carvalho, surveying the New England scene in the 1920s, found that the children of the Portuguese, after having gone through American schools, rarely keep up contact with the "colony" except for business matters and relations with their parents. They are educated people, he added, but nobody would dare consider them true elements of the Portuguese "colony."[5]

Actually the Americanization of immigrants is not always the result of pressure from their children or other sources. Far from being reluctant to shed some of their old-country habits, many Portuguese have been eager to do so, even to the extent of urging their own children to speak English rather than Portuguese in the home. What is involved here is not only a perception of the economic-political advantages of Americanization, but also a low valuation of one's old-country background. Some reference to this has already been made on pp. 204-205.

In 1967, a second-generation Portuguese in New England told this writer: "My mother had for years hidden the fact that she was Portuguese and in general represented herself as French." Similarly, in 1964 New Bedford's Portuguese daily stated editorially: "To this day there are Portuguese-Americans who are ashamed of their descent and try to disguise it behind Anglicized family names, or who even go to the extreme of alleging they are French or Spanish."[6] According to Carvalho, the Portuguese lack confidence in Portugal and consider her old and decrepit; for many New England Portuguese, he explains, Portugal is a dying nation; they know little about her.[7] This is echoed in California, where the *Jornal Português* complained editorially (in 1940) that hundreds of California Portuguese were ashamed of their nationality.[8]

If one's Portuguese background is viewed unfavorably, what then are some of the aspects of life in America that Portuguese immigrants have found particularly attractive? One visiting journalist from Portugal put it this way: "The American flag is like a sentinel standing next to every Portuguese settler. The material comforts and conveniences of the land are like hands extended to him. His children convey to him, from what they learn in school and from contact with other youngsters, a strong sense and pride of being part of a great and powerful country."[9] Carvalho singles out one factor as particularly important: "The individual feels more like a citizen in America [than in Portugal]," i.e., he has more of a voice in public affairs.[10]

The immigrant of peasant background, widely separated from the ruling upper class in the old country, is delighted at the "democratic" informality and relative absence of rigid class distinctions in the United States. Azoreans returning to the Islands from America (as of 1904) rave not only about the money they have made here, but about the fact that in the American democracy everybody addresses everybody as "you"[11] (where the Portuguese language requires different pronouns of address to mark status distinctions). New Bedford's *Diario de Noticias*, in 1953, upbraids a Portuguese diplomat for having stated that it is indecent for men to take off their jackets in the presence of ladies: formality of dress has nothing to do with being well bred; plebeian informality as practiced in the United States is true democracy.[12] In this country, the same paper adds editorially on a later occasion, public officials are regarded as public servants and are simply addressed as "you," whereas back in Portugal the press accords every official automatically such epithets as "illustrious," "egregious," "venerable," or "meritorious," thus continuing to keep the common people in awe of officialdom.[13]

"When I first came to the United States," a young immigrant wrote to a friend back in Portugal, "I felt ashamed to have to work in a factory. But one day one of my own fellow-workers turned out to be the son of the factory owner, and a medicine student. He explained to me that in the United States work is no degradation. Indeed, I have learned in the meantime that this country judges men by their ability and productivity, not by rank or origin."[14] In the words of the Visconde de Alte, Portugal's ambassador to the United States early in the century: "The tremendous assimilatory pull of the American milieu is based not on language nor race nor religion nor love of soil. The force that grabs the immigrant is economic and political; the individual's success here depends on his aptitudes, of whatever kind, on that very will power that enabled him to uproot himself." "In America, the land of the dollar, there is nothing demeaning about work," the viscount added.[15]

The immigrant's willingness to Americanize, in superficial ways and especially at deeper levels, is determined in part by how far he or she feels accepted, welcomed, or else held at bay, rejected by his/her "American" neighbors—and vice-versa. Actually, throughout the period of mass immigration during the second half of the nineteenth century and far into the twentieth, outgroup contacts of Portuguese immigrants, in many urban industrial locations of the Northeast as well as in Hawaii and California, were with other "non-Anglo" ethnic groups, such as French-Canadians, Poles, Italians, Hispanics, Japanese, and other Orientals, much more frequently than with the dominant "Anglo" core of American society. For many Portuguese just as for immigrants from other countries, the Americanization process has had its competitive aspects—invidious friction with other ethnics as to who has gotten here first, who is more American, who looks more outlandish. This sort of friction between the more and the less "Americanized" is currently in evidence among the Portuguese themselves, viz., the old-timers and the recent arrivals from Portugal.

No further reference need be made here to relations between different subgroups of the Portuguese immigrant community, as described on pp. 157-63. As regards relations to non-Portuguese neighbors, "Anglos" or others, we recall what has been said on pp. 113-14 and 118-20 about the low educational level of the masses of earlier Portuguese immigrants, their racial status, and about their ratings as to "intelligence," docility, emotionality, etc. A sort of benign disparagement leveled by one population group at another is reflected in the so-called ethnic jokes (Polish, Jewish, etc.); and the Portuguese in the United States have not been spared a few jokes aimed at them, suggesting dumbness. For example, there is the joke about the "Portagee" who placed his right foot on a chair in order to bend down and tie the shoelace on his left foot. Or the one about the carpenter wearing a pencil behind his ear who is hit by a cement block that shaves off his ear. He climbs down from his scaffold to look for that ear, as he assumes it can be sewn back on again. When a fellow worker finds the ear and hands it to him, our Portagee shakes his head: "This isn't my ear—it doesn't have any pencil!"[16]

There was a time, in the 1860s and 1870s, in ethnically mixed tenements of Boston's North End, when non-Portuguese tenants "cast looks of ineffable scorn" upon destitute Portuguese fellow tenants.[17] The Portuguese consul in that city felt prompted to plead that the character of a whole nation should not be judged from the looks of a few of its immigrants.[18] Almost fifty years later, the then Portuguese consul in the same city still had to report that because of its comparative poverty and lack of distinguished individuals, the Portuguese "colony" in New England was occupying a very lowly position in American society.[19]

That intergroup relations evolved somewhat differently in different places, due to a variety of local factors, is suggested by a number of sources. Comparing New Bedford and Fall River, Estellie Smith finds that, in the former city, the gradual build-up of Portuguese settlement under generally favorable economic conditions (with the smooth transition from whaling to cotton manufacture) led to positive attitudes toward the Portuguese, encouraging community involvement. In Fall River, which developed rather late and rapidly as a textile center, the Portuguese streaming into the mills were drawn into a competitive struggle (against Irish, French-Canadians, etc.) from the start and remained relatively isolated near the bottom of the ladder for a long time.[20] But in New Bedford, too, even though the Portuguese as a whole came to feel more integrated than in neighboring Fall River, the several ethnic groups (including French-Canadians, Lebanese, Puerto Ricans, etc.) remained relatively aloof from each other well into the 1960s, according to Engler.[21]

The Capeverdeans, previously keeping away from the American blacks as well as from other groups, and being racially discriminated against both by Portuguese and other whites in New England, were encouraged by the civil rights movement of the 1960s to draw closer to American blacks in New Bedford and elsewhere. It is claimed that despite racial discrimination, Capeverdean immigrants naturalized more readily (perhaps because of a higher rate of literacy?) than white Portuguese, and by the 1940s appeared at least as Americanized as the other immigrants of Portuguese nationality.[22]

In historic Provincetown some racial and religious antagonism between Portuguese and Yankees around the turn of the century gave way to peaceful intermingling, including some intermarriage. With the former gradually outnumbering the latter, both population elements were closely interwoven in the business of fishing. After World War I, the Ku Klux Klan provoked a new period of severe tension, one which did not die down until World War II. Actually the Provincetown Portuguese have Americanized relatively fast, partly because of their isolation from other larger Portuguese settlements.[23]

For some more examples of distinctive local conditions, we may point to Portsmouth, Rhode Island. About the time of the First World War, there was more free and amiable mingling between the Portuguese farmers and their Yankee neighbors in that rural spot than there was in urban Fall River, where the Anglo element kept distant from the "foreigners."[24] When the Portuguese first settled in Ludlow, Massachusetts, they encountered the hostility of French-Canadians and Scots, due to competitive fears. But with the second generation gaining voting strength, the Portuguese group improved its position. In multi-ethnic Bethlehem, Pennsylvania, where a small number of Portuguese settled generations ago, the ethnic distinction between these and Greeks, Italians, Hungarians, etc., is still strong, although without friction.

What about California? This was new frontier country, and the

Portuguese had a share in building it up from the start, in contrast to New England, where the Portuguese were newcomers in a thickly populated region with a long tradition. Moreover, in California the bulk of the Portuguese settled in rural areas, where there is generally less pressure toward quick assimilation and less interethnic friction than in crowded cities. "Relations between the Portuguese and the other foreign groups here are peaceful . . . , although there is a beginning anti-foreign sentiment on the part of the native Americans," the Portuguese consul at San Francisco reported in 1892.[25]

By 1908, according to another consul in that city, various foreign groups in California had overtaken the Portuguese in overall prestige, largely because of the widespread illiteracy among the latter. They were ignored in political contests. Yet, the same observer continued, the United States exerts an amazing power of assimilation on all immigrants including the Portuguese; these are "overanxious" to switch their loyalty to their "adoptive country."[26] The United States Immigration Commission, in its sample survey of the Fresno area about 1910, found that North European immigrants in this area were fairly well assimilated; to a lesser extent, this was also true of the Portuguese and the Dalmatians. There was little if any prejudice against these groups, largely because, in general, they were part of the American middle class (in an economic sense). The Armenians, German-Russians, Italians, Japanese, and Chinese, on the other hand, were regarded as "foreigners" by the Fresno natives—partly because they had come to the United States more recently than the others and were economically weaker. The Danes, Germans, other North Europeans, and the Portuguese (but not those other groups) were rather freely accepted as members of American fraternal organizations.[27]

Some thirty years later, shortly before the outbreak of World War II, Gerald Estep found that assimilation of the Portuguese in California (as regards language, political involvement, rate of intermarriage, etc.) was trailing way behind that in Hawaii, because, in his analysis, in California the Portuguese were subjected to less discrimination, and hence less pressure to assert and "prove" themselves.[28] In the early 1950s, the California Portuguese—at least the farmers in the San Joaquin Valley—still had a reputation of clannishness: "Up to this present generation (only now coming of age) . . . they seldom associated, or cared to associate, with anyone outside their own group, so that most of the non-Portuguese population regard them as odd, unfriendly, farm-type foreigners, and simply let it go at that."[29] Nevertheless, the postwar years have brought a good deal of rapprochement between Portuguese-Americans and such other local ethnic groups as the Italians and the Irish (but not the Mexicans!), including quite a bit of intermarriage.

Outgroup relations of the Portuguese in the Hawaiian Islands have been dominated by the long-drawn-out effort to escape the low-prestige classification of "plantation laborer," which because of the increasing proportion of Oriental immigrant labor in the islands soon would carry about the same connotation as "non-white" on the traditional mainland prestige scale. Or to put it positively, the Portuguese tried to get as close as possible to the status of the dominant Anglo-Nordic-American Haole group (cf. p. 114) by being bracketed together with the latter as simply "Caucasian" (meaning "white") rather than being singled out as a separate group somewhere between nonwhite and white. (This did not prevent a certain amount of intermarriage with aboriginal Hawaiians and with Chinese, higher on the scale than later Oriental arrivals.)

On the sugar plantations, the Portuguese had been generally placed in separate camps, neither Haole nor Oriental; they were thus kept socially distant by the Haoles, while keeping themselves distant from the Oriental groups. Merging with the "other Caucasians" became easier in urban Honolulu—or else by moving to California.[30] But for a long time yet, a disparaging connotation attached to being called a "Portagee" (as against the more straightforward "Portuguese"), let alone a "pakaliao" (from the Portuguese word for codfish).[31]

To cite an extreme attempt to escape stigma: the probated will of a Portuguese woman deceased in Honolulu in 1928 stipulated that her son-in-law with children could live in her house only on condition that he "not allow any Filipinos or Hawaiians . . . to enter the said premises at any time."[32] A less drastic way to achieve "Americanization" (in one sense of the word) was for Portuguese girls to marry "Nordic" men so as to acquire an English-sounding surname. In the 1930s a person of mixed Portuguese and aboriginal Hawaiian parentage would rather class himself as Hawaiian than as Portuguese.[33] Portuguese membership in the (Protestant) Central Union Church at Honolulu, long considered the church of the rich Haole, rose from about 1 percent in 1934 to 9 percent in 1949.[34]

Today the Portuguese ethnics (or more precisely, persons of Portuguese ancestry) in Hawaii have been pretty much absorbed into a broadened and ethnically rather neutral middle class. They still prefer to stress their Haole status, but no longer consider themselves superior to the Japanese ethnics, who now hold a very strong position in the Islands. With few exceptions, they have become as completely Americanized as Hawaii's multi-ethnic setting will permit—more uniformly so than is true of the people of Portuguese descent in California and in the New England–New York region.

It is probably correct to say that, in the American democracy, assimilation implies a certain amount of active interest and participation in political democratic processes on the part of men and increasingly also on the part of women. But active participation in the form of voting, or of actually running for public office, presupposes citizenship—naturalization in the case of immigrants. Naturalization, in turn, in the twentieth century, has as its prerequisite a minimum of literacy (in English). On the other hand, an alien's desire to be naturalized does not necessarily reflect a substantial degree of assimilation, i.e., approval of all or most aspects of the prevailing American life-style. For instance, naturalization may be sought for economic advantage, and/or to protect one's right to disagree.

Among the earlier Portuguese immigrants, the rate of naturalization was extremely low, at least up to the 1930s. The obvious reason for this was the high degree of illiteracy among them, coupled with peasant apathy or distrust of governmental formalities. The Portuguese consul in Boston summed up the situation like this, as of 1912: The percentage of Portuguese who become naturalized was much lower in small rural settlements than in cities. The principal motives *for* naturalization, according to the consul, were (1) the emigrant's decision to settle in the United States permanently with his family; (2) fear on the part of draft-dodgers of being punished in Portugal if they were to return there; (3) propaganda for naturalization by community leaders, so as to give voting power to the immigrants; (4) the fact that certain occupations were open to American citizens only (notaries, government employees, liquor dealers, etc.).[35]

In 1920, according to the United States census (which may not be entirely reliable[36]), only 16 percent of Portuguese immigrants (aged twenty-one years and over, white, within the continental United States) were naturalized. The rate rose to about 23 percent in 1930—which was still the third lowest among all immigrant nationalities, after the Mexicans and the Spaniards. (By comparison, the percentage of naturalized among the Italian immigrants was then 55 percent, and 68 percent among those from Russia.) In the 1930s, when American citizenship became a prerequisite for a growing number of occupations and when there was an increasing proportion of native-born children urging their immigrant parents to become Americans, the number of naturalized rose sharply. During World War II there were many cases like the one of a woman born in São Miguel who at the time had five sons in the United States Armed Forces and decided to attend naturalization school in Fall River so as to learn some English and become a citizen. Or the case of an eighty-five-year-old Madeiran woman living in Hawaii since 1879 who in the presence of some seventy American descendants filed a petition for naturalization in 1944.[37] Other similar cases have been reported in very recent years.

One cannot know how many of those thousands of Portuguese immigrants who ultimately resettled in their homeland (see pp. 47–48) did so out of patriotic attachment to Portugal and/or inability to adjust to American conditions. Many of the repatriates, especially in the Azores, continued to express very positive feelings about their American experience. Certainly the overwhelming majority of those who did remain permanently in the United States seem to have developed a strong sense of loyalty toward their adoptive country even without naturalizing.

On the other hand, at no time in the nineteenth or twentieth century has there been any official friction or major ideological clash between Portugal and the United States that would have forced immigrants here to experience a conflict of loyalties or to choose sides—with the possible exception of periods during Salazar's dictatorship, when official Portugal veered close to an alignment with Fascist Italy (but short of support for Nazi Germany), and again when she fought against the independence movement in her African colonies.

Early in this century, shortly before and for some time after the fall of the monarchy in Portugal, immigrants in this country were divided in their sentiment for or against ("leftist-anticlerical") republicanism in their homeland. Most of the small number vocal enough to express themselves (in the immigrant press or elsewhere) sided with republicanism, as encouraged by the American climate, but later on were rather neutral about Salazar's corporate state, perhaps under the influence of the clergy. Upon the entrance of the United States into the First World War, the leading Portuguese fraternal society in California was quick to send a telegram to President Wilson pledging support in the war effort.

Again, after the Pearl Harbor attack, Portuguese clubs in the

Newark area joined to cable President Roosevelt: we stand ready to serve America. In 1942 the major Portuguese fraternal society in New England adopted a resolution, sent to Washington: "Whatever attitude Portugal may take, forcibly or voluntarily, the U.P.C. will remain faithful to the cause of the U.S.A." The League of Portuguese Fraternal Societies in California followed up by donating $10,000 to the United States government for the purchase of two antiaircraft guns. In 1960 a proposal originating in Madeira and the Azores for the erection of a "Monument to the Portuguese Immigrant" in New Bedford failed to win support here: a monument to emigrants, in Portugal, may be all right, commented New England's Portuguese daily; but the immigrants on this side of the ocean, instead of asking the United States to take care of a memorial of immigrant self-praise, should express their own gratitude to this country.[38]

As has been pointed out on p. 164, before an individual immigrant comes to identify himself as an American, he usually develops a sense of belonging to his immigrant group, to his "hyphenated" or "ethnic" community—at least if he lives close enough to a substantial number of compatriots to share in such immigrant institutions as clubs or churches. Ethnic block formation, we may now add, is a psychologically helpful way station on the road to integration, at least if integration is to mean more than submersion, namely, active participation in shaping the destiny of American society at large, whether by technically political means or otherwise.

"For the average immigrant a colony of his own race is the natural route to the life of America," concludes John Daniels. "If the immigrant is to escape demoralization by the sudden and complete change from his former life, he must have, during the adjustment to his new environment, some moral support and control of a kind which he will recognize and understand. This function the colony performs."[39] Ultimately, to rise in the social scale and get political leverage, the foreign-born will rely heavily on their American-born offspring. Politically ambitious individuals of the second or even the third generation, in turn, may look primarily to their ethnic group, including the naturalized foreign-born, for support in elections.

If the Portuguese ethnics have been relatively slow, particularly in the Northeast, to produce qualified candidates for public office, this seems to have been only partly due to the low educational and economic level (and low rate of naturalization) among the foreign-born. There has been a correspondingly slow educational-economic advance on the part of the second generation—again primarily in the Northeast. In addition, political bloc formation in support of fellow Portuguese actually running for office has been weak. Many Portuguese-Americans, complained the *Diario de Noticias* on one typical occasion, accuse those among them who have political ambitions of wanting to live an easy life; or they question their qualifications out of envy or an inferiority complex.[40]

In southeastern New England, stronghold of Portuguese settlement, it was only about the time of World War II that the Portuguese element began to enter the political arena on any scale. Actually a major step in that direction was taken within the labor movement: Mariano S. Bishop (Bispo), a native of São Miguel who had come to Fall River as a child, managed to become a director of the Textile Workers Union of America, C.I.O., in 1943, and rose to executive vice-president in 1952 (but he died a few months later). Michael Botelho, born in Fall River of São Miguelian immigrants, was elected to a vice-presidency within the same union in 1953. Joseph F. Francis won a seat in the Massachusetts State Senate in the early 1940s, probably the first Portuguese-American (native-born) to enter a state legislature in the eastern part of the country.[41] By 1952, two members of the Massachusetts State Senate (one of them, Mary L. Fonseca, a woman) and four members of the State House of Representatives were of Portuguese parentage or birth.

In 1957 John M. Arruda, born of immigrant parents in Fall River, became mayor of that city, apparently the first Portuguese ethnic to hold such office in New England. Five years later, there were also two Superior Court judges and one district attorney of Portuguese background in that area. As of 1974, ten out of 280 members of the Massachusetts legislature (both chambers) were Portuguese-Americans. A few more state and municipal offices have been won since then, but New Bedford, the "Portuguese capital of the United States," has yet to elect its first mayor of Portuguese extraction.

In California, the Portuguese won their first seat in the state legislature when Azorean-born João G. Mattos, Jr., was elected to the Assembly as early as the year 1900. He later served several terms in the California Senate and also held a judgeship.[42] A second seat in the Assembly was won in 1910 by Antonio A. Rogers, of Azorean parentage. There is only a meager record of Portuguese Californians holding public office thereafter, until Mrs. Helen L. C. Lawrence (née Silveira) became "mayor" (actually City Council chairperson)

of San Leandro in 1941.[43] As of 1959, Sacramento's mayor was one
Clarence Azevedo, son of Portuguese immigrants ("but he doesn't
speak a word of Portuguese"[44]). Other second-generation Portu-
guese in California's public life in recent years have included Joseph
Freitas, Jr., district attorney of San Francisco,[45] and two State
Assembly men. Finally, early in 1979, Peter ("Tony") Coelho, of
Merced, California, won election to the United States House of
Representatives, probably the first Portuguese-American to reach
Washington's Capitol Hill.[46]

A different picture presents itself in Hawaii, where the Portuguese, partly because Oriental immigrants were barred from naturalization for a long time, managed to acquire considerable political
influence early in the century.[47] In 1894, after the overthrow of the
Hawaiian monarchy, three out of eighteen elected delegates to the
Constitutional Convention (two out of six from the Oahu districts)
were Portuguese.[48] Between 1909 and 1929, no less than thirty-one
members of the territorial legislature were ethnically Portuguese,
including many foreign-born. Thirty of these served as representatives for one or as many as nine terms, four of them also as
senators.[49] One of the latter, Manuel Caetano Pacheco, a native of
Ponta Delgada who had come to Hawaii as a child, and a bookbinder
by profession, also was Supervisor of Honolulu and chaired the
Democratic Territorial Committee.[50]

In addition, Honolulu-born Antonio Perry (Pereira), son of a
Fayalese whaler, entered the territorial judiciary in 1896 to become
Chief Justice of Hawaii, 1926–1934.[51] Perhaps a dozen more
individuals of Portuguese ancestry, some of them foreign-born, have
held judgeships there. Cyrus Nils Tavares, Attorney General of the
Territory in the 1940s, chaired the Hawaii Statehood Commission in
1953 and then was appointed Federal District Judge.[52] The proportion of Portuguese stock in Hawaiian public life has naturally waned
more recently as the Japanese stock has risen in influence. But as of
1961, the Speaker of the State of Hawaii House of Representatives
was Elmer F. Cravalho (or Carvalho?), born on Maui Island of
Azorean parents; the Vice-speaker was Madeiran-born Manuel S.
Henriques (then the only nonnative member of the house).[53]

Portuguese-Americans, like other minorities trying to define their
place within the larger society, have sometimes felt a little unsure
about whether they should play up the "Portuguese" or the
"American" part of their label. For example, in 1944, when some of
those in Fall River proposed the erection of a separate honor roll for

Portuguese-American servicemen in that city, others opposed the idea on the ground that such "separatism" would offend other Americans; there should be a single honor roll for all Fall River servicemen.[54] But the 1950s and 1960s, a time of growing self-assertion for various ethnic groups in the United States, also witnessed a modest swelling of ethnic pride among the Portuguese in New England and California, including some successful publicity for the Portuguese contribution to America.

Thus a memorial to the "Portuguese-American war dead" was unveiled in New Bedford in 1950. A similar one, sponsored by a new "American Portuguese Loyalty Association" and "American Portuguese War Veterans" (with *American* deliberately placed before *Portuguese!*), was dedicated in Fall River the next year, followed by one in Ludlow and perhaps others elsewhere. Peter Francisco, a soldier in Washington's army whose connection with Portugal is tenuous at best (see pp. 15–16) was built up into a Portuguese-American folk hero, complete with an annual Peter Francisco Day.[55] In California the commemoration of Cabrilho (cf. pp. 7-8) was given new impetus through efforts of Cabrilho Civic Clubs, etc.

To close this chapter and this book, we shall attempt a brief, realistic appraisal of the contribution of the Portuguese element to the United States. But is it actually possible to define objectively, in universally valid terms, what constitutes a positive contribution? The definition will depend on the value system of the recipient, as much as on that of the giver or of a third-party judge. Within the context of prevailing American notions of success, one is likely to look around in the first place for named individuals who have claimed leadership positions in politics, in business, or in other large organizations, or who have stood out in the sciences, in the arts, in popular entertainment, or in competitive sports.

Other things being equal, a relatively small immigrant group with a predominantly "peasant" background cannot be expected to produce as many successful individuals as a much larger group or one starting out from a technologically more advanced baseline. A small number of Portuguese-Americans, mostly of the second generation, who have filled responsible positions in regional political life, largely in Hawaii, have already been mentioned.[56]

In the field of organized religion, which bears certain similarities to organized politics, the Portuguese immigrant who reached highest office is Humberto S. Medeiros. Born on the island of São

Miguel in 1915, he settled with his family in Fall River in 1931, "swept the floors of a textile mill for 62 cents a day" for a while, nontypically went on to a doctorate in theology at Catholic University, Washington, in 1947, and was appointed pastor of one of the Portuguese immigrant churches in Fall River about 1958. In 1970, after heading a bishopric in Texas for some years, he found himself chosen to succeed Cardinal Cushing as Archbishop of Boston, the first non-Irish head of that important Catholic district in 124 years; and in 1973 he was elevated to Cardinal of the Roman Catholic Church.[57] In Hawaii, Madeiran-born Stephen Peter Alencastre, raised on sugar plantations but ordained a priest at Honolulu in 1902, became Bishop of Hawaii in 1924.[58]

Quite a different type of religious success story is that of Bishop "Daddy" Grace, founder and lifetime head of the Negro revivalist House of Prayer for All People. Marcelino Manuel Graça (later Anglicized as Charles M. Grace) was born on Brava Island, Cape Verde, about 1882, and first came to New Bedford around 1902, as a cook on one of the schooners then plying between that city and the Cape Verde Islands. He eventually settled down in the New Bedford area, for a while owned a small grocery in Wareham, Massachusetts, and later worked as a dining-car cook on railroads in the South. In 1921 he began preaching independently in New Bedford about miraculous powers of the Holy Spirit operating through him, and by 1926 the self-styled Bishop Grace founded his own first congregation, House of Prayer for All People, in Charlotte, North Carolina.

His evangelist movement spread, drawing Negroes from many other sects and from the general population. In 1930 "Sweet Daddy Grace" entered the Harlem section of New York City, there to become a successful competitor of Father Divine. He was said to perform miracles of healing, representing himself as a prophet and savior. What is certain is that this prominent Capeverdean-Portuguese immigrant, a man of superior intelligence and charismatic personality, gradually gathered about him a following (mostly Negro) of over 3 million people, distributed over about 350 Houses of Prayer in some sixty American cities, with churches and other real estate personally vested in him. When Grace died in 1960, he left an estate estimated at close to $25 million.[59]

In the sphere of business enterprise and economic development, it is difficult to think of individual Portuguese-Americans for special mention. Their contribution is essentially a collective and anonymous one of relatively unskilled labor. Even if there are some Stachanow-type record workers among them, they would not get into the news. In the New England–New York area, a rare example of a successful businessman of part-Portuguese extraction was William M. Wood, founder and longtime head of the American Woolen Company (which as of 1923 operated fifty-nine mills). Born in Martha's Vineyard in 1858 and raised in New Bedford, where he worked in cotton mills in his teens, he was the son of an Azorean whaleman and a Yankee mother, probably originally named Madeira (the Portuguese word for wood).[60]

In recent years, Madeiran-born Joseph E. Fernandes turned the little grocery store started by his parents at Norton, Massachusetts, into a chain of over thirty supermarkets blanketing southeastern Massachusetts. But in addition to heading an enterprise grossing well over $100 million a year, Fernandes has engaged in philanthropies which have earned him citations from the Pope, the (United States) National Conference of Christians and Jews, and the Portuguese government.[61] In California, perhaps a dozen individuals of Portuguese birth or parentage have attained some local recognition as wealthy heads of relatively large dairy or fishing enterprises (e.g., Lawrence Oliver, mentioned in earlier chapters, and Joaquim A. de Silveira, who jointly with Manuel T. Freitas founded and developed the Portuguese-American Bank, in San Francisco).[62]

Portuguese immigration to these shores has included only a bare sprinkling of academically trained or otherwise "intellectual" persons, such as physicians, artists, and writers. (A few who came as children, and especially American-born children of immigrants, received a higher education in the United States and subsequently entered various professions.) For example, Mathias Figueira (1853–1930), born in Madeira and educated at the University of Coimbra, became well known in medical circles of New York and was a founder of the American College of Surgeons. Carlos Fernandes, also Madeiran-born, was director of St. John's Hospital in San Francisco. (He died in 1977.) José Rodrigues Migueis, born in Lisbon (1901), author of short stories and some novels (mostly written in Portuguese), is far better known in Portugal than in the United States, although he has spent much of his adult life in New York. Henrique Medina in Hollywood and Palmira Pimentel in New York, both natives of Portugal, achieved some distinction as painters in the 1930s.

It is significant that Portuguese-Americans, in trying to think of prominent individuals of their own background, point to John Philip Sousa and John Roderigo Dos Passos perhaps more than to anyone else. Actually Sousa (1854–1932), the famous composer of marches and other music, was born in Washington of a German mother and of a father born in Spain of a noble family that had been driven from Portugal during a revolution. Thus Sousa was third-generation Portuguese, and only on his father's side at that. Dos Passos (1896–1970), the celebrated novelist, had only one Portuguese grandparent, a Madeiran who had settled in Philadelphia as a shoemaker. Yet Dos Passos did become genuinely interested in his part-Portuguese ancestry in his later years.[63]

Comparatively fair is Portugal's contribution to America in the area of the performing arts. Most recently Elmar de Oliveira has risen to prominence as a concert violinist. Born of Portuguese immigrant parents in Connecticut, he won first prize in Moscow's Tchaikovsky competition in 1978. Raul da Silva Pereira, a native of Lisbon who settled in California about 1922, was noted as a composer and conductor. Portuguese-born Ilda Stichini, also a resident of California, and Maria Silveira, born in Boston of an Azorean sea captain and a Yankee mother, enjoyed moderate success as opera singers in the 1930s.

Show-business people of Portuguese extraction in the United States have included the comedian Harold Peary, known as "The Great Gildersleeve" on radio and the screen (born in San Leandro as Harold José Pereira de Faria, of Azorean parentage), and John A. Mendes, born in Fall River of Portuguese immigrants, who achieved fame as a touring magician ("Prince Mendes") during and after World War II. Rod de Medecis, born Rodrigo Nóbrega Pinto de Médecis in northern Portugal, acted in many early American films. Henry da Sylva (Henrique Maria Jaime da Silva) came from Lisbon to Hollywood about 1920 to open a ballet school and to direct and act in a number of motion pictures. The California Portuguese community has also laid claim to the movie actor Nestor Pavie and the singer Tony Martin.[64]

In the world of sports, Bernie de Viveiros, born in California of Portuguese parents, was a major-league baseball player (with the Detroit Tigers in the 1920s and the Oakland Oaks thereafter). Other nationally known baseball players of Portuguese extraction were Manuel Gomes and Lou Fonseca. Al Melo (Alfonso Tavares de Melo), boxing champion of New England, represented the United States in the 1924 Olympics. George Araujo, born in Providence of

Capeverdean parents, was a contender for the world lightweight boxing championship in 1953. Other such contenders were California-born Johnny Gonsalves and Irminio José de Souza (known as Babe Herman). A professional wrestler in the 1920s was Justiniano Silva, who had come from northern Portugal. Madeiran-born Henrique Santos won the United States fencing championship in 1942.

One can be inventive at some level without much formal schooling. A number of Portuguese immigrants have proven it through minor technical inventions: Abilio da Silva Greaves, who had come from Faial to be pastor of Boston's Portuguese, invented the Thermophone fire alarm in 1924 and also patented a number of aviation-related devices. Steve Abrantes, who had immigrated to work his way up in a Connecticut factory, invented a new wool carding or combing system in his own works near Providence in the 1940s. José Pacheco Correia, from São Miguel, developed an electric needle machine for cotton combing in his New Bedford plant. In Bethelehem, Pennsylvania, Sebastião Luiz Dias received a patent for a new irrigation control system. A patent for an improved stable cleaner was issued to José dos Santos Fernandes, who lived in the New York area in the 1940s and whose real ambition was to become a writer.

In the late 1920s John C. Lobato, who had studied engineering in Portugal, presented in New Jersey what he claimed was the first model of a combination airplane-dirigible-helicopter. Previously he had developed a new type of armored car or tank, of interest to the United States government. More dramatic and puzzling is the story of one João André (John Andrews), a Portuguese living near Pittsburgh, who in 1916 claimed to have invented a new fuel for combustion engines much cheaper than gasoline. It was allegedly made with water, to which a chemical (unidentified but obtainable in any drugstore) was added by some secret formula. André successfully demonstrated his invention at the New York Navy Yard and in Washington. But he refused to reveal his formula unless he were first paid $2 million, which he did not get; and then he mysteriously disappeared. Approached again during World War II, he claimed to have lost his formula. He died in 1953, taking his secret with him.[65]

So much for a brief list, necessarily incomplete and perhaps somewhat arbitrary, of individual Portuguese-Americans who have made a "name" for themselves. This listing has been included partly for the benefit of readers—many of them presumably of Portuguese extraction themselves—who are looking for a kind of

Who's Who. But it is also intended to demonstrate that Portuguese-Americans as a group have not been lacking in sparks of special talent, in the kinds of individual accomplishment that usually get noted on the record.

Yet the true contribution of a whole nationality of ethnic population within the fabric of American society cannot be measured by the number of individuals who happen to have entered the public limelight. The major "contribution," if that is the right word, the "give" in exchange for the "take," consists in the collective productive labor and in the cultural traditions of the group as described in previous chapters. It is especially appropriate to recall the characterizations of Portuguese immigrants mentioned on pp. 119 ("hard-working", "honest", "law-abiding", etc.), the pioneering efforts outlined in Chapters 1 through 5, the solid muscle they have provided in the factory, on the farm, and on the seas (see Chapter 9).

As a matter of fact, as Americanization and integration proceed, it makes less and less sense to distinguish between "we" and "they," to talk of the contributions of a distinct group which is no longer very distinct from the rest of the population. Ultimately, the question of the contribution of one population group or another resolves itself into the multi-faceted contributions of individuals as such in the give and take of daily living. Simple ordinary people, most of them and most of us.

On this note we conclude—having shown how those who came from Portugal, even though only a minor component of American society, spread across an unusually broad canvas of American history reaching from the beginning of the sixteenth century to the present and from New England to Hawaii.

Notes and References

Documentary sources which are referred to in the notes only once are given a full bibliographical listing in the respective note, without again being listed in the bibliography.

On the other hand, sources cited repeatedly are identified in the respective notes by author's last name, or equivalent key word, followed by a boldface numeral which refers to the correspondingly numbered entry in the bibliography. For example, in notes 1 and 3 to chapter 1, the key word Morison followed by the boldface numeral **148** (followed by a colon and by page numbers) identifies the source as *Portuguese Voyages to America* by Samuel E. Morison, which is entered in the bibliography as no. 148. The cross-referencing numeral thus obviates the need for repetitious full citations.

PREFACE

1. *A Report on World Population Migrations as Related to the United States of America* (Washington, D.C.: George Washington University, 1956); consisting primarily of bibliographies, pp. 85–449; here pp. 250, 344.

2. Several hundred more sources actually consulted but not specifically cited for documentation appear neither in the Notes nor in the Bibliography; but most of these are included in the separately published bibliography cited in note 1 above.

CHAPTER ONE

1. Morison, **148:** 5.

2. Diario, **4:** 24, 25 March, 8 June 1955; 15, 19 October 1959; 28 April 1953.

3. Morison, **148:** 33–41.

4. Prestage, **152:** 270–71. Morison, **148:** 51–55. Eduardo Brazão, *A descoberta da Terra Nova* (Lisbon: Agência-Geral do Ultramar, 1964), pp. 37–59.

5. John Cabot, the Italian navigator in English service, sighted Cape Breton Island and Nova Scotia in 1497, but he did not, apparently, discover Newfoundland. On the other hand, remains of a settlement found in northern Newfoundland in 1963 may possibly be of Norse origin, antedating both Columbus and Corte-Real. In 1965, Yale University announced discovery of a map "proving" that the Norwegian, Leif Ericson, had landed

on the northeast coast of America about the year 1,000 (*New York Times*, 17 October 1965); but this map has since been declared a fake.

6. Cf. Prestage, **152**: 271–76; Morison, **148**: 71–72; Edmund B. Delabarre, *Dighton Rock* (New York: Walter Neale, 1928). For more discussions of Gaspar and Miguel Corte-Real's role in the discovery of North America see Gago Coutinho, in *Boletim da Sociedade de Geografia* (Lisbon), ser. 68, nos. 5–6 (May–June 1950), and Eduardo Brazão, *Os Corte Reais e o Novo Mundo* (Lisbon: Agência-Geral do Ultramar, 1965).

While Brazão and other Portuguese scholars are skeptical about Delabarre's hypothesis, Portuguese-American organizations in Massachusetts and Rhode Island, with their growing political leverage, have managed to gain quasi-official acceptance of Delabarre's view linking the Dighton Rock to Miguel Corte-Real: A "Day of Miguel Corte Real," set for 10 June, was proclaimed by the mayors of Fall River and Taunton, Massachusetts, in 1951, and has been nominally observed since. In 1963, the controversial rock was moved from the bed of the Taunton River to a more protected onshore location at Berkley and declared a public monument by the State of Massachusetts; the access road to Dighton Rock Park was named Delabarre Road. For various eighteenth and nineteenth-century reconstructions of the Dighton Rock "inscriptions," as of Indian or even Phoenician origin, see Garrick Mallery, *Picture-Writing of the American Indians* (New York: Dover, 1972), pp. 86–87, 762–63.

Delabarre's alleged decipherment of the Dighton Rock markings had generated the additional belief that a structure variously called the Old Stone Mill or the Newport Tower, at Newport, Rhode Island, may have been built by Miguel Corte-Real, and not by the Vikings. Cf. Philip A. Means, *Newport Tower* (New York: Holt, 1942); Herbert Pell, "The Old Stone Mill," *Rhode Island History*, (1948), 105–19. Most recently, Fort Ninigret at Charleston, R.I., has also been attributed to Portuguese origin.

The relatively noncontroversial link of Gaspar Corte-Real to Newfoundland was officially acknowledged by the unveiling of a statue of this explorer at St. John, N.F., in 1965, in the presence of Canadian and Portuguese official delegations. The province of Newfoundland has had an officially proclaimed "Portugal Day" annually since that time.

7. Cf. John B. Brebner, *The Explorers of North America, 1492–1806* (New York: MacMillan, 1933), p. 114; António Baião et al., eds., *História da expansão portuguesa no mundo*, 3 vols. (Lisbon: Atica, 1939), pp. 317, 355; Fidelino de Figueiredo, "A collaboraçao portuguesa no descobrimento da América do Norte," *Revista de História* (Lisbon), 15 (1926), 261.

8. For an annotated English translation of the narrative by the Gentleman of Elvas see James A. Robertson, transl. and ed., *True Relation of the Hardships Suffered by Governor Fernando de Soto and Certain Portuguese Gentlemen During the Discovery of the Province of Florida*, 2 vols. (De Land: Florida State Historical Association, 1932–1933), and Theodore H. Lewis, ed., "Narrative of the Expedition of Hernando de Soto by the

Gentleman of Elvas," in *Original Narratives of Early American History: Spanish Explorers* (New York: Scribner's, 1925). According to Jaime Cortesão, *Os portugueses no descobrimento dos Estudos Unidos* (Lisbon: Seara Nova, 1949), pp. 43–44, at least one hundred of the six hundred men that disembarked with de Soto in 1539 were Portuguese; for the ship commanded by André de Vasconcelos, one of the larger ones among the six carrying the expeditionary force, was filled entirely with Portuguese.

9. See George P. Hammond and Agapito Rey, eds., *Narratives of the Coronado Expedition 1540–1542* (Albuquerque: University of New Mexico Press, 1940), pp. 12–13.

10. The name of "Cabrillo" (which may mean "kid," "little buck") was probably given him by the Spanish; the Portuguese spelling would be "Cabrilho."

11. The name of Cabrilho is commemorated nowadays all over California. At Point Loma, near San Diego, the U.S. Government has erected the Cabrillo National Monument, topped by a bronze caravel. In 1935 the California State Legislature designated 28 September as Cabrillo Day, to be celebrated annually. A memorial plaque donated by a group of Portuguese-Americans was unveiled on San Miguel Island in 1937. A statue of Cabrillo donated by the Portuguese government was added to the National Monument at Point Loma in 1949. As for pertinent place-names, there is or was a Point Cabrillo at Mendocino, and a Cabrillo Point at Monterey. (Cf. Erwin G. Gudde, *California Place Names: a Geographical Dictionary* [Berkeley: University of California Press, 1949].) There is a Cabrillo Street in at least five Californian cities.

12. For a summary of the Cabrillo expedition, see, for instance, Charles E. Chapman, *A History of California: The Spanish Period* (New York: Macmillan, 1921), pp. 76–81.

13. Cf. Chapman, pp. 116–21.

14. Cf. George Patterson, "The Portuguese on the North-East Coast of America, and the First European Attempt at Colonization There," *Proceedings and Transactions of the Royal Society of Canada for the Year 1890*, sec. 2, pp. 127–73. See also M. A. Buchanan, "Notes on Portuguese Place-Names in North-Eastern America," in *Estudios Hispánicos- Homenaje a Archer M. Huntington* (Wellesley, Mass.: Wellesley College, 1952), pp. 99–104; Pap, **57**: 125–28; Samuel E. Morison, *The European Discovery of America: The Northern Voyages A.D. 500–1600* (New York: Oxford University Press, 1971), pp. 228–30.

15. Cf. Levinger, **121**:90

16. Isaac Jogues, *Novum Belgium*, edited with notes by John Gilmary Shea (New York, 1862); and John J. Birch, *The Saint of the Wilderness*, *St. Isaac Jogues* (New York: Benziger, 1936), pp. 172–73.

17. Most of the foregoing, regarding Portuguese Jews in America, is based on Levinger, **121**: 59–95; Peter Wiernik, *History of the Jews of America* (New York: Jewish Press Publishing Co., 1912), pp. 77–99; Lee

M. Friedman, *Early American Jews* (Cambridge: Harvard University Press, 1934), pp. 13, 61–89; Morris A. Gutstein, *The Story of the Jews of Newport* (New York: Bloch, 1936). A few details on the Portuguese congregation in New York were supplied by Rabbi D. de Sola Pool. On the Portuguese Jews in various countries, see also J. Lúcio de Azevedo, "Judeus portugueses na dispersão," *Revista de História* (Lisbon), 4 (1915), 105–27, 201–17; Cecil Roth, *A History of the Marranos* (Philadelphia: Jewish Publication Society of America, 1932).

18. Holmes, **52**: 394. For specific arrivals in Pennsylvania, see J. Daniel Rupp, *A Collection of Thirty Thousand Names of German, Swiss, Dutch, French, Portuguese and Other Immigrants in Pennsylvania . . . from 1727 to 1776* (Harrisburg, 1856), pp. 310–36; William H. Egle, ed., *Names of Foreigners Who Took the Oath of Allegiance to the Province and State of Pennsylvania 1727–1775, with the Foreign Arrivals 1786–1808* (Harrisburg, 1892), pp. 566, 629; Frank Ried Diffendorffer, *The German Immigration into Pennsylvania through the Port of Philadelphia from 1700 to 1775* (Lancaster: The Pennsylvania-German Society, 1900), p. 48.

19. For details on The Melungeons and Croatans, see Swan M. Burnett, "A Note on the Melungeons," *American Anthropologist*, 2 (1889), 347–49; Will A. Dromgoole, "The Melungeons," *Arena*, 3 (December 1890–May 1891), 470–79, 745–51; Will T. Hale and Dixon L. Merritt, *A History of Tennessee and Tennesseans*, 2 vols. (Chicago: Lewis, 1913), I, 180–85. More recent references are: Roland M. Harper, "A Statistical Study of the Croatans," *Rural Sociology*, 2 (1937), 444–56; Brewton Berry, "The Mestizos of South Carolina," *American Journal of Sociology*, 51, no. 1 (July 1945), 34–41; William H. Gilbert, Jr. "Memorandum Concerning the Characteristics of the Larger Mixed-Blood Racial Islands of the Eastern United States," *Social Forces*, 24, no. 4 (May 1946), 438–47. See also *Dictionary of American History* (New York: Scribner), vol. 3, s.v. "Melungeons." While some derive the word *Melungeon* from French *mélange*, others attribute it to an alleged Afro-Portuguese *melungo* "shipmate"; cf. Brewton Berry, *Almost White* (New York: Macmillan, 1963), p. 36. The most recent discussion of these mixed-breeds is by T. Thompson, "The Little Races," *American Anthropologist*, 74, no. 5 (October 1972), 1295–306.

In February 1958, the journalistic discovery of sixteen allegedly "Portuguese" families living as a segregated racial group in Gaston Township, Northampton County, North Carolina, created quite a stir in the American and then in the Portuguese press. According to B. Teixeira (personal communication dated 21 March 1958), then press officer of the Portuguese Embassy in Washington, his on-site investigation showed that the families in question were all completely white, related to each other, with Anglo surnames; they claimed to have been in Northampton County since the construction of the Roanoke Rapids Canal, c.1820, when their (allegedly Portuguese) ancestors came either from Pennsylvania or from Portugal to

work on the canal; and they have been locally described as "Portygee,"
never as Croatan or Melungeon, "as far back as at least 100 years." Two
acts of the North Carolina legislature, in 1923 and 1925, had set aside this
small group as a separate "Portuguese" race, assigned to a segregated
school. I have discussed the entire case in Diario, 4: 20 March 1958.
I am indebted to Gerald M. Moser for pointing out (in a personal
communication dated 28 August 1965) that the pilot and shipmaster of Sir
Walter Raleigh, and of others on the first colonizing voyages of the British
to Virginia, was the Portuguese Simão Fernandes (Simon Ferdinando); he
was associated with Raleigh as early as 1578. Could this "substantiate" the
Melungeons' claim of descent from Sir Walter Raleigh's colony, and from
the Portuguese?

20. Charles E. Banks, *The History of Martha's Vineyard, Dukes County,
Massachusetts*, vol. 2 (Boston: George H. Dean, 1911), pp. 18, 22, 208; vol.
3 (Edgartown: Dukes County Historical Society, 1925), p. vii.

21. Cf. Jornal, 7: 13.

22. The first census of 1790 itself did not record any national origins.
Therefore, it seems impossible to check further the claim made by
individuals in 1920 that their ancestry could be traced back to colonists of
Portuguese origin. Actually, no specific claim of "Portuguese" ancestry as
such was required: analysis of the national origins of the 1790 population
was based largely on a study of family names of that year (cf. Bernard, 162:
26).

23. Lincoln Lorenz, *John Paul Jones* (Annapolis: United States Naval
Institute, 1943), pp. 252–54, 268; Gardner W. Allen, *A Naval History of
the American Revolution*, vol. 2 (Boston: Houghton Mifflin, 1913), pp. 444–
49; John H. Sherburne, *The Life and Character of John Paul Jones*, 2d ed.
(New York: Adriance Sherman, 1851), pp. 134–40. Sherburne's book
contains the muster roll, including the names of all the Portuguese crew
members; most of these names appear mispelled (partly as an adaptation to
French—for these Portuguese had arrived at L'Orient as crew members of
two French vessels), but the roll clearly specifies the native country of the
men as "Portugal" ("Fayal" in one instance).

24. See the dramatic account of Thomas J. Malone, "Never Heard of
Him? Then Meet Private Peter Francisco, Portuguese-Born," *American
Legion Magazine*, 31, no. 2 (August 1941), 12–13, 39–41; see also Lessing,
Pictorial Field Book of the Revolution, 2 vols. (New York: Harper, 1851–
1852); Diario, 4: 17 May 1950. Just as has happened in the cases of Cabrillo
and of Miguel Corte-Real, the story of Peter Francisco has become a symbol
and vehicle of the growing ethnic consciousness and political aspirations of
Portuguese-Americans since World War II: In Massachusetts, a Peter
Francisco Day was first proclaimed officially in 1954, and has been
celebrated annually since, on 15 March. The State of Rhode Island followed
suit in 1962; and so did the mayor of Newark, New Jersey, in that same
year. (The largest Portuguese-American communities in the Eastern states

are located in southeastern Massachusetts, Rhode Island, and in Newark, N.J.) In 1964, a banquet in New Bedford to award the annual Peter Francisco prize, sponsored by a Portuguese-American fraternal society, was actually attended by a great-grandson of Peter Francisco, one John R. Francisco resident in Virginia. On the other hand, about that same time, a dash of cold water was thrown in the direction of the developing Peter Francisco cult when George Monteiro, himself of Portuguese extraction, pointed out that, if Peter Francisco was indeed abandoned on the Virginia beach as a three-year-old child, he could hardly be expected to recall his origin; in 1784, as a matter of fact, he merely told a visitor he "had been told" he was either Irish or Portuguese (George Monteiro, "The Unhistorical Uses of Peter Francisco," *Southern Folklore Quarterly*, 27 (1963), 139–59).

25. Cf. W. W. Dobbins, *The Battle of Lake Erie*, 3d ed. (Erie, Pa., 1929). The muster roll printed on pp. 198–202 of this book includes the Portuguese-sounding names of Domingo Alvarez, Peter Fernandes, and John Manuel. At the time he received his commission for the Great Lakes fleet, Perry was living at Newport, R.I., as a naval lieutenant on shore duty; we may conjecture that quite possibly he picked up some Portuguese crew members in or near Newport, as we know that a number of Portuguese settlers or transient sailors were to be found along the New England coast in the early years of the last century.

26. Communication by Mr. J. F. Santos, vice-consul of Portugal in New Orleans, based on account published in the *New Orleans Times-Picayune*.

27. According to a communication from the Louisiana Historical Society, it is certain that there were "many" Portuguese among Lafitte's men and that all of these participated in the Battle of New Orleans on the American side.

28. Zachary F. Smith (*The Battle of New Orleans* [Louisville, 1904], pp. 36–37) states that the pro-British fishermen near Lake Borgne were Spanish and Portuguese, but he adds: "Of this treacherous little colony, the names of Maringuier, Old Luiz, Francisco, Graviella, Antonio el Italiano, El Campechano, Manuelillo, and Garcia became known as connected with this disloyalty." Some of these names are unequivocally Spanish and Italian; Luiz and Francisco might be Spanish or Portuguese. Mitchell U. Charnley (*Jean Lafitte, Gentleman Smuggler* [New York: Viking, 1934], p. 131) identifies the fishermen in British service merely as "Spanish and Italian."

CHAPTER TWO

1. In New Bedford, Massachusetts, the district at the south end of Water Street, where the earliest Portuguese immigrants lived, was known as "Fayal Street" about the middle of the nineteenth century (Daniel Ricketson, *History of New Bedford*, [New Bedford, 1858], p. 55), or (a little later) as "Fayal" or "New Fayal" (Gihon, **140:** 549; U.S., **76:** XXII, 446). Toward the end of the century, the Portuguese immigrant farming com-

munity on Martha's Vineyard was familiarly known as "Fayal" (Peck, **27:** 207). For the Azoreans in general, "Yambub" is another term reported to have become current among Yankee whalemen, just as the Capeverdeans were called "Bravas" (Chippendale, **119:** 134).

A major reason why the early Yankee whalers were attracted to the island of Fayal (according to J. Menezes, writing in Arauto, **1:** 19 April 1913) was a Portuguese government regulation permitting them to unload barrels of oil there without actually anchoring, as long as they paid the harbor fees. This brought commerce and local jobs not only to many Fayalese, but in due course also to men from the neighboring Western Azores islands of Flores, Pico, and São Jorge.

Because of the importance which the Azores, and particularly Fayal, gained for American-Portuguese relations largely as a result of the whaling traffic, an American consulate was opened at Horta as early as 1804 or 1808. The first consul was John Baptist Dabney, of Boston; when he died at Horta in 1826, he was succeeded in that consular post by his son, and later by a grandson of his; the Dabney family with its trading firm remained an influential part of life on Fayal for several generations, until its return to the United States in 1892. (Cf. Greaves, **50:** 24 ff.).

2. For vivid descriptions of the composition of such motley whaling crews, including a proportion of Portuguese, see Hohman, **120a:** 55–58.

3. Chippendale, **119:** pp. xiv, 29–37, 139, 159–61. For the foregoing, see also M. Borges de F. Henriques, *A Trip to the Azores or Western Islands* (Boston: Lee & Shepard, 1867), pp. 28, 102–4; Livermore, **168:** 39–40; Raul d' Eça, "The Portuguese in the United States," *Social Science,* 14 (1939), 365; Digges, **18a:** pp. xiii–xv; Dionis C. Riggs, *From Off Island* (New York: Whittlesey House, 1940), pp. 185–88.

In Herman Melville's famous novel, *Moby Dick, or the Whale* (first published in 1851), there are several references to Azorean seamen on Nantucket whalers. Melville, at one point, also mentions a Nantucket vessel that was shipwrecked off the Azores as early as 1807, and at another point he talks about cruising off the Azores, as well as off the Cape Verde Islands. Cf. the two-volume edition published in 1922 by Constable & Co., I, 149, 216, 219, 259, 293.

4. D. H. Strother, "A Summer in New England: New Bedford," *Harper's New Monthly Magazine,* 21 (June–November 1860), 1–19.

5. Hutt, **86:** II, 582. For the above, see also Montepio, **23:** 81; Diario, **4:** 18 May 1942; Arauto, **1:** 26 April; 17, 24, 31 May 1913.

The first recorded instance of a "Brava" settler in New Bedford is that of one John Adams (obviously an adopted name), from the Cape Verdean island of São Vicente, who arrived on a whaler in 1840.

6. Diario, **4:** 10 April 1942, p. 4; Bradley, **78:** 30.

7. Typewritten report by the International Institute, Providence, 1935.

8. Oscar Handlin, *Boston's Immigrants 1790–1865* (Cambridge: Harvard University Press, 1941), p. 232; Carvalho, **16:**13; Jornal, **7:** 90 (Maria da Conceição came from Flores to Cambridge in 1849 to marry Francisco

Pimentel Baeta; her sister arrived in 1851); John J. Babson, *History of the Town and City of Gloucester, Cape Ann* (Gloucester, 1892), p. 112.

9. When Timothy Dwight, the president of Yale College, traveled through New York about 1812–1813, he found some Portuguese immigrants living there; cf. Timothy Dwight, *Travels in New England and New York*, 4 vols. (New Haven, 1822), 3:469.

10. Robert Ernst, *Immigrant Life in New York City 1825–1863* (New York: King's Crown Press, 1949), pp. 45, 125, 127–29, 199, 213; *Courrier des Etats-Unis* (New York), 8 February 1859; Ella Lonn, *Foreigners in the Union Army and Navy* (Baton Rouge: Louisiana State University Press, 1951), pp. 140, 149.

11. Henry H. Bisbee, *Place Names in Burlington County, New Jersey* (Riverside, N.J.: Burlington County Publishing Co., 1955), p. 78; E. M. Woodward and John F. Hageman, *History of Burlington and Mercer Counties, New Jersey* (Philadelphia: Ruerts and Peck, 1883), p. 399.

12. Portugal, **67**: n.s. 2 (1913), 690. Arauto, **1**: 31 May 1913.

13. Personal communication from Adelaide J. Perry, of Erie, Pa., a descendant of early Portuguese immigrants to that city.

14. Camilo Camara, "Uma sociedade beneficente portuguesa sem membros portugueses," *Portugal-America*, **9**: April 1929, 255–57; *Revista*, **10**: June 1915, p. 6; communication by Mr. J. F. Santos, vice-consul of Portugal in New Orleans; Ella Lonn, *Foreigners in the Confederacy* (Chapel Hill: University of North Carolina Press, 1940), pp. 109–10, 210, 481; V. Alton Moody, "Slavery on Louisiana Sugar Plantations," *Louisiana Historical Quarterly*, 7, no. 2 (April 1924), 246–47.

15. Even though this group of Madeirans found work conditions in Trinidad unbearable, they apparently performed their tasks well enough to earn the praise of Trinidad's governor; for it was his favorable report on these Portuguese immigrants that sparked the beginning of contract labor importation from Madeira into Bermuda, in 1849. Cf. Purves, **170**: 135.

16. George R. Poage, "The Coming of the Portuguese," *Journal of the Illinois State Historical Society*, 18 (1925), 101–35. According to Charles M. Eames, *Historic Morgan and Classic Jacksonville* (Jacksonville, Ill., 1885), pp. 127–28, 173, 214, the first group of Madeiran "exiles" arrived in this country in 1846 (not 1849); and as of 1884, the Portuguese in the Jacksonville area had three churches or congregations: two relatively small ones of the Presbyterian denomination, dating from 1849 and 1858, and a much larger "Catholic" one (!) organized in 1856. It would seem, then, that many of the Madeiran "converts" soon reverted to the traditional Catholic fold, even within the Protestant environment of Illinois, or else had never taken the formal step of conversion.

17. Carl Sandburg, *Abraham Lincoln: The Prairie Years*, 2 vols. (New York: Harcourt Brace, 1926), II, 271. Other personal acquaintances of Abraham Lincoln's among the Illinois Madeirans were Joseph J. Alvies, a grocer and farmer, and Ritta Angelica da Silva, to whom Lincoln made two

mortgage loans. See Joseph Wallace, *Past and Present of the City of Springfield and Sangamon County, Illinois*, 2 vols. (Chicago: S. J. Clarke, 1904), I, 794; and J. D. Fiore, "Mr. Lincoln's Portuguese Neighbors," *Lincoln Herald*, 73 (1971), 150–55.

    18. *Jornal*, **7**: 13.

    19. *Jornal*, **7**: 31, 71, and *Jornal*, **6**: Special issue for 1947, pp. 1–2. On Rocha, see also J. Gregg Layne, *Annals of Los Angeles . . . 1769–1861* (San Francisco: California Historical Society, 1935), pp. 13, 68; Helen S. Giffen, *Casas and Courtyards; Historic Adobe Houses of California* (Oakland: Biobooks, 1955), 9–11; *Diario*, **4**: 31 July 1953.

    According to Hubert H. Bancroft (*The History of California*, II, 681–82), five out of 146 "foreigners" who settled in California before 1830 were Portuguese; these included, in addition to Antonio José Rocha, one Manuel de Dios Pasos (who came about 1823), Joaquin Pereira (1826), Jordan Pacheco, and Manuel de Oliveira (1829). Others came between 1836 and the late 1840s. Cf. Walton J. Brown, *Portuguese in California* (San Francisco: R. & E. Research Associates, 1972), pp. 41–48.

    20. For Gold Rush travel routes to California, cf. Doris M. Wright, "The Making of Cosmopolitan California; An Analysis of Immigration, 1848–1870," *California Historical Society Quarterly*, 19 (1940), 323–24; and Angel, **91**: 119–20. Greaves (**50**: 158) says that the journey across the Isthmus of Panama, in carts drawn by mules, used to last about two months. (The railroad across the isthmus was not completed until 1855.) The overland route by wagon train was popular in the early days of the Gold Rush, but the Portuguese seem to have preferred the maritime route. According to Charles B. Hawes (**120**: 191–95), news came to New Bedford in December 1848 that the crews of sixteen whalers had deserted their vessels in California ports in order to hunt for gold; and by 1849, "men in large numbers shipped on board New England whalers . . . for the sole purpose of getting free transportation to the gold mines. . . ." In 1850, according to the recollections of a Portuguese old-timer in New Bedford, 132 passengers arrived in that city on a small freighter from the Azorean island of São Jorge, bound for the mines in California. About that time also, one Antonio Fiadeiro, a native of São Jorge who had been in California at the time gold was discovered (probably he had been whaling in the Pacific), returned to the Azores to solicit men for the California mines. (*Arauto*, **1**: 7 June 1913). A booklet in Portuguese containing "information and suggestions extracted from official documents concerning California and her gold mines" was published at Oporto, in northern Portugal, in 1849; it recommended increased trading with gold-producing California, and also outlined the ways of reaching that territory (Soares, **39**: 59).

    21. The presence of a small number of Portuguese in California shore whaling during that early period is commemorated in the place-name Portuguese Bend (east of San Pedro), where a shore whaling station was located from 1864 to 1884. There were two whaling stations at San Diego,

between ca. 1856 and 1886 (W. L. Scofield, *California Fishing Ports*, State of California Department of Fish and Game, *Fish Bulletin*, no. 96 [Sacramento, 1954], pp. 128, 150–53). Apart from Portuguese Bend, the placenames Portuguese Point (near Los Angeles) and Portuguese Flat (in Shasta County) date from those early days; in addition, in the 1870s, the place later known as Hazel Creek was called Portuguese (Erwin G. Gudde, *California Place Names* [Berkeley: University of California Press, 1949], p. 270). In the early 1850s transportation between San Francisco and Oakland was handled by some Portuguese operating small launches and whaleboats. Alameda County, and particularly San Leandro, was the first area in which the Portuguese took up farming, shortly before 1858 (Halley, **93**: 134, 198, 553).

22. For the foregoing, see Jornal, **7**: 17, 23, 35, 39, 47, 71, 73, 120; see also Smith, **97**: 412–13; Digges, **18a**: XV, XVII; *Illustrated History of San Joaquin County, California* (Chicago: Lewis, 1890), p. 506(on A. de Costa).

23. Grace R. Hebard and E. A. Brininstool, *The Bozeman Trail*, 2 vols. (Cleveland: Arthur H. Clark, 1922), II, 15–38, etc; Lyle E. Mantor, "Fort Kearny and the Westward Movement," *Nebraska History*, 29 (1948), 175–207; Arthur Amos Gray, *Men Who Built the West* (Caldwell, Idaho, 1945), pp. 213–16; John G. Ellenbecker, "John Phillips' Heroic Ride," *Pony Express Courier* (Placerville, Calif.), 3, no. 10 (March 1937), 13, 15; Jornal, **6**: special issue for 1952, pp. 3–5; Jornal, **6**: 30 January 1953, and 2 August 1962.

24. In 1974, there were about a dozen foreigners in Hawaii, including one or more Portuguese. See Ralph S. Kuykendall and A. Grove Day, *Hawaii: A History* (New York: Prentice-Hall, 1948), p. 37; and Harold W. Bradley, *The American Frontier in Hawaii* (Stanford: Stanford University Press, 1942), p. 34.

25. Cf. Otto von Kotzebue, *Entdeckungsreise in die Südsee und nach der Beringstrasse*, 3 vols. (Weimar: Gebr. Hoffmann, 1821), II, 10–12; Freitas, **43**: 148; A. Grove Day, *Hawaii and Its People* (New York: Duell, Sloan & Pearce, 1955), p. 46.

26. Yzendoorn, **118**: 41.

27. Communication by Joaquin B. de Menezes, a veteran Portuguese-American journalist in California who died in 1949.

28. The cost of building the (Catholic) chapel of St. Patrick at Halawa, Oahu, dedicated in 1860, was defrayed almost entirely by several Portuguese. One Capeverdean sailor became a Protestant preacher about 1860; he was first assigned to Ewa, where there was a "colony of Portuguese negroes," and then became pastor of a native Hawaiian church at Kaneohe (Yzendoorn, **118**: 223).

29. Adams, **100**: 24, 79, 117–18, 134–35; Colonias, **46**: 719; Freitas, **43**: 149.

30. According to Almeida, (**34**: 12), the official total of Portuguese arriving in the United States from 1820 to 1855 was 3,562; to which should

be added a certain number who came to California via the Isthmus of Panama or from Louisiana beyond the reach of immigration officials.
31. For figures, see Colonias, **46:** 341–42.

CHAPTER THREE

1. Based on reports of the United States Bureau of Immigration. See also Graves, **37:** 87ff. During the first two decades of the twentieth century, Portugal attained the second highest ratio of emigration to total population (or to natural population increase) of any country in Europe and probably in the world, after Ireland (Lautensach, **143:** 162; Cerqueja, **132:** 76).
2. Graves, **37:** 41–43, 89–91.
3. Lautensach, **143:** 163; Marvaud, **146:** 172, 194; Costa, **47:** 235: Taft, **30:** 94–95. Cf. also Iliowizi, **142:** 92; Weeks, **159:** 145; A. J. Drexel Biddle, *The Land of the Wine*, vol. 2, 2d ed. (Philadelphia, 1901), pp. 58–61.
4. Andrade, **126:** 323–31; Peck, **27:** 208; Lautensach, **143:** 163; Taft, **30:** 94.
5. Costa, **47:** 235; Marvaud, **146:** 194.
6. This "chain reaction" element in migration patterns must not be underestimated. It has recently been stressed with respect to Portuguese immigration into Canada; cf. Anderson, **161:** 28–29.
7. Eugene T. Sawyer, *History of Santa Clara County, California* (Los Angeles: Historic Record Co., 1922), p. 1392.
8. Tinkham, **99:** 1039.
9. Poole, **28.**
10. *Standard Times* (New Bedford), January 1975.
11. Walker, **158:** 108.
12. C. Alice Baker, *A Summer in the Azores* (Boston: Lothrop, Lee & Shepard, 1882).
13. On the other hand, José G. Maio, writing in 1945, deplored the continued isolation of the Azores from the Portuguese mainland, pointing out that regular passenger service between these two regions had been limited to one steamer twice a month for the past fifty years; the trip from Lisbon to Ponta Delgada would take four days, and to Faial seven days, even as of the 1940s! See José Guerra Maio, *Portugal desconhecido* (Lisbon: Bertrand, 1945), 215, 229.
14. Archivo, **127:** VII, 134–52. Often the sailboat trip from the Azores to New England took forty to fifty days. Cf. Portugal-America, **9:** October 1926, 44; **24:** 63.
15. Portugal, **67:** XII, 746.
16. Evening, **84:** 15, 29 May 1929; Providence, **89:** April 1920, p. 182.
17. Portugal, **67:** n.s. II, 700.
18. Portugal, **67:** V, 471.
19. Portugal, **67:** VIII, 1104.

20. Portugal, **67**: IX, 428; X, 663; XI, 821–22; XIII, 711–12.
21. Portugal, **67**: XII, 746–47.
22. Weeks, **159**: 145; Walker, **158**: 107; Peck, **27**: 208.
23. Oliver, **55**.
24. Baker (cf. note 12 above), pp. 25–26.
25. Evening, **84**: 29 May 1929.
26. Lautensach, **143**: 162–63.
27. Jorge Dias, *Rio de Onor* (Porto, 1953), p. 529. According to Concei-ção (**17**: 18), about 6,000 Portuguese entered the U.S. illegally from Cuba between 1920 and 1930. Since emigration on land routes was uncontrolled, many Portuguese (continentals, not islanders!) would go to Galicia, then embark in Galician (i.e., Spanish) ports under guise of Spanish nationality (Silva, **157**: 113–14, 130).
28. Clandestine emigration from Portugal need not, of course, amount to illegal entry into the United States. Up to 1882, immigration into this country was practically free and unrestricted, although from 1830 to that date the states in which ports of debarkation were located (such as New York and Massachusetts) had regulatory authority. An official count of immigrants (or simply "aliens") arriving in such ports has been kept since 1820. Some of the Portuguese arriving before 1882, such as sailors jumping ship, might go unrecorded, but they could in no case be called illegal immigrants. The Chinese Exclusion Act of 1882 marked the beginning of federal controls of immigration. These were relatively mild (except for Orientals) until the closing days of World War I. Yet the exclusion of persons likely to become public charges, and particularly (since 1917) of illiterates, probably motivated quite a number of arrivals from Portugal to avoid being counted by immigration officials and to become truly illegal residents. Cf. Bernard, **162**: 5–6, 11–13, 279–80; Lawrence G. Brown, *Immigration: Cultural Conflicts and Social Adjustments* (New York: Long-mans Green, 1933), pp. 28–29.
29. Cf. the annual reports by the U.S. Commissioner General of Immigration since 1895, by the U.S. Bureau of Statistics during 1867–1895.
30. Cf. U.S., **76**: III, 4, 44–51, 61; U.S., **75**: table 8; Taft, **30**: 101–3.
31. Graves, **37**: 93. Hawaii does not seem to be considered in this computation.
32. U.S., **76**: III, 289.
33. U.S., **75**: table 9.
34. Portugal, **69**: 241–44.
35. U.S., **76**: IV, 46; III, 372–73, 383–91. These figures do not include Portuguese citizens making merely "temporary trips" (visits) to the U.S. or (while residents of the U.S.) to Portugal.
36. U.S., **75**: table 3.
37. Report in the *San Francisco Chronicle*, as cited in the Portuguese immigrant weekly *O Colonial* (Fairhaven, Mass.) of 18 August 1933. But in the Portuguese population census for 1930, only 1,089 residents of the

Azores declared themselves to be American citizens (Açoreana, **123:** II, 206).

38. *Treaties, Conventions, International Acts, Protocols and Agreements between the U.S.A. and other Powers, 1776–1909*, 2 vols. (Washington, D.C., 1910); II, 1475–76. The convention provided that subjects of one country who become naturalized in the other and have lived there continuously for five years shall be treated by the original country as citizens of the country of naturalization. But a naturalized citizen returning to his original country may be prosecuted there for crimes committed before emigration; and if he remains in his original country for more than two years, he shall be presumed to have renounced his naturalization.

39. Haeberle, **144:** 521.

40. Friedlander, **138:** 22; U.S., **76:** XXII, 539–48; Parsons, **25:** I, p. XII.

41. Casimiro, **133:** 157, 182.

42. Leite, **144:** 68.

43. Ribeiro, **153:** 24–27.

44. Greaves, **50:** 166, 178. There is some similar testimony about the influence of re-emigrants from the U.S. in the Cape Verde Islands, especially in Brava and São Nicolau. See Jacinto José do Nascimento Moura, "Crioulo e folclore de Cabo Verde," in *Trabalhos do 1º Congresso Nacional de Antropologia Colonial* (Porto, 1934), II, 263–96; Lyall, **145:** 102–3, 144.

45. Luz, **53:** 9–15, 23–29.

46. Arauto, **1:** 24 September 1904.

47. Livermore, **168:** 197–98; *A Lusitania* (Boston, monthly), August 1917, p. 104.

48. Carvalho, **16:** 18, 21.

49. Cf. U.S., **74;** U.S., **73:** year 1932, p. 100; Niles Carpenter, *Immigrants and Their Children* (Washington, D.C., 1927), pp. 72–107; Schmitt, **114a:** 75, 120–21.

CHAPTER FOUR

1. Cf. Daniel C. Brewer, *The Conquest of New England by the Immigrant* (New York: Putnam's Sons, 1926), pp. 11–13, 151, 162, 167–68, 226–27, 271.

2. Lang, **22:** 9.

3. Portugal, **67:** n.s. II, 692.

4. Massachusetts, **63;** Rhode Island, **71;** Shippee, **72.**

5. Translated from Montepio, **23:** 33.

6. Oliver, **55:** 13.

7. Oliver, **55:** 16.

8. James M. Guinn, *History of the State of California and Biographical Record of Oakland and Environs*, 2 vols. (Los Angeles: Historic Record Co., 1907), II, 838–39.

9. Merritt, **94:** II, 246.

10. Lang, **22:** 10; *Modern Language Notes*, 3, no. 4 (1888), col. 220.
11. Montepio, **23:** 80.
12. Works, **33.**
13. Goode, **62:** sec. 2, p. 231.
14. Vorse, **31:** 410.
15. Peck, **27:** 207–8.
16. U.S., **76:** XXII, 539–40, 543, 547–48; Edwards, **82:** 49–52; *Boston Evening Transcript*, 16 June 1923, p. 33.
17. North, **88:** II, 11, 59–60; III, 110.
18. William F. Whyte, "Race Conflicts in the North End of Boston," *New England Quarterly*, 12 (1939), 623–24; Robert A. Woods, ed., *American in Process; a Settlement Study* (Boston: Houghton Mifflin, 1902), pp. 45, 58–59, 122, 245.
19. Neves, **24.**
20. Portugal, **67:** n.s. II, 693.
21. Kenngott, **87:** 26–28, 33, 40–53. Frederick W. Coburn, *History of Lowell and Its People* (New York: Lewis, 1920), pp. 396, 406.
22. Private communication.
23. Taft, **30:** 89, 98, 198; U.S., **76:** 39–40; Massachusetts, **64:** 38–39.
24. Providence, **89:** May 1914, p. 389.
25. William Kirk, ed., *A Modern City: Providence, Rhode Island* (Chicago: University of Chicago Press, 1909), pp. 43–44, 47–48, 56–57; Shippee, **72:** 4, 10, 14–15, 27.
26. Cf. Taft, **30,** esp. for Portsmouth; also U.S., **76;** XXII, 445–49.
27. Private communication.
28. North, **88:** 62.
29. Portugal, **67:** I, 375.
30. David J. Viera, *The Portuguese of Rochester and Monroe County, New York* (East Providence, R.I., 1976).
31. Lang, **22:** 9; and private information.

CHAPTER FIVE

1. Portugal, **70:** year 1877, pp. 219–20; Colonias, **46:** 342, 354.
2. Portugal, **70:** year 1892, p. 29. Portugal, **67:** XI, 1041.
3. McEntire, **169:** 13, 78–88, 169–70; Doyle, **166:** 3–17; Carlson: **164:** 42–43.
4. Jornal, **7:** 23.
5. Estep, **48:** 61.
6. Taft, **30:** 105–6.
7. Portugal, **70:** year 1892, p. 31; Portugal, **68:** XI, 1036–41; Graves, **37:** 94–95; Marvaud, **146:** 187.
8. Private communication.
9. Portugal, **68:** n.s. IV, 216.
10. Merritt, **94:** II, 127.

11. Tinkham, **99:** 1151
12. Small, **96:** II, 545.
13. Honoria Tuomey, *History of Sonoma County, California*, 2 vols. (Chicago: S. J. Clarke, 1926), II, 914.
14. Graves, **37:** 93–94.
15. Graves, **37:** 52–53, 58–62, 98; Symposium, **40:** 51–52.
16. Cf. Symposium, **40:** 51–53; Graves, **37:** 52–64 95–114.
17. Symposium, **40:** 38-44; Graves, **37:** 74; Stuart, **98:** 143–51, 187, 233; Roy C. Beckman, *The Romance of Oakland* (Oakland: Landis & Kelsey, 1932), p. 20.
18. Crissey: **36:** 11.
19. Jack London, born in San Francisco, grew up in Oakland. The name of Eden Township (Hayward plus San Leandro) may have prompted him to give the name of Martin Eden to his one novel, set in the Oakland-San Francisco area; Azorean-born Maria Silva and her "brood" play a major role in it. In 1916, Jack London bought a ranch in Sonoma County, to the north of San Francisco; *Sonoma*, in some local Indian language, is said to mean "Valley of the moon"; in the novel by that name, again, we find many references to the "Porchugeeze" in San Leandro.
20. Portugal, **70:** year 1875, pp. 210–11; year 1886, pp. 309–10.
21. Portugal, **68:** X, 256–57.
22. U.S., **76:** XXIV, 326–29, 345–46, 357.
23. Arauto, **1:** 19 December 1914. The reference, if accurate, is to the Portuguese colonies of Mozambique, Angola, Macau, Goa, etc., and the Portuguese part of Timor Island.
24. Jornal, **47:** 47.
25. Bohme, **35:** 235, citing Anne B. Fisher, *No More A Stranger* (Stanford, 1946), p. 237.
26. Goode, **62:** sec. 2, pp. 601–8; Bohme, **35:** 238–39.
27. Bohme, **35:** 239–40; Jornal, **47:** 79, 119–20; Andrade, **13:** 104–5.
28. Oliver, **55:** 19ff.
29. Portugal, **150:** 813, 830–31.
30. Vandercook, **117:** 58.
31. Hawaiian, **107:** year 1887, pp. 74–77; year 1911, pp. 43–44 (reprinted in Freitas, **43:** 151); Portugal, **70:** year 1896, report from Honolulu dated May 1897, p. 14; Vandercook, **117:** 57–58; U.S., **76:** I, 699; Jean Hobbs, *Hawaii, A Pageant of the Soil* (Stanford: Stanford University Press, 1935), pp. 78–79.
32. Social, **115:** III, 71.
33. Jornal, **6:** 21 January 1944.
34. The plantation owners, with government subsidy, had to pay for the transportation of the recruited laborers. The per capita cost was around $90 or $100; but, since the labor contract terms allowed adult males to take their wives and children along, this resulted in an average of close to $300 per male laborer. Cf. U.S., **76:** I, 703.

35. U.S., **76:** I, 708.
36. Portugal, **68:** IV, 127; V, 742.
37. Hawaiian, **107:** year 1911, pp. 44–45 (reprinted in Freitas, **43:** 151). Portugal, **68:** n.s. VIII, 291.
38. Portugal, **68:** n.s. VIII, 291. Portugal, **70:** year 1896, p. 7.
39. Social, **115:** III, 72. The Azorean-born Maria Silva portrayed in Jack London's novel *Martin Eden* (see note 19 above) had moved to San Leandro from Hawaii.
40. Portugal, **70:** year 1890, 1–4; year 1888, consular report from Honolulu dated February 1889, p. 8; year 1892, report from San Francisco dated April 1892, p. 44; year 1893, report from San Francisco dated April 1893, p. 73.
41. Portugal, **70:** year 1896, report from Honolulu dated May 1897, p. 13; Portugal, **68:** II, 436–38.
42. Portugal, **68:** V, 743; IX, 409.
43. Portugal, **68:** XII, 763.
44. According to one source (A. Marques in Hawaiian, **107:** year 1911, pp. 43–45, reprinted in Freitas, **43:** 151–54), fully one half of the approximately 13,000 Portuguese brought to Hawaii during 1878–1899 left the islands again at different times, the bulk attracted to California, a relatively few to return to their old homes. Also, many of those who immigrated in 1906–1909 moved on "immediately" to California. On the small amount of "retromigration," see also Taft, **30:** 105, Russ: **114:** 211–12.
45. For at least part of this period, these census figures do not include Hawaiian-born persons with only one Portuguese parent. Those of mixed parentage were generally subsumed under "(Other) Caucasians." Cf. Adams, **100:** 12–13.
46. Schmitt, **114a:** 75, 120–21. Other sources give slightly different figures.
47. Arauto, **1:** 17 February 1912.
48. Knowlton, **44:** 97; *Mid-Pacific Magazine*, 10, 227–28; Portugal, **70:** year 1896, report from Honolulu dated May 1897, p. 18; Portugal, **68:** V, 743; VI, 663; IX, 408–9; XIV, 967.

CHAPTER SIX

1. For example, several hundred Capeverdeans sailed to New Bedford in 1917, unaware of the new regulation, but were forced to return to the islands (*Boston American*, 3 June 1917) Similarly, of the 200 Portuguese immigrants who arrived in the port of Providence on 27 July 1919, forty were detained because they could not read nor write (Diario, **4:** 27 July 1944).
2. For much of the foregoing see Bernard, **162:** 13–30, 33–38, 304–6; Roy L. Garis, *Immigration Restriction* (New York: Macmillan, 1927), pp. 130–38, 142–57, 182–83, 257; **73:** 112.

3. U.S. Immigration and Naturalization Service figures as cited in Jensen, **19**: 36, and Rogers, **58**: 34.

4. Independente, **5**: 12 July 1934; Evening, **84**: 15 May 1929.

5. U.S., **75**: years 1921 to 1930, table 9 or 24.

6. Conceição, **17**: 18.

7. Diario, **4**: 15 June 1951, and various issues in April–May 1952.

8. Diario, **4**: various issues, September–November 1951; 27 April and 4 May 1953.

9. Portugal, Polícia de Vigilância e Defesa do Estado, *Relatório 1932 a 1938* (Lisbon: Bertrand, 1939), p. 147. As for Bermuda, a number of Azorean plantation laborers (spearheaded by some who had deserted from whaling ships) settled in that British island colony during the second half of the nineteenth century. But most came in the 1920s and 1930s, imported as contract laborers from São Miguel and Madeira—repeating the Hawaiian experience. By 1945 there were a total of aboaut 3,300. See Purves, **170**; Hudson Strode, *The Story of Bermuda* (New York: Harcourt Brace, 1946), pp. 136–39; Diario, **4**: 28 October 1943 and 14 February 1945; Jornal, **6**: 27 May 1949.

10. Harriet Ch. Adams, "European Outpost: The Azores," *National Geographic Magazine*, 67 (January 1935), 34–66.

11. Portugal, **68**: October 1935, p. 28.

12. See Matson for a vivid reportage of such a crossing. Edwin C. Guillet, *The Great Migration* (Toronto: Thomas Nelson, 1937), p. 244.

13. Independente, **5**: 12 July 1934.

14. Cf. Jensen, **20**: 120. The figures cited in Rogers, **58**: 45 are far too low (for 1960, 56,000 foreign-born, 144,000 native of foreign or mixed parentage)—probably because Rogers failed to realize that the census category "Portugal" excluded part of those of Azorean (Madeiran, Capeverdean) descent; but see his postcript, Rogers, **58**: 69.

15. Graves, **37**: 10–11.

16. Jensen, **20**: 121; Montepio, **23**: 80.

17. Hatch, **85**: 73–74; and private information.

18. Private information. Also Portugal-America, **9**: September 1928, February 1929, April 1929, Independente, **5**: 12 July 1934; Diario, **4**: 8 July 1954; Jensen, **20**: 121.

19. Portugal, **68**: year 1935, issue for October 1935, pp. 25–26.

20. U.S., **74**: Walter Laidlaw, ed., *Population of the City of New York, 1890–1930* (New York: Cities Census Committee, 1932); *Yonkers Herald*, 26 May 1928; *Luso-Americano* (Newark), 14 January 1945; private information.

21. Diario, **4**: 25 May 1954; Viera (see note 30 to chap. 4); private information, as of the 1960s.

22. Cf. Henry H. Bisbee, *Place Names in Burlington County, New Jersey* (Riverside, N.J.: Burlington County Publishing Co., 1955), p. 78; letter from Pemberton Community Library Association, 1971.

23. Report as reproduced in Colonial, **2**: 14 April 1933.

24. Arauto, **1:** 6 January 1912.
25. Private communication; see also Montepio, **23:** 68; Diario, **4:** 7 March 1956.
26. Private communication; Jornal, **6:** 6 May 1949. At New Orleans, we recall, a Lusitanian-Portuguese Benevolent Association, founded by a group of Portuguese immigrants in Louisiana in the mid-nineteenth century, was still operating in the 1950s; see p. 24 above.
27. *Christian Science Monitor,* 5 December 1942.
28. Doyle, **166:** 4–6, 21–23; McEntire, **169:** 169–70; Graves, **37:** 11–12.
29. Information based largely on local interviews.
30. Cf. Schmitt, **114a;** Lind, **111:** 120, 123; Adams, **100:** 16–20, 267.
31. Adams, **101:** 55; Ira U. Hiscock, *A Survey of Health and Welfare Activities in Honolulu, Hawaii* (New York: American Public Health Association, 1929), p. 26.
32. Midkiff, **112:** 156; Graves, **37:** 11; Lind, **110:** 47–49.
33. Lind, **111:** 309–10; Lind, **110:** 54–55.
34. Fuchs, **106:** 58.

CHAPTER SEVEN

1. Porfirio Bessone, *Dicionário cronológico dos Açores* (Cambridge, Mass., 1932), s.v. "tremor," pp. 322–39, 367.
2. For summary discussions of the new general and special immigration legislation in the 1950s and 1960s, see *Annals of the American Academy of Political and Social Science,* September 1966, and Jensen, **20:** 116–19. For day-by-day reports on the 1957–1964 Azorean earthquakes and related relief actions, I am indebted to Diario, **4.**
3. Cf. Portugal, Ministério dos Negócios Estrangeiros, *Documentos relativos aos acordos entre Portugal, Inglaterra e Estados Unidos da América para a concessão de facilidades nos Açores durante a guerra de 1939–1945* (Lisbon: Imprensa Nacional, 1946), pp. 47–48; Livermore, **168:** 197–98; Ronald H. Chilcote, "Angola or the Azores?," *New Republic,* 30 July 1962, p. 21; Correia, **136:** 105–6.
4. *New York Times,* 12 September 1971.
5. Diario, **4:** 27 July 1964.
6. Jensen, **20:** 126.
7. As pointed out by Francis Rogers (**58:** 35), these figures from the annual reports of the U.S. Immigration and Naturalization Service do not include Capeverdeans for 1968 and earlier years. Capeverdeans were included starting in 1969.
8. *New York Times,* 18 March 1968.
9. Rogers, **58:** 35–36.
10. Annual Reports of Immigration and Naturalization Service, table 12A.

11. Rogers, **58**: 37.
12. Anderson, **161**: 121.
13. Anderson, **161**: 21, 25–26, 57, 69; interview with Fe. Cunha, Toronto, July 1971; Diario, **4**: 20 February 1956, 28 June 1961.
14. The figures cited in Rogers, **58**: 43, although attributed to Census authorities, are much too low and incorrect.
15. A survey on "language minorities" in the U.S., prepared by the National Center for Education Statistics of the U.S. Department of Health, Education, and Welfare, estimates that as of the spring 1976 there were about 247,000 U.S.-born persons and about 241,000 Portuguese-born persons in the U.S. whose "language background" (defined as mother tongue, or else usual or second household language) was Portuguese. Even if "second household language" is interpreted very broadly to include only occasional or rare household use of Portuguese, and if we include the tens of thousands of new arrivals from Portugal between 1970 and 1976 as well as Brazilian "stock," these figures seem somewhat inflated.

CHAPTER EIGHT

1. According to a survey by the U.S. Immigration Commission of cotton goods manufacturing mills in the North Atlantic States in 1908–1909, involving a sample of 40.5 percent of all the employees in those mills, the majority of Portuguese-born employees in Fall River, New Bedford, and Lowell were males (Massachusetts, **64**: 35–36). The reported slight preponderance of females (51.2 percent) over males among foreign-born Portuguese in Boston as of 1895 (Bushee, **79a**: 16) shows how, while the new Portuguese arrivals were turning preferably to such developing textile centers as Fall River, a more stabilized Portuguese colony such as the one in Boston was relatively quick in attaining a normal sex ratio.
2. In 1909 the U.S. Immigration Commission found that only between one sixth and one third of the c. 3,000 Capeverdeans in the Cape Cod cranberry district (Plymouth, Barnstable, and Nantucket counties) were women and children (U.S., **76**: XXII, 542–43). The same was still true in the Providence area around 1930 ("A Survey of the Foreign Communities of Providence," unpublished report [Providence: International Institute, July 1935]).
3. The Portuguese contract laborers imported into Hawaii between 1878 and 1886 brought along even more women and children than the plantation owners had stipulated: 46 percent of the total arrivals during that period were children, 23 percent adult women, and only 31 percent adult men (Lind, **111**: 120; Porteus, **95**: 54).
4. For example, of the 11,302 Portuguese immigrants arriving in 1974, 50.2 percent were female (Handley, **51**: 11).
5. U.S., **76**: III, 13–51; U.S., **75**: table 7 (in each annual report).
6. Bernard, **162**: 182.

7. U.S., **76:** IV, 23.

8. U.S., **76:** IV, 25.

9. Portugal, **70:** year 1892, p. 31; year 1893, p. 74.

10. United States, Bureau of the Census, *U.S. Census 1940: Population: . . . Mother Tongue by Nativity, Parentage, Country of Origin, and Age, for States and Large Cities* (Washington, D.C., 1943), pp. 35–41.

11. Adams, **100:** 135.

12. Freitas, **43:** 151.

13. Portugal, **67.**

14. Data taken from various issues of Jornal, **6,** and Diario, **4.**

15. Taft, **30:** 137ff.

16. Bernard, **162:** 173.

17. J. V. DePorte, "Inter-Racial Variation in Infant Mortality," *American Journal of Hygiene,* 5 (1925), 479–80. A study done in Portugal found that the average annual infant mortality in that country in 1902–1904 was 138 (per 1,000 live births), as against 147 in England and Wales, 168 in Italy, 104 in Sweden. Within Portugal, infant mortality was higher in the south where there was less breast feeding than in the north; and the most common cause of infant deaths in Portugal, the study concluded (coinciding remarkably with DePorte), was unsanitary nursing, or feeding the baby solid foods too early out of ignorance. See Carqueja, **132:** 298–303, 322–23.

18. Chas. H. Verrill, "Infant Mortality and Its Relation to the Employment of Mothers in Fall River, Mass.," *Transactions of the 15th Int. Congress on Hygiene and Demography* (Washington, D.C., 1913), III, 318–37.

19. New Bedford, Mass., Board of Health, *Annual Reports,* Report for 1915, p. 23; Report for 1918, p. 23. When the economic depression in 1924 curtailed work in New Bedford's mills, the fact that many unemployed mothers stayed home resulted in a drop in infant mortality, according to the Report for 1924, p. 43.

20. Jessamine S. Whitney, *Infant Mortality; Results of a Field Study in New Bedford, Mass.* (Washington, D.C., 1920), pp. 18–20, 31, 33, 45.

21. Frederick L. Hoffman, *The Sanitary Progress and Vital Statistics of Hawaii* (Newark, N.J.: Prudential Press, 1916), p. 71; Midkiff, **112:** 82.

22. National, **54:** 196.

23. Robert R. Kuczynski, *The Balance of Births and Deaths,* vol. 1 (New York: Macmillan, 1928), p. 7; vol. 2 (Washington, D.C., Brookings, 1931), pp. 58–60, 131; Lautensach, **143:** 162.

24. Arauto, **1:** 6 May 1916.

25. Diario, **4:** 3 March 1955.

26. Freitas, **43:** 151, and passim.

27. Cf. Hans Zeisel, "The Race Question in American Immigration Statistics," *Social Research,* 16 (1949), 222–29; Edward C. McDonagh and

Eugene S. Richards, *Ethnic Relations in the United States* (New York: Appleton, 1953), pp. 3–5, 13–14; David F. Bowers, ed., *Foreign Influences in American Life* (Princeton: Princeton University Press, 1944), pp. 8–9.
28. Coon, **165:** 5–11.
29. Coon, **165:** 83–85, 291–93, plate 22 (between pp.399 and 400), 495–98; A. A. Mendes Corrêa, "Origins of the Portuguese," *American Journal of Physical Anthropology,* 2 (1919), 117–45.
30. Arthur Ramos, *Introdução à antropologia brasileira,* 2 vols. (Rio de Janeiro: C.E.B., 1943–1947), II, 65–67; Portugal, **150:** 812, 829; Açoreana, **123** , vol. 2 (1941): 195–211; Taft, **30:** 26–27, 30, 40, 47–49.
31. Almeida, **125:** 51–56; Almeida, **124:** 7–8; Casimir, **123:** 83–85; Lyall, **145:** 56, 59, 63, 142–43.
32. Allan McLaughlin, "Italian and Other Latin Immigrants," *Popular Science Monthly,* 65 (May–October 1904), 348; similarly, Edward A. Ross, *The Old World in the New* (New York: Century, 1914), p. 289.
33. Vorse, **32:** 76, 163–64.
34. Cape, **80:** 16.
35. Jack London, *Valley of the Moon* (New York: Macmillan, 1928), p. 315.
36. Du Puy, **61:** 106.
37. Reid, **122:** 104.
38. U.S., **76:** XX, 540, 552.
39. Lind, **110:** 19–22; Adams, **100:** 12–13, 16–18, 117–20, 134–35; Blascoer, **104:** 47; Margaret Lam, "Baseball and Racial Harmony in Hawaii," *Sociology and Social Research,* 18 (1933–1934), 60, 63; Social, **115:** IX–X, 105, XII, 28, 30; Edward Norbeck, *Pineapple Town, Hawaii* (Berkeley: University of California Press, 1959), pp. 118–19. On the island of Bermuda, the several thousand Portuguese farm laborers (most of them hailing from São Miguel and Madeira) are similarly classified in census statistics as a separate "race," neither white nor colored (Jornal, **6:** 27 May 1949; Rogers, **58:** 54).
40. U.S., **76:** XXXVIII.
41. H. L. Shapiro, *Migration and Environment* (New York: Oxford University Press, 1939); Marcus S. Goldstein, *Demographic and Bodily Changes in Descendants of Mexican Immigrants* (Austin: Institute of Latin-American Studies, 1943). Even in Japan proper, children are now growing taller and more "filled-out" than before World War II, due to a Westernized life-style (*New York Times,* 30 August 1964, sec. 1, p. 7). Americans themselves are getting taller, and wider, than previous generations (*New York Times,* 18 October 1959, pp. 36, 38). On the other hand, American children reared in Brazil were found to grow shorter and slighter than their peers in the U.S., probably because of the tropical climate (*New York Times,* 13 February 1965).
42. Vandercook, **117:** 59.
43. Weeks, **159:** 144–45; Iliowizi, **142:** 88; Crane, **18:** 24; Taft, **30:** 5.

44. Crane, **18:** 24.

45. Poinsard, **149:** 358–59, 370.

46. Anderson, **161:** 141.

47. Portugal, **67** . Some statistics cited in various sources give an exaggerated picture by counting the total of illiterates as a percentage of the total population of all ages—including small children!

48. Anderson, **161:** 141.

49. U.S., **76:** IV, 30; III, 85; **75:** table 7.

50. Taft, **30:** 104, 114–15; Casimiro; **133:** 21; Evening, **84:** 29 May 1929; private communications.

51. Diario, **4:** 10 April 1942.

52. Independente, **5:** 22 October 1942.

53. Jack London, *Martin Eden* (New York: Grosset & Dunlap, 1908), p. 220.

54. Arauto, **1:** 27 February 1897.

55. Nuno Simões, *O Brasil e a emigração portuguesa* (Coimbra: Imprensa da Universidade, 1934), p. 94.

56. Jensen, **19; 20:** 137.

57. Cf. Louis R. Sullivan, "The Labor Crisis in Hawaii," *Asia*, 23 (1923), 512; du Puy **61:** 106; Babcock, **102:** 9; Midkiff, **110:** 88; Adams, **100:** 265–66.

58. Adams, **101:** 20; Midkiff, **112:** 86, 203.

59. Sharkansky, **29:** 44–49, 51.

60. Bouchard, **14:** 54.

61. The Portuguese common people in their own homeland have not always struck observers as industrious: the Portuguese do not like to work, especially in the South (Marvaud, **146:** 174). They attach little value to time or money, spend much time in chatting (Lautensach, **143:** 99–100). The peasant in the Minho region, who owns his little plot of land, is hardworking and thrifty; but the Alemtejo peasant, working for big landowners, is a lazy spend-thrift (Portugal, **151:** xxxiv). The average Capeverdean is indolent and lazy, quick to seek public charity; but once he emigrates, he is willing to work hard on foreign soil (Almeida, **125:** 58–59). Some Azoreans, having worked and saved hard while in America, turn indolent and lazy upon return to the Azores (Arauto, **1:** 24 September 1904). This suggests that industriousness, far from being a fixed personality trait, depends in part on perceived opportunity of reward.

62. S. D. Porteus, "Temperament and Mentality in Maturity, Sex and Race," *Journal of Applied Psychology*, 8 (1924), 68–73; Marvin L. Darsie, "The Mental Capacity of American-Born Japanese Children," *Comparative Psychology Monographs*, 3 (1926), 81; Jack W. Dunlap, "Race Differences in the Organization of Numerical and Verbal Abilities," *Archives of Psychology*, 19 (1930–1931).

63. Kwok Tsuen Yeung, "The Intelligence of Chinese Children in San Francisco and Vicinity," *Journal of Applied Psychology*, 5 (1921), 269;

Notes and References   261

Kimball Young, "Mental Differences in Certain Immigrant Groups,"
University of Oregon Publications, 1, no. 11 (July 1922), 3.
    64. Nathaniel D. M. Hirsch, "A Study of Natio-Racial Mental Differ-
ences," *Genetic Psychology Monographs*, 1 (1926), 244–46, 281–87.
    65. Antonio Augusto, "Inteligência das crianças portuguesas," *A Criança
Portuguesa*, 6 (1946–1947), 241–56.
    66. Parsons, **26:** 89.
    67. Private communications; Taft, **30:** 78, 339–40; Crane, **18:** 24;
Cabral, **42:** 98–100; Elma T. Cabral, "Maezinha's Dilemma," *Paradise of
the Pacific*, 64 (1953), 48; Social, **115:** III, 72.
    68. "Specific evidences of a belief in the evil eye and in the efficacy and
use of divine or faith healing intervention in illness have recently been
collected among new Azorean immigrants in Cambridge, Mass. (1975)"
(National, **54:** 194). The *New York Times* of 15 December 1968 reported on
two trials of *bruxas*, in Lisbon and Oporto respectively, on grounds of
medical quackery.
    69. Aubrey F. G. Bell, *In Portugal* (London: John Lane, 1912), p.13;
Lautensach, **143:** 99, 157; Weeks, **159:** 144–45; Correia, **136:** 82–83.
    70. Maria Teresa de Mendonça Lino Netto, "A linguagem dos pesca-
dores e lavradores do concelho de Vila do Conde," *Revista Portuguesa de
Filologia*, 1 (1947), 82, 89, 118–19; Raul Brandão, *Os pescadores*, 2d ed.
(Lisbon: Aillaud e Bertrand, 1924), pp. 131–32, 153–54, 239; Açoreana,
123: I, 148.
    71. Descamps, **137:** 83–84, 127, 437; Almeida, **125:** 58, 60, 73–74.
    72. Social, **115:** I, 27, 29; III, 70–73.
    73. Estep, **48:** 64.
    74. Ferro, **49:** 204, 206.
    75. Hans H. Leder, "Cultural Persistence in a Portuguese-American
Community" (Ph.D. diss., Stanford University, 1968), pp. 5–6, 25–27, 47,
55, 67, 112.
    76. John T. Cole and Richard Tulisano, "Is Terminology Enough?,"
American Anthropologist, 67 (1965), 747–48.
    77. Graves, **37:** 142–44.
    78. This point was recently emphasized by Estellie Smith, based on case
studies she undertook among Azoreans in New England as well as back in
the Azores; cf. Symposium, **59:** 70–76, 81–82.
    79. Andrade, **13;** Symposium, **59:** 11, 25–27.
    80. U.S., **76:** X, 79–80.
    81. U.S., **76:** XXII, 446–54.
    82. Social, **115:** I, 28; III, 71.
    83. Bannick, **45:** 111, 114.
    84. Symposium, **59:** 12–13.
    85. Ulysse Forget, *Les Franco-Américains et le Melting-Pot* (Fall River,
1949), p. 16; Sharkansky, **29:** 83, 97–99.
    86. Estep, **48:** 63. Between 1912 and 1934, according to Fuchs, **106:** 59,

over 20 percent of Portuguese women in Hawaii married Haole men, but only two percent of Portuguese males married Haole girls. During 1930–1934, according to Adams, **100:** 140, there were 760 weddings of Portuguese to Portuguese and 949 of Portuguese to non-Portuguese.

87. In Portugal, during the period from 1913 to 1925, the total number of marriages concluded per year ranged from about 30,000 to 53,000; the total number of divorces, at the same time, was only about 300 to 600 per year, or roughly one percent; cf. Portugal, Direcção Gèral de Saúde, *Estatística do movimento fisiológico da população de Portugal* (annual bulletins), for this period; Descamps, **137:** 473.

88. Adams, **100:** 305; Estep, **48:** 64. Several divorce cases involving California Portuguese were reported in the immigrant press by the early 1900s. In one of these, a woman was suing her husband on the ground that he had told her she would never go to heaven, and that he considered her capable of poisoning him (Arauto, **1:** 25 June and 1 October 1904, 21 March 1908).

89. Diario, **4:** 31 August and 20 October 1944.

90. Sharkansky, **29:** 88, 163.

91. Diario, **4:** 14 December 1964.

CHAPTER NINE

1. Portugal, **150;** Carqueja, **132;** Portugal, **50;** Correia, **136;** Orlando Ribeiro, *L'Ile de Madère* (Lisbon, 1949); **138;** and various standard references. According to Portuguese census statistics, barely twelve percent of the country's total population were "urban" (living in cities or small towns) as of 1864; in 1920, the percentage was still about the same. According to the same official source, in 1900 and 1911 the percentage of the total labor force engaged in agriculture was as high as 60 percent for the country as a whole (mainland plus Azores and Madeira). The fisheries, at the same time, occupied less than one percent of the working population on the mainland, some two percent in the islands.

2. U.S., **76:** IV, 37.

3. U.S., **76:** IV, 27–28; III, 147–48. See also **75:** tables 10 and 29, showing a similar distribution for the years 1911–1931.

4. U.S., **76:** X, 70–71.

5. Cf. Hohman, **120a:** 218–20.

6. Portugal, **69:** 247.

7. On all of the foregoing, regarding whaling, see also Hohman, **120a:** 53–58, 110–27, 300; Foster R. Dulles, *Lowered Boats* (New York, Harcourt Brace, 1933), pp. 34–36, 90–96, 155–63, 253ff.; Bogart, **163:** 60–61, 202; Hatch, **85:** 62–64; Hawes, **120:** 191–96, 223–26; Greaves, **50;** Poole, **28.**

8. Collins, **60:** 75–76; also cf. Wilcox, **77:** 203, 205.

9. Edwin C. Starks, *A History of California Shore Whaling* (Sacramento, 1922), pp. 6, 17–27; Charles M. Scammon, *The Marine Mammals*

of the Northwestern Coast of North America (San Francisco: Carmany, 1874), pp. 247–51; Portugal, **70:** year 1875, p. 226; year 1877, pp. 219–20; year 1878, p. 193; year 1886, p. 309; year 1892, p. 35; year 1894, Report no. 30, p. 97; Symposium, **40:** 50.

10. A. Hyatt Verrill, *The Real Story of the Whaler* (New York: Appleton, 1916), pp. 91–94, 241–43; Hawes, **120:** 311, 323; Wolfbein, **90:** 7.

11. Goode, **62:** 146; James B. Connolly, *The Book of the Gloucester Fishermen* (New York: John Day, 1930), pp. 299–300.

12. For the New England fisheries in general, see Raymond McFarland, *A History of the New England Fisheries* (New York: Appleton, 1911), pp. 129, 189–90, 247, 288, 291ff; Edward A. Ackerman, *New England's Fishing Industry* (Chicago: University of Chicago Press, 1941), pp. 71–78, 150–51, 164–68, 185, 291; Massachusetts, **65:** 11, 40, 44. For Provincetown, cf. Vorse, **32:** 162–63; **31:** 410–15; Hatch, **85:** 67–74; M. Estellie Smith, "Portuguese Enclaves," in *Social and Cultural Identity*, ed. T. K. Fitzgerald (Athens: University of Georgia Press, 1974). For Gloucester, also see Luis Marden, "Gloucester Blesses Its Portuguese Fleet," *National Geographic Magazine*, 104, no. 1 (July 1953), 75–84; *New York Times*, 25 September 1969, p. 49; 18 April 1971, p. 12.

13. John J. Poggie, Jr., and Carl Gersuny, *Fishermen of Galilee: The Human Ecology of a New England Coastal Community* (Narragansett: University of Rhode Island, 1974), pp. 5, 16.

14. Federal Writers' Project, *Seeing St. Augustine* (St. Augustine, Fla.: Record Co., 1937), pp. 13, 52; Colonial, **2:** 14 April 1933; Diario, **4:** 17 May 1949.

15. Collins, **60:** passim; Wilcox, **77:** 153–54, 189; Fritz Bartz: *Fischgründe und Fischereiwirtschaft an der Westküste Nordamerikas* (Kiel, 1942), pp. 29–33, 47, 103–11, 137–43; Clifford M. Zierer, "The Fishery Industry in California," *Scottish Geographical Magazine*, 51 (1935), 65–79; Max Miller, *Harbor of the Sun* (New York: Doubleday Doran, 1940), pp. 281, 305–11; Symposium, **40:** 6–7; Portugal, **68:** year 1942, pp. 160–62; H. C. Godsil, *The High Seas Tuna Fishery of California* (Sacramento: California State Printing Office, 1938).

16. Symposium, **40:** 23; and private communications.

17. Portugal, **69:** 246–49.

18. Massachusetts, **63:** year 1885, vol. 1, pt. 2, pp. 532–611. For Boston, also cf. Bushee, **79a:** 63–65, 70, 83, 88, 95; according to this source, the Portuguese needle women in Boston were paid only two to three dollars per week, struggling in great poverty to help their men or to support a "fatherless" family. A special note on the barbers: "The more intelligent of the young men . . . choose hairdressing as their profession . . .," wrote Henry Lang in 1892, with reference to the New England Portuguese; "it is among the barbers that we must generally look for the leading members of the social and other societies of our colonies" (Lang, **22:** 10). Even among the earliest Azorean immigrants to New England, in the 1850s and 1860s,

there were a number of barbers and especially hairpiece makers enjoying relatively high prestige, in such different locations as Boston, Lawrence, Lowell, Worcester, Hartford, and New York City—and as far as Philadelphia and Indianapolis. See M. J. Vieira, *The Tonsorial Art Pamphlet* (Indianapolis: Press of the Publishing House, 1877), pp. 68–69, 92–94. (The relatively high status of the "tonsorial artist," among various immigrant groups, can be interpreted as due to an interesting confluence of paramedical, quasi-artistic, and news-mediating functions.)

19. Massachusetts, Bureau of Statistics of Labor, *Race in Industry* (Boston, 1903), pp. 52–55.

20. Rhode Island, **71:** year 1905, table 7.

21. Portugal, **68:** n.s. II, 692–93.

22. Massachusetts, **63:** year 1915, pp. 536–631.

23. Bogart, **163:** 347–48, 376–78; Harold U. Faulkner, *American Economic History*, 6th ed. (New York: Harper, 1949), p. 422; **81:** 118.

24. Hawes, **120:** 190; U.S., **76:** X, 41; Copeland, **81:** 27–30.

25. On the concept of "networks of contact," cf. Anderson, **160** and **161**.

26. For Fall River, see Payson W. Lyman, "Fall River, Massachusetts," *New England Magazine*, n.s. 24 (1901), 291–312; Jonathan Th. Lincoln, *The City of the Dinner Pail*, (Boston: Houghton Mifflin, 1909); see also Bogart, **163:** 347–48, 376–78. For Lowell, cf. Kenngott, **87**.

27. U.S., **76:** X, 9–21. This ranking may not be quite accurate, as it was based on a sample. According to Philip T. Silvia ("The Spindle Ciy" [Ph.D. diss., Fordham University, 1973], pp. 685–88), 3,553 out of a total of 12,654 textile operatives in Fall River ca. 1910 were French-Canadian, only 2,401 were "Portuguese."

28. Massachusetts, **64:** 43–45; W. Jett Lauck, "The Cotton-Mill Operatives of New England," *Atlantic Monthly*, 109 (1912), 706–13.

29. U.S., **76:** I, 384–89.

30. *Jornal de Fall River*, 24 August 1977; Agostinho, **12:** 214–17.

31. Agostinho, **12:** 214–17.

32. Andrade, **13:** 84–85, 89.

33. Diario, **4:** 24 and 31 January, 7 February 1952.

34. Kenngott, **87:** 110.

35. Gertrude Barnum, "The Story of a Fall River Mill Girl," *Independent* (New York), 58 (January–June 1905), 243; Hutt, **86:** 506.

36. Herbert J. Lahne, *The Cotton Mill Worker* (New York: Farrar & Rinehart, 1944), pp. 7, 73, 164, 212–14; Robert W. Dunn and Jack Hardy, *Labor and Textiles* (New York: International Publishers, 1931), pp. 106–14, 178–80, 218–25; Burgy, **79:** 166.

37. Edmund J. Brock, *The Background and Recent Status of Collective Bargaining in the Cotton Industry in Rhode Island* (Washington, D.C.: Catholic University of America Press, 1942), pp. 10–11; Margaret T. Parker, *Lowell: A Study of Industrial Development* (New York: Macmillan,

1940), p. 172; Wolfbein, **90:** 39, 43−44, 80, 140; Sharkansky, **29:** 21−29, 32−36; Portugal-America, **9:** September 1928, April 1929.

38. N. S. Shaler, "Martha's Vineyard," *New England Magazine*, n.s. 34 (July−December 1874), 736−37.

39. Peck, **27:** 207−8. It is probably this Portuguese-American farming community at "Cottage City," on Martha's Vineyard, or one very much like it, that suggested the fictitious village of Melton depicted in the novel *An Island Chronicle* by William Cummings (New York: Knopf, 1924).

40. Holmes, **52:** 401.

41. The first saying is cited in Soares, **39:** 56, in Diario, **4:** 15 November 1941, and elsewhere. For the second, cf. Cape, **80:** 6, no. 9, p. 29.

42. U.S., **76:** XXII, 539−50; Cape, **80:** 1, no. 4. pp. 25−26; 1, no. 9, p. 5; 5, no. 2, pp. 34−36; Albert P. Brigham, "Cape Cod and the Old Colony," *Geographical Review*, 10, no. 1 (July 1920), 16, 20; **65:** 32−34; Josiah C. Folsom, *Farm Labor in Massachusetts, 1921* (Washington, D.C., 1924), pp. 1, 7−8, 19−21; Theodate Geoffrey, *Suckanesset; . . . a History of Falmouth, Massachusetts* (Falmouth: Falmouth Publishing Co., 1930), pp. 152−53; Montepio, **23:** 66; Katherine Smith and Edith Shay, *Down the Cape* (New York: Dodge, 1936), pp. 73−76; Millard C. Faught, *Falmouth, Massachusetts* (New York: Columbia University Press, 1945), pp. 52, 151−52, 169; Agnes Rothery, *Family Album* (New York: Dodd Mead, 1942), pp. 43−45; "Cranberries", *Ebony*, 4, no. 1 (November 1948), 31−33. Capeverdean cranberry pickers on Cape Cod are depicted in the novel *Cranberry Red* by E. Garside (Boston, 1938). For a vivid portrayal of living conditions among Capeverdeans on Cape Cod, see also the reminiscences of Belmira Nunes Lopes (Symposium, **59:** 33−55, esp. 42−48). Born in Providence of Capeverdean immigrant parents, she spent her childhood in cranberry country. After graduating from Radcliffe College with honors, she was refused a teaching job in Massachusetts "because of racial prejudice." But she did eventually have a teaching career in Puerto Rico, and later in New York City.

43. U.S., **76:** XXII, 445−50. Cf. Taft, **30:** passim.

44. Graves, **37:** 49−50. On these mining operations in general, cf. J. W. Wooldridge, *History of the Sacramento Valley, California*, 3 vols. (Chicago: Pioneer Historical Publishing Co., 1931), I, 211−36.

45. Halley, **93:** 134; also 198, 292−93, 477, 505.

46. Bohme, **35:** 241−42. Apparently in a very indirect sense only, the Portuguese have had something to do with bringing the navel orange to California: From Goa (Portuguese India), this citrus fruit had been taken to Portugal and hence to Brazil, where it was propagated in the Bahia area about 1820. In the 1870s, a U.S. Department of Agriculture official heard of the superior Bahia variety and introduced it to California. On the other hand, the Valencia orange, now equally important in California, originated in the Azores, from where it came to the U.S. via England. Cf. Rahno M.

266 THE PORTUGUESE-AMERICANS

MacCurdy, *History of the California Fruit Growers Exchange* (Los Angeles, 1925), pp. 4–5.

47. Ezra A. Carman, et al., *Special Report on the History and Present Condition of the Sheep Industry of the United States* (Washington, D.C., 1892), pp. 972–74. A few Portuguese shepherds in Inyo County (bordering on Nevada) show up in the autobiographical story *The Flock* by Mary Austin (Boston: Houghton Mifflin, 1906), pp. 62, 65, 167–68, 203–4. Some Portuguese remained in the sheep-raising business as late as the 1930s, in the San Joaquin Valley as well as in Nevada.

48. Portugal, **70:** year 1892, pp. 28, 31–33, 36.

49. Carey McWilliams, *Factories in the Field* (Boston: Little Brown, 1939), p. 122.

50. Vaz, **41:** 67–68. Portugal, **68:** X, 264; XI, 1041; n.s. IV, 217. Through several mergers, this bank became a constituent of Wells Fargo Bank in 1960.

51. Arauto, **1:** issue of December 31, 1910 (18 savings bank ads), and miscellaneous earlier issues seen in an incomplete back file.

52. Portugal, **68:** n.s. IV, 218.

53. US., **76:** XXIV, 262–63, 292–93, 334, 489–90. Incidentally, the same Commission report also noted (XXV, 431–34) that in the only two important cotton mills then operating in California, both at Oakland, two thirds of the employees were of Portuguese birth or parentage (presumably transplants from New England). Cf. also Crissey, **36,** for concrete examples of Portuguese farming skill; and Mowry, **38:** 115. Fictionalized references to Alameda County's Portuguese gardeners are contained in Jack London's *Valley of the Moon.*

54. George Digby, *Red Horizons* (London: Collins, 1939).

55. Graves, **37:** 36, 81–86; Jornal, **7:** 117; Portugal, **66:** no. 51, pp. 3–4; Sampaio, **155:** 370–72; Portugal, **150:** 711–12, 715, 723; Portugal, **70:** no. 38, p. 9; no. 75, p. 9; no. 86, p.13.

56. U. S. Bureau of Animal Industry, *Bulletin,* no. 14; Edward J. Wickson, *Rural California* (New York: Macmillan, 1923), pp. 231–38; California State Dairy Bureau, *Reports:* Report for 1904–1906, pp. 5–6, 35–36; Report for 1911–1912, p. 11; Commonwealth, **92:** 411–12; Small, **96:** I, 296–300, 323–24; Eugene L. Menefee and Fred A. Dodge, *History of Tulare and Kings Counties, California* (Los Angees: Historic Record Co., 1913), pp. 207, 224–25; Jornal, **7:** 76.

57. Edwin E. Cox, "Farm Tenantry in California," *Transactions of the Commonwealth Club of California,* 11, no. 8 (December 1916), 455; Jornal, **6:** 26 March 1943, and private communication; Smith, **97:** 413. In Jack London's semiautobiographical novel *Martin Eden* (New York, 1908), pp. 211–12, Maria Silva says her greatest dream is to own a "milk ranch" some day.

58. Ferro, **49:** 180.

59. Jornal, **7:** 117; Graves, **37:** 116–22.

60. Tinkham, **99:** 1039.

61. James M. Guinn, *History of the State of California and Biographical Record of the San Joaquin Valley* (Chicago: Chapman, 1905), pp. 331–32.

62. Graves, **37:** 155–56.

63. Colonias, **46:** 719; Freitas, **43:** 148. In 1880, the Portuguese in Honolulu had twelve general stores, two boardinghouses, four shoe repair stores, two barber shops, three groceries.

64. Portugal, **150:** 813, 830–31; Francisco António Correa, *História económica de Portugal*, 2 vols., (Lisbon: ENP, 1929–1930), II, 208–09; T. Bentley Duncan, *Atlantic Islands* (Chicago: University of Chicago Press, 1972), pp. 31, 72. Madeira's sugar cane production increased shortly after 1900—but chiefly for the manufacture of cheap brandy. See Portugal, **66:** no. 38, pp. 4–5; no. 75, p. 6; no. 86, pp. 6–7.

65. See pp. 24-25 and pp. 46-47 in text. The workers imported by Louisiana sugar planters in 1872 were paid 7–10 dollars per month, plus housing and food; this compared with 3–5 dollars per *day* for free workers off the plantations (according to Portugal, **69:** 241–44).

66. Porteus, **95:** 54–55.

67. Russ, **114:** 212; du Puy, **61:** 105–6.

68. Hawaiian, **107:** year 1892, pp. 11, 15.

69. A different statistic for 1890 lists 2,330 Portuguese men as well as 272 women and 417 children as laboring on the plantations (Portugal, **70:** year 1890, p. 4).

70. Portugal, **70:** year 1888, report dated February 1889, pp. 5–7, 9.

71. Portugal, **70:** year 1890, report dated October 1890, pp. 6–8.

72. Portugal, **70:** year 1895 (*sic!*), report dated May 1897, pp. 11–12, 14, 16, 21.

73. A. Marques, in Hawaiian, **107:** year 1911, pp. 45–46.

74. Adams, **100:** 36, 40, 136, 262, 332–33; Adams, **101:** 20–21; Lind, **111:** 10, 267, 322, 324; Midkiff, **112:** 53, 58, 63.

75. Social, **115:** I, 26–31; reprinted in Blake Clark, *Hawaii* (Doubleday, 1947), pp. 100–102.

76. Freitas, **43:** 156, 160.

77. Nellist, **113:** 714.

78. Commonwealth Club of California, *The Population of California* (San Francisco, 1946), pp. 159–61; Carl C. Taylor et al., *Rural Life in the United States* (New York: Knopf, 1949), pp. 440–43; Bohme, **35:** 242–43; Commonwealth, **92:** 400–401, 410–11. For general background, see Carlson, **164:** 63–67; Doyle, **166:** 5–6, 25–27.

79. Graves, **37:** 131–32.

80. Private communications, including many on-site interviews; Jornal, **7:** 17, 39, 68, 71; Graves, **37:** 136, 142–44.

81. On-site interviews.

82. Cf. Jensen, **20:** 134–36; Symposium, **59:** 11–15, 80; on-site interviews.

83. Carvalho, **16**: 27. Also cf. Luz, **53**: 23−29, 139−45. In popular Portuguese speech, particularly back in the Azores, the term *calafona*, an Anglicism derived from *California*, came to designate an emigrant in, or repatriate from, the United States in general (even including New England)—somewhat with the connotation of "rich uncle from America."
84. Handlin, **167**: 89.
85. Anderson, **160**: XIII−XIV, 23, 97−100, 116, 166. Also cf. Estellie Smith in Symposium, **59**: 83−84.

CHAPTER TEN

1. Hipólito Raposo, *Descobrindo ilhas descobertas* (Porto: Gama, 1942).
2. Graves, **37**: 32.
3. Handler, **51**: 31−32. For example, Terceir ans are teasingly referred to as *rabos tortos* ("twisted rumps or tails") by inhabitants of some of the other islands.
4. Cf. Camara, **131**: 20.
5. The same kind of regionalism is reported for the large and relatively recent Portuguese immigrant communities in Canada; c.f. Anderson, **161**: 95−96, 161; Anderson, **160**: 172.
6. Data taken from newspaper files and interviews.
7. Cf. Arruda, **128**: 25−27, 40−58; Walker, **158**: 160−61; Borges, **129**: 127; Taft, **30**: 343−44.
8. Parsons, **26**: 94
9. Lyall, **145**: 56; also 59, 63, 71.
10. Symposium, **40**: 19.
11. Incident recalled in Diario, **4**: 14 October 1953.
12. Carvalho, **16**: 34.
13. Shippee, **72**: 14−15.
14. Colonial, **2**: 30 September 1932.
15. Rogers, **58**: 50, 54.
16. Copies of bylaws seen. St. Antonio Society (Honolulu), *Jubileu da Sociedade Portugueza de Santo Antonio . . . 1877−1927* (Honolulu, 1927), pp. 17, 33. Luso, **8**: 23 December 1916.
17. Robert A. Warner, *New Haven Negroes* (New Haven: Yale University Press, 1940), pp. 197, 260.
18. David Baxter, "Approaches to Studying Ethnicity among Cape Verdeans in New Bedford, Mass," unpublished paper, 1974; Engler, **83**: 34.
19. Portugal, **70**: year 1896, Report no. 4, p. 14; Blascoer, **104**: 48.
20. Almeida, **34**: 17.
21. Steven S. Ussach, "The New England Portuguese: A Plural Society," *Plural Societies*, 6 (1975), 52−55.
22. Handler, **51**.
23. Carvalho, **16**: 273.
24. Portugal, Secretariado Nacional de Informação, *Social Assistance in*

Portugal (Lisbon: SNI, 1945), pp. 17−25; Miguel de Oliveira, *História eclesiástica de Portugal* (Lisbon: União Gráfica, 1940), pp. 235−38; Baldomero Cerdá y Richart, *Historia y doctrina del mutualismo* (Barcelona: Bosch, 1943), pp. 76, 83, 86, 93−94, 100; **66**: no. 4, pp. 8−76; no. 25, pp. 3−76; no. 27, pp. 13−101; no. 95, pp. 3−82; no. 103, pp. 4−13; José C. da Costa Goodolphim, *Assistance publique en Portugal* (Lisbon, 1940), pp. 7−8.

25. Portugal, **69**: 249.

26. Almeida, **34**: 25−30; Vaz, **41**: 81−84.

27. Private communications; Freitas, **43**: 149, 161.

28. Almeida, **34**: 40−67.

29. Portugal, **70**: year 1892, Report no. 14, pp. 38−41; Angel, **91**: 187; C. M. Gidney et al., *History of Santa Barbara, San Luis Obispo and Ventura Counties, California*, 2 vols. (Chicago: Lewis, 1917), pp. 266−67; Carvalho, **16**: 71; Noel P. Gist, "Secret Societies," *University of Missouri Studies*, 15 (1940), 24, 31−32, 39−41.

30. Almeida, **34**: 73; Vaz, **41**: 92−93, 110; Arauto, **1**: 9 and 23 May 1908; private communications.

31. Various newspaper reports, in Diario (**4**), Jornal (**6**), Arauto (**1**), etc.

32. Data culled from various newspapers.

33. Charles W. Ferguson, *Fifty Million Brothers* (New York: Farrar & Rinehart, 1937), pp. 82−93; Martha E. D. White, "The Work of Women's Clubs in New England," *New England Magazine*, n.s. 28, no. 4 (June 1903), 447, 452.

34. Portugal, **68**: I, 287; n.s. II, 696.

35. Arauto, **1**: 20 April 1912.

36. *União Lusitana Hawaiiana* (Honolulu), 5 March 1892.

37. Vaz, **41**: 119−29.

38. Jornal, **7**: 115; Diario, **4**: 2 May 1942.

39. Arauto, **1**: 13 May 1916; U.S., **76**: XXIV, 493.

40. Private communications; Vaz, **41**: 96, 99, 115; Jornal, **7**: special issue for 1943, p. 11. In 1904, officers of the Supreme Council of U.P.E.C. included Maria Straub, Maria Kilarnovich, Maria J. Smith, and Eugenia Joseph—all evidently married to non-Portuguese; cf. Arauto, **1**: 12 November 1904.

41. Manoel Bernardes Branco, *Portugal e os estrangeiros*, pt. 2, 3 vols. (Lisbon, 1893−1895), I, 33.

42. Montepio, **23**: 125; Diario, **4**: 19 June 1952.

43. Cf. Carvalho, **16**: 172−89; Portugal-America, **9**: April 1929, p. 252; Diario, **4**: 2 May 1942.

44. Vaz, **41**: 221−26; Diario, **4**: 17 April 1957, 26 February 1959; Jornal, **7**: 69, 121; Jornal, **6**: 4 July 1947; Soares, **39**: 62−63.

45. Peck, **27**: 209.

46. *Providence Journal*, 20 October 1916, p. 14.

47. Diario, **4**: 2 May 1942; 2 November 1944; 27 October 1952.

48. Arauto, 1: 4, 11 March 1911; Almeida, 34: 125, 128.

49. Private communications. Some such scholarships are also given out by the Luso-American Fraternal Federation, which resulted from the merger of A.P.P.B. and U.P.C., two medium-sized statewide fraternal societies.

50. Almeida, 34: 44–45. Also cf. Poinsard, 149: 378–400; Handlin, 167: 176–77; Mary B. Treudley, "Formal Organization and the Americanization Process," American Sociological Review, 14 (1949), 46–50.

51. Private communications; Garden Island (Kanai, H.I.), 21, 26 March, 2 April 1940; Honolulu, 108: 10 May 1953, 1 May 1955.

CHAPTER ELEVEN

1. Poinsard, 149: 371–72, 378–81; Weeks, 159: 202; Riegelhaupt, 154: 836; M. V. d' Armelim Jr., "Os Açores," Boletim da Sociedade de Geografia de Lisboa, 40 (1922), 243.

2. Cf. Diario, 4: 15 November 1941; 24 May 1965; Arauto, 1: 25 July 1896; Yzendoorn, 118: 224–25; Sharkansky, 29: 78; Jensen, 19.

3. Cf. Sharkansky, 29: 78; 79–80; Handlin; 167: 127–28.

4. Diario, 4: 9 September 1950.

5. An example of such friction, between the pastor of one of New Bedford's Portuguese parishes and the organizers of the Feast of the Blessed Sacrament, is recounted in detail in Cabral, 15.

6. Bradley, 78: 30–31; Diario, 4: 4 September 1942; Providence Visitor, 19 April 1912; Açores, October 1928, p. 60.

7. Vaz, 41: 189–94; União, 11: 28 March 1938, pp. 2, 20–21; Ribeiro, 153: 20; Jornal, 6: special issue for 1952, pp. 29–30. Yzendoorn, 118: 224–25; Adams; 100: 139.

8. Vaz, 41: 203–9; Diario, 4: 12 October 1945, 9 September 1950; private communications.

9. Portugal, 68: n.s. II, 696; Diario, 4: 15 November 1941, 15 July 1955; Rogers, 58: 27.

10. Since the 1950s Fatima has also become a favorite invocation with many non-Portuguese Catholic churches across the United States. This seems quite unrelated to Portuguese immigration, of course. However, one Portuguese mission priest in New York City made widespread propaganda for this Portuguese Lourdes during the 1940s and 1950s, through his English-language Fatima Magazine.

11. Diario, 4: 27 June 1950. Also see note 16 to chapter 2!

12. Letter from a descendant of the Vicentes; União, 11: 28 March 1938, pp. 3–5; Lang, 22: 9; History of Erie County, Pennsylvania (Chicago, 1884), p. 462. Nelson's Biographical Dictionary . . . of Erie County (Erie, 1896), p. 177.

13. Garcia Monteiro, mentioned on pp. 61–62 in text, directed this paper in 1884; cf. Neves, 24, and Carvalho, 16: 108, 154. An unnamed

newspaper which the same Garcia Monteiro floated or collaborated on unsuccessfully in Boston in 1883 may have been identical with the *Luso-Americano* before it was transferred to New Bedford, or else may have represented a separate effort; in the former case, the founding date of the *Luso-Americano* may have been 1883 rather than 1881.

14. Carvalho, **16**: 108; and private communication.

15. Almeida, **34**: 68; Vaz, **41**: 142, 144. Although the founding date of *Voz Portuguesa* is given as 1884 in Jornal, **7**: 23 and elsewhere, the date of 1880 is evidenced by the first issue of this paper, preserved at the Library of Congress.

16. Vaz, **41**: 142, 144.

17. Arauto, **1**: 28 October 1911. According to Knowlton, **44**: 90, there was a paper called *A Liberdade* from 1900 to 1910.

18. Knowlton, **44**: 89–90; Hawaiian, **107**: passim.

19. See principally Carvalho, **16**: 108–15; Vaz, **41**: 139–49; Knowlton, **44**.

20. Portugal, **68**: n.s. II, 695–96; Arauto, **1**: 25 January, 9 May, 29 August 1908; Knowlton, **44**. If the total number seems excessive, considering the small readership base, it appears small when we learn that in the Azores, 312 different newspapers and magazines were born and died between 1830 and 1886, half of them on the island of São Miguel alone, most of them living a few months to two years (Archivo, **127**: VIII, 485–556). Among the French-Canadians in New England, 200–300 different French-language newspapers had seen the light of day up to 1943; some twenty were still in publication at that time. See Jacques Ducharme, *Shadows of the Trees* (New York: Harper, 1943), p. 127.

21. Pap, **56**: 31.

22. The owner-editor of one of these weeklies confesses (*Voz de Portugal*, 11 May 1944, p. 12): "I don't have the qualifications of a journalist; at age twenty I did not even know how to put together two syllables; but I am fighting for justice, and this is what my paper is for."

23. Up to about 1920, the editor of the *Diário de Notícias* (New Bedford) reminisced in 1944, Portuguese weeklies had usually been produced on presses made for the printing of receipts, tickets, and pamphlets. If this kind of printing prospered, the newspaper flourished too—even if it had hardly any subscribers. But immigrants arriving after 1914 were more interested in newspapers and politics than earlier ones; thus, in 1919, the *Alvorada* (later renamed the *Diário de Notícias*) became the first daily paper. Diario, **4**: 3 May 1944, p. 9.

24. Not untypical although bordering on the grotesque was an incident reported in 1904: the owner-editor of the *Liberdade*, in Sacramento, was arrested on a libel charge at the request of the editor of the *União Portugueza*, in San Francisco. The former, in turn, caused the arrest of the latter, because of insults published in the *União*. In the end, the adversaries settled out of court by mutual apologies (Arauto, **1**: 13, 20 August 1904).

CHAPTER TWELVE

1. Gallop, **139**: 126.

2. M. F. Smithes, *Things Seen in Portugal* (London: Seeley, Service & Co., 1931), pp. 144–45, 147. Gallop (**139**: 158) traces the picnic meals at the *romarias* to the offerings of food that were eaten in common by all the participants at pagan festivals, as acts of propitiation and attempts to gain strength against evil influences. According to Chaves (**134**: 124–27), the *romarias* (which are held on weekdays as well as Sundays, throughout August and September) serve three converging purposes: for the faithful, devotion and fulfillment of vows; for the merrymakers, fun; for the beggars, alms.

3. Weeks, **159**: 204.

4. Anthony J. Drexel Biddle, *The Madeira Islands* (Philadelphia, 1896), pp. 66–67. See also L. F. Ramsey, "Levada-Walking in Madeira," *Living Age*, 307 (October–December 1920), 661.

5. According to Estep (**48**: 65), religious and fraternal festivities have also been relatively rare in Hawaii, compared to California.

6. Chaves, **135**: 49–50; Walker, **158**: 117–18. Cf. also Braga, **130**: II, 289–90.

7. Braga, **130**: II, 284–90.

8. Walker, **158**: 117.

9. Gallop, **139**: 104.

10. Braga, **130**: II, 284.

11. In the opinion of Chaves **135**: 46, 49, the Alemquer cult is closely connected with the "miracle of the roses." But there are two variants of this miracle: According to one, money was transformed into roses when Isabel was defraying building expenditures for the convent of Santa Clara. According to the other, roses were transformed into gold during the construction of the Holy Ghost Church at Alemquer. These two variants mentioned by Chaves are in addition to the one reported in the text above.

12. In mainland Portugal, a Holy Ghost festival in one form or another is still observed in Coimbra (where the body of Queen Isabel is preserved in a silver casket), Braga, Tomar, and some other places in the east-central region. It continues to be popular on the island of Madeira, and in parts of Brazil. See Gallop, **139**: 131; Jaime Cortesão, "O sentido da cultura em Portugal no século XIV," *Seara Nova*, 35 (January–March 1956), 30; Portugal, **151**: 51; *Notícias de Portugal*, July 1973; Emilio Willems, "Acculturative Aspects of the Feast of the Holy Ghost in Brazil," *American Anthropologist*, 51 (1949), 400–408; Riegelhaupt, **154**: 840; Monteiro, **147**: II, 74–75; Social, **115**: III, 70–71.

13. Braga, **130**: II, 285–87; Weeks, **159**: 212–13.

14. For some descriptions of Holy Ghost celebrations in the Azores see Braga, **130**: II, 287–88; Iliowizí, **142**: 88–90; Walker, **158**: 118–20; Henry Sandham, "St. Michael's of the Azores," *Century Magazine* (New York),

n.s. 69 (December 1915), 224–25; Haeberle, **141:** 527; Patricia W. Vaurie, "Festival in the Azores," 28 (April–October 1938), 125–27; Sampaio, **155:** 356–60; Inocêncio Enes, "As festas do Espírito Santo nos Altares," *Boletim do Instituto Histórico da Ilha Terceira,* 6 (1948), 107–23; Rose Dabney and H. Cunningham, "Fayal," *New England Magazine,* n.s. 7, no. 6 (February 1893), 745–46; Correia, **136:** 76–81.

15. Jornal, **7:** 50. According to Revista, **10:** June 1915, p. 6, and Vaz, **41:** 106, the first recorded celebration took place at Sausalito, some time before 1887.

16. Jornal, **6:** special issue for 1942, p. 25; Jornal, **7:** 100; Revista, **10:** June 1915, p. 6; Vaz, **41:** 106–7.

17. University, **116:** Luso, **8:** 17 August 1918; Yzendoorn, **118:** 247; Social, **115:** XVI, 64; Honolulu, **108:** 23 May 1958, 25 May 1961.

18. University, **116.**

19. Arauto, **1:** 15 May 1915 (program notice).

20. Colonia, **3:** 24 June, 15, 22 July 1924.

21. Haeberle, **141:** 527; Iliowizi, **142:** 88; Weeks, **159:** 210–12.

22. Jornal, **6:** special issue for 1947, pp. 18–19; Arauto, **1:** 30 April and 29 May 1904; 25 April 1908; Colonial, **3:** 20 May 1924; Jornal, **6:** 8 February 1946; **41:** 136–37.

23. *Jornal de Fall River,* 29 June 1977. The Santo Cristo festival is also a huge event among Azoreans in Canada, where it was initiated at Toronto in 1963 and a little later at Montreal. In 1974, according to Anderson, **161:** 144, 90,000 people attended the procession and the subsequent merriment in Toronto's Trinity Park.

24. Arauto, **1:** 1 October 1904; Portugal-America, **9:** August 1928, p. 416. Jornal, **7:** 31, 47; Jornal, **6:** 18 June 1943; Jornal, **7:** 19 August 1949.

25. Leite, **144:** 58; Cabral, **15;** Another image by the same name is worshipped at Obidos, continental Portugal (Gallop, **139:** 127, 131).

26. Vaz, **41:** 129–31; Jaime Vieira dos Santos, "Vocabulário do dialecto madeirense," *Revista de Portugal, Serie A: Língua Portuguesa,* 10 (1946), 27.

27. Chaves, **134:** 22–24; Armando de Lucena, *Arte popular; usos e costumes portugueses,* vol. 1, 2d ed. (Lisbon: ENP, 1944), 21–22, 49, 81–83.

28. Vorse, **32:** 51. According to Koehler, **21:** 28–32, the Provincetown Portuguese still put out their creches (as of 1972), but without the traditional arrangement; serenading is now limited to an occasional neighborhood sing.

29. University, **116.**

30. For a very detailed description of the Festa de Serreta at Gustine see A. H. Gayton, "The Festa da Serreta at Gustine," *Western Folklore,* 7 (1948), 251–65.

31. The blessing of the fishing fleet, traditinal in Lisbon each April before the departure of codfishing vessels for Newfoundland, was instituted

by Portuguese-Americans at Gloucester in 1944. The Italians in that town have their own vessels blessed a week or two after the Portuguese (who sometimes combine this event with a Holy Ghost devotion). In imitation of the annual Gloucester event, the predominantly Portuguese fishing people in Provincetown instituted the touristy blessing of their own fleet in 1948. In the late 1930s, the custom had also traveled south to Brunswick, Ga., where the annual blessing of Portuguese shrimp trawlers (in this case under the sponsorship of Our Lady of Fatima) still enjoys considerable publicity. See Diario, **4:** 22 April 1948, 1 June 1948, 15 September 1955; *National Fisherman*, July 1955, pp. 23–25; *Bulletin of American-Portuguese Cultural Society*, Spring 1969; *New York Sunday Times* 18 April 1971 (Travel Section, p. 12); private communications.

32. Jornal, **6:** 1 August 1952; Luso, **8:** 17, 24 August 1918; J. Edith Hutcheon, *Things Seen in Madeira* (London: Seeley Service, 1928), pp. 109–10; Gihon, **140:** 556.

33. For a full history and fascinating analysis of this New Bedford celebration, see Stephen L. Cabral, "History and Traditions of Local Feast Traced," *Sunday Standard-Times* (New Bedford), 27 July 1975, p. 7; and the same author's "The Feast of the Blessed Sacrament" (M.A. thesis, Brown University, c. 1975).

CHAPTER THIRTEEN

1. Portugal, **70:** year 1894, p. 12.

2. Portugal, **68:** n.s. IL, 695.

3. Portugal, **68:** XI, 1042. This is in marked contrast to a report about 1880 to the effect that the Portuguese families in California rear their children in the Portuguese language and do not speak English among themselves (Colonias, **46:** 355).

4. Arauto, **1:** 23 August 1913.

5. Arauto, **1:** 12 August 1911. In 1956, Portuguese classes at the University of Hawaii, originally mandated by law in that multiethnic territory, had to close down for lack of any enrollment. See *Publications of the Modern Language Association*, 75, no. 4 (September 1960), pt. 2, p. 9.

6. Montepio, **23:** 67.

7. Diario, **4:** 7 August 1942.

8. Bouchard, **14:** 72.

9. Inasmuch as we have included the Capeverdeans among the Portuguese through most of this book, we must here recall the fact, already mentioned on p. 164, that for most Capeverdean immigrants the language problem was not simply one of Portuguese versus English: the native speech of Capeverdeans is a Creole largely derived from Portuguese, but so different from standard Portuguese as to constitute practically a separate language. Many a Capeverdean immigrant, unless he or she had acquired a good deal of standard Portuguese in school back in the islands, was

therefore faced with learning not only English, but also standard Portuguese. Creole speech is still used in many Capeverdean immigrant homes, in New England as well as California.

10. Diario, 4: 20 May 1954; Jornal, 6: 22 May 1953.

11. Some of the above examples are taken from a recent list supplied by Francisco C. Fagundes, published in part in Symposium, 40: 8–17. Most of them are taken from Pap (56), which describes Portuguese immigrant speech in more technical detail. (This latter publication by the present author, long out of print, is again available in a reprint edition, on special order from University Microfilms International.)

Some Anglicisms of the sort just cited have a surprising amount of stability as they get passed on from old-timers to new immigrants, and from immigrants (or repatriates) to the folks back home. For example, the term *grossaria* ("grocery"), widely used in Portuguese immigrant centers today in lieu of standard Portuguese *mercearia*, is documented in Hawaii as early as 1885 (*Luso Hawaiiano*, 15 August 1885); *bordo* ("board," "meals") appears in a Boston boardinghouse ad in 1880 (*Voz Portugueza*, 5 August 1880); in California, scattered newspaper issues (Arauto, 1) for 1904 turn up *farm, basket, plow, hall, bordar* "to board," *raiva* "driver," *overalls*, and many more. Many Anglicisms heard among the New England Portuguese by Pap (56) are also current in the popular speech of São Miguel (Camara, 131).

12. For additional examples of Anglicized surnames see Pap, 56: 124–38, and Almeida, 34: 263–66 (a list of over 300 such names!).

13. Thomas W. Higginson, "Fayal and the Portuguese," *Atlantic Monthly*, 6, no. 37 (November 1860), 526–44.

14. Monteiro, 147: II, 59.

15. Cabral, 42: 97.

16. These and many more examples are cited in George Monteiro, "Alcunhas among the Portuguese in Southern New England," *Western Folklore*, 20 (1961), 103–7.

17. Private communications. At the general store in San Leandro, about 1910, a Portuguese individual could carry on business under several names (Mowry, 38: 116).

18. Elizabeth B. Carr, *Da Kine Talk* (Honolulu: University Press of Hawaii, 1972); and private communication from Steven Ussach.

19. On Portuguese influence in North American place-names, see Pap, 57.

20. The subject of Portuguese immigrant literature is being dealt with by the present author in a separate chapter, forthcoming in a volume sponsored by the Modern Language Association, on the contribution of European ethnics to American literature (edited by E. Ifkovic and R. Di Pietro).

21. See Carvalho, 16: 175–89 for specific groups and plays.

22. Colonial, 2: various issues, 1935, 1937.

23. Anna H. Gayton, "Luso Californian Culture and Its Research Needs," *Proceedings of the Internat. Colloquium on Luso-Brazilian Studies* (Nashville: Vanderbilt University Press, 1953), 85; *Bulletin of New York Public Library*, 47: 263–64.

24. Joanne B. Purcell, "Portuguese Traditional Ballads from California" (M.A. thesis, University of California–Los Angeles, 1968); Symposium, **40**: 33–36; Manuel Da Costa Fontes, "A New Portuguese Ballad Collection from California," *Western Folklore*, 34 (1975), 299–310.

25. Parsons, **25.**

26. For Portuguese folksongs collected in the United States, see Maud C. Hare, "Portuguese Folk-Songs from Provincetown," *Musical Quarterly*, 14 (1928), 35–53. See also Florence H. Botsford, *Folk Songs of Many Peoples*, 2 vols. (New York: Womans Press, 1921–1922), II, 282–302. For folksongs and dances in Portugal, see Michel' Angelo Lambertini, *Chansons et instruments: renseignements pour l' étude du folk-lore portugais* (Lisbon, ca. 1904); João do Rio, *Fados, canções e dansas de Portugal* (Rio de Janeiro: Garnier, 1909); Pedro Fernandez Tomás, *Canções portuguesas* (Coimbra: Imprensa da Universidade, 1934).

27. Elma T. Cabral, "Grandpa Was a Troubadour," *Paradise of the Pacific*, December 1946, pp. 17–20; Hawaiian, **107**: year 1886, p. 58; year 1899, pp. 164–66; year 1917, p. 145; year 1925, pp. 77–79; Helen H. Roberts, *Ancient Hawaii Music* (Honolulu: Bernice P. Bishop Museum, 1926), pp. 7–10; Honolulu, **108**: 20 December 1953 (Sunday supplement, p. 10); Honolulu, **109**: 14 July 1954; "How the Ukulele Came to Hawaii," *Paradise of the Pacific*, 35, no. 1 (January 1922), 8–10. Also cf. Jorge Dias, in *Biblos*, 28 (1953); Santos, **156**: pp. xv–xvi, 198.

28. The dance called *chamarrita* in Madeira is quite different from the Azorean one of the same name (Santos, **156**: 53–56).

29. *Cooking with a Portuguese Flavor* by August M. and Elizabeth Vaz (Castro Valley, Calif., 1967) contains over 150 recipes, with delightful interspersed commentary; E. Donald Asselin, *A Portuguese American Cookbook* (Rutland, Vt.: Tuttle, 1966) (over 200 recipes, collected among the Portuguese in Wareham, Mass.); Koehler, **21**: 40–113 (recipes collected at Provincetown); Irene Vizi, *Portuguese Cooking* and *Portuguese Desserts, Cakes and Cookies* (Los Angeles, 1976 and 1977) (several hundred items, including many desserts and cakes). See also Bazore, **103**: 76–80, 11–12, 118, 144–45, and passim; James P. Shenton et al., *American Cooking: The Melting Pot* (New York: Time-Life Books, 1971), pp. 144–51, and several items in accompanying ring-binder book; *As the World Cooks: Recipes from Many Lands* (Lowell: International Institute, 1938), pp. 189–96.

30. Weeks, **159**: 147–48. Since the turn of the century, the sweet potato has replaced corn as the principal staple in the Azores (Andrade, **126**: 433). Corn is still the staple in the Cape Verde Islands (Almeida, **125**: 62).

31. Walker, **158**: 287–88. For São Miguel, also cf. Arruda, **128**: 17–18.

32. Jan and Cora Gordon, *Portuguese Somersault*, 3d ed. (New York: MacBride, n.d.), p. 127.

33. Carlos Bento da Maia, *Tratado completo de cozinha e de copa* (Lisbon: Guimarães, ca. 1903), p. 80. Also cf. António de Almeida Garret, "Costumes alimentícios dos portugueses," *Publicações do Congresso do Mundo Português (1940)*, 17 (1940), 341–44.

34. J. Leite de Vasconcellos, *Tradições populares de Portugal* (Porto: Clavel, 1882), p. 228; Braga, **130:** I, 116–17.

35. Bertha M. Wood, *Foods of the Foreign-born in Relation to Health* (Boston: Whitcomb & Barrows, 1922), pp. 13–14.

36. Charlotte Raymond, *Food Customs from Abroad* (Massachusetts Department of Public Health, 1935), pp. 15–16.

37. Symposium, **59:** 49–50.

38. Honolulu, **109:** 14 July 1954, 8 August 1961; Edgar C. Knowlton, "Portuguese in Hawaii," *Kentucky Foreign Language Quarterly*, 7 (1960), 214; Bazore, **103:** 77.

39. Bazore, **103:** XIII, 76–79.

CHAPTER FOURTEEN

1. Luis da Camara Pina, *Dever de Portugal para com as comunidades lusíadas da América do Norte* (Lisbon: Bertrand, 1945), pp. 36–37.

2. William C. Smith, *Americans in the Making* (New York: Appleton-Century, 1939), p. 347. Also see Smith for an excellent general discussion of the process of Americanization.

3. Edward A. Ross, "The Lesser Immigrant Groups in America," *Century Magazine*, n.s. 66 (May-October 1914), pp. 937–38.

4. Bannick, **45:** 133–34.

5. Carvalho, **16:** 152.

6. Diario, **4:** 26 May 1964.

7. Carvalho, **16:** 251; Gil de Alverca, *Problemas da nossa colônia* (Boston, 1924), p. 11.

8. Jornal, **6:** special issue for 1940, p. 36.

9. Ferro, **49:** 177.

10. Carvalho, **16:** 247.

11. Arauto, **1:** 24 September 1904.

12. Diario, **4:** 9 April 1953.

13. Diario, **4:** 27 January 1954.

14. Revista, **10:** October 1921, p. 5.

15. Silva, **157:** 291–92.

16. Jokes reported by Eduardo M. Dias, in a letter dated 23 July 1979.

17. North, **88:** II, 58.

18. Borges, **129:** 117.

19. Portugal, **68:** n.s. II, 694.

20. M. Estellie Smith, "A Tale of Two Cities," *Urban Anthropology*, 4 (1975).

21. Engler, **83:** 30–34.

22. Engler, **83:** 34; Burgy, **79:** 166; Reid, **122:** 104–6; U.S., **76:** XXII, 551–52; Symposium, **59:** 44, 48, 52; interviews.

23. Vorse, **31:** 41, 416; Everett L. Clarke, "Provincetown," *New England Magazine*, n. s. 47 (1912), 60–65; Edwards, **82:** 51–52, 163–64; Vorse, **32:** 74–77, 160–61. A similarly close integration of the Portuguese and local Yankee element has occurred on the island of Martha's Vineyard, forming a common front against the "alien" summer tourists from the mainland. This is even evident in an English pronunciation feature distinguishing the local folk from the tourists, as noted by the linguist William Labov (in *Word*, December 1963, pp. 273–309).

24. U.S., **76:** XXII, 454; Taft, **30:** 205–8.

25. Portugal, **70:** year 1892, p. 42.

26. Portugal, **68: XI,** 1043; **XII,** 1023.

27. U.S., **76:** XXIV, 664–66. Also cf. Mowry, **38:** 115–17, and the letter to the editor and rejoinder relating to Mowry's article, pp. 290–93 of the same magazine volume (*Out West*, n.s. vol. 1).

28. Estep, **48:** 62–69.

29. Ted Le Berton, "Portuguese in the Valley," *Extension* (Chicago), 48, no. 10 (March 1954), 16.

30. Social, **115:** XIX, 46–47. Also cf. Lind, **111:** 224, 261; Andrew W. Lind, "Backgrounds in Hawaii," *Race Relations*, 5, nos. 1–2 (October–November 1947), 15–16; Adams, **100:** 119–20, 136–37, 284, and passim.

31. Adams, **100:** 136; Franck, **105:** 249; and private communication.

32. Honolulu, **108:** 27 September 1928.

33. William C. Smith, "The Hybrid in Hawaii as a Marginal Man," *American Journal of Sociology*, 34, no. 4 (January 1934), 463–64.

34. Social, **115:** XVI, 41. This may have been due to the merger of the small (Portuguese Protestant) Pilgrim Church with Central Union, but it also suggests one avenue toward Haolization.

35. Portugal, **68:** n.s. II, 696–97.

36. According to an unpublished report by the Reverend M. Conceição, Jr., in 1938, census takers visiting Portuguese immigrant households where the parents spoke no English would "often" address the question about citizenship to some American-born child that was doing the interpreting; and the latter, even though the parents were still aliens, would proudly answer: "We are Americans."

37. Diario, **4:** 29 June 1943; *Voz de Portugal* (New Bedford), 24 August 1944.

38. Diario, **4:** 2 March 1960.

39. John Daniels, *America via the Neighborhood* (New York: Harper, 1920), pp. 96–97, also pp. 338, 393–94, 456–58; Caroline F. Ware, "Cultural Groups in the United States," in *The Cltural Approach to History* (New York: Columbia University Press, 1940), p. 63.

40. Diario, **4:** 16 October 1945. On the slow political awakening of the Portuguese in Fall River, see Sharkansky, **29:** 122–30.

41. Prior to the 1940s, one Manuel Vitorino da Silva was lieutenant mayor of New Bedford in the early 1920s. A Boston lawyer by the name of William Andrews (Guilherme Andrade) is also reported to have represented Massachusetts in the U.S. House of Representatives, and/or to have been lieutenant governor of Massachusetts some time before 1924 (Revista, **10:** 22 May 1924, and private communications). Frank M. Silvia, born in Fall River of Azorean parents, was appointed a county judge in 1920, as was Madeira-born John B. Nunes in 1935. Luiz Cordeiro was elected state vice-chairman of the Democratic party in Massachusetts in 1944. São-Miguel-born Jacinto F. Diniz (Dinis) sat in the Massachusetts House of Representatives in the 1940s, but lost by a narrow margin in the race for U.S. Representative in 1947. Julio F. Rocha, as of 1945, was the first and only Portuguese-American in the Rhode Island state legislature. In 1949, August C. Taveira, born in New Bedford of immigrant parents, was appointed county judge; and Arthur A. Carrellas won a similar office in Rhode Island some years later. Edmund Dinis, son of the aforementioned Jacinto F. Diniz, with whom he immigrated as a child, was a district attorney for southeastern Massachusetts through the 1960s.

As a curio item we might add here that one Joseph H. De Bragga (Braga), born in New York City in 1866 of a father who had immigrated from Portugal as a youngster and had served in the Northern navy during the Civil War, was the Republican party leader in Queens County (N.Y.) from 1904 to 1930 (*New York Times*, 28 January 1939.) The mayor of Jacksonville, Illinois, as of 1945, was one Mr. Vasconcelos, evidently a descendant of the "Madeiran exiles"—and thus representing a fourth or fifth generation (Diario, **4:** 12 January 1945).

42. Arauto, **1:** 24 September and 12 November 1904; Ferro, **49:** 181– 82; Almeida, **34:** 158–59.

43. San Leandro's woman mayor had immigrated as a child from Horta, Faial, where her father had been mayor (Almeida, **34:** 177; Stuart, **98:** 233). E. H. Christian (Cristiano) was a California state senator in the late 1920s. Anthony Brazil became a district attorney in 1934, and a county judge in 1949. Both these men were born in California, of Portuguese immigrant parents.

44. Diario, **4:** 10 February 1959.

45. In 1977, Joseph Freitas headed the newly founded Portuguese-Americans for Political Action, and was a candidate for the office of attorney general of California (*Jornal de Fall River*, 26 May and 2 November 1977).

46. *Portuguese Times*, 19 April 1979. But see note 41 above, re M. V. da Silva.

47. In 1910, there were 2,025 eligible voters among a Portuguese population of 22,303; but only 670 among 21,674 Chinese, and 53 among 79,614 Japanese; on the other hand, 5,783 among 29,711 non-Portuguese whites, and 9,802 among 38,547 Hawaiians. In other words, the Portuguese then constituted about 11 percent of all eligible voters, representing about

12 percent of the total population. Aboriginal Hawaiians and Haoles had disproportionate voting strength, Orientals hardly any.

48. Donald Rowland, "The Establishment of the Republic of Hawaii, 1893–1894," *Pacific Historical Review*, 4 (1935), 212; Sylvester K. Stevens, *American Expansion in Hawaii, 1842–1898* (Harrisburg: Archives Publishing Co. of Pennsylvania, 1945), pp. 270–71.

49. For a full list, see Freitas, **43**: 107.

50. Freitas, **43**: 107, 156.

51. Freitas, **43**: 155.

52. Cf. Freitas, **43**: 98, 121, 158, 176, 220; Nellist, **113**: 225; *New York Times*, 1 July 1953; Jornal, **6**: 15 April 1960.

53. Honolulu, **109**: 19 March and June 1961.

54. Diario, **4**: 20 October 1944 and later issues.

55. Cf. George Monteiro, "The Unhistorical Uses of Peter Francisco," *Southern Folklore Quarterly*, 27 (1963), 139–59.

56. U.S. Supreme Court Justice Benjamin Cardozo, who has been cited in this connection, was a descendant of Portuguese Jews who had left Portugal centuries earlier. So were all four individuals incorrectly listed as American citizens of Portuguese birth on the "Wall of Fame of the American Common" at the 1940 World's Fair in New York.

57. Diario, **4**: 20 April 1966; *New York Times*, 9 September and 8 October 1970; 4 February 1973. Even though the Roman Catholic Church is directed by an international hierarchy centered in Rome, this is at least partly an American success story.

58. Yzendoorn, **118**: 225, 240–41; Franck, **105**: 275.

59. Diario, **4**: 13, 19, 25, 27 January and 4 February 1960; *New York Times*, 13 January and 2 February 1960; Arthur H. Fauset, *Black Gods of the Metropolis* (Philadelphia: University of Pennsylvania Press, 1944), pp. 22–29, 111–13; Elmer T. Clark, *The Small Sects in America*, rev. ed. (New York-Nashville: Abingdon-Cokesbury Press, 1949), pp. 122–24, 129, 225; "Daddy Grace," *Life*, 1 October 1945, pp. 51–56, 58; *Ebony*, January 1952, pp. 17–20, 23 and November 1953, pp. 86–88, 90.

60. Ribeiro, **153**: 11.

61. *Portuguese Times*, 19 February 1976.

62. Ferro, **49**: 221–30; Ribeiro, **153**: 12; Almeida, **34**: 143–44. For a comparison of socioeconomic accomplishments in New England and California, we may note that in the 1920s Merritt's history of Alameda County, Calif. (**94**) included twenty-two Portuguese-Americans among its roughly 450 "prominent men" (subjects of biographical sketches), whereas in Hutt's history of Bristol County, Mass. (**86**), only seven out of over 2,000 biographical entries referred to Portuguese-Americans, which means about five percent as against one third percent.

63. In 1961, Dos Passos accepted the Peter Francisco prize offered him by the Portuguese Continental Union of the United States (a fraternal society centered in New England). In 1969, one year before his death, he

published *The Portugal Story: Three Centuries of Exploration and Discovery.* Cf. Francis M. Rogers, *The Portuguese Heritage of John Dos Passos* (Boston: Portuguese Continental Union of the United States, 1976).

64. According to some reports, the famous actor Otis Skinner, born at Cambridge, Mass., in 1858, was the natural son of the Azorean immigrants Francisco Pimentel Baeta and Maria da Conceição, but ran away from home at age 10 to join a theatrical troupe, and was later adopted by one Rev. Charles A. Skinner. The equally famous actress Mary Astor (a stage name) was born in Illinois as Lucille de Vasconcellos Langhanke, of a German father and a mother who, to judge from her maiden name, may well have been Portuguese—or more probably a descendant of the "Madeiran exiles" who had settled in Illinois. One unconfirmed report has it that Tom Mix, the cowboy hero of early movie days, was born in continental Portugal as Antonio Nunes Pinguelo and emigrated to the United States in 1912. Other artists and related professionals with Portuguese-looking family names were the screen actress Louise Fazenda, the stage actor Howard DaSilva, the producer and song writer George G. DeSylva, the studio production designer and architect William L. Pereira, the landscape painter William Posey Silva, among others. None of these have any connection with the Portuguese immigrant community, although some of them may be distantly descended from Portuguese Jews.

65. Cf. *Esquire*, February 1935, p. 95; *United States Naval Institute Proceedings*, v. 62: 385–89; Diario, **4:** 11 February 1953. According to a report in Jornal, **6:** annual special issue for 1945, p. 23, a Californian automotive engineer by the name of Frank R. Perry developed an automobile running on compressed air mixed with an expanding liquid, propelled quietly by continuous pressure rather than by explosions. His invention was exhibited in Los Angeles streets in 1945. But whether Perry actually was of Portuguese descent as this report implied is doubtful.

Selected Bibliography

As explained in the Preface, the following list comprises only those sources referred to repeatedly in the text. Many supplementary references, cited once each, are listed in the Notes and References only.

1. PORTUGUESE IMMIGRANTS PERIODICALS

1. *Arauto.* Weekly newspaper; Hayward and Oakland, 1896 – 1917.
2. *Colonial.* Weekly; Fairhaven, Mass., 1925 – c. 1950.
3. *Colónia Portuguesa.* Semiweekly; Oakland, 1924 – 1930.
4. *Diário de Notícias.* Daily; New Bedford, 192? – 1971.
5. *Independente.* Weekly; New Bedford. c. 1934 – 1945.
6. *Jornal Português.* Weekly; Oakland, 1932 – 197?.
7. ————, annual special issue for 1938: "Os Portugueses da Califórnia."
8. *Luso.* Weekly; Honolulu, 1896 – 1924.
9. *Portugal-America.* Monthly magazine; Cambridge, 1926 – 1929.
10. *Revista Portuguesa.* Monthly magazine; Hayward, 1915 – 1924.
11. *União Portuguesa.* Weekly; Oakland, 1917 – 1942.

2. BOOKS AND ARTICLES DEALING PRIMARILY WITH THE PORTUGUESE IN THE UNITED STATES

a. New England

12. AGOSTINHO, J. "Um emigrante açoriano: José Gonçalves Correia," *Boletim do Instituto Histórico da Ilha Terceira* (Angra, Azores) 10 (1952): 204 – 38.
13. ANDRADE, LAURINDA C. *The Open Door.* New Bedford, Mass.: Reynolds-DeWalt, 1968.
14. BOUCHARD, ELLEN LOUISE. "The Learning of English by Portuguese Immigrant Children in Providence." Unpublished M.A. thesis, Brown University, 1968.
15. CABRAL, STEPHEN L. "Ritual Change among Portuguese-Americans in New Bedford, Massachusetts." Unpublished paper, 1977 (forthcoming in *Journal for Voluntary Action Research*).
16. CARVALHO, EDUARDO DE. *Os Portugueses na Nova Inglaterra.* Rio de Janeiro, 1931.
17. CONCEIÇÃO, M., JR., "Breve relatório sobre o trabalho missionário de

evangelização entre o povo português na Nova Inglaterra." Unpublished report, 1938.

18. CRANE, W. EDWARD. "Sons of the Azores on Cape Cod," *Travel* (New York), September 1937, pp. 23–26, 42. Reprinted in McLellan, Mary B., and DeBonis, Albert V., eds. *Within Our Gates* (New York: Harper), pp. 275–83.

18a. DIGGES, JEREMIAH. *In Great Waters: The Story of the Portuguese Fishermen*. New York: Macmillan, 1941.

19. JENSEN, JOHN B. "Phonological Interference: A Study of the English Pronunciation of Portuguese Immigrant Children in Fall River, Massachusetts." Unpublished Ph.D. dissertation, Harvard University, 1970.

20. ———. "The Portuguese Immigrant Community of New England: A Current Look," *Studia* (Lisbon), June 1972, pp. 109–51.

21. KOEHLER, MARGARET H. *Recipes from the Portuguese of Provincetown*. Riverside, Conn.: The Chatham Press, 1973.

22. LANG, HENRY R. "The Portuguese Element in New England," *Journal of American Folk-Lore* 5 1892): 9–18.

23. MONTEPIO LUSO-AMERICANO (New Bedford, Mass.). *Os portugueses em New Bedford; o 5.º centenário dos Açores na Nova Inglaterra*. . . . New Bedford, 1932.

24. NEVES, HENRIQUE DAS. *Individualidades; traços característicos, episódios e anécdotas authênticas de indivíduos que se evidenciaram*. Lisbon: Colecção António Maria Pereira, 1910.

25. PARSONS, ELSIE CLEWS. *Folk-Lore from the Cape Verde Islands*. 2 vols. Cambridge–New York: American Folk-Lore Society, 1923. Folklore collected among Capeverdeans in New England.

26. ———. "Folk-Lore of the Cape Verde Islanders," *Journal of American Folk-Lore* 34 (1921): 89–109.

27. PECK, EMELYN FOSTER. "An Immigrant Farming Community,' *New England Magazine* 37, n.s. 31 (1904–1905): 207–10.

28. POOLE, DOROTHY C. "Antone Fortes, Whaleman," *Dukes County Intelligencer* (Edgartown, Mass.) 11 (May 1970): 129–52.

29. SHARKANSKY, IRA. "The Portuguese of Fall River; a Study of Ethnic Acculturation." Unpublished B.A. honors thesis, Wesleyan University (Middletown), 1960.

30. TAFT, DONALD R. *Two Portuguese Communities in New England*. New York: Longmans, Green & Co., 1923. (Columbia University Studies in History, Economics and Public Law, no. 241.)

31. VORSE, MARY HEATON. "The Portuguese of Provincetown," *Outlook* (New York) 97 (January-April 1911): 409–16.

32. ———. *Time and the Town; a Provincetown Chronicle*. New York: Dial Press, 1942.

33. WORKS PROJECTS ADMINISTRATION OF MASSACHUSETTS. "The Portuguese in Provincetown." Unpublished report, 193?.

b. California

34. ALMEIDA, CARLOS. *Portuguese Immigrants; the Centennial Story of the Portuguese Union of the State of California.* San Leandro: Portuguese Union of the State of California, 1979.
35. BOHME, FREDERICK G. "The Portuguese in California," *California Historical Society Quarterly* 35 (1956): 233–52.
36. CRISSEY, FORREST. "Lessons from Our Alien Farmers; Pointers in Profits from the Thrifty Portuguese," *Saturday Evening Post*, November 18, 1911, pp. 9–11, 52–54.
37 GRAVES, ALVIN RAY. "Immigrants in Agriculture: The Portuguese Californians, 1850–1970's." Unpublished Ph.D. dissertation, University of California (Los Angeles), 1977.
38. MOWRY, EMILY YATES. "Portuguese Colonies in California; a Problem in Race Amalgamation," *Out West* 33 (January 1911): 114–17.
39. SOARES, CELESTINO. *California and the Portuguese.* Lisbon, 1939.
40. SYMPOSIUM ON PORTUGUESE PRESENCE IN CALIFORNIA, FIRST (San Leandro, June 1974). *Report.* Available from UPEC Cultural Center, San Leandro, and Luso-American Education Foundation, San Francisco.
41. VAZ, AUGUST MARK. *The Portuguese in California.* Oakland: Brotherhood of the ivine Holy Ghost, 1965.

c. Hawaii

42. CABRAL, ELMA T. "The Romance of Roza das Vacas," *Paradise of the Pacific*, December 148, pp. 97–100.
43. FREITAS, J. F. *Portuguese-Hawaiian Memories.* Honolulu, 1930.
44. KNOWLTON, EDGAR C., JR. "The Portuguese Language Press in Hawaii," *Social Process in Hawaii* 24 (1960): 89–99.

d. Various Parts of the United States

45. BANNICK, CHRISTIAN JOHN. *Portuguese Immigration to the United States: Its Distribution and Status.* San Francisco: R. & E. Research Associates, 1971. Originally an unpublished M.A. thesis, University of California at Berkeley, 1917.
46. "Colónias portuguezas em paízes estrangeiros," *Boletim da Sociedade de Geographia de Lisboa* 2 (1880–1881): 341–42, 355, 719–20.
47. COSTA, JOAQUIM. "Colónias portuguesas nas Ilhas de Hawaii e América do Norte," *Boletim da Sociedade de Geographia de Lisboa* 30 (1912): 233–63.
48. ESTEP, GERALD A. "Portuguese Assimilation in Hawaii and California," *Sociology and Social Research* 26 (1941–1942): 61–69.
49. FERRO, ANTONIO. *Novo mundo. mundo novo.* Lisbon: Portugal-Brasil, n.d. (c. 1930).
50. GREAVES, MANUEL. *Aventuras de baleeiros.* Horta (Azores), 1950.

51. HANDLER, MARK J. "Azoreans in America: Migration and Change Reconsidered." Upublished paper, c. 1977.
52. HOLMES, URBAN TIGNER, JR. "Portuguese Americans." In BROWN, FRANCIS J., AND ROUCEK, JOSEP S., eds. *Our Racial and National Minorities*. (New York: Prentice-Hall, 1937), pp. 394–405.
53. LUZ, DINIS DA. *Destinos no mar*. Lisbon: Portugalia, n.d. (c. 1951).
54. NATIONAL PORTUGUESE CONFERENCE, SECOND (Providence, May 1977). *Proceedings*. Fall River, Mass.: National Assessment and Dissemination Center for Bilingual-Bicultural Education, 1978.
55. OLIVER, LAWRENCE. *Never Backward: The Autobiography of Lawrence Oliver, a Portuguese-Amerian*. San Diego, 1972.
56. PAP, LEO. *Portuguese-American Speech; an Outline of Speech Conditions among Portuguese Immigrants in New England and Elsewhere in the United States*. New York: King's Crown Press (Columbia University), 1949.
57. ———. "The Portuguese Adstratum in North American Place-Names," *Names* 20 (1972): 111–30.
58. ROGERS, FRANCIS M. *Americans of Portuguese Descent: A Lesson in Differentiation*. Beverly Hills: Sage Publications, 1974.
59. SYMPOSIUM ON THE PORTUGUESE EXPERIENCE IN THE UNITED STATES, SECOND (Adelphi University, 1976). *Proceedings* (= *Women in Portuguese Society*). Fall River, Mass.: National Assessment and Dissemination Center for Bilingual-Bicultural Education, n.d. (1978).

3.   GOVERNMENT REPORTS CONTAINING DATA ON THE PORTUGUESE
IN THE UNITED STATES

60. COLLINS, J. W. "Report on the Fisheries of the Pacific Coast of the United States." In United States Commission of Fish and Fisheries. *Report of the Commission for 1888* (Washington, D.C.: Government Printing Office, 1892), pp. 3–269.
61. DU PUY, WILLIAM ATHERTON. *Hawaii and Its Race Problems* (Prepared for Unted States Department of the Interior). Washington, D.C.: Government Printing Office, 1932.
62. GOODE, GEORGE BROWN. *The Fisheries and Fishery Industries of the United States* (prepared for United States Commission of Fish and Fisheries). 5 sections in 7 vols. Washington, D.C.: Government Printing Office, 1884–1887.
63. MASSACHUSETTS, BUREAU OF STATISTICS. Census Reports (*Abstract* for 1865, *Compendium* for 1875, *Reports* for 1885, 1895, 1905, 1915). Boston.
64. ———. *The Immigrant Population of Massachusetts* (= Part 1 of Annual Report on the Statistics of Labor for 1912). Boston, 1913.
65. MASSACHUSETTS, DEPARTMENT OF LABOR AND INDUSTRIES. *Population and Resources of Cape Cod*. Boston, 1922.

66. PORTUGAL, DIRECÇÃO GERAL DA ESTATÍSTICA. *Censo da população de Portugal.*(Census Reports. Title varies slightly). Lisbon: Imprensa Nacional.

67. PORTUGAL, MINISTÉRIO DOS NEGÓCIOS ESTRANGEIROS. *Boletim Comercial.* Lisbon: Imprensa Nacional. Periodical, contains consular reports.

68. ———. *Documentos apresentados ás Cortes . . . Emigração portugueza.* (For legislative sessions of 1874 and 1875). Lisbon: Imprensa Nacional, 1874 and 1875.

69. ———. *Relatórios dos cônsules de Portugal.* Lisbon: Imprensa Nacional. Annual.

70. PORTUGAL, DIRECÇÃO GERAL DO COMÉRCIO E INDÚSTRIA. *Boletim do trabalho industrial.* Lisbon: Imprensa Nacional.

71. RHODE ISLAND, CENSUS BOARD. Census reports. (Title varies). Providence.

72. SHIPPEE, LESTER B. *Some Aspects of the Population of Providence* (prepared for Rhode Island Office of Commissioner of Labor). Providence, 1921.

73. UNITED STATES, BUREAU OF THE CENSUS. *Statistical Abstract of the United States.* Washington, D.C.: Government Printing Office, various years.

74. ———. *United States Census, 1940: Population, Second Series: Characteristics of the Population.* Washington, 1941–1943.

75. UNITED STATES, COMMISSIONER GENERAL OF IMMIGRATION. *Annual Reports.* Washington, 1911–.

76. UNITED STATES, IMMIGRATION COMMISSION. *Reports.* 41 vols. Washington, 1911.

77. WILCOX, WILLIAM A. "Fisheries of the Pacific Coast." In United States Commission of Fish and Fisheries. . . . *Report of the Commissioner for the Year Ending June 30, 1893.* (Washington, D.C. 1895), pp. 139–304.

    4.   VARIOUS NONGOVERNMENTAL SOURCES CONTAINING SCATTERED
         REFERENCES TO THE PORTUGUESE IN THE UNITED STATES

a. New England

78. BRADLEY, FRANCIS J. *A Brief History of the Diocese of Fall River, Mass.* Edited and brought up to date by Rev. M. V. McCarthy. Fall River (?), 1931.

79. BURGY, J. HERBERT. *The New England Cotton Textile Industry.* Baltimore, 1932.

79a. BUSHEE, FREDERICK A. "Ethnic Factors in the Population of Boston." *Publications of the American Economic Association*, 3d ser., 4 (1903): 299–477.

80. *Cape Cod Magazine* (monthly, Wareham, Mass.).
81. COPELAND, MELVIN THOMAS. *The Cotton Manufacturing Industry of the United States.* Cambridge: Harvard University, 1912.
82. EDWARDS, AGNES. *Cape Cod—New and Old.* Boston, New York: Houghton Mifflin, 1918.
83. ENGLER, RICHARD E., JR. *The Challenge of Diversity.* New York: Harper and Row, 1964.
84. *Evening Bulletin* (daily, Providence).
85. HATCH, MELLEN C. M. *The Log of Provincetown and Truro on Cape Cod, Massachusetts.* Provincetown: 1939.
86 HUTT, FRANK WALCOTT, ed. *A History of Bristol County, Massachusetts.* 3 vols. New York and Chicago: Lewis Publishing Co., 1924.
87. KENNGOTT, GEORGE F. *The Record of a City; A Social Survey of Lowell, Massachusetts.* New York: Macmillan, 1912.
88. *North End Mission Magazine* (quarterly, Boston).
89. *Providence Magazine* (monthly, Providence).
90. WOLFBEIN, SEYMOUR L. *The Decline of a Cotton Textile City: A Study of New Bedford.* New York: Columbia University Press, 1944.

b. California

91. ANGEL, MYRON. *History of San Luis Obispo County, California.* Oakland: Thompson and West, 1883.
92. COMMONWEALTH CLUB OF CALIFORNIA. "Land Tenancy in California," *Transactions of the Commonwealth Club of California* 17, no. 10 (November 1922): 397–448.
93. HALLEY, WILLIAM. *The Centennial Year Book of Alameda County, California.* Oakland, 1876.
94. MERRITT, FRANK C. *History of Alameda County, California.* 2 vols. Chicago: S. J. Clarke Publishing Co., 1928.
95. PORTEUS, S. D., and BABCOCK, MARJORIE E. *Temperament and Race.* Boston: Richard G. Badger (Gorham Press), 1926.
96. SMALL, KATHLEEN EDWARDS, and SMITH, J. LARRY. *History of Tulane and Kings Counties, California.* 2 vols. Chicago: S. J. Clarke Publishing Co., 1926.
97. SMITH, WALLACE. *Garden of the Sun.* Los Angeles: Lyman House, 1939.
98. STUART, REGINALD R. *San Leandro: a History.* San Leandro: First Methodist Church, 1951.
99. TINKHAM, GEORGE H. *History of Stanislaus County, California.* Los Angeles: Historic Record Co., 1921.

c. Hawaii

100. ADAMS, ROMANZO. *Interracial Marriage in Hawaii*. New York: Macmillan, 1937.
101. ———, and KAI, DAN K. *The Education of the Boys of Hawaii and Their Economic Outlook*. Honolulu: University of Hawaii Press, 1928.
102. BABCOCK, MARJORIE E. *Applications of Clinical Psychology in Hawaii*. Honolulu: Mercantile Press, 1927.
103. BAZORE, KATHERINE. *Hawaiian and Pacific Foods; a Cook Book*. . . . New York: M. Barrows and Co., 1947.
104. BLASCOER, FRANCES. *The Industrial Condition of Women and Girls in Honolulu*. Honolulu, 1912.
105. FRANCK, HARRY A. *Roaming In Hawaii*. New York: Frederick A. Stokes Co., 1937.
106. FUCHS, LAWRENCE H. *Hawaii Pono: A Social History*. New York: Harcourt, Brace and World, 1961.
107. *Hawaiian Almanac and Annual* (Honolulu, 1875–date; 1925–1935, called *Hawaiian Annual*; after 1935, *Thrum's Hawaiian Annual*).
108. *Honolulu Advertiser* (daily).
109. *Honolulu Star Bulletin* (daily).
110. LIND, ANDREW W. *Hawaii's People*. Honolulu: University of Hawaii Press, 1955.
111. ———. *An Island Community; Ecological Succession in Hawaii*. Chicago: University of Chicago Press, 1938.
112. MIDKIFF, FRANK E. "The Economic Determinants of Education in Hawaii." Unpublished Ph.D. dissertation, Yale University, 1935.
113. NELLIST, GEORGE F., ed., *The Story of Hawaii and Its Builders*. Honolulu: Honolulu Star-Bulletin, 1925.
114. RUSS, WILLIAM A., JR. "Hawaiian Labor and Immigration Problems before Annexation," *Jounal of Modern History* 15 (1943), 207–22.
114a. SCHMITT, ROBERT C. *Demographic Statistics of Hawaii, 1778-1965*. Honolulu: University of Hawaii Press, 1968.
115. *Social Process in Hawaii* (published about once a year by the Sociology Club, University of Hawaii, Honolulu).
116. UNIVERSITY OF HAWAII (Honolulu), SOCIOLOGY DEPARTMENT (pamphlet file). Unpublished autobiographical student reports.
117. VANDERCOOK, JOHN W. *King Cane; the Story of Sugar in Hawaii*. New York: Harper, 1939.
118. YZENDOORN, REGINALD. *History of the Catholic Mission in the Hawaiian Islands*. Honolulu: Honolulu Star-Bulletin, 1927.

290   THE PORTUGUESE-AMERICANS

d. Various Parts of the United States

119. CHIPPENDALE, HARRY A. *Sails and Whales*. Boston: Houghton Mifflin, 1951.
120. HAWES, CHARLES B. *Whaling*. Garden City: Doubleday, Page Co., 1924.
120a. HOHMAN, ELMO P. *The American Whaleman: A Study of Life and Labor in the Whaling Industry*. New York—London—Toronto: Longmans, Green and Co., 1928.
121. LEVINGER, LEE J. *A History of the Jews in the United States*. Cincinnati: Union of American Hebrew Congregations, 1930.
122. REID, IRA DE A. *The Negro Immigrant; His Background, Characteristics and Social Adjustment, 1899—1937*. New York: Columbia University Press, 1939.

5. BACKGROUND MATERIALS ON PORTUGAL

123. *Açoreana* (journal, irregular). Angra, Azores: Sociedade Afonso Chaves.
124. ALMEIDA, ANTONIO DE. "Sobre a terminologia anatómica nos crioulos de Cabo Verde," *Anais [da] Junta das Missões Geográficas e de Investigações Coloniais* (Ministério das Colonias, Portugal) 4 (1949): tomo 5, 3—17.
125. ALMEIDA, JOÃO DE. "A população de Cabo Verde." *Trabalhos do 1.º Congresso Nacioal de Antropologia Colonial* (Porto, 1934) 2: 51—75.
126. ANDRADE, ANSELMO DE. *Portugal económico*. Lisbon: Manuel Gomes, 1902.
127. *Archivo dos Açores* (journal, bimonthly). Ponta Delgada, Azores.
128. ARRUDA FURTADO, FRANCISCO DE. *Materiaes para o estudo anthropológico dos povos açoreanos: Observações sobre o povo michaelense*. Ponta Delgada, Azores, 1884.
129. BORGES DE F. HENRIQUES, M. *A Trip to the Azores or Western Islands*. Boston: Lee and Shepard, 1867.
130. BRAGA, THEOPHILO. *O povo portuguez nos seus costumes, crenças e tradições*. 2 vols. Lisbon: Ferreira, 1885.
131. CÂMARA BORGES, NAIR ODETTE DA. *Influência anglo-americana no falar da ilha de São Miguel (Açores)*. Coimbra: Instituto de Estudos Românicos, 1960.
132. CARQUEJA, BENTO. *O povo portuguez; aspectos sociaes e económicos*. Porto: Livraria Chardron, 1916.
133. CASIMIRO, AUGUSTO. *Portugal crioulo*. Lisbon: Edições Cosmos, 1940.
134. CHAVES, LUÍS. *Portugal além; notas etnográficas*. Gaia: Edições Pátria, 1932.

135. ————. . "A tradičõ nacional da Raínha Santa," *Revista de História* (Lisbon): 12 (1923): 44–66.
136. CORREIA, ANTÓNIO. *Poucos conhecem os Açores.* Lisbon, 1942.
137. DESCAMPS, PAUL. *Le Portugal, la vie sociale actuelle.* Paris: Firmin-Didot, 1935.
138. FRIEDLAENDER, IMMANUEL. *Beiträge zur Kenntnis der Kapverdischen Inseln.* Berlin: Dietrich Reimer, 1913.
139. GALLOP, RODNEY. *Portugal; a Book of Folk-Ways.* London: Cambridge University Press, 1936.
140. GIHON, A. L. "A Summer Cruise among the Atlantic Islands," *Harper's New Monthly Magazine* 54 (December 1876–May 1877): 546–57, 664–76.
141. HAEBERLE, ARMINIUS T. "The Azores . . . ," *National Geographic Magazine* 35 (January-June 1919): 514–45.
142. ILIOWIZI, HENRY. "In the World of the Azores," *Harper's Monthly Magazine* 104 (December 1901–May 1902): 85–94.
143. LAUTENSACH, H. *Portugal.* 2 vols. Gotha, 1932, 1937. (= Petermanns Mitteilungen, Ergänzungsheft Nr. 213 and 230.)
144. LEITE DE VASCONCELLOS, J. *Mês de sonho; conspecto de etnografia açórica.* Lisbon, 1926.
145. LYALL, ARCHIBALD. *Black and White Make Brown; an Account of a Journey to the Cape Verde Islands and Portuguese Guinea.* London: Heinemann, 1938.
146. MARVAUD, ANGEL. *Le Portugal et ses colonies; étude politique et économique.* Paris: Felix Alcan, 1912.
147. MONTEIRO, MARIA DE LOURDES DE OLIVEIRA. "Porto Santo; monografia linguística, etnográfica e folclórica," *Revista Portuguesa de Filologia* 1 (1947): 340–90; 2 (1948): 28–91; 3 (1949–1950): 90–151.
148. MORISON, SAMUEL ELIOT. *Portuguese Voyages to America in the Fifteenth Century.* Cambridge: Harvard University Press, 1940.
149. POINSARD, LÉON. "Le Portugal inconnu," *La Science Sociale* (Paris) 1910 (25ᵉ année, deuxième période): 1–437.
150. *Portugal; breviário da pátria para os portugueses ausentes.* Lisbon: SNI, 1946.
151. *Le Portugal au point de vue agricole.* Lisbon: Imprensa Nacional, 1900.
152. PRESTAGE, EDGAR. *The Portuguese Pioneers.* London: Black Ltd., 1933.
153. RIBEIRO, LUIS DA SILVA. *O emigrante açoreano.* Ponta Delgada: Correio dos Açores, 1940.
154. RIEGELHAUPT, JOYCE C. "Festas and Padres: The Organization of Religious Action in a Portuguese Parish," *American Anthropologist* 75 (1973): 835–52.

155. SAMPAIO, ALFREDO DA SILVA. *Memória sobre a Ilha Terceira*. Angra: Imprensa Municipal, 1904.
156. SANTOS, CARLOS M. *Trovas e bailados da ilha; estudo do foclore musical da Madeira*. Funchal: Delegação de Turismo da Madeira, 1942.
157. SILVA, FERNANDO EMYGDIO DA. *Emigração portuguesa*. Coimbra: França e Armenio, 1917.
158. WALKER, WALTER F. *The Azores or Western Islands*. London: Trubner, 1886.
159. WEEKS, LYMAN H. *Among the Azores*. Boston: James R. Osgood and Co., 1882.

6. Miscellaneous

160. ANDERSON, GRACE M. *Networks of Contact: The Portuguese and Toronto*. Waterloo, Ontario: Wilfrid Laurier University, 1974.
161. ———. , and HIGGS, DAVID. *A Future to Inherit: Portuguese Communities in Canada*. Toronto: McClelland and Steward, 1976.
162. BERNARD, WILLIAM S., ed. *American Immigration Policy; a Reappraisal*. New York: Harper, 1950.
163. BOGART, ERNEST L., and KEMMERER, DONALD L. *Economic History of the American People*. 2nd ed. New York–London–Toronto: Longmans, Green and Co., 1947.
164. CARLSON, OLIVER. *A Mirror for Californians*. Indianapolis–New York: Bobbs-Merrill, 1941.
165. COON, CARLETON S. *The Races of Europe*. New York: Macmillan, 1939.
166. DOYLE, KATHLEEN. *Californians: Who, Whence, Whither*. Los Angeles: Haynes Foundation, 1956.
167. HANDLIN, OSCAR. *The Uprooted; the Epic Story of the Great Migrations that Made the American People*. Boston: Little Brown, 1952.
168. LIVERMORE, SEWARD W. "The Azores in American Strategy-Diplomacy, 1917–1919," *Journal of Modern History* 20 (1948): 197–211.
169. MCENTIRE, DAVIS. "An Economic and Social Study of Population Movements in California, 1850–1944." Unpublished Ph.D. disertation, Harvard University, 1947.
170. PURVES, JAMES. "Portuguese in Bermuda," *Bermuda Historical Quarterly* 3 (1946): 133–42.

Index